# Perspectives in Sociology

## Sixth edition

*E.C. Cuff, A.J. Dennis, D.W. Francis and W.W. Sharrock*

Routledge
Taylor & Francis Group

LONDON AND NEW YORK

Sixth edition published 2016
by Routledge
2 Park Square, Milton Park, Abingdon, Oxon OX14 4RN

and by Routledge
711 Third Avenue, New York, NY 10017

*Routledge is an imprint of the Taylor & Francis Group, an informa business*

First edition published by Unwin Hyman Ltd 1979
Fifth edition published by Routledge 2006

*British Library Cataloguing in Publication Data*
A catalogue record for this book is available from the British Library

*Library of Congress Cataloging in Publication Data*
Cuff, E. C.
 Perspectives in sociology/by E.C. Cuff, A.J. Dennis, D.W. Francis
 and W.W. Sharrock. – 6th edition.
  pages cm
 1. Sociology. 2. Sociology–History. I. Title.
 HM586.C84 2015
 301–dc23                                    2015009675

ISBN: 978-1-138-79353-8 (hbk)
ISBN: 978-1-138-79354-5 (pbk)
ISBN: 978-1-315-76105-3 (ebk)

Typeset in Amasis
by Cenveo Publisher Services

Printed and bound by CPI Group (UK) Ltd, Croydon, CR0 4YY

# Perspectives in Sociology

From its first ⋯⋯ ⋯s of
undergraduate ⋯⋯ ⋯logi-
cal theory. Thi⋯

- a complete ⋯
- all-new int⋯ ⋯fore;
- an updated ⋯
- a compreh⋯

While retaini⋯ ⋯s of
sociology, thi⋯ ⋯lated
disciplines to ⋯

**E.C. Cuff** was ⋯ ⋯bury
School of Ed⋯

**A.J. Dennis** ⋯

**D.W. Francis** ⋯ ⋯ity.

**W.W. Sharro⋯**

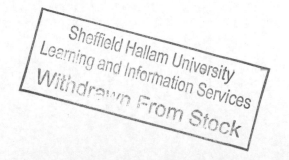

# Contents

## CHAPTER ONE

# Introduction

In the nine years since the previous edition of this book was published, much has changed socially but there has been little theoretical movement sociologically. This is, perhaps, a cause for concern. In 2006 we argued that:

> There remains a sense of crisis in sociology, and realisation of the grand ambition that it should contribute to (if not play the key role in) a rational reconstruction of society for the benefit of all humanity now seems further away than ever. At the present time, there are even suspicions that the discipline has virtually put itself into liquidation.

This has not changed. Although there have been new developments (such as the growth of 'network' approaches, an apparently reinvigorated Marxist tradition, and the development of 'public sociology' – all of which are introduced in this new edition), none have successfully re-invigorated the discipline's core concerns, aims or approaches. There have been no major disputes or crises in the discipline. It remains business as usual.

Viewed another way, however, this lack of movement may be regarded as a fruitful opportunity. As we argue here, the developments in sociological theory that dominated the discipline between the 1980s and 2000s were not without problems. The poststructuralist and postmodernist 'turns' came to represent abandonments of sociology's original rationale: the possibility of progressive social change, the objectivity of social facts, and the orderly nature of social life were all consigned to the scrapheap of 'grand narratives'. The 'return' to social theory offered by Giddens, Bourdieu, Habermas, *et al.* proved to be problematic in its own terms: attempts to synthesise Parsons and his critics ultimately resulted in social theories that were exposed to the same kinds of criticisms Parsons himself endured. And, finally, while pointing towards sociology's liberatory and egalitarian heritage, the 'emancipatory sociologies' of feminism, queer theory and postcolonialism proved to resurrect the same theoretical problems faced by the symbolic interactionists' 'underdog bias' and the relativist traps of postmodernism.

Social theory, we argue, has not changed much over the last ten years but – given where it was ten years ago – that does not necessarily mean it has stagnated. Empirical work is held in higher esteem, and has reasserted itself as central as the 'post' perspectives have declined in influence. Much of this work explicitly locates itself in pre-postmodern positions, such as Duneier's (2000) superb study of itinerant magazine sellers in New York and (Alice) Goffman's (2014) bestselling ethnography of young, black men wanted by the police in Philadelphia – both of which are grounded in the tradition identified here as symbolic interactionism. Analyses of the financial crash (Lanchester 2010) and rapidly increasing levels of inequality (Piketty 2014) owe much to organisational sociology and economic sociological theory respectively, and have found a wide general readership. Piketty's *Capital* topped the bestseller list in 2014, mirroring the success of Hardt and Negri's (2001) more explicitly Marxian *Empire* a decade before. Sociological ideas provide inputs to and controversial foci in a wide range of other disciplines, and to that extent sociology's influence continues to spread.

In short, there seems to be an increasing hunger for the kinds of analyses sociologists have traditionally produced. The events of the 2000s and 2010s raise questions about the nature of society, social change, social order and organisation, cultural difference and integration, the relationship between economy and society – the core concerns of the discipline since Marx, Weber and Durkheim. That a number of influential writers are now addressing these concerns in a sociological manner (or at least in a manner that owes much to sociology) is cause for celebration. That these writers are not self-defined sociologists is, perhaps, less of a worry than it might be for other disciplines. Sociology has been a hybrid discipline for forty years or more, and its willingness to open up to influences from political theory (Althusser), cultural studies (Foucault), literary theory (Derrida) and elsewhere has nourished the discipline even when its 'core' (social theory *per se*) has seemed impoverished. The lack of significant theoretical development in sociology over the last ten years seems to us to indicate a hunger for *genuinely* new ideas as much as a gradual disenchantment with the rather stale concerns of the 1980s and 1990s. We hope this will be borne out over the lifetime of this edition.

The sixth edition of this book is, therefore, an updating and revision of the fifth, rather than a fully rewritten text. We have subdivided the text more clearly into thematic units: the founding thinkers, sociology in the English-speaking world, the European tradition, post-sociological perspectives, and contemporary trends. The text has been updated and revised, chapter introductions provided throughout, and key questions rewritten. A glossary of terms has been added, and references have been updated and corrected. New developments such as network approaches to society, autonomist-influenced Marxist trends and public sociology have been incorporated. More than anything else, though, we have retained our sense that there has been little development in sociological theory over the last ten years – but that this may soon change.

This edition is dedicated to the memory of our friend, E.C. (Ted) Cuff, who was the driving force behind *Perspectives in Sociology* from its first edition in 1979 to his death in October 2014. Our worlds are poorer without him.

# PART I

# Founding thinkers

In this first part, the three founding figures of sociology will be introduced. They are Karl Marx, Max Weber and Émile Durkheim. Although radically different in their approaches to the nature of the social world, they shared a concern with accounting for human behaviour in its social context: as behaviour that takes place in a society made up of other people, which shapes (even determines) what form that behaviour can or cannot take.

This shared perspective reflected a shift in emphasis from the *individual* to the *collective* that occurred in the nineteenth century. The revolutions of 1830 and 1848, the unification of Italy and Germany, the Parisian uprising of 1871, and other events could not be understood as simply the outcomes of particular individuals deciding to act in particular ways. Although key figures were involved, such as Bismarck in Germany and Mazzini in Italy, they were able to marshal existing social pressures and cultural demands to achieve their ends. The social world came to be seen as something which had its own forces, which could not be kept in check, whether by force or by persuasion, for any protracted period of time. As Simmel (2009: 19) had it, 'these are the claims that the science of sociology is concerned to raise: the theoretical pursuit and reflection on the practical power that the masses have acquired in the nineteenth century against the interests of individuals'.

Each of the founders construed this problem in a different way. For Karl Marx, the key question facing social thinkers was why the world is organised in the way it is. The overwhelming majority of the population have to work to support themselves, but they have no say in how this work gets done. Furthermore, they own neither the places they work in and the equipment in them (the means of production), nor the fruits of their labour (their product). Instead, they sell their labour-power – the thing that makes them human, their capacity to transform the world – to members of a different *class*, whose contribution to society is simply to own the means of production and buy (or not buy) the labour-power of the workers. Society, for Marx, is based on a contradiction: the interests of the working class and the interests of the ruling class are diametrically opposed. The former are deprived of what makes them human, the latter are parasitic on the former. Marx's fundamental insight was that these contradictions are the forces that underpin what happens in the social world, and they will, ultimately, lead to its transformation (as they have done before).

Max Weber disagreed. His starting point was that, although the economic relationships Marx wrote about might well be important forces in society, they were not the only ones – and, perhaps, were not even the most important ones. Capitalism, the social system Marx devoted the latter part of his life to examining, appeared in different forms in different places. Capitalism in Catholic Italy, for example, was very different in organisation and form to capitalism in Protestant Britain. The latter was rational and bureaucratic, and the economic success of certain powers (Britain and Germany in particular) could be accounted for with reference to this rational, bureaucratic organisation. Weber tried to show that the form capitalism took in Britain and Germany was the product of particular *ideas*, religious commitments on the part of capitalists, which encouraged the development of the contemporary business enterprise. Weber was thus interested in *authority*, the different ways particular individuals come to dominate others. Furthermore, Weber argued that class conflict – although important – was not the only kind of conflict in contemporary societies. Societies are *stratified* in different ways, by 'party' and by 'status' as well as by class, and the complex relationships between these forms of stratification require description and analysis.

Émile Durkheim was far less interested in individuals than Weber. He argued that society was a reality *sui generis* (unique in its characteristics), and could not be understood as either the result of economic forces (as in Marx's work) or the product of the activities of the individuals that comprise it (as in Weber's). Rather than focusing on the transition from feudal to capitalist societies, Durkheim emphasised the changing nature of social bonds in the *division of labour*. While medieval societies were organised 'mechanically' (each village having more or less the same organisation), contemporary societies are characterised by an 'organic' division of labour (where different parts of society fulfil different roles, like the different organs in a body). Although Durkheim emphasised the orderly, integrated nature of society – accounting for its relative stability over time – he was not, therefore, a conservative thinker. His work on crime and suicide revealed the tensions that exist in contemporary societies, and their effects on those societies' members, and his distinction between 'normal' and 'pathological' social phenomena has been increasingly influential over the course of sociology's development.

Marx, Weber and Durkheim were not alone in founding sociology. Contemporaneous thinkers like Georg Simmel, Gabriel Tarde and Ferdinand Tönnies were also enormously influential, and their works have been 'rediscovered' over the course of the twentieth and twenty-first centuries. Thinkers like Auguste Comte predated all three. Nevertheless, as we will see, the *problematics* and *methodologies* Marx, Weber and Durkheim introduced have been the driving forces behind most subsequent sociological thinking.

## CHAPTER TWO

# Karl Marx

## Chapter overview

In this chapter, Karl Marx's ideas about the nature of society will be introduced, starting with the question of whether Marx was a *humanist*. The roots of his approach in the work of G. W. F. Hegel's *dialectics* will be outlined, and his *materialist* theoretical arguments – centring on *work* – examined. His key concepts of *alienation*, *class conflict* and *ideology* will be introduced, their implications for the study of history elaborated, and the complex relationship between economic *base* and cultural *superstructure* critically examined.

## Introduction

The formative, decisively influential figures affecting, first, sociological theory and, now, social theory remain the trio of Karl Marx (1818–83), Max Weber (1864–1920) and Émile Durkheim (1858–1917). Though the first of these three has now – again – apparently fallen into eclipse, none the less Marx has had a decisive and continuing influence upon the development of sociological thought. Moreover, his *method*, partly derived from G. W. F. Hegel, continues to exercise extensive influence. So does the *problematic* which he played a main role in forming. Durkheim and Weber also, to different degrees, for different reasons and in varying ways, contribute key ideas to the contemporary configuration of social thought.

We begin with Marx, whose 'humanism' has provided, since the 1970s, such a bone of contention.

## Was Marx a humanist?

The influence of Marx's ideas within social theory has been enormous – not just upon avowed Marxists, but much more generally. It has shaped social thinking about fundamental issues to such an extent that the defining issues of contemporary theory are largely of Marxian origin. For example, a common central theme of recent theoretical discussion, which transcends a range of perspectives and approaches, concerns the role of cultural institutions in the analysis of contemporary industrial societies. While concepts and assumptions differ across the theoretical spectrum, there is broad consensus around the idea that cultural institutions – however conceived – have taken over the dominant position in society formerly occupied by strictly economic ones. Loosely speaking, then, the issue concerns the relationship between – using Marx's terms – the *base* and the *superstructure*. While we might now reverse the relationship that Marx posited existed between them, and recognise cultural institutions as being far more significant and powerful in shaping social life than they were in Marx's day, the fact remains that the problem continues to be defined in its most basic terms by reference to a model of society which originates in Marx, and which is explained below. In this sense, the spectre of Marx continues to haunt social thought, even among those who explicitly reject his theories and claim to have outstripped his influence. Indeed, the base–superstructure model as a *method of analysis* is as popular and widespread among contemporary social theorists as it has ever been.

For our purposes, a central question has dominated debates about and interpretations of Marx's thought: 'What does it mean to say that Marx was a humanist?'

## Humanism

The concept of humanism refers to the extent to which social theories account for the organised character of social life in terms of the individual: is social order conceived as constructed out of action? How far is structure explained by reference to the creative powers of a society's members? In this sense, humanism is a theoretical assumption, or, better perhaps, a *meta-theoretical stance*, i.e. a stance looking at theory from outside.

The question we are posing, therefore, is whether this stance is correctly attributable to Marx, and if so, what follows from reading him in this way?

In developing this question, we need to begin not with Marx himself, but with G. W. F. Hegel (1770–1831).

## Hegel: the dialectic of history

Hegel was the most influential thinker of the first half of the nineteenth century in Germany and, arguably, in Europe as a whole. Hegel's philosophy aimed to give an account of history-as-a-whole. The history of all humanity can, he argued, be grasped as a single, unified, organised and *rational* progress. History might look like a mere accidental succession – one thing after another in a rather disorganised, chaotic sequence – but that impression is only superficial. Seen in the right way, history can be recognised as making up a coherent story about development and progress. Progress is not smooth, continuous and cumulative, but, rather, comes through struggle, conflict and discontinuity. Nevertheless, this progress is of an essentially logical kind.

How was Hegel able to make such a counter-intuitive proposal plausible? Surely struggle, conflict and change are inimical to order and logic? Grasping how these apparent opposites are reconciled is the key to Hegel's thought. The crucial idea is that conflict is itself an *orderly* process, consisting in the creation and overcoming of oppositions. Compare the history of human beings to the growth of a plant from a seed. The seed contains the plant, and out of the seed grows the plant, destroying the seed. Thus the life of the plant is the development of the seed into what it has the potential to become: first, the shoot, later, the fully-grown plant. In the same way, consider history as the life of humanity, and see, therefore, that history is merely the unfolding of the potential which was present at the earliest stage of its being. History is the natural expression of the essential nature of human beings, just as the plant is the natural expression of the essential nature of the seed. Humanity *must* itself develop into what it has the potential to become. Note that Hegel takes it for granted that his history is a *collective* one, i.e. it is a history of humanity as a whole, or of large groups of people, not of particular individuals.

Just as the seed is destined to turn into a plant of a specific kind, human beings – Hegel argues – are destined to develop towards complete freedom. What human beings essentially are will never be fully expressed if their capacity for development is restricted, inhibited by circumstances; the potential of humanity will only be fully developed when they are truly free, which means free of *all* circumstantial inhibition. Over the course of history, human beings necessarily represent something less than the true or full nature of humanity. For just as the full potential of the seed is only realised when the plant is fully matured, so the full potential of human beings will only be realised after the period of growth – i.e. history – is over. The achievement of complete freedom will be the 'finished growth' of human beings. Consequently, there will be an end to history. Since history is a process of change through which humanity develops its full potential, then when that has been realised there can be no further development and therefore no further history. History is directed towards an end in two senses: (1) in the form of a particular result; (2) in being directed towards a literal end or finish.

**Teleology**

The notion that something is driven or striving towards a particular end is called a teleological conception; therefore Hegel presents a teleological account of human history.

## The spirit of the age

In what sense does humanity develop? For Hegel, the primary manifestation of development was the development of the intellectual life, of the mind or spirit; the German term used by Hegel is *Zeitgeist* (i.e. 'spirit of the age'). He held it to be plain, if one studied the history of a given people, that their art, religion and philosophy would at any given time have a certain uniformity, a common cast of mind, a shared outlook. This concept reaffirms Hegel's *collectivist* aspect, for it was his firm conviction that the commonality across many different thinkers was not a matter of mere coincidence; individuals were driven by larger, widespread influences affecting them all in similar ways. In short, the mind or the spirit that drives the historical process is the mind of humanity, as manifested in particular peoples and periods, not the mind of individual thinkers.

### Idealism

Hegel's study of the mind was the study of the development of ideas, so naturally he concentrated upon those areas of society that were creative or expressive of ideas: art, abstract thought (particularly philosophy) and religion. Hence Hegel is termed an *idealist*: he thought that the true nature of history and human existence was to be understood in terms of the development of thought, of *ideas*.

## The purpose and logic of history

Since the purpose of thought is to achieve knowledge, the progress of history must be towards knowledge, and the end of history will therefore come with the achievement of full knowledge and full understanding. In other words, history is completed when humanity finally comes fully to understand its own nature. The development of history is humanity's continuing struggle to understand itself, and Hegel's philosophy was meant to provide an understanding of humanity's true nature as a historically, progressively developed thing which consists in self-understanding. Hegel's philosophy amounts to the self-understanding of humanity. It should, therefore, expose the complete understanding of history and humanity's nature – they are, after all, the same thing – and therefore comprise the finale to history. History has completed itself when it arrives at Hegel's conclusions.

What of the nature and role of logic in this process? Since the development of history is a development of thought, and the essential process of thought *is* logic, it follows, then, that the development of history must be an essentially *logical* process. If so, Hegel's initial claim that history-as-a-whole was amenable to rational understanding would be vindicated at this point. For him, history effectively *consists in* thought and its logical operations, and these are, of course, our very means of understanding. Thus, to see history as a rational process is nothing other than to grasp its underlying logic. This approach, however, required Hegel to reform logic; he maintained that the logical process is more complex and roundabout than it is presumed to be in classical logic. What was needed, he argued, was a *dialectical* logic.

Philosophy was, in Hegel's view, the crucial vehicle for the development of thought, since it purported to be the apogee of rational, logical thought. Yet a survey of the logic of Hegel's time shows a preoccupation with absolute distinctions between irreconcilable opposites. Examples are: truth and falsehood, being and non-being, the animate and the inanimate, and the mortal and the immortal. The distinctions were absolute in the sense that things were immutably of one kind or the other. Something false cannot become true, i.e. it cannot change into its opposite. From Hegel's standpoint, this apparent truism was a false conception of the nature of things. It did not recognise the fact that things *could* change; the flatly oppositional thinking of philosophy was too simplified.

### Dialectical logic

Classically, truth is often sought in discussion – in dialogue, or *dialectic*. Hegel bases his logic on the model of discussion exemplified by Socrates in classical times. Discussion originates in disagreement, the conflict of oppositions, which spurs debate. The argument proceeds by the putting of one position and the countering of it by another, opposed position. The search for truth is not about standing pat on one's own position, but about attempting to reach agreement with one's opponent, to arrive at a conclusion both can accept. It incorporates elements of each of the two previously opposed positions, but now combines them in a third, new position that is improved and superior.

In grossly simplified terms, we may glimpse Hegel's dialectical logic as an exposition of the way in which seeming opposites can be reconciled and combined in a new unity. Of course, arriving at an agreed position might end *that* discussion, but it does not end *all* discussion, for this newly agreed position will be put in some other conversation, will provoke a counter-statement, initiate a new debate and a search for yet another more inclusive, mutually acceptable conclusion, and so on.

This logical progression is the very stuff of history. Hegel is saying that history arises from *conflict*. Far from conflict being an undesirable and unnecessary blemish upon the face of human existence, it is the driver of history, the essential motor of progress. Conflict engenders new and better ideas and pushes towards a more comprehensive understanding. Conflict is not only necessary, but also productive, for conflicts are eventually resolved and result in improved outcomes before yet further conflicts are initiated.

We must emphasise, also, that – although the development of philosophy is crucial to Hegel's understanding – his history is a general history of civilisations and their activities, including their wars and other social struggles. At any point in history oppositions or *contradictions* – the logical term for opposition between propositions stating conflicting positions – dominate the mind or spirit of a people and their civilisation. Although philosophy has always concerned itself with oppositions, in fact they affect the whole civilisation; people act out oppositions in their social, political and economic affairs as much as in their intellectual culture. Thus conflicts, and development through conflicts, are an integral part of social existence, involving, in Hegel's rendition, the working through and working out of these contradictions.

For example, the military conquests of Napoleon were just as much part of the logical pattern as were the philosophical arguments of René Descartes or John Locke (1632–1704); the history of society, of its intellectual culture and of philosophy itself were all part of one and the same enterprise. Of course, Napoleon, Descartes and all the other individuals who have contributed significantly to human history were not aware that they were playing a part in this pattern; Hegel spoke of the 'cunning of reason' to refer to the way in which this logical patterning worked itself out in history through the activities of individuals without their awareness of the part they were playing. Only someone equipped with Hegel's philosophy could know about this inherent logic of history.

## Marx's reformation of Hegel

Hegel's philosophy was humanist in treating humanity as occupying a special, central place in the whole historical process, and seeing that the very point of history was to improve and fulfil the human spirit. His ideas certainly had immense impact; he dominated German intellectual life and influenced most young German philosophers of the time. One of these was Marx, who appropriated much of Hegel's scheme, certainly in his early writings. He was, however, sceptical of Hegel's significance as a political thinker. Marx could not accept Hegel's contention that the key to human emancipation lay in the development of philosophy, carrying people to the level of complete understanding of their own nature and thus to complete freedom through his, Hegel's, own philosophical works. After all, this supposed final enlightenment and full elaboration of humanity's progress co-existed with jails filled with political prisoners. Freedom in philosophy, freedom only in the mind, obviously was not the same as real political freedom. Therefore, Hegel's idea of history could not offer an account of the progression of history to a *real*, i.e. practical, political freedom if it only resulted in freedom in theory. For Marx, the real history of human development could not be a history solely of thought or ideas; it would have to be a history of human life *in the real world*, i.e. the world of economic and political being.

Despite this important reservation, Marx initially adopted much of the *form* of Hegel's argument, i.e. the idea of a scheme for history-as-a-whole, and of history as a progressive development of the true character of human nature that could only be fully realised when history reaches its final stage. These ideas were taken over. So was the idea that the driving force of historical change was conflict. Change was structured in the dialectical pattern of conflict, resolution, further conflict and higher, more advanced resolution. It went through a succession of ever-higher stages of development, with increasing degrees of freedom, eventually resulting in a final, full enlightenment and emancipation of humankind.

## Production and human essence

Marx's reservations were about the *inequality* of society. At that stage only a very few individuals had participated in the development of human thought, or spirit, in the sense of its intellectual expression; the vast majority were excluded from the process of creating these purported expressions of human essence. This majority had been engaged in producing human history all right, but not by way of intellectual creation and discussion. Rather, it had produced human history through physical, not mental, effort, creating through its *labour* the actual conditions of human existence and the material conditions under which thinking, for example philosophy, might be done. Marx denied Hegel's view that the human essence was to be found in thinking; he favoured the view that the human essence is to *work*.

**Work**

> Work, involving as it does the physical transformation of the world around us, literally changes our world, whereas thinking makes no physical difference to anything. Work also provides the most basic means to freedom, to liberation from necessity. For, of course, our labour provides us with food, shelter and clothing, giving us some freedom from the challenges and pressures of nature. Further, progress in labour sets us free from the necessity for labour itself by giving us time and resources to do things other than labour, including the opportunity to engage in intellectual thought.

This is not to say that *thinking* does not matter at all because, of course, thinking is part of labour, part of what Marx calls 'practical consciousness', i.e. the thinking involved in, and for the purposes of, carrying out labour. Indeed, for Marx, as for his predecessors Aristotle and Hegel, the capacity for thought marks out human beings as distinctive; the capacity to think about things and to imagine them being otherwise enables human beings to envisage new (improved) ways of making the physical world meet their needs, bringing about changes in the physical environment itself. In this capacity they differ from animals, whose ability to alter the physical world is fixed in instinct-given ways; animals have no capacity for reflection and foresight.

**11**

It is important to recognise that Marx's contempt was reserved for *speculative thinking*. The kind of theorising that Hegel had engaged in had, for Marx, a fundamentally self-deluding character.

## The fundamental division

If labour is the essence of humanity, then special attention needs to be paid to the *division of labour*.

### The division of labour

The division of labour has both a positive and a negative aspect. On the one hand, it is an enormously powerful device for harnessing and maximising the creative potential of human labour; by subdividing work, immensely more can be produced than is possible if all the members of a group pursue the same task. However, such division can – invariably does – lead to separation of human beings into different categories, with some having power over others.

Thus the existence of the division of labour means the dislocation of the human essence, the division of humanity against itself. It also means a division between thought, i.e. between speculative thinking, and practical, physical, world-transforming activity, because some specialise in the former activity, some in the latter. The fateful moment for the division of labour is not when it produces people who specialise in different aspects of a work task, but when it produces a division between those who do the physical work and those who do not. Some are now supported by the products of other people's physical labour; they do not themselves contribute towards it. Those who do not engage in physical labour often occupy themselves with thinking, but their thinking is now freed from a crucial constraint of reality, i.e. from the crucial connection with physical labour and its patent reminder that human existence owes everything to the capacity for labour, that everything of real value in human life is made possible by someone's physical production.

As a consequence, thought can begin to *misrepresent* reality by presenting itself as the source and embodiment of everything valuable, as something more important to human existence than 'mere' physical labour. This misrepresentation of reality not only denies the true facts, but also serves a social use: by elevating thought above physical labour, thinkers also elevate themselves above those who do physical work, thereby justifying their entitlement to the material necessities which they have not produced themselves. Further, they often claim a disproportionately large share. This misrepresentation is the source of an idea fundamental to *all* of Marx's work.

## The fundamental idea

The progress of history and the organisation of society are to be understood as being decisively shaped by the division between those who do and those who do not engage in physical production, those who produce and those who consume a portion of what is produced even though they have not produced it.

The fact that humanity is divided within itself in this way means, of course, that actual human beings cannot be full and proper expressions of the human essence. The human essence is prevented from achieving its full development by two things:

1 Those who engage in physical labour, which is purportedly the fulfilment of their human essence, do not engage in it freely; they are, in one way or another, unfree. The stark example is, of course, the slave, but the medieval peasant and the industrial worker are also unfree in important ways. The industrial worker differs from the slave and peasant in being *legally* free, but this is not the same as being truly free, i.e. free of all external limitation.
2 Those who do not labour are cut off from their true 'species nature', their human essence. They may believe that they are living the highest form of human life possible and feel entirely happy, without realising that they are only very partially fulfilling human potentiality, since their own achievements and privileges are acquired at the expense of other human beings. The vast majority pay the price in deprivation and suffering; the cultural achievements of the few cannot be considered the fulfilment of the potential of humankind *as a whole*.

In such circumstances – which are only too familiar – there is, then, a basis for the criticism of society and the formation of proposals for its reorganisation. Society can be criticised for the way in which it distorts the human essence by limiting freedom, and a case can be made for what needs to be done to move the development of that essence further forward. Hegel himself had used his philosophy in a conservative way, to justify the rule of a tyrannical king, but Marx saw in his method the basis of a programme for *revolutionary* change.

## Alienation

Given his borrowing from Hegel, it is not surprising that Marx's criticism of his contemporary society was initially cast in terms of one of Hegel's key concepts, *alienation*.

13

## Alienation

This concept refers precisely to the separation of human beings from their very essence. Engagement in productive work *should* be the expression of human essence, thereby fulfilling the rich potential of human energy, imagination and creativity. It was clear to Marx that work in the developing industrial societies of the nineteenth century was very different. Far from being the fulfilment of their very being, work for industrial workers was experienced, at best, as a necessary evil and undertaken out of the need for survival. For the overwhelming majority it was a deadening experience – physically unpleasant, mentally unrewarding and spiritually numbing.

Further, the members of industrial society are alienated as a *population*, not just as a collection of individuals. Human essence is not the possession of individual beings, but of the species as a whole, and will be fully realised only when human beings have developed their full potential. The industrial society, however, was divided within itself between those who could enjoy physical comfort and intellectual stimulation, engaging in freely creative activity, e.g. of a cultural and artistic kind, and those who were reduced to being near-sub-humans in the foul and brutal conditions of the factory system.

Another aspect of alienation involves the misrepresentation of reality in the form of the *self-denial* of human essence as people misapprehend their own true nature. In their thinking, people come to underestimate their own powers, failing to realise that certain things are actually the product of their own, human effort and not of some other source. A leading example is religion, where people often take a fatalistic line towards what occurs because they believe God determines what happens to them and that they can have no control over their own fate. But Marx, the atheist, following another critic of Hegel, Ludwig Feuerbach, maintains that there is no God. God is just an idea made up by human beings, partly to muddle up and mislead people, partly to express unsatisfied human longings. By accepting the idea of God and taking such a fatalistic line, people are resigning their own capacity to control their own destiny, are wrongly thinking of themselves as subordinate to great, supernatural forces over which they can have no control. In fact there are no occult beings or forces, so that everything that human beings can possibly be is within their own (collective) control.

A further example of this kind of alienation is Hegel's own philosophy, where the human spirit, made up of ideas, achieves an almost occult existence of its own. This strange, superhuman force directs history from behind people's backs, making use of them as unwitting pawns to carry out its plans. It is human beings, however, who produce ideas, including 'the human spirit', not the other way around, and it is human beings, not quasi-supernatural ideas, who make history. In so far as things are done behind people's backs, then, *other people*, not 'ideas', do them.

For Marx, another most important kind of alienation is the way in which people accept their economic situation, e.g. unemployment or badly paid labour, because they suppose that their fate is determined by economic 'laws' over which they can have no control. The recent tendency of many governments to insist that the market is a near-infallible mechanism for regulating all activities, the possessor of greater wisdom than individuals or their governments are capable of, might show the persistence of this kind of conception. For Marx, the market cannot be some super-human, super-wise entity but only *a set of relationships between human beings*, something which human beings have created (albeit not by any conscious intention) and something which they potentially can control. He maintained that there is no need to accept that we are assigned a miserable fate by the nature of things, to which we simply have to resign ourselves. Human beings make themselves through their labour, they develop their own nature through changing the world about them, and they have (collectively) the capacity to *reshape themselves* by reshaping their physical, economic and social world.

The remainder of Marx's intellectual career, in which his writings principally were concerned with economic ideas, was devoted to exposing illusions of this kind. Such illusions are self-limiting misconceptions of human destiny that must be removed.

## The real basis of society

For Marx, it was not enough to liberate people from a set of illusions; human progress involved liberating them from real social, political and economic conditions. The objective must be to determine within reality itself the way the human essence was developing through the formation and reformation of social, political and economic conditions. He wanted to discover how the movement towards emancipation could be assisted and expedited. In short, the potential for emancipation has to exist in the real conditions of life themselves, and not in the logical potential of ideas alone. For this reason, Marx's attention turned to the analysis of economic and political arrangements, considered as socially organised complexes.

### Dialectical structure

In Marx's version, the conflict was not between contradictory ideas, expressed first in thought and subsequently also in social relations. The reverse applied. The root historical conflict was between opposed *social groups*. Their conflicts would sometimes find their expression in thought, in the realm of ideas, but they originated in differences of *economic interest*. The key to understanding a society was to begin by understanding the way in which it organised its economic activity, the arrangements through which it carried out its physical production.

Marx replaced Hegel's history of ideas by analysis of socio-economic conditions, but he remained attached – at least arguably so – to his conception of an underlying logic, a *dialectical* structure, to history.

The question of the relationship between economic interests and ideas will recur on several occasions below, for central to subsequent decisive shifts in Marxism has been an ongoing dispute over what Marx intended by this relationship. In crude terms, the issue concerns whether or not Marx can be fairly considered to be an economic – even a technological – determinist.

At this point, we simply recapitulate the shift from Hegel's idealism to Marx's materialism.

## Materialism

The human essence is the capacity to labour, to work upon and modify the world about it, to shape it better in accord with human needs, thereby enhancing human existence and potential. In short, labour is human nature – human essence itself. The capacity of labour has a cumulative character, since human beings can contrive new and improved ways of carrying out their work on the world, given their capacity for practical thought; e.g. the creation of tools increases human powers.

## Change: quantity and quality

The cumulative character of labour, however, is not smooth and continuous. Here another Hegelian notion informs Marx's analysis: quantity into quality. Hegel had noted that many changes are continuous up to a point, and then they involve a drastic, discontinuous alteration. For example, if we heat or cool water for a time we get a continuous cumulative change, and the water just gets hotter or colder, but if we continue, then at a certain point there is a change not just of quantity – so many more degrees – but in nature or quality. The water starts to boil and turn into a gas, or freeze and turn into ice. This quantity-into-quality change is characteristic of historical processes, where a society changes in a cumulative way. For example, an agricultural society might expand the area of land under cultivation but, at a certain point, further changes are not possible except through a change in the whole nature of the society, and an agricultural becomes an industrial society.

Human beings develop tools – technology – to enhance their labour power, and in a given period of history a certain level of technology prevails, which is amenable to continuing improvement. At a certain point, however, a new, different kind of technology is created, which is superior. This emphasis upon the development of technology invites the view that Marx is a *technological determinist*, i.e. he sees the development of new technologies of production as giving rise to historical change. However, Marx was precisely concerned to oppose this kind of idea of technology as an independent force, since technology in itself is no more than an inert body of practical and technical knowledge. It takes the social relations between human beings to make a technology conceivable and practical. Economic, productive activity is a *social*, a *collective* affair. The prevailing form of technology might be among the forces of production, but the social relations of production are most critical.

## The social relations of production

A technology implies, so to speak, certain kinds of relations among people. For example, one person can operate a horse-drawn plough, but an industrial plant obviously requires the complex organisation of a team of individuals, involving, among other things, an elaborate division of labour into specialist tasks.

Economic change is never just a change in technology; it also requires a set of changes in *social relations*, and not just in the social relations involved in production itself. For example, an individual alone, someone living in isolation, remote from any neighbour, can operate the horse-drawn plough, but an industrial plant cannot be operated by members of a population that is as thinly scattered across a landscape as prairie farmers. People have to be resident near to the plant if they are to work there. Obviously, there is much more to this idea that economic relations require social relations of specific kinds, but this example indicates its force.

In summary, Marx's idea that economic production is *basic* to the life of a society has at least a threefold justification:

1 Productive activity is definitive of human nature.
2 Productive activity is logically prior to other activities, in the sense that we cannot do anything else until we have met the conditions of our physical existence, i.e. we cannot theorise, or paint, or play sport until we have provided food, protection from the environment and so forth.
3 The structure of productive activity has causal consequences for the form taken by other social activities. For example, an aristocrat and a peasant lived completely differently, i.e. the aristocrat could have a leisure-filled existence, but the overwhelming bulk of the peasant's time was consumed in producing what was needed for his or her own (and, ultimately, the aristocrat's) existence.

## The economic foundations of power

One other element vital to these considerations was the fact that some people controlled and directed the activities of others.

## Ownership of the means of production

In production, there was often the difference between those who did the physical work, and those who supplied them with the means to do that work – access to land, or raw materials or technology – but did not themselves do it. The aristocrat controlled land and granted the peasant permission to work, the industrial employer controls the physical plant and machinery and pays workers wages to use them. The one who possesses the means of production, therefore, has power over the one who makes use of them.

Hence for Marx the crucial division in society became not just that between those who worked and those who did not work in physical production, but more specifically one based on the existence of private property, i.e. between those who possessed – who owned – the means of production and those who did not. In production, the former controlled (and *exploited*) the latter. The exploitation consisted, in crudest terms, in the fact that those who did not work were able to have at least a portion of the product physically created in work handed over to them, though they had contributed nothing to its actual creation.

The relationship of power, of control, which was found in economic relations based on private property, was reproduced in the wider society. Those who dominated within the process of economic production ruled the society; for example, the aristocrats who controlled the land also made up the ruling group within pre-industrial society. The key positions and relationships in society were those of class.

## Class

Under any particular regime of production, there are many people who would stand in the same relationship to one another; in the productive process, as we have said, people either work, or own the means of production. Those people in the same position on one side of this divide were in the same class.

The pattern of this divide not only exists in the economic sphere, but also obtains across all areas of life. Life in society, even in those areas most remote from physical production, is class-divided, class-based. Hence the concept of class is wider than the analysis of economic relations alone; it involves the analysis of the structure of society as a whole. This is another respect in which economic structures are 'basic' to society for Marx, for it is in terms of the relationships established around a given form of economic production that social class is formed, which, in its turn, becomes the fundamental relation around which all other social activities are structured.

## Classes and class conflict

The idea of society as composed of classes is the key to the materialist implementation of Hegel's dialectical concept. To reiterate: by 'materialist' we here mean nothing more than a view of history as the product of real, striving human beings, rather than of any occult or supra-individual forces such as God or the human spirit.

Classes are *relational* entities: one class can exist only if there are other classes; a 'one-class' society must be a no-class society, since to speak of a class is to speak of a collection of people who are differentiated from one or more other collections of people. The relationships between such classes are those of opposition.

### Class interest

The two classes of owners and workers have opposed interests, for the owning class can only meet the conditions of its physical survival – or, indeed, of its much more luxuriant style of existence – if it takes the means from those who create the things that can be consumed.

In Marx's view, someone who does not take part in physical production is not entitled to a share of its product; thus those who do not work exploit those who do.

This conception of the fundamental organising character of class has implications for the way in which the structure of *society as a whole* is to be understood. The class nature of ownership and exploitation has consequences within the economic structure and also carries implications for the organisation of the rest of the society. Since the inequality between the owning class and the labouring class involves a social relationship of *power and control*, it cannot be narrowly defined as simply economic, because the difference of interest between these classes refers to *freedom*. The capacity of the owning class to deprive the physical producers of their physical product is a difference in power, a manifestation of the fact that the owners can restrict the access of labourers to the means of economic activity. When they do grant them access to these means, e.g. by renting land to farm, or hiring them for industrial work, the owners have the capacity to direct what they will do. In other words, those who labour are not free, a fact most starkly apparent in the case of the slave and also, albeit less starkly, in the cases of the peasant legally bound in service to the lord, and of the industrial worker hired for a wage to work under the control and direction of plant management.

## Class conflict

The conflict of interest between owning and labouring classes is, then, a conflict over power and freedom. It must pervade the rest of society's organisation because the owners wish to protect and preserve their position. For them to realise their own interest requires control not only over the immediate circumstances of economic production, but also over the way the rest of the society is arranged.

This broader dimension of power and control is necessary to ensure that the position of the owning class within the economic structure is sustained. If the conflict of interest between the owning and the labouring classes becomes an open and direct confrontation, then the owning class requires that its position – and interests – within the economy be recognised in the society as legitimate and defensible. Accordingly, it is entitled to call on the use of whatever force – police, army – is available. In this way the economic and the political dimensions of society are interrelated; the owning class has *an interest* in the nature of the law and in the disposition of political power in its need to be assured of support in any challenge to its ownership and control.

## Class, economic order and social institutions

This need for support entails more than simply containing direct challenges to ownership and control since the requirement for production must also be reproduced. A given way of organising production depends upon there being a sufficiently numerous and suitable labour force available and able to do the kind of labour involved in the work of the economy. The economy itself does not provide this labour force; rather, it derives from the way the rest of the society is organised. For example, family arrangements must produce enough individuals to fill the places for labour. These family arrangements (perhaps in conjunction with other institutions and organisations) have to ensure that the individuals are healthy enough and suitably educated to be able to do the available work. The owning class has *an interest* in the ways the family, health provision, education and training are organised in the society, for these provide preconditions for the continuation of its own position.

There is one further element. To be suitable, a labour force has to possess not merely the capacity to do the work available, but also the necessary outlook and motivation. Crucially, the outlook should lead to accepting the position of the owning class within the productive process, i.e. workers should be docile and co-operative in the system. This outlook cannot be taken for granted; it has to be produced and reproduced, for the kind of outlook on life people have depends upon their social background, experience and learning. Thus the owning class has *an interest* in the intellectual culture of a society, in the nature of the ideas that are being circulated, and in the ways they are being disseminated.

If ideas challenge the right of ownership or encourage a dissident and uncooperative attitude to work within the prevailing arrangements, then they are not in the interest of the owning class.

The owning class, therefore, has an interest in the way the general affairs of society are organised. In fact, it is *in the interest* of this class either to control the society as a whole, or to have society controlled on its behalf. In short, the interest of the owning class entails a direct concern with the politics of its society. Of course, such control of the whole society is the very focus of politics. Hence the economically dominant class wishes to be also socially and politically dominant; the owning class aspires to be a *ruling* class. This class might rule directly, as in a feudal society, where the rulers are the landowning aristocrats, or relatively indirectly, as in industrial societies. Here the owners of economic production in the form of companies do not themselves operate as the political, i.e. parliamentary, rulers, yet, according to Marxist interpretations, they none the less get their way in matters of politics, exercising sufficient control over parliamentary representatives to ensure that their interests are advanced in law and statute.

As well as political dominance, the owning class also seeks *intellectual* control, which came to be called *hegemony* in the later Marxist tradition (see Chapter 8). Marx himself explicitly pointed out that the ruling class in society controls the channels through which ideas can be created and circulated, and we have indicated its reasons for having an interest in the kinds of ideas that are circulated, i.e. to inculcate in workers an outlook that makes them tractable and compliant. We have also mentioned Marx's view about the way the division of labour produces a separation of physical and mental labour, and how the liberation of thinkers from the practical demands of productive work exposes thought to the risk of self-delusion.

## The nature and functions of ideology

In combination, these views of Marx contribute to the notion of *ideology*. This notion of ideology has been particularly significant in shaping the subsequent impact of Marx's thought upon sociology. Though the appeal of Marx's ideas within sociology is at its lowest point for some time, and though Marx's teachings have been largely repudiated by contemporary poststructuralist thinkers, nevertheless he continues to be hailed as one of the three thinkers – along with Friedrich Nietzsche (see Chapter 10) and Sigmund Freud (see Chapter 9) – who created the idea that individuals' actions are shaped by forces of which they are not conscious. The idea of unconscious determinants of conduct is a vital, indispensable element in both structuralist and poststructuralist thought. Nietzsche, Marx and Freud have been jointly nominated as 'the masters of suspicion' for the collective suggestion of their contributions to the notion of unconscious determinants of action, i.e. the actual determinants of conduct are much more base and unattractive, much more unacceptable, than those which we consciously believe to be governing what we do. In both Nietzsche and Freud, the idea is more of unconscious *psychological* determinants of thought, which originate in the individual's own mind, while Marx's ideas are more about the *social* origins of distorted thinking: the socio-political necessity to keep the real causes of people's actions inaccessible to their conscious thought.

## Ideology

An ideology is a system of ideas that *systematically* misrepresents reality. It does so in ways that serve the interests of social groups, particularly the ruling strata. Ideologies misrepresent reality in various ways: they conceal unacceptable aspects of it; they glorify things which are of themselves less than glorious; they make out things which are neither natural nor necessary as though they were both.

To give a simple and crude example, many theories of human nature created in capitalist societies treat human beings as though they are naturally selfish and unrelentingly competitive, as though it is in their nature to look out only for themselves and to seek every degree of advantage over others that they can find. This kind of idea today comes over as 'scientific', through interpretations of Darwin's evolutionary biological theories, which some crudely summarise as being that evolution is a question of 'the survival of the fittest'. It is presented in popular form. Richard Dawkins (1976) expounds this argument as being about 'the selfish gene' in a book of the same name. The idea here is that selfishness is in the nature of all living things (as a result of the imperative of our genes to survive) and that existence is a matter of competing for the marginal advantages that will ensure the survival of our genetic matter into future generations.

Such a view has two features that are common among ideologies: the suggestion that it is simply in our nature to be selfish and self-interested; and the implication that there is nothing we can do to change this characteristic because it is built into our nature. The Marxist point of view denies that we are innately competitive in this way. To talk about the natural, immutable competitiveness of the human species offers a false picture of our human natures. Such theories serve to justify a socio-economic system – competitive capitalism – that is based upon unrelenting individual competition. These ideas justify such a system by suggesting that, first, it gives full rein to our fundamental human natures and is therefore best suited to us, and, second, there is little point in disapproving of or attempting to moderate its competitiveness since it is our nature to be competitive. If we are being 'natural', no alternative seems possible and therefore competitive capitalism seems to be unchangeable. In one way or another, systems of ideas play this ideological role of convincing people that they cannot change their society, or that it is not worth their effort to try changing it; one of the purposes of Marx's analysis is to expose the ideological character of such ideas in order to encourage the view that change is conceivable, possible and necessary.

The point about such ideologies is that they are instilled into the thought of individuals and become the basis upon which those individuals act. The individuals may think they are freely choosing to do the things they do, but they are, rather, acting in ways which are in the interest of the ruling class only, and in which the system needs them to act if it is to survive and prosper. The systems of thought that exist in society are not shaped by the freely operating minds of thinkers, but are decisively influenced by the needs and structures of the society itself. On examination, these systems will be seen not to be objective and general, but to be specific and partial, developed not because they show how things are in themselves, but because such ways of thinking are necessary to the particular form of society in which they grow up. The individuals subject to these systems of belief are not, therefore, aware of the true reasons for holding these beliefs; from a Marxist point of view, they are misguided about what it would be in their own interests to do. As mentioned, the ideological distortion of thought is an indispensable notion for many current forms of social theory.

## The base–superstructure model of society

We now are well on the way to setting in place two central pillars of Marx's thinking:

- the base–superstructure metaphor, with the concept of ideology;
- the idea of history as a progression through class conflict.

The debate over whether or not Marx was a humanist thinker turns on what interpretation is given to these elements. To set up this issue clearly, it is necessary to say a little more about the base–superstructure model.

The account we have given has set out the general lines of Marx's thinking. At the centre is a model of society that provides one of the main bones of contention about the actual nature of his theories, namely, the model of an economic *base* and an institutional and intellectual *superstructure*. It has been implicit in our discussion above, i.e. in suggesting that the other institutions and the culture of a society are to be understood in terms of the needs of its economic arrangements. We have just been saying that organising and perpetuating a given form of economic organisation requires the whole of the society to be appropriately structured; the economy could not function or persist if, for example, the legal system, the educational arrangements and even the religious beliefs of people were not of a suitably supportive kind. For example, religious beliefs can contribute to economic docility if they teach the importance of accepting authority in all its forms and the spiritual merit of hard work.

## The base–superstructure model

The idea is of the economic structure being the foundation upon which the rest of the social edifice is raised. It fits with Marx's conception that productive activity is logically prior to other things; only after the requirements for survival and sustenance have been satisfied is it possible for human beings to do other things, to engage in leisure and creativity. Consequently, the manner and means by which productive activity meets these basic human needs set limits to the things that people can otherwise do.

## Two readings of Marx

Marx was thus proposing that the form which social institutions and the intellectual life of a society take is decisively shaped by its economic institutions, a proposal which was – at the time he was making it – extraordinarily radical and drastic. A century and a half later it has become commonplace and very widely assumed, usually without any recognition of its affiliation with Marx. The proposal, however, remains controversial, and only comparatively recently has been the focus of heated contention. Is Marx an *economic determinist*? In other words, is Marx saying rather more than that productive and non-productive activities presuppose one another, and a given form of economic activity has certain preconditions for its existence and operations, which must be met by other institutions in the society? Is he going on to say that the economic base of society *dictates* the shape of all the other institutions in society, thereby *driving* the whole history of the society? If the economic base dictates – or *determines* – how the family, legal, religious and intellectual arrangements of the society must be, then the economic base drives the history of the society as a whole.

## Economic determinism

If the economy changes its fundamental character, then the preconditions for its operation and persistence will also change, and will causally necessitate suitably adaptive modifications in the rest of the society. The form of the economy will then dictate the form that will be taken by the family, the political system, religious practices and the rest.

Though many have extracted it, such a picture from Marx's work is often disapproved of as 'vulgar materialism', i.e. the idea that the superstructure is a simple and direct function of the base, changing at the behest and in the manner dictated by the base. For many, this view may have a considerable element of truth, but it cannot be entirely true; they cannot seriously hold that *all* aspects of life and thought are straightforwardly dictated by the requirements of productive organisation. After Marx's death, his friend and close, long-time collaborator Friedrich Engels, keen to dissociate the pair of them from any such implication, suggested that the relationship between base and superstructure was more complex and reciprocal than this 'vulgar Marxist', one-way, rigid determinism.

Dissent importantly focuses upon the issue of *voluntarism*. The strongly 'economic determinist' reading suggests that human individuals are mere playthings of economic forces; whatever they attempt to do makes no difference to anything. This reading, many feel, either makes Marx's theories entirely unattractive, or would do so if it were accepted. Of course, some may find this idea of total determination an attractive one. However, one can read Marx as precisely seeking to distance himself from any such determinist conception; after all, it is one of the main themes of his life's work to demystify economic relations, to dispel any suggestion that they are super-human, quasi-supernatural forces which have human lives at their mercy. He favoured the view that economic relations are social; they are relations between human beings, whose true nature has been obscured behind clouds of ideological falsification. One can read as the message of Marx's work that it is necessary for people to realise that their economic systems and their social institutions are their own creations; if they have created them, then they can recreate them in a new and improved form. Only by the realisation that they are not puppets of supra-individual forces – such as God or the market – can people take proper control of their own destiny.

On this reading, Marx does not deny that individuals *collectively* can make a difference; he does deny that *isolated* ones can. Marx finds laughable the idea that Hegel, just by working out a philosophical system, can bring the whole of humanity to complete freedom. The absurdity of this supposition is manifest in the fact that next to nothing in the real world of social, political and economic injustice was altered by the arrival of Hegel's theory. It is entirely unrealistic to think that one individual, just by writing a book, can get armies to disband, prisons to close and owners to surrender their property. Hegel's underlying idea that history and social change are collective phenomena is correct, but Hegel himself failed to apply it properly. A given historical, socio-economic system can be changed, but to turn such a system upside down requires considerable collective, concerted effort. In short, only the might of a large and well-organised social group (properly directed by the right understanding of social reality) can bring about full human freedom.

Indeed, organised social groups (not technology or economic systems) have been the driving force of social change; they will bring the process of change – history itself – to completion. It is the process of *class conflict* that makes up the story of change.

## Change and conflict

Hegelian logic can be seen in Marx's treatment of the pattern of social change. If we treat an actual society as built around a central conflict of interest, i.e. an irreconcilable (or seemingly irreconcilable) opposition, then, after the fashion of Hegel's dialectic, we should expect this situation to be unstable. There are pressures to change, to escape from and to overcome this conflict. Also from Hegel can be taken the idea of conflict as a productive, creative force, i.e. the attempt to overcome a conflict will result in a more developed situation, in which the initial conflict will be resolved, but within which a new opposition can be expected to arise. At the heart of any given society, then, we should expect to find a central opposition which defines the whole character of the society, and, on Marx's reinterpretation of Hegel, we should expect to find that that opposition will take the form of class conflict. The system of economic organisation gives rise to two classes, those who own and control and those who labour, and their opposed interests will place them in mutual struggle, with the ruling group seeking to establish its pre-eminence within the whole society.

The decisive moment for change will not come, however, from this confrontation of ruling class with labouring class – at least, not until the final stage of the historical process with the full development and final overthrow of the capitalist system. In the first instance, the capacity of human beings to envisage and create new and improved ways of production provides the impetus to ensure that, within a society dominated by a given economic system and a property-owning class, a new way of organising economic affairs will begin to develop, and new ways of organising relations between owners and producers will begin to form. Since the new means of organising production are an improvement, they have the potential to replace the existing system, thereby providing a threat to the existing system and the class whose ruling power is based upon that existing system. The system as it stands does not favour the development of the full potential of the new ways, but those new ways will continue to develop, and those who own and control the new economic forces will have the characteristic desire to have things arranged to maximise the realisation of these forces. In so doing, they will want to control the whole society. Those who dominate within the newly emerging system will find themselves in conflict with the existing ruling class, and will begin to see the need to replace the ruling class if they are to realise their own objectives.

Consequently, a struggle will develop over the question of who is to be the ruling class. For example, the Marxist version of the history of Western Europe was the struggle between the aristocrats, who dominated within the agricultural system that prevailed across the whole of Europe for such a long time, and the bourgeoisie, the city-based businessmen, who controlled the emerging industrial plants. The latter system eventually became the prevailing mode of production throughout Western Europe and the USA; its powers, needs and products enabled these societies to dominate and to make use of the rest of the world, which had not developed such production. With the shift towards industrial production as the dominant system, the owners of industrial property became the true powers in society, influential enough to reshape the law in the interests of their type of property, and decisively to direct political policy, even though they did not hold political positions themselves. But trouble was storing up in such societies.

As we have seen, on the Hegelian, dialectical model the progression from one stage of history to the next involves the development of something, which is already present in the current stage, beyond the point at which it can continue to exist within the confines of this current stage; the transformation, which Hegel referred to as 'quantity into quality', is involved. Applying this logic to capitalism, the system, like other forms of society before it, ought to contain the seeds of its own destruction, producing something that will, eventually, have to carry development beyond the capitalist stage for its realisation. The relevant development within capitalism is the *proletariat*.

## The proletariat

This is the force of urbanised industrial workers, whose ranks were relentlessly expanded as all kinds of other individuals (farmers, individual artisans, etc.) found their livellhoods destroyed by the superior productive power of capitalist production; they had no choice but to seek work in the expanding industrial plants.

At the same time, of course, capitalism was expanding the working class across societies, as well as within them, as its system continued relentlessly to grow internationally.

## The logic of capitalist expansion

This expansion was 'driven' by competition: the system is such that every member of the bourgeoisie is in competition with others. The capitalists have no choice; they have to expand their industrial capacity for economic survival. The logic of competition brings a relentless drive for efficiency and, as the potential for efficient production is greater the larger the productive unit, there is a continuing drive towards bigger industrial plants. An inevitable consequence is the continuing expansion of the industrial working classes; the process of expansion serves not only to increase their numbers, but also to provide the basis for their unification.

## Workers' unification

Industrial expansion concentrates the working classes in urban areas, and provides them, through the wonders of capitalism's products, with an increasing capacity to communicate with one another and, therefore, to organise.

At the same time, the expansion of the system also provides them with the motivation to organise and to oppose the capitalist system itself, for, in Marx's most simplified model, the development of capitalism involves: (1) the *simplification* of social relations, the concentration of the overwhelming mass of the population into two sharply divided social classes – those who own, and those who do not own property; and (2) the *intensification* of the exploitative relationship that obtains between the two. It results in (3) the *immiseration* (i.e. impoverishment) of those who are exploited. These developments, together with improvements in communication, mean that it becomes increasingly apparent to the proletariat – especially if aided by Marx's theory – that their miseries are the result of the system; all their important interests starkly oppose them to the ruling class of capitalist entrepreneurs. In brief, here is a very promising basis for the revolutionary uprising of a working class who could destroy capitalist society.

Viewed from a historical perspective, the destruction of capitalism is not a negative but a positive change, albeit not, of course, from the standpoint of the bourgeoisie, whose domination of society would be terminated. It would remove the causes of massive human misery and, even more importantly, would involve making the productive power created by capitalism into a collective possession, thereby releasing its tremendous powers and benefits to serve the needs of all, not just a few.

## Conclusion

On the reading we have given, Marx is a humanist because he is understood as having inherited Hegelian ideas that human beings are at the centre of history, and that history is the story of the development of their essential nature (i.e. the mind in Hegel's case, the capacity for creative labour in Marx's). In both accounts the whole of history focuses centrally on a particular, unifying theme. This theme, to be seen in each phase of history, is that society embodies a dominant contradiction: it is formed around a central opposition that determines all other aspects of its existence. Such a contradiction can be found in the succession of each stage of history, as the next stage of society takes up the further development of the unfolding nature of the human species.

## Yet to come

We have said little in this exposition of Marx's thought about his last writings, especially his largest work, *Capital*, which consisted much more in technical economics than his previous works. This is not to say that the underlying logic of those writings could not be absorbed to the above scheme, since a Hegelian reading can encompass writings from all phases of Marx's career. However, the inclination to read Marx in this way has been contested fiercely, with great consequences for contemporary analysis, by the French Marxist Louis Althusser. He insisted that while Marx, in his early work, had indeed been a humanist under Hegel's influence, he had later come to see that such a way of thinking was not truly scientific. Marx saw that essentialism is unscientific, being, in reality, ideo-logical, so he purged *all* Hegelianism from his thought. He moved from ideology to science and stated the scientific position in *Capital*. Accordingly, we continue the story of Marx's thought and a consideration of *Capital* at a later point when we encounter Althusser's structural Marxism (see Chapter 9). Before that, we will continue the account of the Hegelian reading of Marx in our remarks on Western Marxism, particularly with respect to the writings of the Frankfurt School, which were the epitome of everything that Althusser condemned (see Chapter 8).

## Questions

1 Explain the differences between a humanist and non-humanist approach to the social world. Find an example of a contemporary social conflict (a strike, a war, a riot, a protest, etc.). What would a humanist description of it look like? How would a non-humanist one differ?

2 How does Marx's concept of 'alienation' relate to other ways the term might be used? Are these different meanings related to one another? Which might be related to the division of labour, and which have different roots?

3 Why does Marx conclude that 'work' is so important in understanding modern societies? Does his definition of work make sense to you, and why? What things have you done this week that might count as 'work' in Marx's sense? Which don't seem to count? Can you think of any non-work activities that would count as 'work' in Marx's terms?

4 What does Marx mean when he uses the concept of 'class'? What, according to Marx, are the relationships between class and power? Can you think of any contemporary examples of how these relationships manifest themselves today? What contemporary social institutions might reflect the class basis of power?

5 What does Marx mean by 'ideology', and how does it differ from other kinds of knowledge? In what ways can you understand a contemporary news story as an ideological product? Are there any news stories that are *not* ideological?

6 What does Marx mean by 'superstructure'? What contemporary institutions are parts of this superstructure? Can they be understood as ideological? Can they be understood as being determined by economic relations? Does it make sense to you for these things to be understood in this way?

7 Does Marx believe that the 'individual' is important? Are people the basis of Marx's analysis or are they just pushed around by economic forces? How do you think this question relates to disputes about whether or not Marx was a humanist?

## Next steps

Bottomore and Rubel's (1970) *Karl Marx: Selected Writings in Sociology and Social Philosophy* is still a useful selection of original texts. A longer selection can be found in McLellan's (2000) *Karl Marx: Selected Writings*, which covers the full range of Marx's thought.

A good short introduction to Marx's thought can be found in Carver's (1982) *Marx's Social Theory*. The classic exposition of Marx, and his influence on later thinkers, is Kołakowski's (2008) *Main Currents of Marxism*.

## CHAPTER THREE

# Max Weber

---

**Chapter overview**

Max Weber was one of the most important sociological thinkers, and his work can be understood as a reaction to – and development of – Marx's ideas. In this chapter his methodological approach to the study of history will be described, and its implications for doing sociological studies drawn out. Weber's understandings of the nature of the social individual and the role of ideas in social life will be examined, and their place in his description of the development of capitalism clarified. The importance of religious belief in this account will be emphasised, and the ways in which this allows us to distinguish between Marx and Weber examined. Weber's analysis of social inequality – *stratification* – will be outlined, and the *forms of authority* described and explained. Weber attempted to use these concepts to compare different societies, and to show what is distinctive about the contemporary Western world: we will conclude with an examination of this work.

---

## Introduction: methodological commitments and substantive themes

Weber's sociology is much closer to Marx than Durkheim's is, and comprises a critique of so-called vulgar Marxism, i.e. the idea that social life, including culture, is a simple function of the economic structure. Weber took Marx for a vulgar Marxist – understandably, given the unavailability to him of Marx's early writings, which unequivocally contradict such vulgar readings. Coming from a very different philosophical background from that of Marx, Weber was allied to the Neo-Kantian rather than the Hegelian tradition in German thought. Neo-Kantians were philosophers of the late nineteenth and early twentieth centuries who followed the teachings of Immanuel Kant (1724–1804). Kant saw human beings as existing only partly in the world of natural causality, and partly in a realm of freedom, governed by moral rules rather than causes.

Consequently, human beings could not be understood entirely by natural science; the study of their moral and spiritual life would have to be pursued by other means. Nevertheless, Weber shared some of Marx's key assumptions and also his core concern with the nature of capitalism. However, he held very different conceptions of the nature of history, and also of the methodology of historical and sociological studies.

One legacy of Immanuel Kant's philosophy is a sharp distinction between the realm of physical nature and that of human mental life. Physical nature is a realm of rigid, mechanical determination, while human mental life is one of freedom and the absence of causality. At the end of the nineteenth century, this distinction gave rise in German culture to a hot debate over the limits to scientific inquiry: were cultural phenomena, the topics of history, by their very nature precluded from the kind of scientific study applied to natural phenomena? This debate framed Weber's own preoccupations. For him, the difference between natural science and history was not basically a result of the different natures of natural and social phenomena; rather, it came out of our relationship to them, out of the interests that we take in them. With respect to nature, we have, on the whole, an interest in understanding its general patterns; the difference between one rock and another hardly matters at all to us and certainly does not matter for its own sake. Rather, we are interested in the way in which rocks in general behave; we can therefore be satisfied with an understanding that is abstract and generalised. However, when it comes to human beings, their *individuality* captivates us. For example, our interest in Adolf Hitler derives not from the characteristics he had in common with other human beings, but from his distinctiveness, the extent to which he was quite unlike other politicians. Similarly, in England we are interested in the study of English society because, for us, England holds a different place in our lives from that of other societies; after all, it is our home. Thus we are not satisfied by studies that take out all that is distinctive about the historical figures that have affected us and shaped our lives, i.e. by studies of our society which give a highly generalised account of people and societies. Weber did not conclude that there is no room for generalities in the social sciences; rather, that they are not their be-all and end-all in the way they are within the natural sciences. Generalities can be useful in the study of history and society as means to another end, i.e. in so far as they help us to understand better the individual case.

## Individuality

For Weber, sociology as a generalising approach was subordinate to history; it provided abstract concepts, which could be useful in understanding concrete, complex, *individual* historical cases. Such concepts were created not for their own sake but precisely for their usefulness in informing historical studies.

Weber's own studies were wide-ranging geographically and historically; they encompassed the civilisations of the West from the time of the Greeks, and

Asiatic societies such as India and China over thousands of years, and were meant to include the world of Islam also (though his study of Islam was barely launched, and most of the other studies, though lengthy, were unfinished). Their purpose was to tackle questions about the role of religion in social and economic change, and also the relationship between ideas and economic conditions of the sort posed by Marx. Nevertheless, understanding of the general issues and of the other societies was not sought for its own sake, but gathered with respect to its relevance to the situation at home, i.e. understanding the individuality of the Western European and North American capitalist civilisations (especially Germany, for Weber was strongly nationalist in sentiments) in the nineteenth and early twentieth centuries. The 'individuals' with whom history was concerned could be quite large complexes, such as 'Western civilisation in the modern world', and not just individual human beings. Further, historical/scientific knowledge had only a relatively subordinate role in relationship to politics. Weber wrote two major essays on politics and science as vocations, putting views that provoke controversy to this day.

## Objectivity and value freedom

Most contentious is the idea that science should be 'value free'. A major political concern of Weber's was to ensure civic responsibility within modern society, where technical and scientific expertise was assuming ever-increasing importance. Weber worried about the blurring of the roles of scientist and citizen and the use of the prestige of science to bolster the claims of demagogues. He feared that those who occupied the role of scientist would often be irresponsible enough to take advantage of the prestige given them by their position of scientific eminence, and of the authority deriving from their expertise, in order to advocate political policies, which can have no scientific basis or authority. He believed that in the universities of his time the professors were exceeding the bounds of their scholarly competence in the lecture hall by delivering impassioned speeches about political issues in the guise of scholarly disquisitions. Academics and scientists are no less entitled to the right to present their political viewpoints than anyone else, but they are no more privileged in the political arena than anyone else and should therefore confine their political persuasion to the public, political arena. There the greatest historian, physicist or sociologist is just one more citizen, one more voice. The responsible discharge of scientific obligations requires sober compliance with the usual rules of scholarly investigation and evidential proof, and abstinence from political polemics in the classroom.

### Facts and values

The distinction between the scientific and the political was, for Weber, the recognition of a long-standing philosophical distinction between *facts* and *values*. A very standard position, which

Weber shared, is that values cannot logically be deduced from facts. Scientists can only report upon what happens and how things are; they cannot tell us how they should be, how we should live, or what we should do. The provision of research and evidence cannot relieve us of the necessity to make choices at the level of values.

This distinction was a key to Weber's conception of human existence as well as sociological method: there is an irreducible variety of incompatible human values; and there is no possibility of a scientific or rational basis upon which to choose between them. We cannot excuse ourselves from the need to make a choice by arguing that science shows one value to be preferable to another, for science cannot do this. We have to make up our own minds about which 'Gods or Demons', as Weber put it, to affiliate ourselves to, which gods to worship, which leaders to follow and which causes to fight for. Such choice is a tragic aspect of human existence and surely a source of terrible conflicts within and between individuals. Consequently, Weber is sometimes spoken of as a *decisionist*, i.e. we have to choose our values, the things we treasure and strive for, from a range of possible and irreconcilable values, and must therefore make a decision to go one way rather than another and, having made it, live with its consequences. Therefore, science can never displace politics, and the scientist can never, acting purely as scientist, be a political leader. The (legitimate) role of science in politics can only ever be advisory. Scientists understand what happens and how things work causally. They can, therefore, give good advice on how to make a certain thing happen. They can tell us, on the basis of their expertise, that certain ways of attempting to make something happen are more likely to bring about the desired result, but they cannot, from that same expertise, tell us whether we should desire that result or a different one. The question whether we want *x* or *y* is a *political* decision, a matter for the political leadership to deal with. Scientific knowledge can be of great value to politics, but it cannot displace or substitute for politics. It is an illusion to think that politics can be made scientific, for politics entails struggle between values, not the facts of empirical knowledge.

Weber never sought to keep the social scientist out of politics but merely to keep distinct the two roles a scientist might play, as disciplined inquirer and as active citizen. Within the sphere of scholarship, the scientist can be objective, since objectivity requires only sober compliance with the obligations of the scientific role to proceed according to the standard rules of evidence and proof. Within politics, the danger is that the difference between the scientific and political roles is obscured, giving a false authority to someone who just happens to be a scientist. In the administration of politics, those serving as scientific advisers to politicians might exceed their role, might begin to usurp the decision-making prerogative of the legitimate political leader through attempting to reduce real issues of value decision to matters of mere technical choice or by obscuring the political issues in talk that sounds like science. Science itself, as Weber recognised, also rests upon values. For example, if we do not value knowledge for its own sake, then what would be the point of pursuing scholarship? 'Value freedom' as Weber understood it operates within the framework of accepted scientific values. He himself was not abashed at being politically active or in seeking to use scientific knowledge in the formation of social policy. Indeed, he was concerned about the absence of decisive, heroic political leadership, leading some critics to see in his ideals a prefiguration of the kind of leadership Hitler would shortly offer the German people.

## The particularity of Western capitalism

The 'individual' that captured Weber's scientific interest was the capitalist civilisation of the West. It was unique and unprecedented. It had arisen only in Western Europe and the USA, and had not developed in other societies. What was special about it? Why did Western civilisation have this individuality? What had given rise to it?

Weber certainly rejected all-embracing historical schemes of the sort employed by Hegel and Marx and decried any suggestion that capitalism was 'one stage' which *all* societies must go through in their progression from the most primitive to the most developed. The idea that there is anything supra-individual, anything super-human about history was anathema to him: history and society consist of human individuals and nothing more. Abstract sociological statements and laws are, in the end, statements about the activities of those individuals and nothing else. Talk about the actions of a social class, such as the working class, makes assertions about the behaviour of the typical or average individual in a certain socio-economic position; ideas of the Marxian type about the members of a social class having the interests of the class to which they belong but of which they are unaware are simply nonsense in this context. Since history consists only in the decisions and actions of individuals, then any idea of history itself having an overall purpose or direction is also nonsense. Thus Weber's inquiries into the origins of modern Western, capitalist society were into a specific set of conditions, and not directed towards identifying any necessary, general tendencies of history.

Weber's fame rests upon his account of *The Protestant Ethic and the Spirit of Capitalism* (1987). Marx was certainly right that the modern Western societies were capitalist. Yet though capitalism might be their dominating feature, it was not, of itself, their distinctive one. Capitalism – the organised pursuit of profit – had taken many forms in different societies across history (including, for example, the pirate ship). What was distinctive – not to say peculiar – about the capitalism in the West was its highly *organised* character and, even more, the highly *moralised* tone of profit seeking. Thus Weber's account was not of capitalism in general, but of one of its forms, the *rational* form, found in the modern West, i.e. Europe and the United States. For Weber, the capitalist business in this period had two crucial characteristics: (1) it was kept in continuous existence and operation; (2) it was a ceaseless operation in the relentless pursuit of accumulating profit. Throughout history, capitalist business had been a sporadic venture, undertaken in pursuit of sufficient profit for purposes of utility and consumption. On completion, the venture was placed in abeyance until another foray for profit became opportune. The modern Western capitalist business was organised on the basis of a continuing operation, utilising the most advanced calculative knowledge of how to link means to ends in both delivering its products and also structuring its own internal financial and organisational affairs.

## Rational capitalism

This unrelenting commitment to means–ends efficiency makes rational capitalism what it is. The capitalist business continues to accumulate profit even though there is no practical need for it, even though the level of profits exceeds what its recipients can ever spend. Rather than being acquired for use, seemingly wealth is sought for its own sake, and the aim of business is the ceaseless expansion of profits. This pursuit of ever-greater profit is not, however, driven by greed or grandiosity of ambition. Instead, it is seen as morally righteous, with the resulting profit being the capitalists' just deserts for their industry.

Indeed, capitalists share with their workforce and the population at large the conviction that a life of dedicated toil is the good life; this conviction provides the true distinctiveness of modern Western, rational capitalism. In most civilisations, work has not been so regarded; rather, it is seen as a necessary evil, endured only when unavoidable. In the capitalist West, however, 'lazy' is a term of severe disapproval and those who are without a job may well be regarded, and may even regard themselves, as 'worthless'.

## Linking the capitalist spirit with Protestantism

Weber's view is that this kind of remorselessly hard-working, endlessly productive society, i.e. the capitalism we know, could not exist without this attitude to work (or 'spirit', as he terms it). What needs explaining is the origin of this vital element. Whence could 'the spirit of capitalism' develop? Weber looked for any precedents for such a spirit in the part of the world where this capitalism developed. He located an attitude that was very similar to the spirit of capitalism in regarding work in one's business or occupation as morally worthy. It differed in one important respect: it was religious and held by Protestants, particularly those influenced by the teachings of John Calvin. For Weber, the spirit of capitalism looked very like a secularised form of 'the Protestant ethic', as he called it. That the similarity may not be wholly coincidental is indicated by the spirit of capitalism developing in the same regions of Europe as those in which the Protestant ethic had earlier formed. Furthermore, in the historical evidence available to Weber – though subsequently questioned – Protestants were disproportionately successful in business.

The Protestant ethic was distinctive compared to other religious attitudes to the world of daily life. Very often, religions deny value to the world by contrasting mundane, everyday existence with the truly religious life; they insist that daily life is meaningless in itself and is of importance only relative to the life in the next world. From this viewpoint, the affairs of daily life should not matter much to the individual, who should, ideally, withdraw from them. Indeed, the medieval Catholic Church was one of a number commending the ascetic life as the ideal existence, and supported a monastic existence, cut off from the secular world. One of Weber's essays focused on such religious rejections of the world. By contrast, the Protestant sects of the European Reformation entirely rejected monasticism and embraced the world of daily life, commending the vigorous fulfilment of obligations within mundane society as serving God's greater glory. This sense of living vigorously, fully and unrelentingly up to the responsibilities of one's secular role at God's behest shows the same energy which those in capitalist society invest in their work, and the righteousness they also bring to it.

## Capitalism and Protestantism

The Protestant ethic and the spirit of capitalism are much alike, except that God commends one and the other is a freestanding, secular morality, held for its own sake. The one could, then, easily be the predecessor of the other: the spirit of capitalism could have grown out of the Protestant ethic.

Weber's views of sociological method are again relevant here. The broad methods of science apply to sociology as to natural sciences, but the subject matters are rather different. Since human beings are not inanimate objects there is the possibility of *understanding* them, whereas there is no possibility of doing so with natural phenomena. We can ask questions of human beings and otherwise attempt to get into their minds in order to see things from their point of view and to grasp the framework of assumptions in terms of which they live. Weber's approach to sociology is often known as the *verstehen* (German for 'understanding') approach. He certainly thought a most important element in studying what people did was to seek such an understanding. This kind of understanding was just what he attempted in making a meaningful connection between the Protestant ethic, the spirit of capitalism, and capitalism.

How could the teachings of the Protestant sects, which condemned materialism and the accumulation of wealth, give rise to the spirit of capitalism and the valorisation of industrial work? Weber's argument employs a two-step process.

The first established the radical orientation of the Protestant mentality. Martin Luther had certainly made a major change in people's attitudes towards the mundane world when he had introduced the notion of 'the calling', i.e. one had been called to one's earthly position by God, and it was, therefore, God's will that one should conscientiously fulfil the duties of that trust. For Weber, this move, though in the right direction, was not assertive enough to be sufficient to inspire something like the spirit of capitalism. Luther's notion called upon the individual conscientiously to fulfil the duties of a position that had been traditionally defined, but it would not be enough to account for the genesis of an attitude that – for Weber as for Marx – disdained and usurped all tradition. Although Luther took the first step, the decisive moves were made in John Calvin's teachings, albeit largely as an unintended result. Calvin's teachings put the believer in a difficult position in having a psychologically, not a logically, contradictory character. Calvin taught predestination. In his wisdom at the beginning of all things, God had chosen only certain individuals for salvation. This decision was fixed for all time, so that among the living only a few were of God's Elect. God's decision of salvation had been settled in advance, and could not be altered, but God had not made it known to mortals. As a consequence, Calvin taught that one's conduct in this life was no means to salvation, that one's actions here on earth could not alter one's ultimate fate. But he offered no licence to live howsoever one chose. Instead, Calvin commanded that whatever God's decision, be it 'saved' or 'eternally damned', one was none the less called upon to live for God's greater glory and to abide rigorously by his commandments. The psychological contradiction for the true believer results from the tension between the doctrine of predestination, on the one hand, and the intense seriousness of the question of salvation of the immortal soul on the other. How to cope with an existence in which one's fate was settled yet unknowable? How to live a religious life faced with the knowledge of the ultimate irrelevance of one's conduct for one's standing in the eyes of God, a standing that is not even known?

Here again is a point of contrast with Marx, who regarded religion as a form of ideology, referring to it contemptuously as 'the opium of the people', because it simply justifies and props up earthly arrangements. For him, religious beliefs concern illusory matters and were to be derogated – at least in vulgar Marxism relative to 'real', economic, i.e. material, interests. For Weber, by contrast, people's religious interest is not to be gauged against the sociologist's idea of what is really important to them; for him, it is simply an observable fact that, for many people, religious concerns and interests, such as the fate of their soul after death, are just as real and at least as important as any material interest. Indeed, people's religious interest in salvation is often greater than their material interests, to the extent of sacrificing their lives for it. So, for a religion as spiritually demanding as Calvinism, believers must have been intensely concerned about religious matters, above all the fate of their soul. Yet they were told that their actions could not influence what mattered more than anything else to them and, also, they could not even know what that fate was.

On Weber's reading, this element is the key to the situation that led to the faithful adapting Calvin's teachings, albeit quite against the grain of their meaning. If God had indeed discriminated between the Elect and the condemned, would he truly have made it so that those who were saved could have no inkling of his choice? Would it indeed be the case that God would have given salvation to those who would flout his commandments, and was it not more likely that those whom God had saved would live in accord with his law? Might not one's conduct be a *sign* of one's salvation? Not a means to salvation, of course, but a manifestation of one's inclusion in the Elect? Since this notion of ascertaining one's own salvational status through one's own conduct was against the tenor of the teachings, any conclusion about salvation would be fragile. If one's conduct were such a sign, then it would only be so if it were flawless, if there were not the slightest hint of deviation from God's law. Even the faintest such failing might indicate one's damnation rather than salvation. Thus the closest self-monitoring and control of one's entire conduct was introduced into the life of the religious layperson.

## Self-discipline and rational capitalism

Religions often demand rigorous self-control, but normally only on the part of their most advanced practitioners, not of the mass of believers. It was the introduction of such thorough and stringent self-discipline into the activities of daily life which struck Weber as providing another parallel with secular – especially business – conduct under capitalism, namely, its extensively *rationalised* (i.e. worked out and consciously controlled) nature.

One further element of Calvinism was noted: the teachings of Calvin emphasised that opportunities within the world were gifts from God; it would be sinful to refuse such opportunities, which should be seized and exploited as the opportunities to magnify God's earthly glory. Here was the crucial step beyond Luther; Calvinist doctrine, rather than teaching resolute fulfilment of obligations within the bounds of tradition, recommends the taking of all opportunities, even if they go beyond the bounds of tradition.

This amended teaching resolved the psychological tension within Calvinism. Weber argued that the immediate consequence of the creating of a conviction that one could at least know if one was saved would be the introduction of a rigorous, systematic self-control into the conduct of everyday affairs, including economic activities. Economic success and expansion would be the almost inevitable consequence of such dedicated application. Since the official Calvinist teachings railed against the dangers of earthly wealth, it could certainly not be used for consumption. Successful Calvinists could do nothing with their wealth apart from reinvesting it, for to leave wealth idle and not increasing itself was, in this new, activist climate, also sinful. Reinvestment would of course only ensure even greater wealth, and so on.

## Ideas as causes

Weber had taken a first step and made a connection at the level of meaning: he had tried to show how in the minds of Calvinist believers the official teachings provided an unresolved problem of their own salvation, and how its resolution led them to impose iron self-control over their everyday affairs, resulting in their coming to look upon economic affairs as righteous activity, to be conducted in a way which did not respect tradition. This attitude has clear parallels with the spirit of capitalism. In Weber's method, success at the level of meaning establishes a possibility; that is, he claimed to have shown what he calls 'an elective affinity' between the Protestant ethic and the spirit of capitalism, i.e. to have shown they were naturally drawn to each other.

But a second step was needed. He had gone far in establishing a case for the Protestant ethic actually giving rise to the spirit of capitalism, and thus to capitalism itself, at 'the level of causality'. Weber had made an *intelligible* connection between the two crucial elements, the ethic and the spirit; we can see (i.e. understand) how the one could have given rise to the other. But the causal question remains: *did* the Protestant ethic actually create the spirit of capitalism? Did the Protestant ethic actually play a part in making capitalism happen? The study of the Calvinist outlook added one element: the compulsion to reinvest made a strong contribution to capital accumulation as a necessary precondition to the rise of capitalism. Nevertheless, Weber was far from claiming that the case at the level of causality was conclusive.

Weber was raising the general issue of the causal role of ideas; religious ideas were one kind, although in his judgement they were historically very important. Weber was consciously arguing against Marx, but how much he disagrees crucially depends upon how one interprets Marx. If Marx is interpreted as holding that ideas are *epiphenomena* of society, i.e. phenomena without real substance or causal force which operate at best as mere rationalisations for things that they misrepresent and cannot control, then Weber is completely opposed on this point. If, however, Marx criticises Hegel for overestimating the power of the ideas of the individual thinker and for not realising that ideas can only matter in history when they are associated with collective movements, then he and Weber are not very far apart on this point, since both agree that ideas can have causal force in history. It is not the teachings of Calvin himself that matter in the above account, but the way his ideas are taken up by the mass of believers.

## Marx and Weber on ideas

If Marx is construed as supposing that only economic interests are real interests and other interests, e.g. political, national and religious, are mere smokescreens for economic interests, then Weber is adamantly opposed. For him, arguments of this kind err towards what we should nowadays call *reductionism*, i.e. seeking to reduce every kind of phenomenon to just one, here the economic.

*The Protestant Ethic* is about the way a religious interest can lead to decisively influential historical activity, which is indispensable to the creation of capitalism as we know it.

So does Weber become an idealist in reacting against Marx's materialism? No! Weber is as much a materialist as the early Marx in recognising that, of course, the substance of history is the existence of real, material human beings (and not occult forces of any kind). Weber is certainly opposed to a materialism that gives the most prominent place in understanding history to economic relations. For Weber, economics is vitally important to sociological understanding, as shown by his main, extended theoretical statement, which comprises a very large (characteristically incomplete) work translated under the title *Economy and Society* (1978). Yet not everything in social life boils down to economics. The interplay between economy and society is complex, two-way and many-sided. In summary, his overall judgement on Marx might be that Marx (as Weber encountered him) provided altogether too schematic an account of things, attempting to tie up in rigidly formulaic ways relationships that were more open-ended and variable.

It should be clear, then, that Weber was certainly not saying that the Protestant ethic alone created capitalism, that the Protestant ethic was capable of bringing capitalism about, regardless of material conditions. Weber's argument about capitalism was that the truly distinctive feature of modern Western capitalism is an attitude, a particular moral outlook, which he dubs 'the spirit of capitalism'. Without this outlook, it would not and could not be the same, for part of its nature as a system resides in its capacity for disciplined, systematically organised work. The motivation for such work is now mostly built into the system, and its whole organisation reproduces the attitude of diligence in its members. This necessary attitude could not have been conjured from nowhere; it must have had roots. Since these roots had to have grown up with capitalism itself, they could not have originated in capitalism, but must have first developed elsewhere. The Reformation provides a likely historical location.

Of course, the attitude is only part of the story. In many respects, Weber accepts that other parts of the story have been told by Marx and others concerning the rise of a whole range of material conditions for the development of modern capitalism, e.g. the productive conditions, the rise of urban areas, the development of urban-based business and trading classes, the freedom of labour from agricultural work, and the development of a money economy. Far from giving importance to only one element, Weber emphasises the large plurality of elements involved. The development of a certain attitude, the spirit of capitalism, was essential to the formation of capitalism only in the sense that the existence of a set of material preconditions for a social development will not, of itself, bring about this development. The mere fact that there were suitable technology, currency, property laws and so forth would not have given rise to the capitalism that we know without the *motivation to exploit the opportunities* that those conditions presented. A given state of economic development presents many different possibilities; which ones are realised depends on other aspects of the situation. Thus the economic preconditions of capitalism could have been developed in very different ways or perhaps not at all; they would not have developed in the direction they have gone were it not for the motivations provided by the 'Protestant ethic', with its associated spirit of capitalism.

# The contingency of history

## Historical events

In Weber's eyes, historical events are a matter of the coming together of independent causal chains which have previously developed without connection or direct import for one another.

There is nothing remotely predestined about the rise of modern Western, rational capitalism. At the time of the Reformation the economic situation could well have turned out otherwise. The rise of the Protestant sects did not happen 'in response' to those conditions, and its effect on them was purely fortuitous. The development of the Protestant ethic mainly arose out of matters internal to religious life and thought, and just happened to occur at the same time as changes in manufacturing technology, etc. were beginning to develop; it was simply the way things worked out that the two developments – coincident in time – became interwoven into the origins of modern, Western, rational capitalism. In reality the spirit of capitalism is only one contributory cause among many; it is no more significant a cause than the others. Weber gives it such prominence to ensure its recognition as one of the indispensable causes of the specific complex of modern Western, rational capitalism along with the numerous – even uncountable – many other indispensable causes. Giving it such prominence acts as a corrective to those who, as a matter of policy, deny to the ethic and spirit (and ideas generally) any causal role in such developments. To make out that the ethic/spirit had either more or less of a role than that of being one cause among many others would be to misrepresent the complexity of causal situations.

It follows from the logic of Weber's argument that an explanation at the level of causality can be tested if he can find a parallel case of *embryonic capitalism* which differs in only one vital respect, i.e. the absence of a Protestant ethic. In his view such a situation had (virtually) existed in traditional China. It had had the material capability for the same kind of dynamic economic expansionism as Western Europe, but this capability had not been taken up because there was a quite different 'economic ethic' attached to its religions. The development of such a case dominated the remainder of Weber's life work, especially in the form of his comparative study of the world religions. He managed to complete substantial work on the religions of India and China, and on ancient Judaism, as well as to write a book-length account of the general evolution of religious practice and thought, and several other related essays. Weber's interests were wider than the study of the world religions, though everything had some connection with the core issue of the origins and distinctive character of the modern Western civilisation. For example, his work on the development of music was designed to show that even the form of Western music was shaped in relation to the rationalising tendencies of the civilisation.

## Power and the forms of social inequality

Weber also provided some general concepts for sociological analysis, which shaped the form taken by his descriptions of the world religions. Most basically, Weber looked upon the organisation of society as involving struggles for power. For Weber, no less than for Marx, social life is about inequality, which can take many forms. In a given situation, inequality is not necessarily economic. Economic inequality is important and frequently plays a leading part, but it is only *one form* taken by inequality. Inequalities are the basis for the organisation of groups, and the struggle over inequalities is most commonly between groups. Therefore, the key element in Weber's account of society is his account of stratification.

### Stratification

Inequalities are arranged on three dimensions, but all are forms of power. In Weber's terminology, power is the capacity to get done what you want despite resistance from others. For example, economic wealth is a form of power, giving the capacity to get what one desires. All forms of inequality are inequalities in power. The three dimensions of power are (1) economic, (2) prestige and (3) pure power. They are the basis for three characteristically different forms of grouping: the class, the status group and the party. It is among and between these three kinds of groups that the historically decisive struggles over power are apt to take place.

Weber's conception of social class is much akin to Marx's. Class is defined in terms of position in the process of economic production, specifically in terms of one's relationship to a market: what does one have to sell on the market? Is it labour power, or does one have products, or what? Weber does not think of classes as real groups, i.e. persons self-consciously interacting with one another; rather, they are merely categories, the product of a sociological analyst's definitions.

### Classes

A class is more a category than a group, i.e. a collection of people identified together on the basis of some common characteristic. We can have as many or as few classes as we like, depending on how grossly or finely we draw the criteria.

We can reduce the number of classes basically to two, by making the distinction between those who sell labour power on the market and those who buy it, i.e. Marx's proletariat and bourgeoisie. Within just the one category, e.g. those (workers) who sell labour power, we can increase the number of categories by distinguishing the broad kinds of labour power sold, e.g. is it skilled or unskilled, manual or non-manual? We can multiply it up to an enormous number of classes by making the criterion of common position the specific kind of labour power being disposed of, e.g. is it the capacity to fix plumbing, to repair electronic wiring, to lay bricks, or to dig ditches? Contrary to Marx's assumption, there is nothing *naturally* unified about a class, and the social conditions which cause classes to act as co-ordinated social units in the struggle for power only rarely arise. The members of a class often react to situations in the same way – what Weber termed 'mass action' – because, of course, they share a similar background and experience, but they are not aware of one another's response and are certainly not acting out of any sense of a joint venture in so responding.

The second form Weber describes is the *status group*. Status groups are real groups: the very specification of such a group involves and is dependent upon mutual recognition by its members. The inequality which separates classes is economic, the kind of returns which can be expected from the market relative to the things to be sold there, but status groups are differentiated by prestige, i.e. the level of esteem in which people hold themselves and are held by others.

## Status groups

A status group is a collection of people who recognise themselves as equals, who look upon one another as equally worthy, and who look up to and down on other social groups. A status group involves shared understandings, mutual recognition among its members and, of course, acknowledgement from its superiors and inferiors of its standing in the general scale of social position.

Thus there is mutual awareness and some – at least diffusely – co-ordinated action integral to the very existence of a status group. The mechanism of such a group's existence is *closure*. It includes some and excludes others; it takes steps to ensure that those who are not equals are kept out.

From an economic point of view, a status group is defined in terms of consumption, not production. What makes someone an equal is how he or she lives, the *lifestyle*, as Weber termed it. For example, to lead the life of an educated, cultured and leisured person might be the basis for mutual acknowledgement. In the end the status group is dependent upon economic inequality because the capacity to lead a certain kind of life presupposes the wealth to fund it. It is not the wealth as such, however, that is decisive. Further, the status group's attempt to preserve its existence and identity through closure characteristically involves economic intervention in attempts to restrain the operation of the market in order to prevent the hallmarks of a lifestyle becoming available to mere purchase (which would directly link them to wealth). The Indian caste system is the extreme case of a status group system, where the operation of the market has been restricted to such an extent that even jobs are retained within the various caste groups through inheritance. Inevitably, class and status are mutually inimical forms of social organisation, since the existence of one – status group – involves some reduction in the operation of the conditions – the market – conducive to the formation of class. The conditions under which the status group can thrive, Weber held, are those of long-term social stability – which is why they occupy such prominence in his discussion of traditional China and India. In situations of rapid social and economic change, social class possesses greater prominence.

The *party* is the third element in Weber's scheme. Whereas the status group has a diffuse sense of solidarity and common interest, providing a more promising basis for the organisation of co-ordinated collective action than that available to the class, this capacity for collective action is not easily going to amount to the focused, carefully calculated pursuit of common interest, which is what the party is all about.

## Parties

The party is a self-conscious organisation for the pursuit of power. As a body created specifically for the purpose of struggling for power, it therefore works out its objectives and organisation to maximise its chances of attaining power.

The party, as Weber intends this term, is an analytical notion and does not just refer to formal political parties. It includes any and all associations developed purely for the sake of winning power. For example, it can include factions in business, leisure and religious organisations as well as large-scale political power. Such a group has self-awareness, mutual recognition among its members of shared specific purposes, and the capacity for closely concerted action in pursuit of them. It is the most effective vehicle in the struggle for power in society. Parties can, of course, attempt to base themselves in specific social groups; they can set out the goal of winning power in society for a specific category, e.g. a socialist party might aim to take political power for the working class, setting out to recruit from among its members, and therefore actively seek working-class members. However, they need not do so, and may seek power for goals and interests that are not those of one, or any specific, class, and may draw their membership from different social categories.

## The forms of authority

Despite this view of society as a struggle for power, Weber is not offering a general model of all social relations in terms of conflict pervading all aspects of social life. His emphasis on the role that conflict plays is far from suggesting that all relations between people are a struggle for advantage on the lines of Thomas Hobbes's (1588–1679) idea of a 'war of all against all'. On the contrary, the passivity of the great mass of people is most striking. The characteristic of power is in achieving results even over resistance, but the fact is that for those who hold power there is often comparatively little resistance. The behest of the powerful is often readily obeyed. Power is often legitimate, i.e. some people are recognised as leaders or commanders and so are accorded the right to command obedience from others. Such relations of legitimate domination are broadly of three kinds, each differing in terms of the source for obedience: charismatic, traditional and rational-legal domination.

## The three kinds of authority

Charismatic domination is based upon the power of the leader's personality; traditional domination depends on the existence of traditional entitlement to position and to compliance; rational-legal domination derives from occupation of a position in accord with the proper requirements, such as the satisfaction of legal conditions. The charismatic leader comes to power by self-assertion, power over others deriving from the strength of his or her personality and will. The traditional ruler has power very typically by inheritance (or similar mechanism, e.g. the selection of the Dalai Lama). In the rational-legal case, power comes from holding an office by formal appointment, paradigmatically through an electoral process.

The *charismatic* can take many forms: as the leader of a religious cult or a military group, or as a political demagogue. Such leaders claim to be special persons either because they have powers specially granted to them by greater forces, as with religious leaders (e.g. Jesus claiming to be God himself come to earth), or by virtue of some special mission they alone can realise (e.g. Adolf Hitler leading Germany towards its national destiny). In this way they assert themselves over their followers by personal power. Loyalty is entirely personal, and all members of the group are loyal to the leader, who, being an 'inspired' individual, is very often apt to be lax about matters of organisation and regularity of arrangements. Taking care of these matters has to be done, but it is a secondary consideration and delegated to particular followers not because they are best at it, but because they are the favourites of the leader. The leader's own capacity to lead is under constant test, for it exists only by continual proof in action. The leader can make things happen, and *must* therefore make things happen, and continue to do so; failure is a massive setback to the leader's claims and, thus, authority. And, of course, the leader will most probably eventually fail, because the likelihood of endless dramatic success is small, and sooner or later even the most successful charismatic will certainly die.

Thus true charismatic authority lasts less than a lifespan and, upon the death, if not the earlier discrediting, of the leader, either the end of the movement or its transformation into a more routinised form comes about. The basis of authority changes either into tradition, where the new leader has power by dint of holding the position that the original leader held (e.g. the Pope holds power by holding the office that is the surrogate position of Jesus), or into the rational-legal type, where the leader's powers derive from formal appointment according to explicit rules and procedure. While it exists, however, charisma is irruptive power. By virtue of the intense loyalty and emotional identification which members have towards the leader, the charismatic movement can create vital and dynamic impetus for change, impetus that can suddenly and unpredictably challenge and break up established structures of power. Typically, this dynamic is short-lived and inherently unstable, being moved by the leader's whims. It lacks any solid administrative structure.

The authority of *tradition* comes from time immemorial. Things are done this way because they have always been done like that. The authority of the traditional ruler resides, characteristically, in the fact that the ruler's family have always held power. The classic form of traditional authority is the royal court, which is attached to the ruler and made up of the ruler's friends and family. The court is also the pool from which the principal administrators are drawn, and their selection depends upon the trust the ruler has in them. The extent to which the ruler might be interested in administration varies and so does the interest in and capacity for administration of those whom the ruler appoints to office. As with charisma, traditional administration is founded on personalised, particularised relationships, and appointment to administrative positions has nothing necessarily to do with proven competence in the work.

*Rational-legal* authority is founded upon some formalised code of law, and awards position on the basis of formal appointment consistent with impersonal principles explicitly laid down. Such principles typically require – for positions of leadership – the holding of elections, or – for those in administrative positions – appointment on the basis of attested competence. Rational-legal authority is associated with what Weber regards as the most efficient form of large-scale administrative structure: the *bureaucracy*. This identification of bureaucracy was made with awareness that bureaucracies are not perfect organisations and they have their own inefficiencies and deficiencies. Historically, the relevant comparison, however, is with the two identified alternative kinds, charisma and tradition.

## Bureaucracy

The bureaucracy is an administrative system built – at least in principle – on the appointment to administrative posts of specialists in such work. It is organised in ways meant to ensure the impartial devotion of their expertise to the organisation and management of administrative affairs.

The bureaucracy is a system of administrative positions, of offices (or bureaux) in a hierarchy, itself involving increasing levels of administrative competence. The activities of the incumbents of these offices are governed by written rules; the authority of the senior over the subordinate figure derives from having greater expertise. Appointments are made on the basis of competence largely assessed through formal examinations. The office-holder's loyalty to the bureaucracy is ensured, ideally, by that person's exclusive dependence for livelihood upon the employing organisation. Thus the 'ideal' bureaucracy, i.e. in the ideal case when all these criteria are satisfied, involves the concentration of administrative expertise within the structure. The organisation of relations and distribution of work within the structure optimise the way expertise is focused upon administrative problems in as objective and dispassionate a way as (humanly) possible. For this reason, administrative decision-making in the bureaucracy (whatever its actual shortcomings) should ideally be superior, since charismatic and traditional administrations are, in the end, at the arbitrary mercy of the leader's whim.

If anything, with bureaucracy the situation is reversed: the political leader is at the mercy of the administration. The leader may have the formal political control over the bureaucracy, but may not have the administrative competence to keep it under control. Weber certainly thought that there was a need for strong, determined and visionary leaders in democratic society who could counter the strength of the bureaucracy. Such leaders must keep an eye on the main issues rather than being persuaded into looking at all decisions (including the important ones) as if they were mere matters of administrative technicality. The Civil Service, as caricatured in the *Yes Minister* television comedies, is exactly what Weber had in mind as threatening the role of the political leader, who is the person entitled to be making the decisions and exercising leadership.

## Weber's comparative sociology

We now return to Weber's comparative studies of the world religions, which are centrally concerned with the *economic ethics* of these various religions. They extend to providing broad analyses of the structure and dynamics of the civilisations where these religions developed in order to highlight the situations within which the social groups, acting as bearers of these economic ethics, were situated and influential. In other words, the comparative studies of world religions were also studies of the cultural dominance of specific status groups.

The Protestant ethic is a case study of the economic ethic of the Protestant sects, of the attitude that they formed towards economic conduct. They viewed it as a morally worthy pursuit within which proof of salvation could be sought. In contrast, we noted the Roman Catholic conception that it is inferior to a truly religious life.

### Economic ethics

Weber held that all religions develop an economic ethic, but it is seldom so favourable to economic activity as Calvinism.

> Some religions come to dominate whole civilisations, and their attitudes set the tone for the whole culture. If such religions have an economic ethic unfavourable to economic activity, economic development is inhibited, preventing the growth of anything like Western capitalism despite otherwise favourable material conditions.

Weber thought that this analysis was particularly true of traditional China, which had developed science and technology as well as socio-economic conditions comparable to those of the Reformation.

Weber was particularly interested in a status group that occupied a key position within the social structure of traditional China. It was the collection of officials who administered the state's business, the mandarins, who were not the ruling economic or political group yet had a powerful influence on the culture at large. Although the mandarins were as worldly and economically acquisitive as any modern capitalist, their Confucian religion took a completely disdainful view of industry and trade. It encouraged an exclusive concern with personal development, i.e. turning oneself into a cultured and aesthetically sensitive individual through literary and artistic concerns. It also encouraged practical indifference to the existing order of things. Piety towards elders and superiors was required, and life had to be conducted in accord with the conventions in order to prevent disturbance to the harmony and well-being of the entire cosmos, of which human existence was seen as a small and orderly part. There was no obligation for the believer to proselytise these beliefs; Confucian beliefs owed their cultural dominance to the strategic position of their *bearers*, i.e. those who held and perpetuated the beliefs within the stratification system of the society. Within the population at large, however, other religions and magic held sway. Weber maintained that the inward-looking nature of Confucianism prevented the mandarins from making any assault upon magic in society. By contrast, a feature of the Christian tradition was an opposition to magic, which came to the fore most decisively in the Protestant phase. Indeed, Weber thought that the elimination of magic was a precondition for the development of a thoroughly rational organisation of economic activity.

The religions of India presented a very different situation from the worldliness of the mandarins. They were predominantly otherworldly, e.g. Hinduism and Buddhism greatly disvalued earthly involvements and extolled a contemplative religious existence. Weber was again much interested in the position within the caste system of a particular status group, the Brahmins. Though only teachers and preachers, without economic or political power, they were also culturally dominant, being the group that provided the yardstick for the measure of the proper life.

In summary, these two great oriental cultures had dominant, religiously inspired economic ethics which would discourage economic activity of the kind favourable to the development of capitalism; their religious outlooks inhibited the development of the rational approach so prevalent within the West.

# The rationalisation of social life

On several occasions we have used the term *rational*, persistently mentioning it as a leading feature of modern Western capitalism.

## The rational

In Weber's usage, 'rational' refers to the attempt to work out means to ends, and to the attempt to develop a systematic understanding of things so that ends can also be worked out systematically and can even be ranked by calculation.

Weber thought that all actions could take only a few basic forms. Many actions are traditional or habitual in character, i.e. they are done without thought or calculation. There are two kinds of action worthy of the title 'rational'. One type he calls *value rational* actions, where the means have no practical relationship to the end, but are simply a way of acting out, of realising, a value the actor holds. His own example is the captain who goes down with the ship; his action does not achieve anything practical, but it does continue the commitment to dignity, integrity and honour which the captain may have made the hallmark of a whole life. The other kind of rationality is the *practical*: the working out of the best, most effective means of getting towards the end that one desires. It is most prevalently exhibited in our economic affairs and our civilisation, drawing extensively and dependently upon scientific understanding. Because we have such a worked-out understanding of the natural world, we are able to calculate with great effect and in very fine detail the best technical solution to any practical business, administrative or other problem.

In the West there has been a progressive process of *rationalisation*, i.e. the extension of this practical kind of action, thereby giving a systematic understanding and calculability of practical means–ends relationships throughout the whole of society. This development has been massively accelerated under capitalism and has been especially associated with the rise of science. Though distinctive in its particular character and in the sheer extent of its development in the modern Western world, the process has very deep roots in Western culture. Weber traced its origins not only to early Greek civilisation – with its scientific mentality – but also, as part of the comparative studies of world religions, to the traditions of ancient Judaism, which were formatively influential upon Christianity. For example, he argued that Judaism was notably hostile to magic, a hostility that it bequeathed to Christianity. In itself, magic is intensely traditionalising in binding people to the repetitive performances of prescribed actions; to be effective, the magical action must be done in the same way on every occasion. Consequently, the possibility of attempting to think out the conditions of effective action, of envisaging how the action might be made more effective by being reorganised, is inhibited. In these ways, the rationalising process has remote roots in Western civilisation and a long history of development. Its apotheosis came with the capitalist phase, when we have not only rationalised our understanding of nature and our mastery of practical actions, but also rationalised our human relations in the form of bureaucracy. For bureaucracy is nothing other than an attempt to rationalise, i.e. to make calculable, predictable and controllable, our own relations and activities. For Weber, it was one of the most inimical features of life today.

We have discussed religion in relation to its economic ethic, which was, indeed, the aspect on which Weber's studies were centred. Yet religion is certainly something more in Weber's eyes. It is a major source of meaning, of significance, in human lives; it gives people a sense that their lives are more than mere reactions to situations, their activities are part of a greater order of things, and their fates are connected to some greater purpose. Weber noted the role of religion in giving sense to otherwise meaningless suffering; it gave those who suffered the idea that the suffering was *for something* and there might be compensation in another life. The development of rationalisation has given us an immense understanding of the world and nature, but at a considerable price, namely the *disenchantment of the world*.

### The disenchantment of the world

Our capacity to see meaning in the world and to understand our relationship to it has diminished. Paradoxically, the capitalist West has given people conditions of hitherto unmatched material satisfaction, but a civilisation of happy people has not emerged. Rather, people complain about the emptiness and spiritual barrenness of their lives.

The future, as Weber could see it, would be grim, with rationalisation and bureaucratisation expanding unchecked and becoming more and more oppressive upon the citizenry until the sense of life would not be of prosperity and freedom, but of containment within an iron cage.

### Conclusion

In recent years, there have been arguments about whether Weber's life work was indeed a unified whole and, if so, what the unifying theme might be. Rationalisation has been nominated, and we can see how such a case could be made. We suggest that it does not really contradict the claim that his central concern was with the individuality of modern, rational capitalism in the West, since rationalisation is such a distinctive and integral feature of capitalism as a social system.

It will become clear just how much influence Weber has had, even on Marxists. Weber's emphasis upon the necessarily irrational sources of seemingly rational phenomena, such as administrative structures and procedures, and his bleak view of life in a society subject to bureaucratic domination, were strongly endorsed by the Frankfurt School (see Chapter 8). Similarly, Michel Foucault (perhaps the most widely acknowledged and influential of recent thinkers, and not a Marxist: see Chapter 11) gives a critical account of the rise of modern society and of the pervasive spread of administrative control which, though formulated in an utterly different fashion to Weber's, is none the less very close to Weber in its characterisation of the structure of modern society.

With the decline of class as the most prominent social division, and the loss of Marx's direct influence, Weber's approach to the analysis of inequality, with its emphasis upon the heterogeneity of status groups, has been seen as a more suitable strategy for the analysis of social stratification in a world in which nationality, ethnicity, gender and religion are more prominent bases of division (and the source of dissident social movements – see Chapter 15).

## Questions

1 How does Weber differ from Marx in his treatment of the 'individual'? Is Weber saying people can do anything they want, or are they also constrained by social forces? Which theorist makes most sense to you and why?

2 Does Weber disagree with Marx about the nature of capitalism, or is he trying to amend Marx's argument? Which contemporary issues make sense in Marxian terms and which make more sense in Weberian ones? How can you choose which approach is better?

3 Is Weber's argument about the Protestant ethic a *psychological* one? Is he arguing against Marx's idea that capitalism is a *social* product? What difference does it make which one is right?

4 Can you think of some contemporary instances of 'status groups' and 'parties'? Which are more important? Can they be understood as 'really' based on class relations, as Marx would argue, or does that remove what is distinctive about them?

5 Marx would describe much of what Weber argues about power and authority as *ideological*. Do you think this is a fair criticism? Are there alternative ways of looking at power that seem more convincing to you?

6 What are the different forms of authority according to Weber? Can you think of historical examples of each? Can you think of contemporary examples? Which seem to you to be most important in different settings? Why?

7 Is Weber nostalgic for the past? Is he more pessimistic than Marx? Which approach do you think is most realistic?

## Next steps

There are two good collections of Weber's writings, both of which reflect the range of his thought: Gerth and Mills's (1948) *From Max Weber* and Runciman's (1978) *Max Weber: Selections in Translation*. Weber's methodological writings are collected in Bruun and Whimster (2012).

A good short introduction to Weber's thought is Collins's (1986) *Max Weber: A Skeleton Key*. Bendix's (1960) *Max Weber: An Intellectual Portrait* remains the best longer exposition of Weber's writings.

## CHAPTER FOUR

# Émile Durkheim

---

**Chapter overview**

In this chapter the work of the third founding figure of sociology, Émile Durkheim, will be introduced. Durkheim was explicitly opposed to individualism (in contrast to Weber and, perhaps, Marx), and took a *positivist* approach to sociological study. His emphasis on *social solidarity* and social integration, perhaps unfairly, led him to be characterised as a conservative thinker. In contrast to Marx and Weber, he characterised contemporary societies as operating on the basis of an *organic* division of labour: one in which different institutions and roles 'fit together' like the organs of a body. This does not mean, however, that modern societies are without problems: Durkheim investigated both crime and suicide to determine where the 'normal' ends and the 'pathological' begins. His later work on religion deepened his analysis of social solidarity, and laid the basis for a powerful theory of the social basis of knowledge. Finally, his work on politics and education will be considered to re-examine the charge that Durkheim is a conservative theorist.

---

## Introduction: the denigration of Durkheim

We have noted that the reputation and influence of Marx within sociology have recently waned. Durkheim's reputation too has undergone travails, though in his case the decline came a good deal earlier, and there are now signs of recovery. With the rising popularity of poststructuralism there are moves to revisit his thought. Even so, Durkheim's influence in contemporary sociology is much less than it was forty years ago. In the immediate post-World War II period it seemed that Durkheim's influence was to be greater and more sustained in sociology than Marx's or Weber's. A main reason was the pre-eminence within Anglo-American sociology then of Talcott Parsons's theoretical scheme (see Chapter 5), which was understood to be a consensus theory and, therefore, owed more to Durkheim than to the other two great founders. Another source of Durkheim's reputation was his methodological writings, exemplified in his study *Suicide*

(1951), which was widely regarded as his most significant work. If Durkheim's concern with social solidarity rather than conflict was dominant at the theoretical level, then his manipulation of suicide statistics in *Suicide* made him for a time the very model for sociological method. He had given a decisive lead to the development of more sophisticated statistical techniques, which were seen as the key to scientific progress in the discipline.

The turning of the tide against Durkheim involved a reaction against both elements of his reputation. He was condemned on two main grounds: his conservatism, and his positivism.

The accusation of conservatism took its force from Durkheim's emphasis upon society as a moral unity. His concern with social solidarity and the containment of damage to it was understood by his critics to mean that the application and development of his approach would necessarily serve the existing social order. This interpretation downplayed – in fact, wholly neglected – the social criticism in Durkheim's writings, together with his reputation in his own time as a socialist and a radical.

The charge of *positivism* was more justifiable.

## Durkheim and positivism

Durkheim argued for his own methods on the grounds that they were essential to the development of a 'positive science', i.e. an approach seeking to find law-like relations among phenomena and modelled on the physical sciences. In this respect, Durkheim was an inheritor of the legacy of his French predecessor Auguste Comte (1798–1857), a founder both of positivism and of sociology in the mid-nineteenth century.

In *Suicide*, Durkheim subjected official figures on suicide to statistical analysis, indicating how sociology might be taken in a *quantitative* direction. For a time in the 1950s and early 1960s this approach had ensured Durkheim much attention from methodologically minded social scientists. The idea that sociology could and should be a science was very strong; so was the notion that science required the discipline to be quantitative. However, with the *interpretative turn*, which began in the mid-1960s, talk about sociology as a positive science and about quantification became hallmarks of the *positivist* outlook, by then anathema to many in sociology. Indeed, Durkheim came to emblematise all that was politically and epistemologically unacceptable in sociology.

To dismiss Durkheim from serious consideration on such grounds would unjustly diminish his stature and would overlook other aspects of his work which continue to influence sociological thought and social theory today. Camille Paglia (1993: 223–26) has observed, for example, that if Americans were aware of the debt that the (currently) immensely fashionable work of Michel Foucault owes to Durkheim, they would be much less impressed by his apparent originality.

She is not alone in noting the links between Durkheim's thought and current concerns; several eminent writers have asserted the contemporary relevance of his ideas.

## Against individualism

In line with our earlier consideration of the theme of humanism in Marx, we begin with Durkheim predominantly as a critic of individualism. His critique has two main strands:

- It is a fundamental misconception to suppose that society is (only) an aggregate of individuals, i.e. he opposed the view that the properties of society are merely the properties of individuals writ large.
- Individuals cannot pre-exist society, i.e. individualism as a doctrine is only conceivable in a certain kind of society; individuals, as represented by this idea of individualism, are only possible in this kind of society.

Durkheim's major target, then, is the idea, the doctrine, of 'individualism', which he seeks to expose as an ideology, to use a Marxist term.

### Individualism

In Durkheim's sense, individualism prizes unconditionally the distinctness and independence of individual human beings, who are to be treated as inviolable in their freedom and autonomy. The idea that individuals should be subordinate to any collective authority is to be borne, if at all, only in the most limited and necessary circumstances.

The doctrine of individualism is in many respects a *political* doctrine – its classical statements remain the political theories of Thomas Hobbes and John Locke – about the relationship of the individual to the rest of society and, in particular, to the putative representative of that society, the state. However, individualism also has a potentially *scientific*, *methodological* aspect to it in suggesting that the constituents of social reality are only and exclusively individual human beings.

According to this view, 'society' is merely a name for the other individuals in relationship with whom a given individual co-exists. The only way to understand society, then, is to understand the general nature of all those individuals as an aggregate. To take a simple example of the kind Marx railed against, the competitive nature of capitalist society is understood as a result of the natural competitiveness and acquisitiveness of human beings generally. Indeed, individualism often conceives of human nature as essentially anti-social, for the individual is conceived of as being motivated only by self-interest. In a picture explicitly painted in Hobbes's *Leviathan* (see Chapter 5), individuals lack all concern for others; they exist in society most reluctantly, conceding to the collective some of their freedoms and rights only for the sake of the benefits to be derived. Durkheim maintained that such conceptions were quite false: to attempt to apply them was entirely the wrong method for a genuine science of society. Nevertheless, Durkheim was unswervingly confident that society could be studied scientifically.

How is a science of society possible? Durkheim assumed that for there to be a science it has to have a subject matter. On the face of it, the appropriate science of society is psychology, the science of the individual mind. After all, if we can understand the mind, we shall understand why individuals behave as they do, and will have no need of an additional science, sociology. Durkheim was eager to dismiss this assumption, but was aware, also, that it has a natural appeal; individual human creatures are tangible, we can encounter and observe them in the flesh, whereas society seems to be no more than an abstraction from their behaviour. We do not meet society in the street, exchange words with it, and watch it going about its activities. Surely individuals are real but society is not. However intuitively true this view may seem, Durkheim insists it is false. True, society is not directly observable, perhaps, but it is observable *in its effects*. It does exist; it may not be detected by the conscious awareness of those individuals, yet it causally affects their actions.

In this way Durkheim argues that sociology can be a science that treats of a genuine subject matter because society exists as an authentic natural reality. It is as much a reality as physical nature, though different in character. Early on, in the way he set out in *The Rules of Sociological Method* (1966), he tried to present the lineaments of his general strategy. There he argued that the way to establish, in principle, the reality of society was to reveal the criteria that define something as a reality. They are general criteria, which include physical reality as a special case.

## Criteria for reality

To say something is real is to say two main things:

- It is *external*, i.e. exists outside our individual consciousness.
- It is *constraining*, i.e. its existence sets limits to our actions.

For example, a brick wall is patently a reality because it exists in the world out there and it resists our actions if we try to walk through it. If these are the criteria of *facts*, i.e. of real things, then Durkheim says that society satisfies them.

How can this assertion be justified? It cannot sensibly be disputed, of course, that the patterns of life in our society are not simply individual inventions. The law is not something that I or any other individual has invented. The law has been developed *collectively*, built up over a long time by many individuals.

It now confronts me as a thing that exists in the world, whether I will it to do so or not. One test for reality is satisfied; such social facts are external. Further, if I try to act in the world, the law may offer me resistance. I cannot simply do anything that I want to do. Yet the law is not necessarily constraining from a subjective point of view, even though objectively this is the case. For many of my actions, I take account of the law in a way which affects those actions, but I do not perhaps experience it as resistance to my individual will. I have simply become accustomed to doing things in ways which comply with the law. For example, when I decide to get some cash, I go to the bank, confirm my identity and account details at an electronic terminal, and am given the cash in return. Consequently, it may seem that I freely do what I want. However, I am doing it in conformity with the law, the way I have to do it if I want my actions to be unimpeded. Suppose I decide to do otherwise, by entering the bank armed with a pistol. In that case I will meet resistance, people will try to refuse to give me the money; they will try to capture me and, eventually, to incarcerate me in prison. The law exists, then, as something which, in designing my actions, I must take into account as a real consideration, just as much as I take into account the brick wall adjoining the door which I use to pass through to the next room. Consequently, the second test of a social fact is demonstrated, i.e. it constrains actions.

## The nature of social solidarity

By such arguments, Durkheim proposes the reality of society and the existence of a phenomenon for sociology to study. It cannot be appropriated by psychology, for that is the study of the content of individual minds. In many ways the law may be the product of individual minds, yet it exists outside them. Just as there are natural facts, so too are there social facts. Having established this point, Durkheim is left with two questions:

1   What kind of existence does this external reality have?
2   On what aspect of this reality is social science to focus its attention?

Throughout the rest of his life he was concerned with answering them in terms of the relationship of society to the individual, and the *solidarity* or *cohesion* of society. Durkheim's concern with the second of these questions legitimately categorises him as a *functionalist* sociologist, thereby earning him much criticism as a conservative. We note that Durkheim insists on the moral unity of society. To speak about 'a society' is to speak of some kind of unit. If we are to talk about English society as opposed to French society, then there must be some sense in which each is a self-subsistent unit, distinct and distinguishable from the other. In this sense, English society must hold together and have some persistent identity as a single whole, however much, and in whatever ways, it is otherwise internally differentiated. Obviously societies have boundaries, and in respect of the society's existence as a bounded, unified entity Durkheim sets in train a very consequential line of thought.

## Social unity

> If a society is to be said to exist, then it must satisfy certain conditions for unity (otherwise, as a matter of simple tautology, it would not exist, and we could not say that it did).

Durkheim's functionalism originates in the notion that for a society to exist it must be ordered in such a way as to meet these conditions.

If a society exists, and is bounded, in what way is it bounded? It must have an inside and an outside, but what does the line between the two differentiate? A tempting idea might be geography, for, of course, societies are often identified with territories. In Durkheim's view this cannot be an answer, not least because of the methodological rule, which he has laid down, that a social fact cannot be explained by any other kind of fact, physical, biological, geographical, climatological or psychological, but only by other social facts. The boundary that demarcates a society must be social: it must relate to *membership*, which includes or excludes people. For example, French persons visiting England do not, thereby, become part of English society, although they are present on English territory, since they do not have the relevant membership. Further, the boundary is moral in nature. The line of demarcation runs between acceptable and unacceptable conduct; those who transgress basic rules – criminals, the mentally ill – are outside the society. That the very existence of society presupposes such a demarcation, Durkheim illustrates with an ingenious account of the nature of crime.

## Crime

> Crime exists even in societies which do not have laws, courts and the police. Durkheim asserts that all societies have crime, since all societies involve a differentiation between two kinds of actions, those that are allowed and those that are forbidden. He calls the latter type *criminal*.

Theories of crime – of which there are many – comprise attempts to understand the basis for this distinction. In seeking a rational basis for determining the nature of the contrast between the criminal and non-criminal, something about the nature and consequences of criminal acts as such is often assumed, e.g. they are harmful to society. Also, attempts to understand the punitive reactions to criminal actions are often regarded as a rational kind of response, with the punishment fitting the crime, or deterring it.

However, these rationalist conceptions do not really fit the facts about the relation between the crime and the reaction it gets. First, if punishment were a rationally worked out form of response, then we would expect a proportionate relationship between the extent of harm caused to society by the act and the punishment inflicted. In fact, actions that do not harm society, e.g. many 'crimes without victims', such as prostitution, elicit punishments, while actions that *do* harm society, such as spreading pollutants, often do not. Second, the punitive reaction to crime is not rational and calculative, but intensely emotional; the sense of outrage, which fuels the desire to exact punishment, is often a substantial component. Having established that this rationalist line of thought does not capture the nature of the response to crime, Durkheim next says that the intrinsic nature of the action involved is essentially irrelevant to the matter. It is not the specific nature or result of the offending action as such which matters, but the fact that the action transgresses widely shared and strongly held sentiments, whatever these might be in any particular case. The reaction to crime is not reparative, it is punitive; an expression of the outrage and anger against the offender is precipitated when strongly held convictions are transgressed. Reaction against criminals makes of them social outcasts, sometimes literally outcasts. The offender is regarded as falling outside normal society, and the punishment provides a display of the fact that some individuals are being set apart from everyone else, at least symbolically. Often they are excluded from the rest of society by denial of full membership rights or by physical separation, i.e. being locked in prisons, or even put to death.

Thus there is a boundary drawn between those who are proper members of society, and those who engage in improper actions and so are not true members of society. The boundary is, therefore, moral. In a way, then, the reaction against crime is a *community* reaction that both vents and creates feelings of mutual solidarity among those who react against the criminal. Being together on the right side of the line gathers in 'the decent people' and sets them against those whose conduct is unacceptable. The reality of society consists, then, very much in moral phenomena, in conceptions of right and wrong and, therefore, of what conduct is permissible.

For Durkheim, society must be something more than a collection of individuals, and in many ways he twisted and turned to say what that 'more' might be. In *The Rules of Sociological Method* he was really arguing that the 'something more' is the product of association, which can only exist in relationships. For example, to disagree we need others; disagreement is a relationship between two or more individuals. For Durkheim, the 'something more' is not mysterious. It is what is shared between individuals, primarily the *conscience collective* (i.e. the beliefs and sentiments shared within the community) and the *representations collective* (i.e. shared ways, such as language, of expressing thoughts and representing things). Both sets of collective phenomena have been learned from others and depend for their operation on being held in common. Here we note in passing the germ of an idea that what people want to do, i.e. their ends or goals, is not random but shared, an idea that Talcott Parsons expanded on greatly (see Chapter 5).

Durkheim's opposition to individualism was spelt out in his first book, *The Division of Labour in Society* (1984). He aimed to prove that the very idea of the individual, and the realisation of that idea, is only possible in a certain sort of society. Durkheim was developing a line which was to come to full fruition in his later work, namely, that it is only possible to think certain sorts of thoughts under specific social conditions. Far from its being self-evident that society acquires its characteristics from its component individuals, Durkheim argues that, on the contrary, individuals acquire their characteristics from society itself.

## The foundations of society

Durkheim's rejection of individualism takes the form of a thoroughgoing critique of the *utilitarian* school of thought. Some thinkers have argued that individuals make up the ways and practices of society on the basis of their practical usefulness to them. For example, Thomas Hobbes (1588–1679) offers the picture of individuals setting up a sovereign authority as a means of regulating their relationship between themselves and restricting the mutually destructive tendencies that unregulated competition would produce. Herbert Spencer (1820–1903) had the idea that society consists of individuals, who devise contractual relationships as a way of facilitating their transactions with one another. This explanation does not work. It is an illusion that a contract is created purely by the individuals who are party to it. Certainly, individual parties do make up any one specific contract, but these parties expect this particular contract to be like all contracts in general, i.e. to be created within a *pre-established moral framework*. After all, if contracts were merely a matter of individual-to-individual agreement, then what would be the point of creating them? If individuals did not trust one another to do as they say, then there would be no point in attempting to improve one's position towards the other by getting him or her to make an explicit, formal agreement obliging the required actions. If one's word were not to be trusted, then why would a mere signature on an agreement be any more reliable? The value of a contract resides in its being made against the background of institutional arrangements. It does not simply bind the actual parties, but also involves obligations on others who are not party to the contractual agreement. The forces of law and order will support the claims of someone who has made a contract if that contract is validly made. Furthermore, society lays down what a contract can validly be; it is defined in terms of understandings in the society at large so that, for example, in our society one cannot make a contract to sell oneself into slavery.

### Non-contractual elements in contract

A framework of moral understandings and of social arrangements of enforcement is presupposed in the making of a contract. The parties to the contract do not establish this framework, but it is necessary if their action of making a contract is to have any sense.

Consequently, the idea of society being *founded* in some sort of contractual arrangement between individuals – invoked by Jean-Jacques Rousseau (1712–78) as well as Hobbes and Spencer – is a non-starter. Hence Durkheim's argument about non-contractual elements in contract opposes the idea that the actions of individuals can antedate the existence of society, since the capacity to perform actions, and not just those of contract-making, extensively presupposes the existence of a social framework, i.e. shared rules and forms of social organisation.

The idea of the individual – which we described above as 'political' – is essentially one of distinctiveness and autonomy, of someone entirely independent of others; individuals should, ideally, be left free to do whatsoever they want (within distinct but very broad limits). This idea is not a conception of human nature, though it offers itself as such. Rather, it is only thinkable in a certain kind of society, namely, the complex, modern society we now inhabit. The individual, in this sense, cannot exist in the simplest, most basic form of society – one which Durkheim terms 'mechanical'.

In the very simplest societies (as Durkheim conceived them) there is little specialisation; the individual human beings engage in similar activities on a self-sufficient basis. Self-sufficiency means that there is little interdependence within the society: any single part of the society – an individual or family group – is not significant to, or essential for, the group's continued existence. The solidarity of such a group derives from *likeness*, not interdependence; the members feel bonds of unity because they are much alike in their pattern of life and also in outlook. Under such basic conditions, life is homogeneous, and the space for the development of distinctive patterns of thought or outlook is severely restricted. Individuals learn their convictions from others and have little or no reason to challenge or depart from them. Since the variety of their own experience is so limited, it serves only to confirm those same shared beliefs in the eyes of each individual.

The analogy underpinning this notion of *mechanical solidarity* comes from the conception in physics of the mechanical structure of a gas, which is made up of identical individual and independent atomic units. Of course, in line with Durkheim's argument about crime, it follows that if a mechanical society ensures such standard existence and uniformity of belief, then there will be strong, widely shared sentiments and, therefore, intense, punitive reaction against crime, i.e. against anyone who might become different.

Under pressure of population growth, such a society will begin to change its nature, for it cannot simply continue to expand while remaining the same. Here Durkheim is echoing Hegel's idea of quantity into quality. The need for a society to cope with increasing numbers gives rise to the development of specialisation, i.e. a division of labour.

## Effects of the division of labour

Here the analogy changes to one borrowed from evolutionary theory: the capacity of an area of territory to support life is greater if the inhabitants are diversified. If they all have the same needs, they will all be competing for the same scarce resources relevant to that need, but if they are different species, with different needs, then they will not be in such direct competition for resources. The pressure of population leads to increasing diversity within the population through specialisation in the parts

> people play in society. With specialisation, the basis of social solidarity shifts from mechanical into *organic,* i.e. from likeness to *interdependence.*

'Organic' draws on a biological rather than a physical metaphor. The living organism is a composite of differentiated structures; metaphorically there is a division of labour among its parts. For example, the heart functions to pump blood, the lungs function to transfer oxygen to the blood, the eyes function as instruments of sight. Clearly, the parts are different, but interdependent – the loss of one has consequences for the rest, e.g. if the heart stops, then everything stops. Comparably, in a complex society with much specialisation there is interdependence; an individual's capacity to specialise in doing just one thing depends upon others doing the complementary things that the first requires for his or her survival. For example, someone practising medicine requires that someone else be producing food; someone producing food depends on others for clothes. Here specialisation is not just in economic activity, but in all areas of life, for Durkheim has in mind a *social* and not just an economic division of labour. Consequently, the members of such a society are held together by their need for one another. Hence with specialisation evaporates the basis for likeness, which derived, of course, from the commonality of experience. Increasing specialisation in society brings on complexity, making for a vastly wider range of possibilities of experience out of which are formed very different conceptions and convictions. Under such circumstances, one individual's life can be very different from another's. Thus the idea of individuals *as* individual, i.e. as distinct and different, can gain a hold and seem convincing. Only in such a context is there any real individuality to be prized and any toleration for autonomy of outlook and sentiment. Under such conditions there cannot be uniformity of sentiment throughout the population; there will be fewer widely shared and strongly held sentiments, so that for anyone to offend by mere difference from the prevailing pattern will no longer comprise crime. Durkheim contends that the role of law in organic society is not so much to repress differences as to reconcile the results of differences. The law has to settle damage to the society resulting from dispute and disagreement arising from the different needs, interests and outlooks of different kinds of persons.

The individual is, then, a creation of organic solidarity in the sense that a creature with individuality is only truly conceivable and possible within a certain kind of society. The very characteristics of the individual derive from the kind of society in which he or she is involved. Thus society creates 'the individual' and not the other way about.

## Diagnosing social pathology: suicide

The attachment of previous social theorists to individualism is, for Durkheim, symptomatic of the fact that the idea of the autonomous individual has such a powerful hold on modern society that it bids to become ever more extreme, threatening the well-being of society itself and, thereby, the individuals living in it. With mechanical solidarity, the society overwhelms individuality; with organic conditions, it seemed to Durkheim that the opposite threatens. Much of Durkheim's later work was motivated by his concern with the appropriate balance between individual and society; he tried to identify the threats to it and to theorise solutions.

In arguing the social foundations of individualism, Durkheim recognised that a degree of individualism was 'natural' to modern societies. He was not against individualism as such, but opposed its rampant, *pathological* forms. The issue, therefore, was how to strike a balance between independence and individual freedom, on the one hand, and subordination to the collective, on the other. He thought individualist doctrines were partial and one-sided; they put absolute priority on the individual's freedom over any restraint by the collective. He felt that such doctrines did not express the true desires of individuals, but only one aspect of the ambivalence that is characteristic of the modern mind. Part of it revolts against all restraint by the collective, but another part clings to and yearns for such restraint. Durkheim aimed to specify this requirement by formulating a conception of the correct proportions of individual autonomy from and individual dependence on the collective. What was the proportion required for general social and individual well-being?

Durkheim's study of suicide needs to be set against this background.

## Suicide

For Durkheim, suicide was a result of imbalance in the independence/autonomy relationship. In brief summary, suicides occur among those subject to too much or too little social solidarity.

*Suicide* is notable in taking what appears to be the most individual of acts, which seems therefore least likely to exhibit any regularities of a social kind, and then going on to demonstrate that suicide varies *according to social ties*, to their presence or absence, their strength or weakness. We noted earlier that *Suicide* had a considerable methodological impact through its manipulation of statistics in order to reveal the interconnection of various facts about suicide rates. It is important to remember that it is differential rates between social groups that Durkheim sought to explain, e.g. Protestants commit suicide proportionately more frequently than Catholics and Jews, single men more frequently than married ones, and urban dwellers more than rural. Durkheim argues that these differentials reflect differences between the social groups, i.e. the different ways individuals are connected to society, and the kind of social support that results.

Durkheim proposed four basic types of suicide: the egoistic and anomic reflect social ties that are too weak; the altruistic and fatalistic types arise from connections that are too strong so that in this case the group suppresses individuality.

*Egoistic* suicide results from the social isolation of the individual. It occurs among those who have fewer social ties, such as those who live alone in rooming houses rather than with a family, or those burdened with an intense spiritual loneliness. For example, Protestants have a higher suicide rate than Catholics since Protestant teachings emphasise that one is face to face alone with God, that one's relationship is entirely direct, and that one must, therefore, carry the entire burden of effort essential to one's salvation. Roman Catholic teachings, however, make the church and its practices the basis for one's relationship with God and provide mechanisms, e.g. the confessional, to share the burden and so to give social support in life.

By contrast, *anomic* suicide was occasioned by insufficient social regulation of the individual. In effect, the moral code of society fails to maintain its hold over the individual. The seemingly paradoxical feature of suicide is that although suicide rates rose during times of economic recession, as we might expect, they also rose during times of economic boom and prosperity, when we might expect them to decline. The superficial element of the explanation is that both situations – boom and bust – occasion dislocation between the individual's social position and the socially prescribed morals which relate to them. Within a socially stratified society there are different norms (moral standards) for the different social classes, and they specify different tastes and aspirations for the members of the respective groups. For example, middle-class people may expect to go to university, while lower-class people may not expect or even aspire to do so. Such norms develop on a collective scale and over time; since they arise from the real situations of the group, they have a realistic character. Even if lower-class people aspire to university attendance, they are less likely to succeed. However, economic bust and boom both result in abrupt movement of people up and also down the social scale. Middle-class people find themselves in greatly reduced circumstances in crashes, while lower-class people can be rendered enormously prosperous by economic booms. In other words, the standards to which they have become accustomed become inapplicable, precipitating suicide. How so?

We noted above that Durkheim's ideas principally have been understood through the writings of Talcott Parsons. The significance of the anomic form of suicide is a case in point. Mainly due to Parsons's influential interpretation of Durkheim, anomic suicide has been held to be a particularly notable category in Durkheim's typology. The idea of anomie, Parsons argued, represented a shift in a key feature of Durkheim's concerns. Previously he had talked about the constraining nature of social facts, identifying them as *moral* facts, which set requirements on how people should act. In his earlier work, however, Durkheim had emphasised the external nature of those constraints, as though society's moral rules were simply a fact in our environment (in the manner of the brick wall) of which we have to take practical account. Therefore, our compliance with society's rules seems a rather *instrumental* matter, i.e. we obey because we fear the disapproval and punishment that would follow any infraction. Durkheim's development of the concept of anomie is very different. For him, the standards of life become part of the individual's personality, the requirements of society's moral order become – to use a post-Durkheimian vocabulary – *internalised*. In short, we do not refrain from doing things which society forbids just because we fear the consequences, but because, very often, we do not want to do them; we feel that it would be wrong to do them.

Durkheim argues that the individual personality would be insatiable if unrestrained by social upbringing. It would have endless wants and, furthermore, would have no realistic basis for working out which of them could be realised. Individuals simply cannot work out the practical possibilities of life for themselves; to have any realistic sense of them, they must pick them up from other people, from their social settings, where cumulative, collective experience has provided the requisite exploration by trial and error. Individuals with insatiable and unrealistic wants would lead utterly frustrating and, eventually, unbearable existences; this fate is prevented only by learning the appropriate social standards. Rapid and extreme movement up and down the social scale disrupts this social learning, putting individuals in a situation in which there is no realistic guide on how to live, allowing them to develop unrealistic expectations and inevitable frustrations, which may finally become unbearable and self-destructive. For Parsons the importance of this argument in Durkheim is in conceiving social restraint as internal and not purely external. We will develop this point further when we come to discuss Parsons (see Chapter 5). The more immediate import of the anomic case is Durkheim's suggestion that an element of socially imposed discipline is essential to individual well-being, i.e. socially prescribed limitations on otherwise natural human appetites are an essential for sheer survival.

Altruism and fatalism are at the other extreme. Altruism involves individuals seeing the pre-eminence of the group over themselves to the extent that the group's needs seem greater than theirs. In fatalism, the group dominates individuals so intensely and oppressively that they are rendered entirely powerless over their fate. *Altruistic* suicide is instanced by cases such as the suicide of military officers for the honour of the regiment, or the self-sacrifice of a leader's family and retinue on the leader's death, or the self-sacrifice of suicide bombers. In such cases the bonds within the social group are so strong and intense that they create among the members a powerful sense of group identity. Individuals are so dependent upon the group for their sense of identity, in fact, that they think themselves less important than the group and are willing to give up their lives in order to respect and preserve it and its values. The *fatalistic* form, which receives barely a mention from Durkheim (one brief footnote), occurs when individuals in a group are placed in a position of such restriction that they feel nothing can be done to control their own life save to exit from it, e.g. suicides among slaves.

This argument for a balance between social regulation and individual autonomy concludes that the problem in modern, i.e. organic, society is that the balance has swung too much towards freedom from social regulation. Durkheim's concern was with understanding the mechanisms which structured relations between the individual and society, with a view to working out how to readjust them in the desirable direction.

As for making out a case for a science of sociology, in the analysis presented in *Suicide* Durkheim felt he had succeeded in demonstrating the existence of supra-individual patterns in terms of which individual fates were decided. In any given society the rates of suicide did not vary much over time, and

Durkheim wrote of society as 'demanding a certain rate' of individual deaths. This kind of remark might seem to justify the impression, which alienated many from Durkheim, that he was giving far too great a reality to society. He seemed to treat it as something not only arising from association among human beings, but also as having a life of its own. Arguably, however, Durkheim did not intend any such suggestion. After all, he did point to *collective* phenomena to justify his talk about the reality of society's existence and did seek to avoid conveying the impression that society was something utterly dissociated from its members. From this point of view, his remark about society 'demanding' a certain rate of suicides was really only a way of saying, admittedly loosely, that the conditions which exposed people to the risk of suicide remained constant for comparatively long periods of time. Rather than unjustifiably *reifying* society (see Chapter 8), Durkheim can be read as emphasising the fact that our membership of society is neither of our choosing, nor something we can cast off at will.

## The social foundations of religion

The topic of religion provided Durkheim with a further opportunity to examine the relationship between the individual and the society and to investigate what he perceived to be a major mechanism of social solidarity. As an atheist, Durkheim could not accept that the ostensible point of religion – to worship a god – could be its real explanation. Here he was not alone, as numerous anthropologists and sociologists before him had sought to explain what religion was 'really' about. Many of these explanations were of an individualist and psychological sort, seeking to understand religion as the product of properties of the individual mind, e.g. as a result of mistaken apprehensions of natural phenomena. Durkheim, entirely in accord with his own past practice, wanted to demonstrate that religion was a collective and not an individual phenomenon.

He reasoned that since religion was such a widespread phenomenon, it could not simply be dismissed as entirely false. If it were, then surely people would see through it, and not so many would be in its sway. There must be something to it – but what?

It was characteristic of Durkheim's approach to empirical analysis to take his point of departure from a general definition of the relevant phenomenon, be it suicide or religion. Thus the first task was to develop a definition of religion which would include all its diverse forms across the span of humanity that count as religions. He rejects the most obvious answer as too narrow, i.e. that the notion of a god or of supernatural beings is a universal feature of religions. For example, Confucianism involves no belief in deities. The essential feature of religion is its association with the notion of the *sacred*, i.e. something quite special, which has to be treated with exceptional levels of awe and respect. The sacred can include such things as the national flag, which is in one sense secular, but which, for many, would be *profaned* by being treated as just an ordinary thing.

## Sacred and profane

Durkheim says that religion divides the world into two spheres, the sacred and the profane. On the one hand, there is the ordinary, everyday world of practical, material and other concerns; on the other is the world of the special and ritualised, which must be sharply separated. For example, changes in dress, attitude and manner can be required of people when what they are doing involves them in contact with the sacred. This distinction is also connected with collective existence, since a church is an organised group, a collectivity of believers. The church requires of its members certain beliefs and, above all, the performance of certain sorts of actions, namely, *rites*.

In *The Elementary Forms of the Religious Life* (1976), Durkheim worked on a now outmoded evolutionist conception of society's development. To examine the essential forms of religion he felt it necessary to study what were then seen as the simplest, least developed societies, here those of the Australian Aboriginal peoples. If religion has an essence, then it must be present in all cases and will be easiest to detect in the most basic, simple ones. Aboriginal religion, 'totemism', had been closely studied and was subject to much controversy before Durkheim took up the topic.

## Totemism

Totemism involves the worship of specific things in the environment – animals, plants, particular places or objects – and the making of representations of these things in the form of symbols (called *churinga* and usually carved on wood) that are used in religious rituals.

Durkheim drew upon other people's studies of the totemic system to argue that it is misguided to look at the totemic object, the item worshipped by a particular group, in order to find a solution to the question of what totemism was really about. The totemic object, which seemingly could be almost anything, was certainly sacred. For example, if it were an animal it could not be killed or eaten. Yet why should these ordinary objects be the recipients of such exceptional treatment? There seemed to be nothing to distinguish them from other, quite ordinary, objects, but surely there must be something.

Durkheim held that imagining ways these ordinary objects acquired such special status couldn't work. It is not the objects themselves but what they stand for that is the key. These objects derive their exceptional character from that with which they are associated. Vitally, Durkheim recognised their symbolic dimension; totemic items are, in fact, *symbols*, and their symbolic meaning is the source of their power. This finding is indicated by the fact that the prohibitions relating to the items themselves – the animal or plant – could be lifted under certain exceptional circumstances, yet the symbolic representations used in the ceremonies are still accorded special status and strictly governed by the prohibitions. What is it, then, that is symbolised? What is there in the environment of the Aborigines that can have such respect-inspiring status? Given Durkheim's proclivities, there can be only one thing: society. The above analogy with the national flag is apposite: in representing the social group, the totem is very like the national flag, for it was an emblem of a social group: those whose totem was the kangaroo would call themselves 'the kangaroos', and they would differ from 'the emus' and so on.

The role of the totem symbolises something not explicitly understood by the Aborigines: their dependence as human individuals upon their society. The totem expresses things which people know in their experience, but cannot comprehend or express in an overt, intellectual way. That religion is a symbolic, rather than a discursive, activity we know but cannot say in so many words. We know through our practical lives the extent to which society is something greater than each of us individually. The life we lead is dependent upon other people and the support of our social group. Moreover, the society of which we are members is much mightier than any one, or even a group, of us. In comparison with us, society is immortal, as it continues to exist though individuals pass away. Given Durkheim's initial assumption that religion must have some essential truth to explain its widespread acceptance and persistence, then religious beliefs must be about something *real*. Religions assign to the sacred immense power and eternal persistence. These must be the properties of something in the world. In Aboriginal life there is only one such thing: Aborigines' society itself. Thus the attitude towards the sacred, the posture of worship, is a posture towards society, an obeisance before the power that truly gives us purpose and rules our lives.

In Durkheim's account, then, the totem is connected with a worshipping group, for which it functions as an emblem. The totem involves various beliefs about its special nature, which are symbolic expressions of the nature of society. Only the rites remain to be considered.

The Aboriginals' way of life involved a cycle of dispersion and reassembly. The occasions of reassembly were those of rituals, called corroboree, in which those involved would get themselves into an emotionally intoxicated state. Here, Durkheim saw further testimony to the power of society; the association between human beings has potent effects upon the feeling states of individuals.

## Collective effervescence

Involvement in the group activity created *collective effervescence*, i.e. an unusual state of shared excitement, involving exceptionally intense feelings. The shared expression of these emotions served to heighten them still further.

More mundanely, the effect is akin to the feeling of being at a good party: one feels different and better because of the occasion. The exceptional states of the corroboree, however, are not attributed to the persons present as such, but rather understood as expressions of the totem's power. To the Aboriginal peoples, the totemic animal or plant has the capacity to induce exceptional states in people, e.g. enabling men to mutilate their bodies without feeling any pain. For Durkheim, the individual's participation in such a common occasion explains such things. Collective involvement renews and strengthens the feelings towards the totem, and the benign and intense character of the emotions created extends to others present in the same situation. The feeling of commonality with them is intensified by the fact that they share the same exceptional experiences. The rites reinforce the solidarity of Aboriginal society in two ways: through the symbolic relationship to the totem; and through the relationship of shared experience between the individuals who make up the group.

Now Durkheim's contention that religion is 'society worshipping itself' becomes somewhat plainer. The members of society collectively give symbolic expression (through ceremony and ritual) to their sense of membership of the large, less transient collective within which they live and upon which they depend. Durkheim supposed that people's reactions are subject to attrition and that over the course of daily life, capacities for certain kinds of feeling will diminish if they are not periodically stimulated. It is the role of both the criminal offence and the ritualised religious life to provide periodic stimulation to feelings, to keep them alive, to restore them to their prior strength. The criminal stimulates feelings of outrage in connection with society's rules, and reinforces our sense of what we have in common with others who endorse those rules, while the religious rite revitalises the senses of attachment and solidarity which we have with others who belong to our group.

## Durkheim on knowledge

Finally, there is one, slightly discontinuous, aspect of *The Elementary Forms of the Religious Life* that served to sustain Durkheim's influence when the conception of him as a positivist and a functionalist cast his ideas into disrepute in many circles. Toward the end of the book he offered the view that the categories of thought have a social origin. The philosopher Kant had maintained that the fundamental categories of thought, e.g. thinking of things being distributed in space and time, or as standing in causal relationships to one another, are innate in the human mind. Durkheim's study of the anthropological material on the Aborigines and his collaboration with his colleague Marcel Mauss in a study titled *Primitive Classification* (1973) convinced him that conceptions of space and time vary from society to society. In short, not all humanity shares our conception of space as something that extends out evenly in all directions. (Indeed, after Einstein we no longer hold such a view, for space now 'curves' – while some other people think of space as circular.) Of course, we all have the capacity to apprehend space; it is an innate part of our capacity to see that the chair is across the room, or that the ball is off the ground and moving through the air. What Durkheim has in mind, however, is not our subjective experience of space, but the conception of space as an objective environment within which we are located. For example, we do not think of ourselves as dwelling at the centre of all things as once we used to; we do not think of ourselves as specially located in a space that radiates out from us. Such conceptions of space could not be figured out from our individual experience of space, but must be acquired collectively. Consequently, the concept of space as something possessed of an overall order must have a social origin.

Durkheim reasoned that human beings could not truly originate conceptions out of nothing; we can only contrive things on the basis of some given model. He held, therefore, that concepts of space (and, on the basis of comparable arguments, time) were social in the sense that they are collectively created, and also they are social in respect of their content. Again, as far as Durkheim could see, the only things on which the comprehensive schemes of space and time could be modelled are *social arrangements*.

### The social construction of knowledge

The concept of space held by a group is modelled on the spatial arrangements of the group's social life. For example, the layout of its camps provides the group with a concept of space as circular, deriving from the circular layout of its huts. Similarly, temporal concepts are based upon the rhythms of the group's collective life, just as the Western year is still structured around feasts and holidays like Christmas, Easter and the New Year. A notion of time as having a structure, a rhythmic pattern, is stimulated by such facts about our social life.

Though much criticised in its specifics, this idea of Durkheim's has been enormously influential upon the sociology of knowledge. The idea of knowledge as socially shaped and socially constructed has become central to many recent strands of sociological thought, structuralist and poststructuralist included, as we will see in Chapters 9 and 10. Consequently, far from being simply an outmoded positivist and functionalist, Durkheim is once again coming to be regarded as a major thinker whose work is a source of profound sociological insights.

### Durkheim the radical reformer

We remarked earlier in the chapter that Durkheim was regarded in his own time as a socialist and a radical and not as a conservative. For example, he played an active role in the 'Dreyfus affair', which began with the false imprisonment for treason of Captain Dreyfus, a French Jewish army officer, and ended by dividing

French society into disputing factions in the final years of the nineteenth century. Durkheim's activities as a 'Dreyfusard', i.e. a supporter of the unfortunate officer, were hardly those of someone entirely anxious to defend the social and political status quo. In his sociological writings he also allied his interest in social reform to his critique of individualism and his theme of the need for collective identity and social integration. For him, the purpose of a scientific sociology was very much to guide social reform along effective lines, based on an objective understanding of society and its problems. His basic diagnosis of modern society as subject to an increasing lack of integration, with the relationship between the individual and society becoming increasingly attenuated, led him to focus upon ways in which this situation might be reversed. The conditions of organic society meant that there was great diversity in outlooks, including moral ones, but Durkheim thought that there was a need to strengthen attachment to shared morals, and also to provide better support for the individual's connection to society.

Since the 'internalisation' (using a Parsonian term) of society's moral code occurs in childhood and largely through the process of education, Durkheim was profoundly interested in education and educational reform. Indeed, he has a strong claim to being the originator of the sociology of education. He was more interested in education's role in the transmission of a shared moral sensibility than in issues around the relationship between education and social inequality, since this role might serve to reunify an increasingly divided society. In *Moral Education* (1961) he argued for the idea that the fundamental purpose of education is the inculcation of moral values and a 'spirit of discipline'. This idea might now sound rather right-wing in tone, but to jump to this conclusion would be to miss the point. Durkheim was indicating something more fundamental: a complex and differentiated society places demands upon its members to be able to co-ordinate their activities with others, thereby requiring individuals to be capable of controlling their conduct in specific ways in order to align it closely with other people's. Furthermore, such control has to be second nature, not requiring individuals to stop and think and consciously plan how to fit their conduct to that of others. Consequently, the general moral attitudes of individuals not only have to be similar, but also require each person to be able routinely to monitor her or his own and others' conduct with respect to these moral assumptions. In modern society the child first becomes involved in complex, collective activities in the school classroom; therefore, the 'spirit of discipline' is acquired in school.

## The classroom as a moral order

Durkheim was pointing to something that has only become fully appreciated by sociologists of education in recent years: underlying the content of schooling, e.g. the teaching of subjects by teachers and the taking and passing or failing of examinations by students, is a more fundamental social reality, the classroom as a *moral order*.

Long before the concept of the 'hidden curriculum' had been coined, Durkheim was arguing that the *social form* of the teacher–student and student–student relationships is what above all shapes the educational experience. These relationships are infused with values, and the role of the teacher in relation to the student is to exemplify society's values.

Durkheim was also led into the field we now call 'industrial relations' by his concern at the breakdown of order and loss of collective morality in modern society. Like Marx, Durkheim believed that the direction in which industrial societies were moving, with ever bigger enterprises and ever greater competition, meant the destruction of any sense of morality guiding economic activities. Economic life was becoming dangerously amoral: the expansion of capitalism was accompanied by polarisation and atomisation, i.e. workers were increasingly isolated from their employers and from one another. The result was the rapid increase in social conflict and more individualised forms of pathology, while civic morals were in decline. Given his methodological view that social facts can only be explained by other social facts, Durkheim believed that social solutions had to be sought, since the causes of these problems were social. New social structures were required to counter these trends. He believed one such structure was the professional association.

### Professional associations

Since workers in the same or similar occupations experienced the same treatment, economically and socially, Durkheim, like Marx, saw a basis for collective action around common interests. Forming occupational groupings such as trade unions or professional associations to pursue these common interests on the basis of shared values would not only tie individuals more strongly to one another, but also provide society with an intermediary form of collective existence between the individual and the nation state.

In arguing for the need for such organisations, Durkheim anticipated much of the subsequent debate about *mass society*, the dangers of which so exercised later thinkers, e.g. those in the Frankfurt School (see Chapter 8). These 'moderate-sized' bodies would bridge the gap between the massive edifices of the state and the capitalist enterprise on the one hand, and the individual on the other. Paradoxically, though Durkheim was himself somewhat leftward-leaning in his politics, this idea of a set of corporate groupings between the individual and the state seems close to the kinds of ideas that the Fascists were subsequently to develop.

### Conclusion

Durkheim's influence on Anglo-American sociology (and British social anthropology) was considerable. He was one of the key figures that Talcott Parsons (see Chapter 5) identified as making a decisive break with the limitations of nineteenth-century thought. Important parts of Parsons's theory derived directly from Durkheim, and it was through them that he figured as a major influence on mid-century sociological theory. However, the reaction against Parsons on the grounds of the conservatism of 'functionalist' and 'consensus' views (which allegedly emphasise agreement and harmony in society, and downplay conflict) meant that Durkheim too came to be reviled for the conservatism of his outlook. At the same time, there was also a strong reaction against methodological views, which held up Durkheim as a heroic precursor on the grounds that he had attempted to make sociology scientific by making it quantitative, by means of the sophisticated use of statistics in *Suicide*. In this connection Durkheim was attacked as a positivist, which became a term of abuse applied to all those holding that sociology might be scientific. At present these harsh and dismissive judgements are being reconsidered and the radical implications of his thought are being stressed. His consideration of the social basis of ideas has also been influential on what are currently considered radical ideas, such as those of contemporary French theory and the Anglo-American sociology of science.

## Questions

1 What do you understand by the term 'positivism'? Can you show how Durkheim's *Suicide* is a positivist account in ways that Marx's or Weber's works were not? What contemporary examples of positivist social research can you think of?

2 Does Durkheim deny the existence of 'the individual'? If not, what role does the individual have in his thought? How does this contrast with Weber's analysis? Which do you think is most useful and why?

3 What kinds of non-contractual social phenomena must be in place before contractual agreements can be reached? Why does Durkheim think these are so important? In what ways might these phenomena represent a challenge to Marx's work?

4 What are the differences between mechanical and organic divisions of labour? How does the organic division of labour differ from Marx's analysis of capitalism and Weber's of bureaucratic rationality? Which makes more sense in accounting for the changes that occurred between pre-capitalist and capitalist social organisations? Why?

5 Why do suicide rates allow one to talk about the nature of a society's moral order? What contemporary measures might serve the same function? Is modern society anomic or fatalistic, egoistic or altruistic? Do these categories make sense in terms of explaining individuals' behaviour?

6 What are the key elements of religious belief and practices in Durkheim's thought? Is he right? In what ways does his

account of religion differ from those of Marx and Weber? Which is most useful? Are different theories better at explaining different religions? Which makes most sense overall and why?

7 Durkheim argues that *ritual* marks the division between the sacred and the profane. What does this mean? What contemporary examples of this can you think of? What non-religious forms of ritual might there be? Do they serve this function?

## Next steps

Durkheim's key texts now all have excellent translations, and are best read in their original form: *The Division of Labour in Society* (1984), *Suicide* (1951), *The Rules of Sociological Method* (1966) and *The Elementary Forms of the Religious Life* (1976).

Giddens's (1978) *Durkheim* is an excellent short introduction to his work, while Lukes's (1975) *Émile Durkheim: His Life and Work* is longer, comprehensive and lucid.

# PART II

# Sociology in the English-speaking world

American thinkers dominated the development of sociology in the mid-twentieth century. Two independent traditions, loosely associated with Harvard and Chicago Universities, moved forward on the question of what kind of discipline sociology might be. The former, dominated by the work of Talcott Parsons, sought to develop a *general theory* of the social world, building on the work of – in particular – Weber and Durkheim. The latter, which came to be labelled 'symbolic interactionism', focused more on empirical studies of what people actually do together, minimising abstract theory and remaining sceptical of claims about sociology being a 'science' or society being a 'system'. A third approach, ethnomethodology – generally associated with work undertaken across the campuses of the University of California – took an even more radical line, attempting to 'respecify' the 'big' problems of social theory by conducting studies of mundane, apparently trivial, social activities.

Talcott Parsons's working life was devoted to trying to understand, theoretically, how societies work. Starting with his *Structure of Social Action* (1937), he argued that Weber and Durkheim were *both* working in similar ways: they rejected individualism, and moved social thought from a 'utilitarian' perspective to a properly sociological one. Parsons pointed out that societies are, broadly speaking, orderly because people want to do the kinds of things that maintain that order. This means that three elements of the social world have to work together: culture (prescribing what people should do), social system (the pattern of activities and relationships between people) and individual personalities. Parsons's developing theory was an attempt to show how this 'working together' is achieved – and what kinds of things might go wrong when it fails. Often criticised for abstraction and an apparent lack of interest in real-world activities, Parsons was nevertheless the greatest American sociologist of the twentieth century. His ideas dominated English-speaking sociology over the 1950s and 1960s.

At the same time that Parsons was developing his theoretical system at Harvard, sociologists at the University of Chicago were developing a radically different way of approaching the study of the social. Influenced by Robert E. Park and his colleagues, graduate students were encouraged to conduct detailed descriptive studies of the city's institutions, neighbourhoods and occupations. Starting from an interpretative position, they argued that people act on the basis of their understandings, the ways they define the situations they find themselves in, and so sociology must try to describe how those definitions are arrived at.

Instead of treating the world as a set of systems, the symbolic interactionists treated social order as the outcome of patterns of interaction, a set of 'social worlds' produced by their participants' interactions. Sociology was not to be a science, with abstract forces operating according to laws, but rather a collection of studies, allowing different kinds of social interaction and different kinds of social institution to be compared with one another. The key 'theoretical' statements of the symbolic interactionists – Blumer's (1969) *Symbolic Interactionism* and Glaser and Strauss's (1967) *The Discovery of Grounded Theory* – are thus rejections of the grand theoretical and 'scientific' claims of Parsonian sociology, and emphasise the need to develop adequate descriptions of the social world from deep immersion in everyday settings.

Many of the symbolic interactionists' ideas have now become commonplace tropes in sociology: working with qualitative data, understanding people's activities in social context, and being agnostic – if not suspicious – of claims that sociology is a 'science'. A more radical approach to sociology, ethnomethodology, which developed in the 1950s and 1960s across the campuses of the University of California, has proved far harder to integrate. Ethnomethodology takes the problem of social order – as identified in Parsons's *Structure of Social Action* – to be something that is worked out by members of society in the course of their routine activities. In this, it is indebted to phenomenology, in particular to the work of Alfred Schütz. Schütz was concerned to demonstrate how members of society experience their world(s), and how that experience has a particular structure: he was thus interested in what he called the 'natural attitude' and 'common sense knowledge'. Harold Garfinkel, the founder of ethnomethodology, took this interest further: how, he asked, do members of society construct the orderly world they live in through their ordinary, mundane activities? By pursuing studies of these mundane activities in close detail, the ethnomethodologists were able to demonstrate, first, that social order is not a systemic or structural phenomenon but rather the product of interaction itself, and, second, that it has a logic and orderliness all of its own: one which is part and parcel of the activities themselves. The apparent abandonment of theory, attention to the detailed workings of trivial activities, and principled indifference to the concerns of other forms of sociology made ethnomethodology a controversial development that was difficult to digest.

CHAPTER FIVE

# Consensus and conflict

---

**Chapter overview**

Talcott Parsons was the dominant sociological theorist in the English-speaking
world for much of the twentieth century. His work was an attempt to show what
was common to Weber and Durkheim (and other theorists), and to develop a
*general* theory of the social on the basis of this. He developed an integrated way
of thinking about both social action and the social system, where each elaborates
the other in complex ways. Parsons is often (unfairly) thought of as a conservative
figure, making society out to be harmonious and free of conflict, and denying
the possibility of social change: these criticisms are considered and evaluated.
The response to Parsons's analysis of power is used as a case study of both
these criticisms and their weaknesses. Finally, both reactions to Parsons's work
(in approaches that stress stratification and social change) and contemporary
developments of his ideas (for instance 'systems theory') are introduced.

---

## Introduction: Parsons – the project for a systematic sociology

The impact of 'the classics' on Anglo-American sociology was, in the first
instance, very much the achievement of Talcott Parsons (1902–79), whose
graduate studies in the UK and Europe in the 1920s had familiarised him
with the work of, among others, the trio of Marx, Weber and Durkheim (see
Chapters 2–4). In the 1930s Parsons set out to construct a major work of theoretical synthesis, drawing especially upon the work of Weber and Durkheim.
The result of his efforts, *The Structure of Social Action*, appeared in 1937.
The work consisted in large part in the presentation of four thinkers, two of
whom – Alfred Marshall, the economist, and Vilfredo Pareto, the economist/
sociologist – have not enjoyed such continuing significance for sociology. This
book provided the world of English-speaking sociology with its first significant
and systematic presentation of the ideas of Weber and Durkheim.

We have mentioned above, in Chapter 2, that Parsons was also familiar with
Marx's work and even sympathetic to some of his views. None the less, Marx

was deliberately excluded from Parsons's grand synthesis. Parsons acknowledged Marx to be a great thinker, but argued that he remained firmly within the prevailing nineteenth-century way of thinking in the social sciences, while Weber and Durkheim had, by contrast, contributed to breaking it down.

One of the main targets of Parsons's criticism was utilitarianism, which, as we saw in our discussion of Durkheim (see Chapter 4), involves the idea that people's actions follow fundamentally practical objectives, and that the human mind is essentially a mechanism for calculating the most effective way to get the most rewarding results. This picture captures the very essence of economics, where 'the economic human' (*homo œconomicus*) is an individual with a clear set of wants and the economic capacity to fulfil some of them; he or she then sets out to figure out a way to get the most rewarding assortment of goods in terms of the resources available. In constructing its theories upon the assumption of such a rational, *maximising* individual, economics is building upon the model that was very widespread in pre-twentieth-century social thought. This model, as previously noted, found its most explicit and, in some ways, most crucial expression back in the seventeenth century, in Thomas Hobbes's *Leviathan*.

Very briefly, Hobbes's argument was that human beings are selfish creatures living in a world of scarce satisfactions. Each individual has wants, and seeks to satisfy as many of them as possible. In working out the most efficient way of getting what they want, individuals realise that they are in competition with one another, that one person can only gain at another's expense. Thus individuals are by nature truly selfish and see others only as obstacles or possible resources in their own pursuit of maximum satisfaction. The most logical way to achieve one's ends, then, is either to eliminate the competition – remove others by killing them – or to turn them towards the service of one's own ends, by forcing or deceiving them into compliance with one's will. However, if every individual is conceived as a rational being, i.e. someone who operates logically, then each person will reach the same inevitable conclusion, making social life a state of perpetual struggle. Hobbes called it a 'war of all against all', colourfully characterising it in a justly famous passage as 'solitary, poor, nasty, brutish and short'. Of course, for most of us human life is not that bad, as Hobbes himself explained: valuing their own lives above all else, these rational individuals can perceive the slippery slope to mutual misery and destruction, down which they would slide if they did not accept some restrictions on their freedom of competition. These restrictions are in the form of society, as represented by the sovereign ruler to whom individuals effectively cede their autonomy.

## Hobbes's idea of society

This expressed three ideas that were immensely influential over the next three hundred years:

1   Society is to be understood in terms of the characteristics of its individual members, as an association of individuals.

2 Those individuals have the kind of absolutely self-interested and calculating outlook that the utilitarian model supposes.

3 Therefore, if they were strictly rational, the only basis for deciding how to act towards others would be to employ the most ruthlessly effective means of getting their own way.

Hobbes held the basic *individualistic* conception of human beings, drew out its strict logical implications, but then backed away from it by invoking 'the sovereign'. For Parsons, to do so was a theoretical cheat since the individuals had to act together – and be social!

Similarly, it was Parsons's view that Marx, for all his emphasis upon social classes, i.e. *social groups*, nevertheless remains within this individualist tradition by virtue of conceiving social life in terms of struggles over material interests. This reading of Marx is not unique to Parsons, as more recent commentators such as Jon Elster (1985) argue a similar view.

Parsons was interested in Durkheim, Weber, Pareto and Marshall because they were all, in their different ways, concerned to think their way out of the framework of utilitarian assumptions. The key move, which they all made, was to reject the utilitarian assumption that people's ends are random. In a scheme like Hobbes's, it does not matter what kinds of things people want, only that they have plenty of wants, more than can collectively be satisfied by the finite resources of the world, and it is this simple fact which makes them competitors. In such reasoning, the way people come by their wants, or the nature of these wants, is essentially irrelevant; viewed as a theoretical system, the ends might as well be random. Durkheim, Weber and the others had perceived, however, that people's ends are not random; they are *socially* acquired and, in consequence, are related to one another in *systematic* ways. For example, Durkheim examines the notion of anomic suicide in terms of the way people's wants are patterned; they are shaped by social arrangements which accord with the hierarchy of stratification and embody normative requirements which prescribe proper and acceptable wants.

Hobbes's thought had bequeathed the problem of social order: how is it possible for people to go about pursuing their individual ends without falling into the state of war of all against all? He had provided an answer, but it was unprincipled. Parsons's four theorists had begun to offer a principled solution which rejected the individualistic picture, since they recognised that human beings develop and form their wants within a social context. Furthermore, the very acquisition of these wants is made possible *by* the social order, by what Durkheim calls society's 'moral order' with its systems of 'collective sentiments' and 'collective representations', i.e. what we would nowadays call *culture*. Far from being random, wants are formed through this social order; individual wants are often common and shared. Moreover, in being shared they are viewed as right and proper wants for anyone to possess. In other words, they have a moral character. In this way, Weber, for example, provided a very different conception of capitalism to Marx's in so far as he brought out the moral nature of the emphasis upon disciplined hard work in capitalism; this emphasis had its origins in religion and the desire for salvation rather than in the calculation of material benefit.

## The project takes shape

On this basis, Parsons thought that a start could be made on developing a general scientific scheme for understanding human life. Between his first major work and his next there was a fourteen-year break – though Parsons did publish many essays in that time. Then, in 1951, he published two books, one self-authored, *The Social System*, the other a collaborative work, *Toward a General Theory of Action*. In a way, Parsons had retreated from the ambitions he had held in 1937, but the plan laid out in these two books was none the less grandiose. *Toward a General Theory* drew its contributors from across several disciplines; necessarily so, for Parsons sought to lay out a ground plan for a large range of the social sciences – or 'sciences of action', as he called them. Thus psychology, sociology, economics, political science and other disciplines were all to be unified within a single theoretical framework, which was basically devised by Parsons. *The Social System* was the sociological element in the project, showing how this general scheme, this general theory of action, would be developed in sociology.

Parsons drew from the work of his four theorists a picture of social life involving *motivated compliance*.

### Motivated compliance

Social life does work, rather than disintegrating into Hobbes's war of all against all. It works not only because people go about their activities in ways that are socially prescribed, but also because they believe these ways to be right and therefore they actually want to follow them.

He proposed that the actual operating life of a society is made up of the following elements:

1   The abstract patterns of behaviour, which prescribe what individuals should properly or appropriately do in particular cases. For example, the highway code prescribes how fast drivers should drive under what conditions and how they should co-ordinate with fellow motorists.
2   The pattern of ongoing activity, i.e. how actual people in actual situations behave in ways which (roughly, more or less) accord with the abstract patterns. For example, in traffic on the road, drivers are busy looking out for what others are doing, and tactically adjusting their driving to accommodate and avoid one another, such action depending in various ways upon the conventions of the highway code being respected by most, if not all, drivers.

3　The personalities, or characteristic patterns of preference, of reaction and so forth of the individuals carrying out these patterns. For example, in traffic they act as drivers, and they interact with one another in terms of their characters: some drive much more quickly than others, some are more respectful of others' rights on the road, some get angry with traffic conditions, and others remain calm. However, the great majority of these drivers abide broadly by the rules of the road and do so not merely from prudence, for safety's sake, or from nicely calculated considerations as to just how much adherence to the rules would maximise their self-interest, but because they think it is the right thing to do. They regard these rules as binding on themselves and on others. They can become indignant with other drivers just because those drivers show disregard for the rules of the road, even though the infraction of these rules may cause them no danger, nor harm them in any way.

'Motivated compliance' means no more than the drivers being motivated to abide by the rules of the highway code, but this illustration of the idea draws attention to the way actual situations in society are made up of three 'action systems', as Parsons called them:

- *culture*: the pattern of ideas, principles, etc. which abstractly specifies how people should behave;
- *social system*: the ordered patterns of activity and relationship among individuals as they go about their affairs in conjunction, even collaboration, with one another;
- *personalities*: the psychic make-up of individuals which affects how they behave in actual situations, how they go about doing things and how they react to other people.

Parsons argues that any society has to provide somehow for the *integration* of these three elements.

## Integrating culture, social system and personalities

Somehow, things will have to work out so that:

- Culture will prescribe what people should do in ways which will prove practically effective, relative to what people want to do.
- The pattern of activities and relationships in which people engage will prove capable of allowing the prescriptions of the culture to be effectively followed (a good deal of the time).
- The personality structures of the parties to social life will have that which will enable them to associate with others, to participate in conjoint, collective ventures, and to accept and comply with the demands that the culture lays on them.

The key word here is 'somehow'. Parsons made the examination of this 'somehow' the focal concern of the remainder of his long career.

Cultures, social systems and personalities have to interact in integrated ways if there is to be any social order. Cultures have to be organised in ways such that their prescriptions will be viable in practical affairs (if cultures demand impractical things of their members, then those members will soon either abandon the culture or die out).

The different prescriptions for the actions of an individual have to fit together with those that other individuals abide by, otherwise they would always be acting at cross purposes, nothing requiring their joint participation would ever get done, and no social system would have even temporary stability. Imagine if drivers had different cultural instructions as to which directions they were to drive in on the roads.

Social activities themselves have to be organised in ways that will offer sufficient involvement of the personality types who will participate in them; if people are utterly frustrated and completely alienated by the demands of participation in some activity, e.g. they have a pathological fear of competition, they are going to be very resistant to being involved in society, e.g. in competitive sports.

Parsons insists that these are the *minimal conditions* for social order. A society can, of course, tolerate the fact that there will be some, relatively few, people who follow different prescriptions, or have personalities incongruous with (say) the generally competitive character of American culture, but it can only operate if the 'lack of fit' in such cases is confined to a *relative* few. Without sufficient integration between the culture, the social system and the individual personality, social relationships cannot be organised and carried on. Of course, 'sufficient' is far from being a precise notion.

In view of the hostile response which Parsons's work eventually met, we should draw attention here to the fact that he does not see the integration of culture, social system and personality as either automatic or complete – far from it. In dealing with something as complex as the order of a society, its pattern of institutions and relationships, its culture built up over its history, and the varied personalities of its numerous members, we should recognise that integration is *highly problematic*. In any ongoing society which is not collapsing into internecine strife, it must be the case that there is a level of integration, since things are getting done, people are acting broadly in line with their cultural prescriptions, and many individuals are engaged in and committed to activities. The perceptible stability of society indicates that its members (or the great majority of them, for most of the time) are not alienated, in the sense of 'turned off'. However, there may not be thoroughgoing integration, since some aspects of the culture may conflict with the way the social system is organised, and the way both are organised may impose deprivations on participants' personalities. In any real society, many people may not be so disenchanted with their jobs that they would rather give them up, so opposed to authority that they would rather fight their supervisor than do what he or she says, or so contemptuous of the law that they would happily violate it. Nevertheless, those same people may be unhappy in their work, reluctant to comply with their supervisor, and so uncommitted to a law-abiding existence that they may not pass up every temptation to transgress. Parsons recognises just such possibilities. They are partly what we mean by the integration of culture, social system and personality being problematic, i.e. the working out of the interconnections between them is neither automatic nor guaranteed. Although any real society must have exceeded the 'minimal' requirements of integration – as testified to by the sheer fact of its existence – none the less it is an empirical question as to how far beyond this minimum the integration extends. It is also a logical consequence of Parsons's systems analysis that there will be tendencies for the system to counterbalance tendencies towards disintegration, to contain dissidence, to keep dissidents isolated from one another, thereby preventing them from building up collectively organised opposition to the dominant culture, and redirecting their deviations into ways that do not damage overall integration. The system 'handles and channels' social disturbances, although there is no theoretical guarantee that disturbances will never overwhelm the system.

In talking about the achievement and surpassing of this 'minimal' level, Parsons is not discussing the ways the members of the society, through conscious, deliberative processes, 'work out' solutions to the problem of integration between these three aspects of social reality. Such matters do not exercise the members. The terms in which these issues are formulated are analytical and sociological; Parsons is talking from a 'system standpoint' about the way things work themselves out; how the social order through the interaction and mutual effects of the culture, social system and personality becomes at least minimally integrated. If societies did not satisfy these minimal requirements then they would not be there for us to study; the fact that there is a society to study means that it has *somehow* met the minimal requirements of social integration. How far it is integrated depends on how much more than the minimum has been effected.

It is important to note that the three elements Parsons identifies are 'integrated' in the minimal sense that any actual, concrete social situation is made up of all three of them. These three elements are all mixed up in actual situations. In fact, says Parsons, they *interpenetrate* one another. People in social relations do not just stand in purely personal relationships, but relate to one another on the basis of social positions (the status, or status roles) they occupy. Hence two individuals in a workplace stand not just as 'Joe' and 'Jim' but as, say, a worker and his supervisor. Their respective positions are not just a matter of what they are doing, but of rights and entitlements, e.g. Jim may be entitled to give Joe orders, and Joe required to do as Jim tells him. In other words, a work relationship, like any other, is a matter of rights and responsibilities, i.e. it includes cultural elements, and these cultural elements go to make up the social system. In its turn, the social system becomes part of the personality of its participants; the position that one holds, the job one occupies, is not merely a matter of external requirements, but is, obviously, bound into and constitutive of the way one thinks of oneself. The kind of position one occupies is contributory to one's self-esteem. Further, in so far as one identifies with one's job, then of course one comes to regard the things one is entitled to do and to be responsible for not simply as things to be done because they are formally required, but as things one would want to do even if not required to do them. In this way, the cultural requirements and responsibilities of a job become part of one's personality.

In Parsons's terms, the social system is made up of cultural elements and of personalities. The social system and the culture interpenetrate because the latter is *institutionalised* in the former. In one sense, a social system is a pattern of institutionalised culture, i.e. a set of rules and requirements which have become accepted as defining how people should act and relate to one another, just as the highway code is ubiquitously accepted as saying how drivers should handle their vehicles and communicate with and respect the drivers of other vehicles. The connection between the social system and the personality is through *internalisation*.

## Internalisation

This concept refers to the ways the members of society come to make the requirements of their various positions an integral part of their personality by 'taking over' these requirements and building them into their own convictions about how and what they should do.

For example, when we see other persons breaking a rule of the road we may become indignant because we feel that we personally have been affronted by what was done. Since a social system is itself significantly institutionalised culture, when people internalise the social system, i.e. identify with their position in it, they also internalise culture because their position in the social system is made up of institutionalised culture.

## Parsons's functionalism

'Functionalism' is often a bogey word: to characterise an argument as functionalist is enough, in some circles, to condemn it. Parsons's work gave the debate over functionalism prominence. His work developed from earlier thinkers – Durkheim, Bronislaw Malinowski and A. R. Radcliffe Brown in social anthropology (both also influenced by Durkheim) – as well as Parsons's contemporary, Robert K. Merton.

Parsons proposed, as a kind of theoretical half-way house and not as an ultimate objective of sociology, the adoption of *structural functionalism*. His original idea had been to approach society from the bottom up, analysing it as a complex composite of *unit acts*, i.e. actions performed by individuals. Moreover, he had imagined representing the relations between actions as a set of mathematical equations, rather in the way the behaviour of a gas can be expressed in equations capturing the behaviour of its constituent molecules. However, he had realised that such an objective was, at least in the short term, quite unrealistic and so, to work towards it, he would adopt a different, top-down conception of society, i.e. one taking the viewpoint of the society-as-a-whole in order to look down upon the behaviour of individuals. From this point of view, sociological knowledge was equated more readily with biology than with chemistry, since the elements of the whole are understood in terms of their relations to the whole. The emphasis is on the functions of the elements, i.e. the contributions they make to the continuing operation of the whole, such as the part played by – the function of – the kidney in eliminating noxious elements from the circulatory systems of the body.

Remember that Parsons's problem was to understand how the integration of culture, structure and personality was achieved. This tripartite scheme was the basis of his structural functionalism. He makes a very simple but crucial assumption: human beings are sensitive to one another and they treat one another's reactions as meaningful, as either rewarding or punishing. It is not just materially rewarding satisfactions which gratify people; they are pleased and pleasured by the approval and affection of others, are hurt by others' disapproval and rejection, and treat one another's reactions as expressions of feelings of liking, approval, distaste and so on. This assumption now structures Parsons's account of the way in which social order is produced through the co-ordination of people's activities through their occupancy of social roles, which are internalised through socialisation.

## Socialisation

Sensitivity is the lever of *socialisation*. Socialisation is simply learning to be social and works through the giving and withholding of affection and approval in the relation between parents and children. Consequently, children come to adopt the parents' attitudes and standards as their own. Internalisation goes together with *identification*: children do not behave in certain ways simply to produce parental approval; in addition they want to become like the parents, to identify with them. They do so by taking on the parental attitudes as their own, wanting and approving the same things themselves.

On the basis of favourable and negative reactions, then, people can build up patterns of stable interaction. Each knows what the other wants, and each wants the other's approval, so each will act in ways that are expected to win the other's approval and solicit an approving, rewarding response. On the basis of this simple, uncomplicated case, Parsons developed the notions of *expectation* and *role* as key elements of social order. Strictly, Parsons's notion was of the *status role*, since it involves a position (the 'status' element) and an associated pattern of approved or expected behaviour (the 'role' part).

## Status roles

To know that persons occupy certain status roles is to know what they *should* do, to have some *expectations* as to how they will behave and, in relationship to them, to know how one should behave *oneself*.

In this way we can imagine two individuals working out a balanced pattern of expectations about each other's behaviour until they arrive at a stable arrangement, so that each acts in ways which he or she knows the other will approve of and avoids acts he or she knows the other will not like.

Parsons asks us to imagine such a process working out across society as a whole so that the expectations that people attach to particular statuses are standard throughout the society. Then, of course, a high level of social order is possible; people who have never met before can immediately enter into a co-ordinated transaction if they know what roles they respectively occupy, since they will have mutual expectations about appropriate, matched behaviour. For example, if we see someone sitting in a vehicle recognised as a cab, we identify him or her as the cab driver and feel entitled to climb into the vehicle, to give some address, and to be driven to that place. Social life would not be possible on any scale of complexity if we had to work out our social relations from scratch each time. Parsons holds that we do not have to do so, for we acquire through socialisation these cultural elements, these expectations, about one another's appropriate conduct, to which we attach *moral* force: we not only expect but demand this behaviour. If it does not result, we have punitive reactions to the other person.

Furthermore, the patterns of expectations – the *norms*, as he often called them – that pertain to different roles cannot be altogether dissimilar. A moderately complex society requires persons to be involved in many different kinds of status roles and in many different activities, e.g. a manager and secretary in office life, and pupil and teacher in education. It is not possible, Parsons argues, for the expectations attached to one relationship to be utterly incongruous to those attached to another; it would be neither practically nor psychologically tolerable for the kinds of things expected/allowed in one context to be utterly at odds with those in another. There must be some broad consistency across the range of status roles in respect of the kinds of things they allow.

## Values

This consistency derives from the *values* which persons hold and which a society centrally institutionalises. Somehow, a society develops a set of cultural elements, beliefs about how things are, about how things should be, and what people should do; these are installed in its main parts and regulate the broad pattern of its arrangements.

For example, US society has been heavily influenced by its Protestant heritage; the idea of success through hard work has been powerfully impressed upon its members' lives. Most spheres of US life are pervaded by this idea, and hard work is everywhere recommended as the ideal for conduct: in the workplace, in the school classroom and so on. That people are commonly attached to such a shared ideal, such a value, makes for a measure of compatibility between the ways in which activities are conducted in different spheres of life. Here we recall the notion that Parsons found in Durkheim and Weber: ends are not merely random but are held in common.

Parsons is not by any means suggesting that everyone shares the same ideas or does so in the same degree, nor is he suggesting that there is nothing but thorough and detailed compatibilities between patterns of expectation in one area of life and another. Hence our frequent use of the term 'broadly', since Parsons is well aware that social life is complex, varied and subject to exigent circumstances. His project was to explore how a complex social unit, a social system, could be organised so that at least the minimal requirements for its survival could be satisfied. He wanted to know how it could so organise itself in order to interrelate the perpetuation and dissemination of its shared culture with the socialisation of incomers into the system. Further, how can both of these requirements be related to whatever business the system is supposed to do – whether that is to educate small children in the school classroom, to produce goods for sale in a commercial business, to prepare for battle in a military platoon, or to witness to God's glory on a religious occasion?

## Systems theory

In Parsons's usage the idea of *system* is important. It is an abstract general term used to capture anything from a two-person conversation to the international system of nation states and underpins Parsons's whole analysis.

### Systems

A system has persistent identity in an environment; it is distinct from its environment, but must transact with it so it is an *open* system. For example, a mouse as a living creature is an open system; the mouse is not the same as its environment, but it must take in necessities (air, food) from the environment and must release waste products into it. The overriding task of the system to maintain its own identity in the face of that environment involves two main aspects:

- the regulation of transactions with the environment;
- the maintenance of effectively operating relations inside the system itself.

On the basis of these very simple assumptions, Parsons attempted to provide a completely general analysis of the way social systems operate.

After the books of 1951 Parsons saw a new way to develop his analysis, largely (or so he claimed) as a result of an association with Robert F. Bales, a social psychologist who had been trying to develop a general model to describe the behaviour of task-oriented small groups. Bales saw such groups as going through four *phases*: (1) they gather together the things they need to do a task; (2) then they organise themselves into carrying out the task; and, in doing so, (3) they manage their own internal relations, e.g. stifling quarrels and keeping people interested; and when they have successfully completed their task, (4) they relax for a while into task-unrelated activities before gathering themselves for the next task. Parsons adapted these four phases into the *four-phase model of system exchanges*. The elaboration of this model and its application to various situations was the abiding focus of his subsequent work.

Since a system must transform its environment, activity is initiated by the gap between the way that the world is now and the way that the system (be it an organism, a small group or a large society) requires it to be for the satisfaction of its needs. Systems are 'goal oriented' in that there are ends they must achieve, situations they must bring about, if they are to survive and operate. The pattern of activity in the system will vary over the course of the attempt to realise a goal, much of this activity being involved in goal attainment, i.e. whatever is necessary to deliver the desired end state – see 2 above. The pattern of such activity often begins with preparing the conditions for goal attainment, for the acquisition and assembly of the means necessary to the pursuit and realisation of the goal. This phase (see 1 above) Parsons terms adaptation; it involves extracting from the environment (be it the physical or the social environment) the means towards the goal, which includes, of course, people capable, suitable and willing to do the work to get to the goal. The pursuit of the goal involves problems and troubles, and stresses and strains in the relations of those involved in the group (see 3). Therefore, things have to be done to maintain working relationships or to restore fractured ones: this is what Parsons terms the 'integrative' phase (see 4). Systems do not remain permanently in activity; people are members of many different systems and, after a group has attained a goal, a system will often dissolve as people go about other activities and contribute to the goal attainment of other groups. The group continues to exist: the fact that all one's family is out of the house, at school or at work or whatever, does not mean the family ceases to exist, only that it is in a 'latent' state, i.e. not currently active as a unit; that is, after goal attainment, the group can enter the 'latency' phase. During this phase, however, things have to happen to ensure that the system's capacity for collective action is kept up, that people will be able to recuperate their energies and commitment for another phase of its activity.

## The AGIL system

Thus the sequence of phases can run (1) adaptation, (2) goal attainment, (3) integration, (4) latency (or *pattern maintenance* and *tension management*, as Parsons terms the keeping up of attachment to the system's objectives). This four-phase system is often known as the AGIL system.

Of course, within a complex system not all parties will be involved to the same extent in all phases, and different parts of the system will specialise predominantly in one or other of these activities on behalf of the rest of the system. We can structurally dismember a system in terms of the priorities that the different parts give to the functional phases of the system as a whole.

It is important to note that for Parsons it is systems all the way down, i.e. the question of 'what is the system?' is relative, depending upon the purposes of analysis. For example, the family can be treated as a part, i.e. a sub-system, of the society's social system; or it can be treated as the system itself, so that the relation of husband and wife, of father to daughters, of mother to daughters, and so on, are seen as sub-systems of the family system. Thus Parsons's categories apply to systems and their sub-systems and their sub-sub-systems. Of course, any sub-system will not engage purely in one of the four functions, for each sub-system will have to satisfy its own functional requirements. For example, within the four phases of society the family can be allocated to the latency phase, for people at home with their families are often taking time out from other social commitments, relaxing, engaging in leisure pursuits and building up their capacity to face another day at the office or whatever. However, if we decide to analyse the family as a system in its own right, then its activities will also have to go through the AGIL cycle, and we might find that within the family some members specialise in one or other of these functions. For example, in the traditional nuclear family the wife/mother specialised rather more in integrative activities than other members; she was held responsible for smoothing relations between the others, providing comfort and support for those in distress or under pressure.

In the AGIL model the issue of internal relations within the system came to dominate the latter phase of Parsons's work. He sought to understand the *interchanges* between the functionally differentiated phases. For example, the adaptive phase (A) involves the accumulation of the means for transforming the environment for the system, but if these means are to be put to use in goal attainment (G), then they have to be handed over to those engaged in these goal-attaining activities. There has to be some incentive, some return, if those involved in the A phase are to make resources – or *facilities*, as Parsons often talks of them – available to the G phase. If people keep on handing over things without any reward or return, they are likely to feel resentful and, eventually, will become fully alienated. For any system to work there have to be some (at least minimally) balanced exchanges between the various phases.

For an overly simple example, the government fulfils the goal-attainment function for the society, seeking to direct the society as a whole towards its objectives (such as economic growth or national glory, or some combination of both). The economy is the adaptive component of the society, i.e. producing resources out of the society's natural and social environment. Obviously, the running of government consumes resources, both to support its existence as an organised structure and to pursue its policies, so the adaptive system must hand over some of its product to government. Equally clearly, the government has to deliver something to the economy, and we can see that some of its policies sustain, enhance and gratify those who work in business. Parsons's scheme is intended to be used in subtler, delicate ways, but it should be possible to see how it can be elaborated. One way is with reference to the patterns of interface and exchange between the different phases (for example, the I and L phases also need facilities). Another is the way that these exchange patterns are nested inside each other, as we uncover by investigating the hierarchy of sub-systems, their interrelations with the system in which they are included, and their own internal exchanges. Since the AGIL model applies to a two-person situation as well as to the level of the total society, and to everything in between, the elaboration of these patterns is necessarily complex and sophisticated.

## Parsons and his critics

Parsons was much criticised, more so than any other figure in modern sociology, even his inability to write plain, concise English being held against him (see Chapter 14). Much of this criticism is superficial as well as repetitive and can be placed aside without too much difficulty. Three initial points of criticism need to be dealt with:

- Society is portrayed as a perfect harmony, devoid of conflict.
- This portrayal partly derives from Parsons's neglect of the source of social conflict, namely, the unequal distribution of power.
- By emphasising harmony and excluding conflict, Parsons's theory cannot explain social change.

All three of these criticisms are false. That Parsons did not consider change, conflict and power in the same way as his critics is not to say that his theory could not deal with them. In fact, in his later writings Parsons went out of his way to do so. From the start, the assumption behind Parsons's theorising is that the functional organisation and integration of the society are problematic; the integration of such complex arrangements involved in a whole society must take place in an intricate and thorough way, with difficulties and failures. Any real society has to be less than completely integrated, and it is only to be expected that there are many discontinuities and incongruities in society between and within its different spheres and their organisation. Such discontinuities and incongruities show up as tensions, if not outright conflicts. Further, Parsons does not assume that a highly (though not perfectly) integrated society would not and could not change. After all, to assume in biology that a living organism must be meeting its functional requisites for survival does not translate into the assumption that the organism is immortal, continuing interminably to fulfil its functional requirements, or that while surviving it will remain unchanged, never ageing, or developing illnesses.

An idea of a functional system attaining an internal balancing between its parts introduces an idea of equilibrium, of things developing to a stable point and then remaining unchanged, and Parsons's model might suggest that this is what he has in mind. Though the idea of equilibrium certainly has its place, he eschews the idea that there is only one kind of equilibrium, for there is the type known as the moving equilibrium, commonly found with respect to living organisms.

An organism can be in equilibrium in that its organs or parts are all healthy and functioning well, but it does not mean that the organism does not change, for, of course, the organism, while remaining healthy and surviving, grows and ages. Parsons had this kind of equilibrium in mind for society, and change is integral to this idea. Among his very last works were two short books (1966, 1971) prepared for an introductory series in which Parsons sought to give a general account of the long-term evolution of Western society, from its origins in (particularly) ancient Greek and Judaic culture (an interpretation heavily indebted to Weber).

## Parsons on change

The process of long-term change was to be understood in terms of the *cybernetic hierarchy*. Parsons drew this analogy from systems designed to provide automatic control for machines such as heating systems, dishwashers and automatic weapons. The idea is that the control and direction of such machine systems involve an inverse relationship between information and energy, i.e. the higher levels of the system use little energy but are rich in information, while the lower levels use less information and more energy. The heating thermostat uses little electrical energy to operate, but it is sensitive to information (in the technical, engineering sense of that word); it responds to fine variations in temperature, and sends out signals as the temperature rises and falls. The central heating unit, however, uses much more energy than the thermostat to run its output, the heating, and does not use much information in its operations.

Parsons proposes that the social system can be understood as structured in a similar way.

### Cybernetic hierarchy in society

Culture is itself mostly information and little energy; e.g. symbolic codes, such as language, are a major component of culture and are very rich in information, but they are not much dependent on physical energy. The social system, however, is much more intensive in its use of energy.

Sending someone a page of instructions can initiate and direct them through a very large task, immensely energy-consuming. Parsons argues that culture is quite like the specific kind of control device represented by the thermostat in the heating system or the programme in the washing machine: a small amount of electric current from the programmer initiates the movement of the heavy drum of the washer; the programmer uses little energy in its own right and yet provides enough information to point the whole system in a given broad direction, thereby guiding it towards its goals.

In summary, Parsons's account of the evolution of the West is very much dominated by the formation of new ideas and outlooks, by *cultural attitudes*.

He adopted from Weber much of his characterisation of the principal cultural attitude of the modern Western society as a type; he calls this attitude *instrumental activism*, i.e. the desire actively to dominate the world in pursuit of practical purposes. For example, the ecological movement testifies to the accuracy of Parsons's judgement since its members regard just this attitude as the cause of ecological change, which is deeply rooted in Western societies, and which they desperately need to change.

He also follows Weber in placing great emphasis on what he, Parsons, calls the 'seed bed' societies of ancient Greece and Israel. With respect to Israel, he argues that the Jewish idea of a god who prescribes morality eventually became, through Christianity, the basis for the concepts of generally applicable (i.e. universal) laws and standards, which are such an important feature of our contemporary outlook. In adopting this evolutionary approach to cultural change, Parsons is recognising that culture is a long-term phenomenon. Cultures are considerably more long-lasting than social systems, personalities, or organisms. Personalities and organisms last only a human lifetime while social systems can survive over many generations. Nevertheless, the pattern of social structural arrangements tends to change many times during a period in which a culture may be judged to continue and to be relatively unchanging. For example, in two hundred years or so, US society has undergone many changes, from a small, agricultural society to a huge industrial and then post-industrial one. In this period key cultural elements like the Constitution have remained the same and the Protestant ethic has continued to provide the dominant ethos of the society, though, obviously, the ways in which they play their part in the society, and, indeed, what they mean, have changed considerably. Social systems may also change in evolutionary rather than revolutionary ways, with basically the same culture needing to be adapted to quite different social structural arrangements, an evolution that Parsons alleges to have happened in the West. He does not, however, rule out either drastic shifts in culture, or revolutionary changes in society as such. His close theoretical associate Neil Smelser studied the conflict-afflicted, near-revolutionary change in the cotton areas of eighteenth- and nineteenth-century Lancashire, and also wrote a general book on the theory of revolution (Smelser 1959, 1962).

## Parsons on power

Parsons complained that his critics saw power as the base for social conflict because they conceived of it in what he termed a *zero-sum* situation, i.e. someone's gain must mean another's loss (the classic Hobbesian view of things). If someone wants a bigger piece of the cake, then someone else must have a smaller one. The potential for conflict in dividing up a cake is apparent, as there may not be enough to satisfy everyone's desires. The picture is clear, but it depends on an assumption: that a fixed quantity is being shared out. If the quantity is not fixed, if it can increase, then it is possible for the amount available to everyone to increase. For example, the overall amount of wealth can expand through economic growth, enabling everyone to have more (though not necessarily in the same proportions). Just as we can look at wealth from the point of view of the whole system as an aggregate and can talk about the wealth of the society, so, too, Parsons argues, we should first of all look at power from the point of view of the system rather than from that of particular individuals or parties.

Taking the societal perspective, it is easy to see how the amount of power available overall can increase; it is clear that the total amount of power available to and required in a society will increase as the society grows, as it becomes both larger and more complex. For example, more power is involved in the modern US than in a small hunter-gatherer group. Therefore, the total amount of power in a society is not a fixed quantity. Further, the necessity to regard power as a means of domination, as a matter of one person having power over another – which is an assumption that usually goes with the zero-sum conception – also dissolves when looked at from the point of view of the system. The distribution of power is to be understood not in terms of individual possession, but as a distribution relative to the functional needs and internal exchanges of the system. Power *is* a way of controlling people, but not of controlling them just for the sake of domination; rather, it is a means of directing and co-ordinating them in the pursuit of collective objectives. Basically, power is a means for getting things done.

The idea of 'exchange' among the four AGIL phases suggests an analogy with economics, for economic exchange is the very paradigm of exchanges (Parsons had started his career as an economist). Economic exchange through barter is a difficult, problematic and inefficient system; money greatly facilitates exchanges. We exchange things for money with a view to using the money in exchange for other things. Money is a medium of exchange and is not itself the object of exchange. Further, money is standardised and therefore can be exchanged for anything. In barter, one thing is exchanged for another, and we have to find the right person who has what we want and is willing to give it up for what we can offer to effect an exchange (i.e. a mutual coincidence of wants), but money eliminates this problem: money will exchange for anything, it is a generalised medium. However, not all the exchanges in society are economic or take place through money. If these other kinds of exchanges are not to be undertaken on a barter basis, presumably immensely inefficient and perhaps entirely impractical for any moderately complex society, then there must be other *generalised media* to facilitate the four kinds of exchange.

Power, Parsons suggests, is a second such generalised medium. He names *influence* and *commitments* as the other two of the four generalised media he thinks necessary. Although he published essays on power and influence (1969), he did not elaborate his thoughts on commitments before his death.

### Power as a generalised medium

Power is to be understood as playing a role in facilitating the pursuit of *collective* objectives, rather than as being essentially used divisively and in pursuit of sectional interests (though it can be, of course). Like money in economic affairs, it oils the wheels of society's organisation. Hence power is heavily concentrated in the polity sector of the social system and is related to the G phase, or goal attainment.

The criticisms we have discussed so far were not the only objections to Parsons's systems theorising. In fact, the reaction of so-called conflict sociologists to his work came relatively late in the day in comparison with objections from other directions. Thus though predominant in American sociology for a time, Parsons's approach also met widespread and fierce opposition from the early 1950s. Symbolic interactionists and ethnomethodologists (see Chapters 6 and 7) objected to the level of abstraction from observable, everyday activities, and even Parsons's functionalist colleague Robert Merton was critical of the very high level of generality of the theory. However, in terms of its impact in shaping the general direction of sociological thinking, it was the attack on Parsons by his conflict critics that was the most influential. At the centre of it was the charge of conservatism: by neglecting possibilities of change and conflict, Parsons's theory was guilty of purveying an ideology that justified the status quo.

## The reaction to Parsons: conflict theory

We have noted that many of sociology's current concerns – as well as its current troubles – have their beginning in the 1960s, with the resurgence in the popularity of Marxism and also the 'interpretative turn' in sociological thought, discussed in Chapters 6 and 7. As much as anything, the criticisms were directed at the perceived political implications of mainstream American sociology in general and of Parsons's thought in particular, which were seen essentially as the acceptance of a – very broadly defined – conservative attitude to contemporary society. Yet, as we have pointed out, Parsons did deal with power and change. Not only did he address what he called 'strains' in systems, he also commented on the conflicts of his time. For example, he wrote on the sources of Nazism, on the tension which the contemporary family structure, i.e. of the 1940s and 1950s, was creating for women, on the problems in integrating blacks into American society and culture, on the rise of the radical right, on the nature of social stratification, and on the causes of social deviance. In political terms, Parsons was a liberal, not uncritical of many aspects of American society, albeit a loyal and conventional enough citizen. He looked for a solution of such problems as the position of blacks or of women in terms of adjustments of the system, rather than in its total, revolutionary overthrow. For many of his critics, however, a liberal was not significantly to be distinguished from a conservative; anyone who did not totally oppose the status quo was perceived to defend it.

Such was Parsons's stature that conflict theory virtually defined itself by its wholesale opposition to his ideas. The complaints about change, power and conflict were themselves expressions of deeper objections, of which we can identify two main ones:

- Parsons was an idealist and neglected the importance of material interests.
- Parsons failed to give any account of *systemic* sources of change.

Idealists are, of course, the *bêtes noires* of Marxists. Hegel had been one. He inspired Marx thoroughly to reject any idealist elements (see Chapter 2).

Hegel believed that the nature and change of reality result from the emanation of ideas and are products of thought. In *The Structure of Social Action* (1937), Parsons explicitly dissociated himself from such idealism at the very start. His position was very much influenced by Weber, whose critics often prefer Marx on the grounds that Weber is too much of an idealist as well. The basis for the accusation against Parsons is his strong emphasis on culture in the solution of social order, especially the stress on the concepts of values and norms. However, this emphasis is certainly not idealism in the Hegelian sense. Moreover, Parsons's point, just like Weber's, is to deny that ideas alone, culture by itself, can provide or regulate social order. Weber emphasised the importance of ideas in relation to what he called 'material' interests. Parsons throughout emphasised that it was culture as *institutionalised* and *internalised* that mattered, and that the processes of institutionalisation and internalisation required articulation with many other phenomena. Even though the cybernetic hierarchy accords a broadly directive role to culture in regard to long-term change, it is not Parsons's view that culture, as some ghostly emanation from the skies, produces such change. Rather, the explanation is to be found in the way the institutionalised cultural patterns are interwoven into the organised affairs of the whole society, thereby providing the 'second nature' of socialised individuals.

It might be suggested, however, that to take the picture of society as Parsons paints it, in terms of shared values and expectations, is to give a very partial and distorted portrait; it presents society in a misleadingly abstract way and fails to highlight the fact that these values and norms are shared (if they are) in the context of considerable *material* inequalities. In other words, Parsons plays down the role of inequality, especially in the form of social stratification, in his portrait of society. As already noted, of course, Parsons was well aware of the existence of social stratification (and of ethnic and gender inequalities as well), but he regarded stratification as just one institution among others, and not as the central or essential institution in society. While important, it is not given pride of place in the analysis of a social system. Instead, it is analysed in terms of the four-phase model, just like any other feature. Parsons himself, his onetime associate Edward Shils (1978), and Robert Merton (in his notorious account of deviance as anomie, 1957) all wrote papers in which stratification figured significantly. Parsons himself wrote two directly about it (1940, 1953).

## Accounting for stratification and change

If we take Shils and Merton as expressing at least parallel, if not strictly Parsonian, views, their position may be summarised as follows: the society is *unevenly* structured around its core values, and certain institutions within the society are very closely articulated around them. Indeed, some institutions are taken as representatives and expressions of these values, e.g. the established church and monarchy in the UK. The monarchy was taken as being not merely a family, but representing the very ideal of family life for many people. Hence revelations of royal marital trouble in the 1990s made an enormous impact, inducing an unprecedented erosion of support for the monarchy.

## Stratification

Institutions in such a position as the UK monarchy in society are what Shils termed 'the centre', while other sectors standing in an attenuated relationship to the centre provide a 'periphery' within the society's overall value system. The ranking of people in terms of closeness to the centre of the society is certainly a matter of their perceived prestige.

In Durkheimian terms, the values of society are the sacred element; the more people are associated with the sacred core, the more highly they are regarded. Though the Parsonian scheme presupposes shared values and norms, they are not supposed to be simply and evenly distributed; it recognises that the intensity of attachment and position relative to values are a variable matter.

Further, Merton attributed deviance to the fact that stratification involves not only variable esteem, but also the sharing out of resources. Of course there can be a discrepancy between what the values and norms of society (the culture) prescribe and the actual, real social circumstances of people in society. It is all very well to hold up certain cultural ideals to all people, but it is more than likely in a complex society that stratification will make a difference in the extent to which people can realistically hope to live the kind of life prescribed in those ideals. For example, Merton argues that the ideal of economic success through hard work is widely disseminated in US society, an ideal (in the guise of the American dream) that has reached all corners of the society. For most people it is unrealistic to expect such success, given where they start in the stratification system and what opportunities are open to them. For most, rising out of poverty by legitimate means, through employment opportunities, is well-nigh impossible. Consequently, under certain circumstances there are pressures on individuals to deviate from the ideal of success through honest hard work and to resort to illegitimate means, such as gangsterism and racketeering.

However, Parsons does not see society – and certainly not American society – as centred upon class conflict: the relationship between stratification and social values means that the inequalities in the society are – widely – accepted as legitimate, as expressions of the respective social worth of people ranked in their terms. Hence class conflict as such is not a significant, let alone a systematic, source of social change. The idea, bequeathed from Marxism, is that an account of social change has to be given, and that it must involve systematic change from within the society. Marx's idea (taken from Hegel) is that each society contains the seeds of its own destruction, the source of its transformation into another and different form. If we take this idea as *the* essential form of a theory of social change then, certainly in its terms, Parsons has no account of social change. In fact, Parsons has a very different idea of what gives rise to social change.

## Social change

Parsons's root notion is that there are many different sources of social change. Social revolutions and civil wars are not inconceivable in society because there is no guarantee that any society will meet its functional requirements to the extent needed to prevent collapse into internal division. Whether or not such situations do develop, however, depends upon the particular character of a society, its mechanisms of integration and so forth. In reality, most social changes do not result from either revolution or overt class warfare, let alone solely from these sources.

Evidently there are sources of conflict built into society itself. They occur in the very way culture, social system and personality fit together: in the internal contradictions of culture, in the discrepancies within the organisation of social systems, and in the inadequacies of human personalities. What they are, and how serious, depends on the case. However, there will be problems of malintegration in any society, and some of these problems might be so stubborn and persistent as to give rise to frustration, alienation and even organised dissent, while others may work themselves out so that dissatisfactions do not continue to build up. In either case, changes will occur, but characteristically they will be changes *in* the system that are compatible with its general character, rather than changes *of* the system into another, i.e. very differently organised, system.

Not all sources of change, however, originate within the social system. Many originate in the system's environment. One major source of change for a given social system is other social systems. A social system can be invaded in a military or a cultural sense; it can be colonised by an army or by an external religious or political ideology, e.g. the role of Islamic fundamentalism today, and social conflict and change produced, but there is no *internal* or systemic source necessarily generating such a change. Similarly, a system can be affected by changes in its technical or natural environment. Since Parsons conceives of a social system as the pattern of relationships between people, then such things as technology and the environment are *external* to that system. Clearly, changes in technology (as with the origin of capitalism itself) can have a major role in producing social changes, but they do not originate systematically in the structure of social relations themselves. Here capitalism is something of a special case, in so far as much of its activity is organised to generate technological change, but the point remains that there is no generalisable basis for technological change from society's structure. The natural environment can also bring about social change. In the Middle Ages, the Black Death reduced population, producing consequences for the agricultural labour force and resulting in changes in feudal relations. In short, there are many different sources of change. Some are internal to the society's organisation, but many are not. That Parsons's theory does not offer a systemic account of change in the way

Marx's does is merely to say that Parsons has a very different idea of what a theory can do.

These observations did not satisfy some critics. They reacted against Parsons's alleged consensus view of society by forming a loose front of arguments on behalf of a 'conflict' approach.

## Consensus view of society

This sees society as centred upon agreement and dominated by co-operation rather than conflict.

Frequently the case for such an approach was made by default, i.e. by simply pointing to alleged deficiencies in Parsons's approach. For example, he underestimated the importance of material interests and neglected the ways cultural elements such as values were the expression of sectional interests, imposed upon or instilled into others in order to rationalise their domination. Conflict theorists produced no body of work comparable to Parsons's in its systematic quality, perhaps because the central ideas of conflict theory were essentially a restatement of Marxian and Weberian conceptions.

Weber's concept of society as an arena of conflicts in which groups compete for domination through economic, cultural and political means (Bendix 1960: 265–69) provides the essence of conflict theory. Whereas Parsons was concerned to provide an analytical framework applicable at all levels of social order, conflict theorists focused almost entirely on the level of the whole society. Like Weber and, to an even greater extent, Marx, they emphasise as society's paramount phenomenon the contest for domination within the system of social stratification. Stratification is taken as the central organising feature of society, mainly with a view to demonstrating the degree to which other institutions and features of the culture are shaped in its image and structured to serve the interest of one stratified group rather than another. This view is given much contemporary acceptability through the work of Pierre Bourdieu (see Chapter 13). The Weberian view of stratification is more apt to be drawn upon than Marx's, since Marx's theory of society, construed as holding that all social conflicts are, at bottom, class conflict, is regarded by many conflict theorists as unduly reductive. They prefer Weber's view that classes, status groups and parties are all forms of stratification and can each be involved in contests for domination. Society comprises a plurality of conflicts, cross-cutting and exacerbating one another. Some centre on class inequality, but others are between what Weber calls status groups, involving ethnic, nationalist and gender conflicts. Domination and exploitation can take many forms; Marx's account of nineteenth-century capitalism, with its emphasis on power as founded in economic position, is simply regarded as a special case by the conflict theorists. For them, economic position is only one form of the distribution of power. Weber argued that there could be a struggle for power itself. The reasons differ, e.g. possession for its own sake, or in order to improve one's position in society, or for the sake of some religious, political or economic purpose. In any actual case, of course, an individual's motives for seeking to dominate others are likely to be a mixture of these elements, though with one being somewhat more prominent than the others. As we will see, an important further development of this kind of thinking has emphasised that domination need not be either overt or direct, that people do not necessarily recognise that they are being dominated, and that the reality of domination running all through the society has been hitherto concealed (see Chapter 9).

In trying to crystallise the substance of the disagreement between Parsons and his critics as best we can, we have tried to show that the differences between them do not lie where the critics try to locate them. Complaints that

- Parsons is an idealist;
- Parsons's theory postulates society as a complete functional harmony; and
- Parsons's theory does not provide for the possibility of conflict, of radically disruptive social change, and does not acknowledge the role of power

are all false, as we have tried to show. In many respects, the real difference between Parsons and his critics was most basically that his account was not a Marxist account of contemporary society, so it did not give priority to the existence and role of class in social explanation. But this was as much a disagreement over the analysis of American sociology as of anything else. Parsons's theory does not rule out the prospect of deeply divided societies, or ones that have disintegrated into civil war. Nevertheless, Parsons did not think that there were such divisions in American society, or in Western capitalist societies more generally; he felt that class conflict had so very little role there that it could not produce substantial structural transformation. Parsons did not deny that there were divisions in American society, but they were relatively superficial and did not engender sustained and cumulative conflict, thus denying that there were systemic forces propelling deep social dislocation. In this respect, surely Parsons has been vindicated: American society has undergone, since the 1950s, many structural reorganisations, but not ones that came from overt conflict between groups. He has been vindicated also by the diminishing role that the notion of class conflict and overt social struggle more generally has played in social theory. Indeed, 'critical sociology' has largely abandoned Marxism, even in its conflict theory version. The emphasis has shifted from arguing that class conflict will transform society to explaining why class conflict has not transformed society, and looking for an alternative means towards the emancipatory results that working-class insurrection was to provide (see especially Part V). Marxism has reached the point at which it must entertain the idea that the point of view of the working class has to be dissociated from the actual working class – a view rather reminiscent of Lenin's idea of the Communist Party as a vanguard movement, but going even further in disconnecting workers from 'their' point of view. Much of the history of Western Marxism (see Chapter 8) involves steady retreat from the idea of the transformative power of class struggle and even from the idea that the notion of class struggle, as such, is relevant to the analysis of Western societies.

## Parsons's contemporary influence

In the face of these assertions, disillusionment with Parsons's version of sociology became rife, and the emphasis upon conflict rose to pre-eminence. Although conflict theory itself did not develop into anything theoretically substantial, into anything beyond elaboration of Weberian points, it was influential in getting other schools of thought to try to draw in conflict more explicitly. For example, Randall Collins (1975), an American Weberian, who talked about 'conflict sociology', certainly had an influence on the direction taken by latter-day symbolic interactionism (see Chapter 6), persuading many of its more recent affiliates to give more explicit attention to conflict theory.

Parsons's sociological reputation reached its lowest point in the 1970s. After his death in 1979 and during the 1980s his theories made something of a comeback. Some sociologists – among them Parsons's former associates and students – talked of 'neo-functionalism'. Under this heading, attempts were made to modify his thought in order to accommodate some of the objections from conflict theory. In addition, some serious revaluations of Parsons's work, e.g. by Jeffrey Alexander (1984), and by Robert Holton and Bryan Turner (1986), reject – as we have done – many of the standard criticisms as simply ill-informed and unjust. Furthermore, in recent years Parsons's work has had some impact upon important figures in German sociology, among them Jürgen Habermas (see Chapter 13) and, more substantially, Niklas Luhman, who sought to develop the idea of systems theory.

## Luhman on the social system

Luhman seeks to combine Parsons's systems theory with his own *general systems* theory. It was derived (originally) from engineering, and the concept of *autopoiesis* as taken from biology (or, rather, from philosophy of biology), together with a *phenomenological* element. The Parsonian notion of system invites connection with general systems theory. For a counter-view that argues that general systems theory is nothing more than a spuriously mathematical pseudo-science, see David Berlinsky's *On Systems Theory* (1968).

### General systems theory

This proposes that many types of phenomena take the form of systems, for which there ought to be general laws referring to the properties of systems as such. If this were so, then many of the properties of social systems would result from the fact that they are merely systems, not *social* systems.

The root idea of systems theory is that a system is less complex than its environment since, after all, the environment is everything which is not in the system, i.e. everything else, and in reality everything else must be more complex than just one item, however complex that item is as a system. Consequently, the properties of the system must be such as to enable it to relate to a more complex environment. The system cannot deal with everything at once; it can only survive by reducing the complexity of the environment with which it must deal.

To Luhman, a system is by definition a composite of interconnected parts. All systems have an internal organisation, but social and psychological systems, while fitting into general systems theory, differ from mechanical or organic systems because their parts are connected through meanings, not through causal interactions; i.e. the connections between different parts of the social system must be made through, must exist as, processes of communication. In addition, the parts of a social system do not exist only in contemporary connection, but derive part of their present connection from their relationships to the past and the future. Since human beings have both memory and foresight, to comprehend the nature of the connections between different parts of the system one must pursue a phenomenological approach, i.e. look at them through the eyes of society's members. Thus the interconnection between system parts is 'in the mind' of members, in the meaningful connections that people see between them. The production and perpetuation of the system's *systemic* being demand that the connections in the minds of different individuals be the same; the individuals must understand things in the same way. The existence of social structures pre-structures meaning for individuals, i.e. by forming pre-given interpretations and responses, these structures reduce the complexity of action situations.

Two philosophers of biology, Humberto Maturana and Francisco Varela, influenced Luhman. They formulated a notion – autopoiesis – designed to identify an essential property of *living systems*.

### Autopoiesis

This is really the notion of systems as self-organising. It views a system's operations as being engaged only in reproducing the system's own features, an important reversal of Parsons's approach.

Parsons's model conceives the system as being organised to sustain itself in the face of an external environment, while the idea of autopoiesis dispenses with the notion of any such independent, external environment. In its terms, the system defines its own environment relative to the needs of its own self-perpetuating arrangements.

For Luhman, the social system exists as, exists in, processes of communication. From this point of view, everything that is not communication is external to the social system. For him, as for Parsons, modern society is a differentiated entity, with sub-systems specialising in such functions as producing economic resources, knowledge, and trained individuals, which are discharged by the sub-systems of the economy, science and education respectively.

These sub-systems simplify the complexity of dealing with the environment by specialising in one aspect of it, and also provide intellectual simplifications in their internal operations by each operating according to a simple binary opposition, e.g. 'true/false' in science, or 'guilty/innocent' in criminal law. Given the vastly multiple differences between any two things, their operation provides simplification of the environment in that they point up the things to be taken notice of, the ones that matter.

Further, contrasted with traditional society, modern society is headless. In the traditional society there is no functional differentiation; stratification is the only form of differentiation. Consequently, the dominant group in the stratification system could count as the 'centre' of the society; as such, it could be regarded as capable of conceiving things for the society as a whole. Hence the system could be represented within the system. Modern, complex society, however, with its numerous differentiated sub-systems, has no comparable functional group; it therefore has no function of comprehending itself as a whole. Here again, albeit in a very different way from Althusser's (see Chapter 9), the system is 'decentred'. Consequently, there can be problems both in the interaction between the system and its environment, and between the various constituent sub-systems of the system, which do not automatically operate in effectively adaptive or reciprocally stable ways.

The issue of ecology and of ecological movements has provided one occasion for Luhman to apply his scheme since, of course, there are problems along both the external and the internal boundaries of the system. Luhman is critical of environmentalism as such on the grounds that these movements involve sloganising and moralising; they suppose that a simple change in outlook is what is called for. Consequently, they underestimate the complexity – the structured complexity – of the problem as it really exists, in terms of the interface between the society and its environment, and at the interfaces of the numerous sub-systems involved in the collective movement of the system. For example, the very complexity of reductions of social systems can result in insensitivity to environmental consequences; the fact is that the autopoietic processes of the system are dedicated to their own perpetuation, regardless of their environmental consequences. Thus the system is to an important extent insulated against its environment.

With respect to internal sub-systems, however, it is a different matter, for these must be sensitive to one another, must be affected by and react to one another, but the ways in which they respond need not invariably be proportionate. There are disproportionately large reactions in one part of the system to small disturbances in other parts, e.g. when a potentially minor event such as a comparatively few deaths from Creutzfeldt-Jakob disease can precipitate a massive, indeed international, ethico-political explosion, as happened with the reaction to BSE (bovine spongiform encephalopathy) in the mid-1990s.

Luhman contrasts his own sociology, in which the notion of 'relation to the environment' is a primary element, to that of other sociologists (such as his contemporary, Habermas) in which the main social (not sociological) problem was conceived to be the discrepancy between society's ideals (of freedom, justice, etc.) and its actualities, rather than the reciprocally destructive potentials of environment and social system.

## Conclusion

Parsons was a crucial figure in the development of modern sociology, as much through the reaction against him as through his positive influence, though he continues to have contemporary adherents (see neo-functionalism, Chapter 13). However, the conviction that Parsons ignored conflict, power and domination in society moved these issues to a central position, where, for most sociologists, they remain to this day. Indeed, the views which subsequent to the 1960s have had most appeal for the sociological community have been those that have given central significance to power relations.

### Questions

1 What is Hobbes's model of human action? Can you think of any contemporary arguments that are based on similar ideas? What were Parsons's criticisms of Hobbes? Are they right? How might they apply in the modern world?

2 Parsons argued that culture, personality and social system had to be *integrated*. We illustrated this with an example about motorists. Can you show how this integration might take place in, for example, conduct in a restaurant? What other everyday example or examples can you think of that show this integration operating?

3 Parsons argued that there were *systems* operating at a number of levels. What does this mean? Is this an accurate description of his work? Does this make sense to you in thinking about the ordinary world? Why?

4 Parsons has been criticised for neglecting social change. Is this criticism fair? How does his account of social change differ from those of other theorists? Are there cases in which one might apply more effectively than another? Why is this?

5 Parsons's analysis of power makes it out to be relatively benign, in contrast to the analyses of, for instance, Marx and Weber. Do you agree with this statement? Does Parsons play down the importance of power or do other theorists make it out to be more important than it is? When does power operate in your everyday life? Which theoretical position best describes that operation?

6 It could be argued that Parsons understood conflict as being based on a pre-existing consensus. Is this an accurate description of his views? Is he right in this? Is society based on conflict or consensus? Why? What examples can you think of that would support each position?

7 What are the problems in Parsons's theory that Luhman attempts to solve? Is he right about these? Does his solution make sense? In what ways is it similar to Parsons's own arguments? How does it differ? Which is better? Why?

## Next steps

Mayhew's (1985) collection of Parsons's writings is comprehensive and a good place to start. Parsons's own *Action Theory and the Human Condition* (1978) provides a good summary of his positions on ethics, history and society at the end of his career.

Hamilton's (1983) *Talcott Parsons* is a good short introduction to his work, while Savage (1982) provides a more advanced analysis, which has been influential in rehabilitating Parsons's reputation.

## CHAPTER SIX

# Symbolic interaction

---

## Chapter overview

At the same time as Parsons's work reached theoretical dominance in sociology, questions about the 'scientific' nature of the discipline were being asked. Peter Winch's criticisms of the idea of a social *science*, based in Wittgenstein's philosophy, were the most coherent and radical example of this questioning. *Symbolic interactionism*, developed by (among others) Herbert Blumer and Everett C. Hughes at the University of Chicago, represented one alternative to the 'scientistic' mainstream. Originating in the pragmatist social philosophy of George Herbert Mead, symbolic interactionists sought to ground sociology in studies of actual situations of social activity, rather than starting with a theory of 'the social'. Blumer's elaboration of Mead's ideas, combined with a trenchant critique of conventional sociological methods, provided a fruitful alternative to the more 'systemic' approach of Parsons and his colleagues. Studies of urban life, professions, institutions (such as schools, universities, asylums and hospitals) and deviant activities revealed the possibilities of such an approach. While theoretically sidelined, symbolic interactionist ideas and approaches to investigation continue to have a strong influence in contemporary sociology.

---

## Introduction: the reaction against scientism

During the 1950s and 1960s, developments in the philosophy of science combined with other developments in sociology and in philosophy to erode confidence in the ambition to create an objective method notionally modelled on the quantitative natural sciences. Summarising this opposition, it has been common practice to identify it as moving emphasis from the *objective* to the *subjective*. This characterisation is accurate only to a limited degree, and in many respects is quite misleading. However, the idea that the core opposition is between those who hold a view that sociology must adopt an objective approach and those who demand a subjective one has captured many people's imagination. One consequence has been the move on the part of a number of more recent, more traditionally inclined sociologists – such as Bourdieu, Giddens, Alexander, Habermas and Luhman, just to mention those discussed below – to make a main part of their theoretical effort that of reconciling this opposition, taking a middle way, and arguing that society is both an objective and a subjective reality.

Our present task is to explicate the reaction against the idea of scientific method, and thereby to offer an answer to the question once posed (rhetorically) by Egon Bittner (1973): how is it that a discipline committed to the goal of objective method came to abandon it in favour of something looser and more subjective?

The idea of method, which became dominant in Anglo-American sociology after 1945, was controversial from the outset. We have already referred (in Chapter 3) to the *Methodenstreit* (dispute over methods, i.e. whether the human and cultural studies should have basically the same, or very different, methods to those of the natural sciences) in German thought around the turn of the twentieth century as the context that formed the problems that Max Weber sought to resolve. As early as the 1920s and 1930s it had widespread impact on sociology at large by raising objections to the idea of basing sociological method on the natural sciences. Despite these objections, the positivistic view that all disciplines seeking the status of rigorous science must conform to the same broad methodological principles and assumptions proved compelling. The logic was simple: making sociology into a science – into the desirably successful science – required making it fit the pattern of science in general and, following the standard scientific method, to proceed methodologically in the same way as the natural sciences.

## The misconceived idea of a scientific sociology

The controversy over whether sociology should try to be a science was renewed when Peter Winch's small book *The Idea of a Social Science* (1990) appeared in 1958, followed later by a companion paper, 'Understanding a Primitive Society' (1964). These publications provoked what is often called 'the rationality debate'. They are frequently taken as his translation of the ideas of the philosopher Ludwig Wittgenstein (1899–1951) into arguments applicable to the social sciences. Wittgenstein was by any standards one of the major philosophers of the twentieth century, who played a massive role in the so-called linguistic turn, which came to dominate intellectual thought during the period after 1945.

The title of Winch's book conveys an air of contempt for the idea it names. He argues that the idea that we will not truly understand our social life and ourselves until we have created a science deserves comprehensive rejection. The attempt to impose a sociological method – a scientific method – modelled on natural science procedures on the study of social phenomena is precisely that, an imposition; it is misguided and can only distort the nature of the phenomena of social life, since their character is different from that of natural, physical phenomena.

As science would seem principally to be concerned with patterns and generalities (often thought of as laws), Winch tries to make his point by reference to regularities. He argues that in many prominent cases the *regularities* of social life are not the same kind as those of physics. The contrast is between *law-like* regularities and *rule-following* ones.

> ## Law-like and rule-following regularities
>
> The difference is between the way in which a billiard ball colliding with another, as a matter of invariant regularity, causes the second ball to move, and the way in which, when counting, we proceed 'one, two, three, four, five, six', etc. In the case of the billiard balls, the prior movement of the propelled billiard ball causes the other ball to move. It is not, however, the prior pronouncement of 'one' that compels us then to say 'two', with that in its turn making us say 'three'. Indeed, when we count, it is not inconceivable that we could actually go 'one, two, three, five, six', or in some other way deviate from this pattern. We do not count in the order that we do because some physical law compels us to make these sounds, to make us say these words; rather, we just carry out the activity by following a set of rules that prescribes the correct way of counting.

The regularity of counting, just like the regularity of stopping at red traffic lights, is *conventional*, not causal. It is not the wavelength of red light that causes us to brake, but the fact that the colour red acts as a signal, an instruction to stop. In stopping the car at the red light, then, we are obeying a rule (in this case, one enshrined in a legal, not a scientific, law). There is, Winch maintains, another important difference between a natural law and a rule, namely that with respect to a natural law the phenomenon governed by it cannot do otherwise than what the law states. A law in physics does not admit of exceptions, but we can violate a rule, e.g. we can miscount, or jump the lights. In other words, a rule often – not always, because there are different kinds of rules – states the right way to go about something, and it is possible for people to deviate from what the rule requires. Winch overgeneralises his case, but makes an important point when he emphasises that one of the defining features of rule-governed action is the possibility of *making a mistake*. By contrast, the tide on the beach cannot come in by mistake.

Winch next argues that the methods for identifying laws and rule-governed regularities are not the same. Thus the method of the natural sciences cannot be appropriate to the social studies (i.e. Winch uses 'studies' not 'science' in order to avoid any carry-over association with the idea of science and its supposedly general method). Understanding a rule does not just involve seeing a regular connection but – to simplify a great deal – involves seeing *the point* of the connection. Traffic lights will do again as our example. We could establish a regularity by observation, noting that cars stop at the red light, and on green move on. Establishing this regularity would not give us understanding of 'stopping at a traffic light', for the colour itself is not the key to the regularity, but what the colour means, what the signal says to drivers. The red colour is not essential to the effect it achieves; the colours could be the other way around, with the green in place of the red. Yet the pattern could remain constant: when the top light showed, then cars would come to a halt. (In Chapter 9 we will find that structuralism has much to say about the arbitrariness of signs.) Of course, the position of the light is no more an absolute factor than the colour in achieving the effect of stopping the cars. In some rail systems, the same set of colour lights is arranged horizontally rather than vertically.

If we look only for some causal connection between the light and driver reactions, we shall never, says Winch, understand why the cars stop for the lights. We stop because the lights act as a remote means of conveying a message between people, between the authorities who regulate road use and drivers. The lights are signals, and the red light, as it happens, signals an injunction: stop now. To understand the point of the red light's power to bring traffic to a halt, then, we cannot simply study the regular connection between the light becoming red, and a car's stopping; instead, we need to understand how this pattern is part of a much more inclusive one – a pattern of meaning rather than causation. The red light and the car form just a small part of a complex pattern involving road use, regulation by authorities and so on. By grasping this complex pattern we are able to see what traffic lights do: they serve a purpose, which is, of course, to secure safe transition for cars at road junctions.

Clearly, Winch is not suggesting that such observations come as revelations to us; we are not astonished to hear that traffic lights let cars alternate through road junctions to minimise collisions. He holds that as members of society we are aware of these patterns, but we do not find them out by studying concurrent events and seeking to infer causal connections between them. We become aware of these patterns and of the point of a particular activity within that pattern *by being taught the rules* (in the main).

## Identifying rule-governed regularities

Learning to understand and follow a 'rule' is a different sort of thing to establishing through observation and inference a 'law-like regularity', Winch maintains. Someone who studies a society – one's own or an alien one – proceeds much more in the former way, i.e. by studying rule-following.

The anthropologist, for example, does not painstakingly observe the regularities of life among those native to the society he or she studies and then go on to hypothesise law-like regularities to cover them. Rather, the anthropological fieldworker more commonly talks to the people under study and gets them to explain what the point of a particular (strange-looking, hard-to-understand) activity might be. In large part, the anthropologist characteristically learns about an alien society by learning *from* those who inhabit it. This is perhaps the pithiest possible way in which Winch's whole argument can be put, and it brings out the similarity with part of Weber's position on meaning (*verstehen*, see Chapter 3). However, Winch does not think that the sort of explanation in terms of rule-following that might be given of the role of traffic lights requires the sort of back-up in terms of causal laws that Weber deems necessary.

There is a further element to Winch's position that decisively separates him from Weber. One of the cornerstones of positivism is the notion that description and explanation are distinct activities. Crudely, on the one hand science consists in describing the facts to be explained; on the other, it shows how these facts are to be explained with reference to a general theory. Thus there is a *descriptive phase* and an *explanatory phase* to scientific method, each governed by different criteria. Although Weber is no positivist, his thinking has some resemblance to this distinction. Here again, Winch finds an essential difference between science and the social studies.

### Description and explanation

Winch argues that we cannot *first* establish any regular kind of connection between two activities and *then* appeal to, or invent, a rule-like relationship to explain that regularity. Making the regular connection, and correctly identifying the connection and the two activities joined by it, cannot be done independently of the rule.

For example, to say that the traffic lights change to red and the cars stop does not properly, correctly, say what is happening, i.e. in stopping for the light, the drivers are obeying the injunction that the red light signifies. That the braking of the car is a *response* to the light is an integral part of what is happening here, and the idea of stopping as a response, complying with an injunction, etc., only makes sense if one already understands the relationship of red lights to the rules of the road, and their role as signals. To Winch, Weber's idea that one would need to observe causal regularities to confirm the connection in terms of meaning seems gratuitous, since getting the nature of the connection established aright in any one case requires the determination of the connection in terms of meaning, i.e. the traffic light signals 'Stop!' in the imperative mode.

### Witchcraft and rationality

In his small but densely packed book, Winch says various other things, in particular about the relationship between language and reality. This relationship arises from the above arguments and has caused much controversy. By trying to clarify his ideas through the example of primitive magic in the accompanying paper 'Understanding a Primitive Society', Winch perhaps only made things worse. Certainly he regenerated in sociology a debate which had been going on for over a century among anthropologists, and which Lévi-Strauss, in his very different way, was taking up through his structuralist approach (see Chapter 9).

The debate was over the comparative rationality of so-called primitive people, on the one hand, and us, the inhabitants of 'advanced' and 'civilised' societies, on the other. Winch's discussion of primitive magic rejects such a patronising view, holding that 'primitives' are no less intelligent and sophisticated than we are. Some early anthropologists had maintained that there was a distinct primitive mentality, that tribespeople were incapable of logical thought. Their use of magic was seen as proving the point: the fact that in such magic people would try to injure others by (say) burning the toenail clippings or hair of the person they wished to harm showed the lack of logical thought, since, of course, logic tells us there is no real causal connection between burning toenail clippings and injuring the person to whom they belonged.

In the 1930s Edward Evans-Pritchard made a careful, very detailed study of the belief in witchcraft, and of the associated magical practices, found in an African tribe, the Zande. Evans-Pritchard argued that the very idea of people being harmed by witchcraft and of measures being taken to identify witches and to mitigate the effects of bewitchment might sound utterly bizarre to us. Yet after living among this people for a period of time, he ceased to find these ways so bizarre or unreasonable as practices for managing day-to-day affairs. Further, close observation of these people showed that they were not – as we might suppose – making childish errors about causal connections between natural phenomena. In many respects, the Zande made just the same causal connections as we do. For example, if a building standing on wooden supports fell down, then they checked, as we would (if we lived in Zandeland), for termites in the supports and, finding them, concluded that the termites were the cause of the collapse. And so on for all kinds of natural occurrences.

However, understanding these natural connections did not stop them wondering whether witchcraft might have played a role. Identifying the physical cause of some event did not necessarily exhaust their curiosity about it; if the event involved a trouble or misfortune for someone, then they asked the question 'Why did this building collapse and cause injury or death to an individual resting from the sun beneath it?' What explanation for this misfortune befalling this person can there be? After all, given that there are termites in the supports, the building might have collapsed at any time – why just now? As part of their culture, the explanation they were entitled to consider was that the misfortune resulted from witchcraft. Central to that culture is belief in both the existence of witches and the power of witchcraft to do harm. Since this explanation is not, as such, in direct conflict with the kind of ordinary, empirical causal connections we make, i.e. between the termites and the collapse, it is enough to justify Evans-Pritchard's major point: the practice of magic and witchcraft in 'primitive societies' cannot be attributed to the feebler mentalities of these so-called primitives, for they show themselves every bit as capable as us of grasping causal, empirical regularities.

However, having made this step, of which Winch approves, Evans-Pritchard provokes Winch's ire by taking a further one: he suggests that while we cannot say that these people are mentally more primitive than us, none the less we cannot deny that their system of thought is misguided, while ours, based upon science, is correct. If we studied their witchcraft practices scientifically and statistically we should soon prove that these practices do not really work. They cannot work because, of course, science (which is the cornerstone of our system of thought) tells us there are no supernatural forces. The fact that their witchcraft beliefs are baseless and do not work is kept from these people by certain self-preserving features of their beliefs: they can explain away evidence. For example, the failure of witch doctoring to cure a patient, in terms of the magical system itself, is due to witches acting to counter steps taken to reveal their identity or to remove their spells. Evans-Pritchard is, then, saying that in the end we *are* superior to them because we know what reality is *truly* like, while they are locked into a self-deceiving and false system of misconceptions.

By taking exception to Evans-Pritchard on this point, Winch in his turn outraged those who thought he was denying the claim of science to tell us about the nature of reality, or at least was denying that science is any better at telling us about the nature of reality than witchcraft.

Consequently, Winch's work became one of the key provocations for worry about *relativism*.

## Relativism

This is the view that the notion of truth is not universal, but relative. Rather than saying that one person (or group of people) possesses the truth, and that other individuals and groups are mistaken, one should hold that what is true for one person or group of persons may not be true for others, for whom something different is true. Relativism asserts that it is up to individuals or groups to decide what is true, and that their decision settles the matter.

Such views are anathema to those – we might mention Stephen Lukes (1982) and Ernest Gellner (1985), and the biologist Lewis Wolpert (1992) – who think that science is something entirely distinct in human history; it *does* attain to the truth (or comes as close as anything can) and one cannot say that witchcraft is as good, or anywhere near as good, as science at explaining things.

However, Winch himself does not actually aim to say what the critics accuse him of. As his book title is meant to indicate, he has deep doubts about *The Idea of a Social Science* on the grounds that the kind of explanation supreme in the natural sciences is not appropriate to understanding the kinds of things about social life that require explanation. This view is very different, however, from arguing that witchcraft is as good as science. The temptation to assert or to deny this view is due to the inclination to think that religion/magic and science are competitors in the same kind of business, so that we must say either that one is better at this business than the other, or that each is as good as the other. Winch's point is that religion and magic, on the one hand, and science, on the other, are actually different kinds of enterprise. It is absurd to ask whether one is better at its business than the other. In other words, the persistent tendency to make an invidious comparison of religion or magic with science (which is the basis for the argument about relativism) supposes that religion/magic competes to provide the same kind of understanding as science. This premise makes it seem (if we adopt the standpoint of science to view the situation) that no one could possibly believe magic could work, for in scientific terms there is no way it could work. Therefore, anyone who does believe in magic must be less than rational.

Winch complains that though Evans-Pritchard has eschewed many of the grounds for patronising 'primitive people' as irrational, his study none the less contains residual elements of such patronising. Evans-Pritchard supposes that the scientific version of how things work is obvious and the fact that witchcraft does not work is equally obvious. It is only because the witchcraft system provides various means of explaining away the failures of their witchcraft practices that the Zande are able to sustain their belief in it. Without recourse to such *secondary elaborations*, they would be forced to acknowledge what any rational person knows: witchcraft is simply false.

Winch is not concerned to counter Evans-Pritchard's argument for science and against witchcraft by arguing the opposite case on behalf of witchcraft against science. Winch's argument actually consists in two elements, one concerning similarities between the Zande and ourselves, the other concerning differences between witchcraft and science as social practices.

The first element queries whether Evans-Pritchard's own beliefs in science stand in any different relationship to those of the Zande people's beliefs in witches. Is it likely that Evans-Pritchard would have given up his confidence in Western medicine because it often fails, because people have incurable illnesses, or die? No, he no doubt accepted in particular cases of illness and death the doctor's explanation as to why it was not possible to cure the illness or prevent the death. Let us remember, too, that the natural sciences themselves are constantly getting things wrong. After all, the refutation of scientific theories and the making of new findings often involve asserting that previous conceptions were mistaken: Newton has been displaced by Einstein. The explanation of what was wrong with the previous ideas is, of course, given in new scientific terms, yet by the logic Evans-Pritchard applies to witchcraft we should conclude that, in the cases of both medicine and science, it is only by the explaining away of the facts that these ventures claim to grasp reality, since plainly they are always making mistakes. Of course, Winch's point is not that we should dismiss science and medicine as well as witchcraft, but only that we should not dismiss witchcraft as obviously mistaken on these grounds.

It might seem that Winch is saying that witchcraft is not mistaken, or not obviously so, and thus committing himself to the view that there are (or might well be) witches. He has been criticised in this way, but to make that objection is to suppose that his argument is directed towards judging whether either witchcraft or science is right when, plainly, he is entirely concerned with whether there is any formal difference in the reasoning pattern of someone brought up within the system of science, who takes it for granted, and of another raised within the system of witchcraft, who takes this different system for granted.

Winch's second – and even more crucial – point is that the determination to compare witchcraft with science results not in demonstrating the superiority of science, but in distorting the understanding of witchcraft. Hence it is seen as a perverse kind of science when, Winch maintains, it is not any kind of science at all. Since it is not any kind of science, it cannot be better or worse than, or even just as good as, our science. Religion and magic (including witchcraft) are not centred on the matters that preoccupy science, but have to do with other matters that pertain to the meaning of life and to the ethics of how people should relate to one another. We would understand this latter point better if, instead of approaching religion and magic on the basis of science-derived presuppositions about what they must be, we were simply to try to understand them. To do so does not involve us in actually accepting their terms. We do not have to believe in witches in order to grasp that believing in them is not a stupid mistake. Neither should we take our own disbelief in them as testimony to our superior rationality. On Winch's argument, the possibility of championing witchcraft against science, an approach which has caused so much agitation, is one which simply does not arise.

## Alternatives to scientistic sociology

Winch's capacity to cause agitation within sociology was complemented by provocations from two American-spawned schools of sociology, both having intellectual roots extending back to the 1920s, but not much noticed until the 1960s. These two schools were symbolic interactionism and ethnomethodology.

*Symbolic interactionism* originated in the work of the social philosopher George Herbert Mead (1863–1931), whose ideas were translated into a sociological doctrine principally by one of his students, Herbert Blumer (1900–1986). Mead published little during his lifetime; his ideas mainly spread through his teaching at the University of Chicago, where there was a sociological tradition of field studies of urban life. This kind of *Chicago sociology*, initiated by Robert Park and Ernest Burgess, continued there through the 1930s, 1940s and 1950s under the leadership of Everett C. Hughes. The symbolic interactionist school was the product of a loose amalgam of Mead's theories – mainly as interpreted by Blumer – and a commitment to field studies championed by Hughes.

*Ethnomethodology* is also commonly associated with a geographical base, being frequently derogated for its Californian origins, with the intendedly disparaging implication that its mode of thought reflected the disreputable, irresponsible, drug-crazed culture of the Hippie movement of the late 1960s. Its actual origins, however, were in 1920s Germany, where a young scholar, Alfred Schütz (1899–1959), undertook a systematic criticism of the philosophical presuppositions of Max Weber's account of the meaning of social action. Schütz based his criticism on *phenomenology*, which was an approach founded by the German philosopher Edmund Husserl (1859–1938). Schütz became an exile from the Nazis, escaping to America, where, during a career as a banker, he continued part-time to publish in sociology, though his work was little known until after his death and the publication of the first of his *Collected Papers* (1962, 1964, 1966) in the 1960s. During the 1940s Schütz's work was very influential upon a student of Talcott Parsons at Harvard University, Harold Garfinkel, who was to develop Schütz's ideas into the position of ethnomethodology. Garfinkel published little, and in relatively obscure places, until a number of his papers were collected into *Studies in Ethnomethodology*, published in 1967. From the 1950s Garfinkel was based in Los Angeles, and in the early 1960s his influence was spread across many campuses of the University of California, attracting a large number of graduate students, among whom the most notable was to be Harvey Sacks. Largely through lectures delivered (between 1964 and 1972) at the Irvine campus, Sacks developed an original extension of Garfinkel's ideas, which became known as *conversation analysis*.

Like Winch, though in different ways, both these schools raised the questions of meaning and rationality, doing so in ways that challenged received conceptions of method as being akin to the procedures of natural science. They often contend against a notion of rationality very similar to the one opposed by Winch. The notion was given specific form in, for example, Talcott Parsons's influential theories (see Chapter 5), against which in the 1960s both symbolic interactionism and ethnomethodology in their different ways were reacting. Essentially, Parsons defined rationality as conduct that accords with the best scientific information. Thus the findings of science are made the yardstick of rationality, and their application is to be undertaken by the sociologist. The sociologist will judge whether the conduct of members of the society is based upon conceptions that correspond with, could be endorsed by, the most up-to-date scientific knowledge. If it does not, then the action involved is irrational. Both schools dissented from this approach in favour of what we might call a *contextual* judgement of rationality.

## Contextual judgements of rationality

Whether or not some action or pattern of activity is judged rational is decided by reference to the particular conditions within which it is undertaken rather than to some abstract, general (scientific) standard.

If we isolate an action from its context, simply describing what someone does without any reference to its circumstances, and compare the understandings which the action seems to express with those of up-to-date science, we may find – almost certainly *will* find – that there is a considerable discrepancy. Consequently, we declare the action to be quite irrational. However, this approach simply shows that an action undertaken in a particular context may well look bizarre if taken out of context and described in a way insensitive to its circumstances. This was precisely the point of Winch's objection to Evans-Pritchard.

## Action in context: an example from Goffman

We can take an example from Erving Goffman, symbolic interaction's most successful exponent in achievement, influence and commercial terms – his books reached an unprecedented bestseller status. Goffman, studying mental patients, noted that they often seemed obsessive about trivial things such as pieces of string or tin foil, often hoarding them. How are we to think of what they are doing? Seemingly, a good way is to think that this behaviour is a symptom of their mental illness, perhaps manifesting obsessions or anxieties.

However, Goffman's point is that though such a description mentions the fact that the patients are in hospital, it says nothing more about the circumstances which life in the mental hospital provides for them. If we fill out some of those details and also consider them from the point of view of those patients as the conditions under which they have to live, a very different picture emerges. At the time of Goffman's study, patients in large mental hospitals were typically deprived of all personal possessions upon committal, e.g. made to wear hospital garb in place of their own clothing, and were allowed neither easy access even to trivial things (such as string, toilet paper, tin foil, etc.), nor any provision of secure places for storage. In these circumstances, small, otherwise valueless items become significant, either as commodities (as cigarettes do in prison) or simply because they are one's own; they come to stand for vestigial autonomy in face of powerful institutional authority. Therefore, anything can become desirable to possess; even if one does not use something oneself, one can exchange it. Being desirable, they are things that other people may try to steal. If one cannot lock one's personal cabinet, then it is not a safe place in which to leave anything – the sensible thing to do is to keep things close, to carry them about in one's pockets, for example. Far from being irrational, then, the patients' behaviour begins to seem perfectly rational in the circumstances; it is conduct imposed upon them as much by the institution's administrative arrangements as by any expression of their mental state.

Goffman argues that we can understand a great deal of inmate conduct in mental hospitals on the assumption that the inmates are psychologically normal rather than that they are insane. His study also makes the more general point that judgements on the rationality of conduct are best made by relating the conduct to its circumstances and by considering how the circumstances confront those involved as the perceived circumstances of their conduct.

## Rethinking sociological inquiry

Both symbolic interactionism and ethnomethodology raise the possibility that a conception of sociological method centred upon a general, abstract and *a priori* conception of rationality will encourage the sociologist to misunderstand and misdescribe social life. What purport to be objective and scientific descriptions can turn out to be partial and distorted, lacking a grasp upon the contextual conditions of the activities concerned and the meaning of those circumstances and activities for those who are situated in them. Thus the main trouble with a theorist like Parsons, according to these arguments, is with the very way he went about putting together a theory. The objection, articulated explicitly by Harold Garfinkel, was that Parsons's theory (like so much sociological theory) was built up in advance of acquiring an understanding of how actions relate to their context or circumstances, and how circumstances and actions acquire or possess their meanings. Rather than argue with specific parts of Parsons's theory, this response requires us to step back from the very starting point of such theorising and to set about sociology in a different way. We must seek general theory in a very different way, or even go so far as to give up the search altogether for a so-called general theory.

One of the most influential statements on method, deriving from a broadly symbolic interactionist outlook, was called *The Discovery of Grounded Theory*. The very title carries the implication that most sociological theory (such as Parsons's) is ungrounded, i.e. it is not rooted in an understanding of what actual situations are like.

## Grounded theory

Barney Glaser and Anselm Strauss, the authors of *Grounded Theory* (1967), held that sociological theory was usually preconceived, and then situations were selected and studied in order to provide data to test the theory. Consequently, the theory was based on only a limited grasp of actual social settings, since the research attended to the nature of situations only in very selective ways, normally those relevant to testing the theory. Sociologists complained widely about the weakness of theory, but why, then, did they not seek to ground their theory? Why not build theory starting from case studies? Why not first make close and intensive observation of some domain of life and then seek to work out a theory that would capture the nature of the area of social life that the case study has revealed?

Not everyone was persuaded by the idea of grounded theory, though it has had considerable popularity over the years and contributed to a broadening of the conception of sociological method. Ethnomethodology, however, sees no need for theorising in the traditional sense at all, and certainly does not accept the need for a method for grounding its theory. We will have more to say on this issue in the following chapter, where we set out its ideas in some detail. However, the current point is: one way or another, symbolic interactionists and ethnomethodologists reacted against the tradition of building all-embracing theories for sociology in advance of getting to know the social phenomena to be covered by the theory. Instead, what was needed – and both ethnomethodology and symbolic interactionism agreed – was to break away from the traditional efforts to construct an apparatus of mock-scientific theory and method. Instead, we should seek to observe social life as it occurs and to observe people as they go about their affairs in order that we might, at least, have access to the circumstances in which their actions are done, to the meanings which are employed in perceiving their circumstances, and therefore to the basis on which actions are undertaken. In other words, abstract theoretical schemes (based largely upon how theorists imagine how people would act) were to be replaced by much fuller depictions of actual conduct in real circumstances.

## The origins of symbolic interactionism: Mead's conception of behaviour

In the remainder of this chapter we consider the approach of symbolic interactionism in more detail. Symbolic interaction is a very loose categorisation not particularly welcome to many of the sociologists commonly counted as part of it. The name itself provides a succinct summation of the key claim of Mead's social psychology, which holds that interaction between people is a matter of communication, through *symbols*. Mead aimed to understand how the capacity for communication by symbols developed among humans, and how it develops in the maturation of each human individual. He aimed to establish through this argument two (anti-Cartesian) points: the mind is a *natural, biological* phenomenon and, also, an *essentially social* one. René Descartes (1596–1650), a French philosopher, had contributed immensely to the formation of Enlightenment ideas through his emphasis upon the acquisition of knowledge through reason, and upon the regulation of the search for knowledge through rigorous method. He had also contributed the view (known thereafter as *Cartesian dualism*) that the human being was composed of two distinct elements, the mind and the body, which had to be understood separately. Mead set himself against the traditional dualism and, equally, against the idea that the mind is a purely individual phenomenon.

### Mead's view of the self

The human mind – which Mead termed *the self* – develops in and through the process of symbolic interaction, enabling an individual to acquire a sense of himself or herself *as* an individual.

The development of the human mind was to be understood in strictly Darwinian terms as a product of the evolutionary process; the evolution of the human organism and the social nature of human individuals were both part of their biological nature. Hence Mead was certainly confident that social life could be studied scientifically, since his social psychology was in essence an application of biology, but he was none the less critical of many attempts to understand human social life scientifically. This was not because they sought to be scientific, but because they had an impoverished conception of:

- what science involves (the methods); and/or
- what the science is to study (the subject matter) in the case of human life.

For Mead, the mind can be studied scientifically because its workings are displayed in people's conduct, not concealed behind it.

The capacity of humans to respond in a more complex and flexible way to their environment than other animals is a product of human biology and its evolution into its specific form. For example, no small part of the crucial linguistic/symbolic capacity of humans is a result of the evolution of the vocal cords. Mead emphasises the contrast between the way animal response is tied to the immediate situation and the way humans can transcend it; they are able to reflect upon and respond to past situations well after they have occurred, and can anticipate and prepare for future situations before they happen. How we shall react in a situation can depend on our preparation and planning, not just on an automatic link between a certain occurrence and a fixed, instinctual reaction as in the case of a reflex action, e.g. the knee's reaction on being hit. We do have reflex reactions, but not only those. Thus Mead is putting the case that we ourselves can control our own behaviour; we do not simply react to a stimulus that provokes our reaction.

The capacity to transcend immediate circumstance in this way requires the development of symbolic capacity.

## Symbolic capacity

This is our ability to be able to represent, i.e. recall or envisage, past and future situations to ourselves, to conjure them up when they are not actually present, are in the past, or have not yet happened.

Part of this capacity for representation involves our ability to represent ourselves to ourselves. If we are to prepare our conduct for future situations then we must be able to imagine not just those situations but, also, what we would do in them. Thus we must have the capacity to think of ourselves in the way that we think about (other) objects; in Meadian terms, we can be objects to ourselves. That is, we can think about ourselves in just the same way as we can think about the objects (including other people) in the world about us, we can step back from our immediate involvement in a situation and reflect on it, and we can also envisage how others in our situation will look upon us and see ourselves as others see us. This, then, is the capacity for self-consciousness.

The individual is not, of course, merely a body, but an identity, a person with a distinct core of psychological character, which Mead terms 'the self'. It is the basis of, the driving force for, an individual's conduct. Mead refers to 'the social self' to emphasise that the self develops in interaction with and is modelled on other people and their ways of acting. The child, for example, learns first by imitation, by copying the behaviour of others in playful form, acting now like the postman, now the shopkeeper, then the mother, and so on. In this way, the individual learns what is involved in social roles, i.e. learns what people expect of one another. Through imitating these roles, the child is learning how other people look upon the world, how they see it relative to their role responsibilities. The child is learning not only to take account of things from its own situated, particular point of view, but also to assess its situation from the point of view of others. Such assessment is a basis for the co-ordination of activities with others, allowing one to adjust one's own actions to what one can expect/anticipate, because one can consider things from their point of view as well as one's own. The child does not develop a detailed conception of how every other kind of person in a society would view things, for that is far too complicated a task, but forms, rather, a general sense of how other people, broadly and typically, look upon things. Mead called this general orientation *the generalised other*.

## The generalised other

This is an important element in the individual's psychology. It is the standard outlook of the community in which the child grows up, and the attitudes that are shared within it form part of each individual's personality.

## Blumer: a method for symbolic interactionism

Herbert Blumer formulated a version of sociology strongly affiliated to Mead's theories. Like Mead, he was critical of the misapplication of the idea of science, and he wrote several papers criticising the 'scientistic' method then widespread in American sociology, one which prided itself on its use of mathematical symbolism. Blumer did not object to every use of mathematical symbols in sociology, but argued that there was an indiscriminate and meaningless imitation of the natural sciences in its use of mathematics. Mathematics was fine in areas like demography (the study of populations), where it plainly had real application, but it was often out of place in other areas of sociology, where the mathematical representations had no genuine grip on the phenomena they purported to represent.

For example, it was common for sociologists to talk about variable analysis as though they were doing the same thing as natural scientists. Variable analysis entails breaking down a complex phenomenon into a number of specific dimensions, which could vary – hence 'variables' – along those dimensions. For example, an object can be located by variables such as speed and direction. Blumer observed, however, that the so-called variables of sociology failed to meet the minimal requirement for comprising a variable, since they did not have actually measurable dimensions with clearly defined properties. In fact, they were not variables at all; rather, they were 'abbreviated terms of reference' for complex patterns of social organisation, which the researcher had not described and, usually, could not describe, e.g. 'alienation', 'the spirit of capitalism', 'social cohesion'. Thus the use of these pseudo-variables to describe social life unduly simplified and arbitrarily represented it. The methods involved in attempting to develop variable-type schemes cannot capture the true character and complexity of social relations – the ways society through communication is built up of elaborate chains of co-ordinated activity among many individuals. Moreover, such schemes tend to reduce the very concept of individual action itself to the stimulus–response relationship that Mead had decried.

Sociology needed to get away from playing with mathematical models of phenomena with which it was not really familiar in order to get on with increasing its knowledge of the range of social phenomena by making first-hand acquaintance with them *in their course*. In particular, it should attend to the ways individuals manage to co-ordinate their activities within the complexes of activity that make up organised social settings. Instead of starting out with ideas of rigorous and precise measurement, sociology should acknowledge that its theoretical concepts are vague and loose; they give no precise expectations about what we can expect to find in any actual situation. We should think of sociology's concepts as sensitising ones, rather than as elements in definite social laws that specify invariant regularities. Sensitising concepts point researchers towards a broad range of diffusely identified phenomena, perhaps enabling them to be more sensitive to connections between phenomena, and to notice relations that otherwise might have been missed. The notion of *career* employed by Blumer's contemporary, Everett Hughes, is just such a concept.

## Career

This invites us to look at a range of social situations in terms of the notion of the professional or bureaucratic career – as a development punctuated by *turning points* rather than as a smooth progress from a starting point to an end – even though such a notion may seem initially to be inappropriate.

For example, we might notice that even in the most supposedly irregular life, such as that of the criminal or the insane, there is orderly arrangement and progression, as illustrated by Edwin Sutherland with *The Professional Thief* (1961) and Erving Goffman with 'The Moral Career of the Mental Patient' in his *Asylums* (1961).

Blumer held that recognising the vague state of sociological thought is not an acknowledgement of disgrace, but a realistic appraisal of where sociology stands in the process of building its body of knowledge. The fact is that precise knowledge is the *goal* of empirical inquiry, not its starting point.

Blumer maintained his dissenting position in American sociology from the 1930s to the end of his career, albeit reformulating his arguments to encompass newly appearing sociological theories, prominently those of Talcott Parsons. Symbolic interactionism's critique was that many techniques, especially of the quantitative kind, were inappropriate to the nature of the phenomena they were intended to capture; they involved basic misconceptions about the nature of social life. Blumer held that symbolic interactionism, drawing upon Mead, had a distinctive conception of social life. He maintained that it was more inclusive than either of those involved in the conflict-versus-consensus debate, which, as we saw in Chapter 5, is the way that the major lines of dispute between Parsons and his critics were framed. Blumer argued that symbolic interactionism recognised that people come together in very different ways, sometimes co-operatively, sometimes competitively and, sometimes, in conflict. It is absurd to attempt to reduce the variety of possible forms of human interaction to one essential or basic form, e.g. either consensus or conflict.

## Society and individuals

As viewed by symbolic interactionism, society is nothing other than people living their lives; it is a large-scale construction produced out of and through the actions and interactions of many individuals. There is, then, no basis for conceiving of 'society' as a self-sufficient entity with needs of its own that could be satisfied by 'functional' arrangements.

Here again, Parsons's views are put aside. If society is viewed as a vast network of individuals, each of whom responds from his or her position in that network and in terms of his or her picture of that situation, the problem of social order is not to be solved by treating society as a centralised entity engaged in the production of its own existence; rather, it is to be understood by treating it as a distributed network, to use contemporary computing terminology. To use terms rather closer to Blumer's, the need is to see society as a product of joint action, to examine it and its other constituent patterns of complex organisation as being assembled out of the independent, but (frequently) concerted, lines of action put together by the individual members of society.

Blumer accepted that if one were to give what he called a 'skeletalised' picture of the complex of institutions and organisations which comprise society at any one time, then the picture given by symbolic interactionism would not look very different from that provided by functionalists or their Marxist critics. The difference lies not in the mapping of society's gross, molar organisation, but in the understanding of how that large-scale pattern comes about. Even though it is a very large structure, it is nothing other than the pattern of individuals going about their lives; the understanding of society consists in understanding the way that action is organised.

## The significance of process

Blumer's dissenting view has two aspects: one pertains to the relationship of structure to what we will call process; the other pertains to the emergent character of lines of action.

Talcott Parsons made a distinction between, and affirmed the (analytical) priority of, structure over process. Parsons analogised his procedure to anatomy, where we seek to understand the (static) layout of organs. First, we describe the locations and physical interconnections of the heart, kidney and spleen. Then we attempt to understand the processes, the changes that take place in the organism and the ways those changes interconnect and contribute to the functioning of the organism, e.g. the flow of blood and the circulation of oxygen. Blumer reverses Parsons's priority. It is true that a society can develop a relatively enduring set of institutions and organisations, which then stand in relatively stable arrangements to one another, but to give these structural patterns priority is, once again, to seek to present social life as simpler than it actually is by making out one aspect of it to be the basic, even essential, element. True, some social phenomena do stabilise out, but many do not. There are many phenomena within society that are transient, short-lived and ephemeral, or which do not settle down into stable patterns. A properly comprehensive account of society would encompass both kinds of phenomena. Blumer himself took a keen interest in *collective behaviour*, the name given to a heterogeneous assortment of ephemeral phenomena, ranging from the spread of rumour, demonstrations, riots and insurgencies, to the movements of fashion; they do not crystallise into a stable structure during the course of their (typically brief) existence. These phenomena, however, should be directly comprehensible in terms of the same theory that explains the development of stable, structured arrangements. Thus society in general consists of the *process* of social action.

## The process of social action

Individuals undertake actions through which they build up together patterns of joint, or shared, action in many cases. Some of these actions may comprise and sustain long-lasting patterns of joint action, but others do not.

The point is to understand the dynamics of both kinds of action and not to treat one or other situation as the leading instance.

It is Blumer's complaint, then, that the picture of stable, shared expectations as the basis of action is best fitted to – in Parsons's case, developed for – the analysis of stable, structured arrangements of joint action, where activities have become routinised into patterns that are highly familiar and predictable to participants. It is not suitable, however, for fluid, developing and changing situations, which involve the rise, transformation and disappearance of some instance of collective behaviour. In the latter cases, joint action does not settle down into stable patterns, yet people are none the less able to organise and carry out their affairs. Indeed, Blumer argued that though a concept of shared expectations like Parsons's might best fit the stable, structured complex of joint action, it did not fully fit even the case for which it was designed. It overestimated the degree to which action, even in the best-regulated circumstances, is (so to speak) worked out in advance, thereby underestimating the need to make problematic what we may term 'joint action in a distributed environment'. This point is perhaps best illustrated by considering symbolic interactionist approaches to the study of formal organisations, such as Anselm Strauss's conception of organisations as negotiated orders, in which people work out the arrangement of their relationships and work practices through person-to-person bargaining (see Strauss *et al.* 1964).

We can now turn to the second aspect of this part of Blumer's position, i.e. the emergent character of lines of action. With respect to the organisation of action and joint action, he argues three points:

- Action involves interpretation (or definition).
- The course of action is emergent.
- There is a process of formation of joint action.

Symbolic interactionism is often associated with a slogan formulated by an earlier Chicago sociologist, W. I. Thomas (1863–1947): 'If men define situations as real, they are real in their consequences.' Making much the same point, Blumer himself talked about the issue of 'interpretation'; hence this kind of sociology is often called 'interpretative' sociology. The key point is that people do not respond to situations as they are identified in terms of the latest scientific categories; rather, they respond to situations as they perceive (or define) them, even if they may not be real in scientific terms.

## Reality

What people take to be real and what according to science may actually be real may differ, but people respond to what they perceive as real.

For example, it may be that witchcraft does not exist, but, as we have already seen in this chapter, it remains the case that people in some societies take witches to be real, and many of their actions are, therefore, undertaken as protection against, or repair to, the damage they believe witches can cause. In Thomas's terms, the fact that people define witches as real has real consequences, i.e. it has a tangible effect on their behaviour, leading them to engage in witchcraft-preventive action.

Clearly, there is, then, nothing inherent in situations, such that their meanings are clear to everyone; scientists and people in them may see them differently. How, then, do people come to define, to interpret, their situations in the ways that they do? The meaning of the situation for the actor is viewed, then, as *originating* with the actor, as being a meaning with which the actor endows the situation. Consequently, the investigation of defining the situation involves exploring the actor's interpretative procedures.

Obviously, the way people define or interpret their situation must draw upon their culture, but that culture cannot anticipate all the possible situations which can confront the individual, nor even the full detail of any one of the specific situations which will confront him or her. It follows, then, that the actor's interpretative efforts have to go beyond what is given by the culture.

## Culture and action

Culture does not predetermine action; even in a situation which is so familiar and recurrent in an individual's life as to be readily defined and identified in a rapid and unreflective way, action will have an element of *Improvisation*, since a current situation will never be precisely the same as ones previously encountered.

Of course, many situations which an individual will experience even in the course of a day will not be of this familiar, recurrent kind, and defining them will be, for the actor, more or less problematic. Thus cases of collective behaviour can often consist in a co-operative effort of individuals defining together, interpreting, and giving meaning and sense to some new phenomenon with which social change confronts them. For an example – ours, not Blumer's – the 'Cargo cults' involved the reactions of Polynesian islanders to the imposition of colonial domination, by generating beliefs that the Europeans had magical powers to produce material things – the Cargo – through access to the Bible. These cults were the indigenous people's way of defining, making sense of, their relations with the Europeans. The practices of the cults comprised an amalgam of traditional native and Christian rituals, together with elements copied from the conduct and way of life that they had observed among Europeans.

## Emergent action

For Blumer, the conception of action which was cultivated in Parsons's scheme, as throughout sociology more widely, seemed to suppose that all that was needed to understand why people acted in the ways that they did was to identify whatever initiated action. For example, the idea of status/role seemed only to involve individuals in a situation identifying one another and thereby knowing which roles they were playing. Then everything else followed automatically, rather like the acting out of lines from a script. By contrast, Blumer held a conception of a course of action that we shall term *emergent* (to use a term coined by Mead, Blumer's intellectual mentor, to refer to the way a course of action is built up as it goes along).

Action characteristically involves a *course of doings*, some sequence of behaviour on the part of its performer. Blumer's point is that though we may have a rough idea of how and where some course of action is going when we set out on it, we do not start with the whole situation of action defined and the course of action fully set. A situation in which we act will itself change or evolve as we act. Therefore, defining the situation is not done prior to and preparatory of the course of action, but must be a continual part of the course of action itself, involving the further defining and redefining of the situation. Further, the way a course of social action develops has to respond to aspects of the situation over which we have no control, e.g. other people may not react to our actions in the way we anticipate. In doing something that requires their co-operation we may have to adapt our intended actions to their responses.

### Emergence

How a course of action will turn out very commonly develops over the course of action, i.e. it *emerges* over the spontaneous development of the course of action itself.

This property (which we have called 'emergence') means that the building up of lines of joint action is to be rendered (analytically) problematic, not treated as simply following from a set of pre-given relationships, however long-standing and well entrenched these might be. Blumer suggests that even a long-standing, perhaps officially and organisationally prescribed, course of action must be renewed on each occasion; the fact we have done something the same way every day for a long time does not guarantee that this time everything will go as before; that remains to be seen. Even when things go exactly as anticipated, their trans-action none the less requires interpretation; it may often prove an effortful task to keep matters on their usual footing and course, since the capacity to repro-duce them is

> subject to pressure as well as to reinforcement, to incipient dissatisfaction as well as to indifference; they may be challenged as well as affirmed, allowed to slip along without concern as well as subjected to infusions of new vigour…A gratuitous acceptance of the concepts of norms, values, social rules and the like should not blind the social scientist to the fact that any one of them is subtended [underpinned] by a process of social interaction – a process that is necessary not only for their change but equally well for their retention in a fixed form. It is the social process in group life that creates and upholds the rules, not the rules that create and uphold group life.
>
> (Blumer 1969: 18)

*Interaction*, then, is the basic notion for symbolic interactionism.

## The basis of symbolic interactionism

This means that the regularity and repetitiveness in social patterns, in rules, norms and values, must be understood as produced by and implemented through action and interaction, which must not be treated as the product of underlying rules, norms and values themselves. The production of large-scale, enduring complexes of repetitive actions is not to be viewed as automatically arising out of joint actions; instead, they are endlessly built and rebuilt, worked and reworked.

After Blumer, the title 'symbolic interaction' acquired its significance much more from the emphasis upon processes of social interaction as the very stuff of soci-ety, and no longer quite so much from the emphasis upon the symbolic nature of interaction among humans.

Lastly, Blumer's conception involves viewing the complex patterns of joint actions as being produced from within themselves by individual people in their positions and situations. To quote Blumer again, it is a mistake to think of society as some kind of system, for one should

> recognise what is true, namely, that the diverse array of participants occupy-ing different points in the network engage in their actions at those points on the basis of using given sets of meanings…the sets of meanings that lead

participants to act as they do at their stationed points in the network have their own setting and localised process of social action – and that these meanings are formed, sustained, weakened, strengthened or transformed, as the case may be, through a socially defining process.

(Blumer 1969: 20)

## Symbolic interaction as an urban anthropology

Everett Hughes, the other key symbolic interactionist, played a different role to Blumer. He wrote little of a theoretical kind, but promoted a tradition followed by many distinguished colleagues and students – including Howard Becker, Erving Goffman and Anselm Strauss – of producing case studies, which were often written rather informally and in the style of essays. Hughes favoured the idea of sociology as a scholarly rather than a professionalised scientific pursuit, which should welcome contributions from wheresoever they might come. It should not attempt to construct exclusive barriers around itself and impose uniformity within. He disagreed deeply with Parsons and Merton on this point, a decisive one for the future of American sociology and resulting in Hughes's defeat. Attitude as much as ideas made for the difference between these Chicago sociologists and those who were becoming the establishment in American sociology. In particular, Blumer and his followers regarded theory as more of a limited, modest enterprise, aiming partly to provide lightly developed guiding concepts, partly in order to bring some direction and order into studies, but primarily to serve in opening up the sensibilities of researchers to aspects of social life that might otherwise seem beneath notice, since, for them, theory was not an end in itself. There was much reflective concern with the practice of fieldwork since research itself could be understood in terms of symbolic interactionism, i.e. as an interactional and an emergent process. Fieldwork was not to be reduced to a strict method, to be followed recipe-like. Rather, the role of the field researcher was loosely defined and open-ended, its actual character being determined through interaction between those under study and the one(s) doing the research. The sense was, very strongly, of research as an *exploratory* activity, especially when the field studies were of areas of social life remote from the day-to-day experience of middle-class professional sociologists. Thus the studies sponsored by Hughes typically have an 'anthropological' character and have been characterised as *urban ethnographies*.

### Urban ethnographies

Studies were often of people remote from conventional middle-class lives, either in class terms, e.g. people in 'low-class' occupations such as janitors and assembly-line workers, or in moral terms, e.g. drug addicts, thieves, prostitutes, the mentally ill.

Studies were also made of middle-class professionals themselves, often focusing on their ways of dealing with the aforementioned socially remote groups, and there was a marked tendency for the tone of these studies about the professionals to be much more sceptical. This orientation gave rise to disputed accusations – as in a famously heated debate from a conflict-theory perspective between Alvin Gouldner (1968) and Howard Becker (1967), the latter taking the interactionist side – that they were based on an excessively sentimental identification with the underdog and the outsider.

The studies of occupations were no doubt motivated by the fact that in modern society the individual's sense of self, of identity, of who one is, has been tied up with one's occupation.

## The sense of self

A main element in the sense of self is the degree of self-worth that (1) one feels one has, and (2) one is regarded as having. It is, of course, closely interwoven with the occupational system, given that occupations are ranked in terms of prestige, and people are judged to be high or low in the scheme of things according to (though not exclusively) the kind of work they do.

For example, the professional is someone of high standing, while the janitor or the rubbish collector is looked upon as a lowly type. Barney Glaser and Anselm Strauss, in one of their studies of medical work (1968), pointed out that one's life could well depend upon where one stands in the status scheme of things. Life-preserving resources are often scarce relative to the demands made on them. When overwhelmed with cases needing emergency medical treatment, staff have to make decisions about whom they are going to try, seriously, to save, and whom they will have to let die. Glaser and Strauss call the criterion they use 'social loss', and seek to capture by this term the practice among medical staff of making such judgements about social worth, i.e. who matters more in and to society, and whose death will represent the least significant loss. For example, a prominent citizen or businessperson, or a family member with dependants, will be chosen over a vagrant.

The occupational studies undertaken by Hughes, his colleagues and students covered both highly esteemed and humble jobs, but the attitudes which the researchers took towards each were rather different. The professions are jobs that have higher ratings and advertise themselves as occupations involving such levels of competence in their routine practice that they can only be carried out by highly skilled individuals who have been prepared through long and arduous training. Because the work requires such skill, the occupation seeks what Hughes called 'licence and mandate' from the society; i.e. it seeks to have itself recognised as dealing in matters requiring such expertise that it needs to be given independence from broader forms of social supervision, and allowed to regulate its own ethics, practice and training. Many sociologists used these features as elements in their models of professions, but the symbolic interactionists took a more sceptical view: the professed high-mindedness of the professions, setting themselves out as virtuous servants of their clients, was often a cover for justifying the elevation of their occupation in the competition for prestige and prosperity, and was to be contrasted with their exploitation of the client's ignorance about what was involved in order to deliver inferior service. For example, Abraham Blumberg (1969), writing about the criminal law as a 'confidence game', described how lawyers would organise their defence work in such ways as to send the client away (even to prison) happy with their lawyer, even though, in fact, the outcome was not the best, but simply the one the lawyer could obtain with least trouble. Similarly, the claim to expertise and the necessity of training was questioned: legal work is often done not by the lawyer who heads the practice, but by clerical staff with no legal training or supervision. Howard Becker's 'The Nature of a Profession', in his *Sociological Work* (1970), is a sustained polemic against the usual admiring concept of a profession.

On the other hand, the studies of the humble occupations and of socially degraded groups were sympathetic, being motivated to take the viewpoint of those in these lowly positions, to ask how they defined their situation, and to look at things from their point of view. The inclination was to emphasise the unappreciated aspects of these positions in society and, as with the studies of professions, to attempt a corrective to popular conceptions. People in lowly positions and social outcasts were subject to unfairly derogatory popular conceptions, which dismissed their lives as disorganised, irrational and disgraceful. In these cases the point of the studies was to claim that the lives were very much ordinary for those who lived them, i.e. organised and routine. Those who live them face and contend practically with much the same array of problems of living as anyone else; crime, for those who do it, involves work no less than do other occupations. Just like the legal profession, crime too might have a kind of professional career structure. At the same time, though, these studies recognised that the people involved had low or negative esteem in the eyes of the world at large. An interest was therefore taken in how people in these positions contend with it: how could they maintain any sense of self-worth in a society that told them they were worthless individuals?

## Goffman and the interaction order

Many of these studies were drawn together to provide the empirical stuffing for Erving Goffman's conceptual structures. As we mentioned above, Goffman was the most successful symbolic interactionist in terms of the distinctiveness of his conceptions, the influence they have had, and the financial rewards from his bestselling, well-received books. In a series of linked books, Goffman gave an account of the way the individual constructs and communicates a sense of self in the course of interaction, and how interaction is produced as an autonomous order of social organisation.

An example Goffman favoured was taken from restaurants. It concerned the abrupt change that would overcome the waiters as they moved through the door dividing the kitchen from the dining area. Before the public, the waiters' behaviour was courteous, constrained and respectful, but entry into the kitchen would transform it into a less restrained mode, often manifesting contempt for those who, only a moment before, had been treated in a servile way. For Goffman, this example illustrates a widespread pattern, common to organisations of the form he termed 'establishments', which included hospitals, department stores, hotels and business offices. These establishments are open to the public and tend to be divided into two separated areas, one part on display to the public, the other closed to it.

## The presentation of the self in establishments

In an analogy with the theatre, Goffman termed these areas the 'front' and 'back' regions, using their existence to argue that the presentation of the individual self is a collective affair, very often the work of a team. As with the theatre, what goes on before the public is organised to convey a particular conception. In the case of organisations, it is often the competent, professional delivery of the relevant service, accompanied by an appropriate attitude.

For example, clients and customers often want not only the specific service, but also its delivery in a manner that treats them with respect, if not subservience. People visiting hotels do not want merely to be provided with a room; they also want to be treated as important and with courtesy. The staff, then, mount a collaborative performance to project themselves as the capable and committed deliverers of that service; they play back the clients' own self-conceptions as the well-regarded, gratefully and gracefully serviced clients. Putting on this performance is often stressful, for the attitude being projected is not actually held. Further, it involves withholding all negative reactions, like irritation, as well as having to fulfil physically demanding and mentally wearing responsibilities such as standing still impassively for long periods. The back region, private to the staff, is where they can physically and emotionally relax, let off steam, loosen tight clothing; they can express the reactions they have restrained during the performance, especially by reversing the relationship of servility they have been acting out. In the back region they can reciprocally express and mutually sustain feelings of disdain for their clients, thereby reinforcing their sense of themselves as being more and other than they must appear to be in the front region.

## Deviance

The 'asylum', i.e. the large state mental hospital, was of interest to Goffman because it did not conform to the front/back region pattern, at least for those who were its inmates. From the point of view of those consigned to the mental hospital, the place was not experienced as a therapeutic environment devoted to the repair of their damaged psyches, but, rather, as custodial, dedicated to attacking their self-image and eradicating any remaining residue of self-respect. For the inmates, notions of psychiatric treatment seemed like mere rationales for an oppressive, disciplinary regime. Medical and psychiatric procedures seemed to be used more as modes of control, even punishment, than of healing; their application seemed to be dictated more by the requirements for administering a large and unruly population than by patient symptoms. As previously mentioned, Goffman held that the inmates are better understood on the assumption that they are psychologically normal, rather than psychologically disorganised; much of their behaviour can best be understood as a perfectly reasonable reaction to a depriving environment. In the earlier example, psychiatrists construed hoarding behaviour as a symptom of mentally disturbed behaviour, but it can as well – if not better – be viewed as a reaction to a lack of privacy and a paucity of resources.

For Goffman, the lack of privacy for inmates was crucial. For them, there was no obvious division between front and back region; they were continually under surveillance and in the presence of many others. Affairs were so organised as persistently to thrust upon the inmate a conception of himself or herself as a flawed, failed individual, deservedly reduced in the social scheme of things to a most humble position, someone crazy or insane. Any protestations that inmates might make that there was nothing really wrong with them were criticised and undermined in the name of therapy until the patient came to realise that the only way out of the institution was to accept the judgement of the staff. Indeed, a first, necessary step in 'progress' towards release was to 'admit' that one was mentally ill; it was deemed 'insight'. Goffman records the detailed, marginal ways in which the inmates none the less struggled in the face of such an assault on their self-esteem to maintain some shreds of self-respect. Even in such a rigorously controlled environment they were adept at creating and exploiting opportunities for shielding themselves and their activities from surveillance:

Free places are backstage to the usual performance of staff–inmate relationships. Free places in Central Hospital were often employed as the scene for specifically tabooed activities: the patch of woods behind the hospital was occasionally used as a cover for drinking; the area behind the recreation building and the shade of a large tree near the centre of the hospital grounds were used as locations for poker games.

(Goffman 1961: 206)

The assumption behind symbolic interactionism's analytical strategy can be understood thus: the formal patterns of social organisation are general and remain the same across the whole range of behaviour; they do not alter as one crosses the line between respectable and disreputable social groups. Combined with the objective of seeing things sympathetically from the point of view of those under study, this approach encourages playing down the difference between those on different sides of morality or the law. Out of it – especially through the work of Edwin Lemert (1967) and Howard Becker (1964) – emerged a concept of deviance, which was to be notorious, controversial and influential as developed by Becker, and became known as *labelling theory*. It was a theory of deviance rather than crime – even though crime is often the leading instance of deviance – and included all kinds of socially disapproved behaviour and outcast groups, i.e. all those infringing social rules, not only those breaking the law.

Theories of deviance traditionally sought to establish just how deviants differed from 'normal' people, i.e. taking it for granted that they did. A common tactic was to look for characteristics – biological, psychological or social – which distinguish 'deviants' from 'normals'. The attentive reader will have noted that such an assumption would not appeal to symbolic interactionists. Goffman explicitly rejects it as a supposition for his study of the 'insane'. Further, symbolic interactionists noted that studies which sought to compare deviants with normals did nothing of the sort. Instead, they compared *identified* (i.e. convicted or diagnosed) deviants with a general population that would also contain unidentified deviants. If a deviant is defined as someone who has broken a social rule or law, then there can be few of us who are not deviants, for we all break rules and laws at some time or other. For most of us there are no consequences – we do not even get fined for parking illegally.

## Labelling theory

Labelling theory picks up on a Durkheimian conception, though developing it to very different effect: deviance is very much a public matter, and deviants, as they have traditionally been studied, are people who have been publicly identified as such, i.e. they have been taken through the courts, the psychiatric admission process and so on. The difference between deviants and normals is not, then, in their individual characteristics. The difference between them is how they have been treated by, broadly, the agencies of social control, i.e. the various administrative bodies engaged in enforcing social rules.

Some people who break rules or laws may be picked out by the police, social workers and so on, while others who break the same rules or laws may continue their lives unmolested. If we want to understand the difference between someone who is convicted or diagnosed and someone who is not, we do not need to study their individual characteristics; instead, we need to look at the practices of the administrative organisations which publicly identify someone as a criminal, or as mentally disturbed. The difference between a deviant and a supposed normal may result from how they are treated by the staffs of such administrative bodies. An outcome might be as incidental as, say, the fact that police patrolmen, bored and wanting a change from sitting in their car, might decide to arrest somebody for an offence that, under other circumstances, they would have done nothing about.

Becker's arguments responded to an issue raised by Durkheim about the fact that all societies create 'crime' (as Durkheim called it, or 'deviance' in Becker's terminology), as a class of prohibited actions. Becker took a different tack in suggesting that we must study the ways people in society, rather than society itself, create and enforce rules. This approach involves recognising the frequently political nature of these actions; since rules are formed out of contests among social groups, the ways favoured by some social groups are enforced on other groups. The outcomes of such contests are not the expression of any will of society, but are very much prone to the contingencies of the (literally) political process. For example, unrepresentative groups, such as temperance movements, can gain a very strategic position, and get their policy imposed generally, e.g. prohibition of alcohol in this case. We can say, then, that the making of the laws *creates* deviance. It does so in two ways:

- by making a set of previously legal actions illegal;
- by giving rise to new kinds of actions which are also criminal; they are responses to the new situation created by the prohibition of the first action (Lemert called them 'secondary deviance').

For example, prohibition brought into existence gangsterism organised to bootleg liquor, just as, some argue, the prohibition of drugs today creates and sustains the illegal drug trade.

The understanding of how the rules are brought into existence, however, is only part of the necessary programme of study, for the fact is that those who enforce the rules once they are made are not the same people as those who create those rules in the first place.

## Moral entrepreneurs and bureaucratic professionals

Becker wrote of 'moral entrepreneurs', who campaign to obtain new law, and noted that the interest of these enthusiasts often extends as far as securing a prohibition. Those charged with enforcing the prohibition are often bureaucratic professionals, who are less likely to care as strongly about the merits of the rule as those who made it, since enforcement is only their job, not their passion. They adapt the enforcement of the law to the practicalities of their work: their interests are in job-relevant considerations like career advancement, a quiet life, avoiding distasteful work, providing amusement during dull periods, keeping the boss happy, etc. In short, the way a rule gets enforced may be very different from how it was envisaged by those who framed it.

Jerome Skolnick's *Justice Without Trial* (1966) provides a compelling portrait of the way the police typically traded off law enforcement against peacekeeping. Police officers treated as first priority the calming of difficult, disturbed situations, and mollifying the upset and angered parties to them; they preferred to disregard the fact that there had been an arrestable offence. That a law had been broken, allowing the possibility of an arrest, was often used as a threat to control the immediate situation. The police knew that if they made arrests every time they could, they would overwhelm their own and the court system's capacity to cope. Also, in many cases they refrained from arrest because it would cause them unnecessary work; they believed that when they had satisfied the demand of an injured party for an arrest, and done all the paperwork, the injured party would probably then drop the charges.

It follows that an understanding of the difference between deviants and normals will not result from a focus upon the individuals who are publicly labelled as deviant. Instead, we must focus on the operations of the individuals, groups and organisations in society which promote and install rules, policies and standards, and on the organisations that implement and enforce these standards. Rather than ask what makes a deviant do deviant things, we might – Becker suggests – ask what stops people from engaging in such acts. We all are subject to impulses to do 'wrong' things at one time or another, but most of us do not follow through on these impulses, or not sufficiently frequently or carelessly to fall foul of the authorities and thereby have our lives transformed into those of outcasts. He suggested that many of us are careful to avoid this outcome because of the *commitments* that we have accumulated in our lives. Even though we have the impulse to do something, thinking of the risk involved to the things we value in the life we currently lead prevents us.

Defenders of more orthodox conceptions responded to labelling theory as a form of relativism, for which it was often fiercely condemned. The theory maintained (or seemed to maintain) that deviance existed purely in the eye of the beholder. Deviance was a purely subjective state; deviance was what people believed it to be, and nothing else. Since people had different beliefs, then they would believe different things to be deviant and, by this logic, these things were deviant. In a way, everything would at once be both deviant and not deviant. Becker explicitly argued that the characteristic 'deviance' is not intrinsic to a given action, because a certain action, such as drinking alcohol, can be legal before and illegal after midnight, legal in one state of the US and illegal in another, legal if done by an adult and illegal if done by an adolescent.

### Defining deviance

If, then, deviance does exist in the eye of the beholder, any action can be deviant, for in the eyes of one group an action may be normal, but in the eyes of another abnormal. According to labelling theory, something is deviant only because there is a law (or rule) against it, and someone is a deviant only if the law (or rule) is enforced and she or he is publicly identified as infringing it.

Here critics complain that if there were no law or other prohibition against, say, beating up old people in the street, it would not be a deviant action. Despite such criticism, however, labelling theory was influential, and its studies of the way the identity of deviant was conferred through the workings of the bureaucracies of social control contributed to the formation of the influential and even more controversial *social constructionist* doctrines, which emphasised the role of organisational arrangements in bestowing all kinds of identities, not just deviant ones (see Chapter 13). Consequently, the way people were identified as 'mothers' or as 'sick', or even 'dead', would be studied in this way.

The heyday of symbolic interactionism was in the 1950s and 1960s, when the pioneering thought and work of Blumer and Hughes was applied in highly creative and imaginative ways by many investigators, including Goffman, Becker and Strauss. The approach has continued to be productive, and there is a substantial and constant flow of writings on a wide range of everyday activities, characteristically based on field studies. However, these are mostly conducted under the auspices of the general and reasonably well-defined approach, rather than involving real innovations. Recently, there has been an attempt to reassert the relevance of the approach with the claims that (1) it is reconstructing itself in such a way as to enable it to deal with topics which are now regarded as essential elements in sociological understanding – social structures, institutions, power and ideology – which, hitherto, symbolic interaction could have been accused of neglecting; (2) it can accommodate to recent postmodern sensibilities, which have tended to minimise the significance of the subject or, in interactionist terminology, 'the self' in modern society, treating it as an illusory phenomenon. Against this poststructuralist and postmodern disposal of the self, it is argued that the self remains a proper topic for empirical investigation, which can be done in a way that is compatible with some main features of the postmodernist position (see Chapter 13).

## Conclusion

Symbolic interaction continues to be practised and remains productive of research investigations, but it has become marginalised relative to the mainstream of sociological thought. Credited with making an important contribution to the relativising of social thought, especially through the ideas of labelling theory, it is none the less regarded as having been left behind by the more drastic and all-encompassing relativism of poststructuralist and postmodernist doctrines. In sociological *practice*, however, qualitative methods, the definition of the situation, underdog bias, and so on, are now mainstream tropes. While symbolic interactionist *theory* is less influential, the study practices of Blumer and Hughes, and their followers, have proved both resilient and compelling.

## Questions

1 Peter Winch argues that the idea of a *science* of society is misconceived. Why? Is he right? What are the implications of this view for government statistics? Do these criticisms just apply to positivist approaches or are they an attack on any form of conventional sociological theory?

2 Do contemporary debates about science and religion parallel Evans-Pritchard's analysis of Zande witchcraft? How might Winch's ideas be useful in considering these debates? Can his ideas be applied to, for example, 'belief' in astrology? What other modern phenomena have similar features to Zande witchcraft?

3   How does George Herbert Mead understand the 'self'? Why is this important? How does this differ from the ways psychologists understand the concept? Why were his ideas used by Blumer to criticise mainstream sociology? Was Blumer right?

4   Blumer, like Marx, Weber and Durkheim, had a particular concept of the 'individual'. How did Blumer conceive of such a thing? How does his account of the individual differ from that of Weber? Can Blumer be understood to be the opposite of Durkheim?

5   W. I. Thomas argued, 'if men define situations as real, they are real in their consequences'. What did he mean? Is he right? How might this be applied to political, ethnic or religious fanaticism? What more mundane matters might it apply to? Can you think of some modern situations that this slogan describes?

6   Hughes argued that there are many similarities between the work of, for example, lawyers and prostitutes: they both have clients, they must both keep secrets, and so on. Does this make sense? Is this an analytical point or about the politics of egalitarianism? What contemporary occupations might be understood to have more in common with one another than first appearances suggest? What are the implications of this kind of analysis for Weber's approach to prestige and status?

7   What is labelling theory? What is secondary deviance? Is there such a thing as 'primary deviance'? How does this approach differ from Durkheim's analyses of crime and suicide? Are there similarities? Is this a relativist approach to sociology? Would it be a bad thing if it was?

## Next steps

Winch's (1990) *The Idea of a Social Science* remains the classic controversial critique of 'scientific' sociology. Blumer's (1969) *Symbolic Interactionism* contains the key papers that systematised the perspective, and Becker's (1964) *Outsiders* remains the best starting place for interactionist studies of deviance. Many excellent symbolic interactionist studies are collected in Rose (1962), Manis and Meltzer (1972), and Stone and Farberman (1970).

Rock's (1979) *The Making of Symbolic Interactionism* is a good overview of the perspective as a whole, while Fine's (1995) *A Second Chicago School?* provides a more detailed analysis.

## CHAPTER SEVEN

# Ethnomethodology

## Chapter overview

Ethnomethodology is a more radical alternative to Parsons's system than symbolic interactionism, but it has different roots – in part, stemming from Parsons himself – and is a very different approach to what doing sociology might consist in. It is based in *phenomenology*, in particular Alfred Schütz's work, an attempt to devise a theory of the ordinary, mundane ways people conduct themselves in the world. These ways are very different to how, for example, social theorists or scientists think about things – *as social theorists or scientists* – but are typically not considered as 'interesting' in their own right. Ethnomethodology is an attempt to reconsider the 'problem of social order' in the light of these mundane understandings: the methods members of society use to make sense of the world. An analysis of these methods reveals a number of features of such sense-making that are incompatible with conventional theories of the social world: their *situatedness* and their *reflexive* nature, for instance. Studies of the organisation of conversation (*conversation analysis*) represent a perspicuous example of what ethnomethodological studies look like.

## Introduction: ethnomethodology – a relativist, subjectivist sociology?

In the debates surrounding symbolic interactionism, a recurrent charge was that it endorsed a relativist stance which denied any objective reality whatsoever to social life by reducing it entirely to the perceptions or definitions of individuals. In so far as the notion of *defining the situation* was taken seriously and to its limits, it was seen to combine with other arguments, e.g. Winch's, in inducing a relativist current into sociological thought. The accusation was most prominently made in relation to the notion of labelling, which, as we have shown in Chapter 6, can be seen as adopting a strange attitude to social reality, i.e. deviance exists only in the eye of the beholder. If symbolic interactionism appeared to encourage such relativist developments, then ethnomethodology was regarded as carrying them even further, to the extreme.

As we noted in the previous chapter, in some ways ethnomethodology is close to symbolic interactionism. Yet in other, and generally more important, respects it is very far removed. It certainly derives from different sources, i.e. directly from European philosophy, and most particularly from Alfred Schütz's application of the phenomenology fathered by Edmund Husserl to the problems of the social sciences. For Schütz, the *locus classicus* of these problems was the methodological writings of Weber. Therefore, he began by subjecting to critical inspection Weber's most basic assumptions about social action. Weber put the actor's point of view, i.e. the subjective point of view, at the centre of his project, but he made no sustained effort to reflect on the way that point of view must be structured, and did not try to give any systematic account of how society appeared to someone situated within it. Nor did he resolve adequately the implications of the assumption of the actor's point of view for sociology's stance towards its subject matter. Schütz proposed to fill this gap. He began his critique of Weber in the 1920s, publishing it in the early 1930s before going into exile in the USA.

## Basics of ethnomethodology

The starting point for the study of ethnomethodology is the writings of Schütz since, in key respects, ethnomethodology is nothing more than the working out of the implications of Schütz's arguments about the nature and foundations of sociological knowledge. In particular, ethnomethodology focuses on how we study the world: the issue of *method* best elaborates its ideas. For ethnomethodology, the notion of method goes far beyond sociological methods conventionally conceived, such as field-work and the social survey. The key to an adequate understanding of ethnomethodology lies in comprehending just why it is called what it is, particularly the significance of 'methodology' in its title.

## Schütz and phenomenology

Schütz owed inspiration to the *phenomenology* of Husserl, which, in its way, had been critical of the 'positivist' spirit in Western thought, especially in science and philosophy. As we have seen in Chapter 3, at the heart of this positivist tradition lies the view that the new, immensely successful natural sciences are the source of a definitive conception of reality, one that is secured by scientific methods. The epitome of these methods is to be found in physics, the most successful of the sciences; this view holds that if we want to know what reality is really like, we had best look into the textbooks of physics. But there we shall find a world very different from the one that we ordinarily know. The natural world familiar to us in our daily life does not appear in physics books; many thinkers of a positivist persuasion have read these books as telling us that this world of daily life does not really exist: it is a form of illusion.

The prevailing stance in sociology throughout much of its history has been shaped by such positivist assumptions, i.e. if sociology follows the path of the natural sciences, then it too will come to define reality in terms of scientific methods. Genuine social reality will be defined *through* these methods so that only when we have finished our sociological studies shall we know what social reality really is. On such assumptions we can expect it to look like nothing we now take it to be. Our current perceptions of social reality will come to be seen as the result of false beliefs.

This contrast was strongly opposed by Husserl. He did not accept this picture of the relationship between the world-according-to-science, on the one hand, and our lived-in-world (*Lebenswelt*), on the other. Husserl certainly did not reject (did not even question) the achievements of the natural sciences as sciences, for his doubts were about the way its findings were being construed. In particular, he argued that serious misconceptions about the way science relates to our pre-scientific understandings had crept in, giving rise to a false picture of the two in conflict. Crudely, science does not provide a picture which displaces the lived-in-world as we experience it, since it cannot do so because the scientific picture both originates in and depends upon the lived-in-world itself. An X-ray photograph does not compete with or displace our passport photograph.

To start by comparing an X-ray with a snapshot and asking which is the correct picture of someone is to go about things the wrong way. Rather than starting with the (supposed) scientific picture already in place and then asking how that compares with our experience of the lived-in-world and how there can possibly be room for both, Husserl thought we should not take the presence of the scientific picture for granted. Instead, we should ask about its *origins*, i.e. how the possibility of looking at the world in a scientific way, as opposed to a common-sense way, developed.

Husserl linked the rise of science as a way of thinking to Galileo, who most influentially promoted the idea that inquiry into the nature of things could begin from assumptions quite distant from those we commonsensically accept. Furthermore, Galileo argued that the development of scientific understanding involved the questioning and, if necessary, abandoning of reliance upon perceptions provided by our unaided senses. Here then were the origins of a distancing of science from everyday ways of knowing the world; they were built into thinking about the natural sciences and what was necessary to their success virtually from the start. Husserl's inquiries comprised the backdrop to Schütz's thinking about the relationship between science and common sense as ways of knowing. Schütz, however, shifted the focus from completely contrasting the world-as-portrayed-in-science, on the one hand, and the world-as-seen-by-common-sense, on the other.

## The natural attitude

Instead, Schütz emphasised differences within the *natural attitude*, i.e. an attitude that begins by taking the existence of an external world for granted. It has two forms, the *common-sense* attitude and the *theoretical* (or *scientific*) attitude. They are very different and in important respects incongruous, but even so, they are far from being altogether distinct.

The reason – and the deep implication of Schütz's argument – is that we cannot give up the common-sense in favour of taking up the theoretical (or scientific) attitude. Consequently, we cannot replace the common-sense with the scientific. Here he connects with the approach of Descartes (see Chapter 6). Descartes recommended the *method of doubt* as a means of reaching the ultimate, unquestionable certainties for which he thought philosophy should search. This method involves doubting everything that can possibly be doubted in order to determine whether anything remains which cannot possibly be doubted, i.e. we are left with certain knowledge. Descartes thought that one could doubt almost everything, even the existence of the external world. The one exception – the only thing seemingly capable of this kind of resistance – is one's own mental existence. In doubting, one is thinking, and being able to think presupposes one's own existence, or, more strictly, it presupposes the existence of one's own mind.

However, the Cartesian method of doubt has its function within the strictly defined domain of pure philosophical inquiry in order to establish the grounds for certain knowledge through the operation of pure reason. Someone who wants to do other than merely think, who wants to *do* something, cannot operate with Descartes' method of doubt – a point that Descartes himself appreciated since he was concerned with purely philosophical questions concerning how to establish certain knowledge. Acting requires dependence on one's body and on the external world: these are presupposed in action. The method of doubt can go on entirely in the mind and without the use of the body or its movement in the external world, whereas actual lives in society must be conducted on some other basis.

## The natural attitude

The natural attitude is contraposed to the method of doubt. As they go about their lives, people do not doubt the reality of everything that could possibly be called into question. They take most things for granted. However, to notice this attitude is not to point to a failing on the part of people going about their daily lives. Of course, people in the natural attitude do doubt, but do not, in practical terms could not, make doubting anything like their first priority. They only doubt when they have need to, when something goes wrong in their practical affairs. We might suppose that people could doubt whether when they do something this time things will happen the same way as last time. For example, if they turn on the tap which last time produced water, will it this time produce water, or nothing, or poison gas? If we had a serious doubt about it, truly thought that a fatally poisonous gas was as likely as water, we would not turn on the tap without first trying to ensure that water will come out. At the very least, an ordinary, routine activity would be made deeply problematic and extraordinarily time-consuming. But note what follows if we assume such scepticism not about a specific activity in particular, but in general. It is not simply that the problem would be endless if we adopted a comparably sceptical view towards everything else that we might use; the problem would be where and how even to begin the task. How are we to be sure that what we take as a tap actually is one? But if we do not assume it is a tap, then what possible sense can be given to the idea that we cannot trust what might come out of it?

Of course, the key point is that we do not carry on like good Cartesians because in our normal lives we just assume, just take for granted, that this time will be like last time and the tap will deliver water we can drink and wash with. Doubt occurs if we turn on the tap and nothing comes out, or foul sludge drips forth. Then we have doubts, and start to check things out, but, even so, we do not start to doubt everything, only those things relevant to the working properly of the tap, e.g. we look out of the window to see if the water-service repair crew might have dug up the road. Doubt in the natural attitude is an occasioned, stimulated occurrence and not the general condition of our lives. The implication for sociology, of course, is the need to study how people *operate under the natural attitude* if we want to understand how their social lives are organised. Schütz's career was entirely devoted to this enterprise.

Importantly, Schütz is analysing an *attitude*, i.e. an approach to their affairs, which the members of society not only overwhelmingly exhibit, but also are required to exhibit. When we refer to 'common sense', we are neither recommending nor supporting particular actions or beliefs. Otherwise, we would be open to the objection (often made by those who misunderstand even the elementary features of this line of argument) that common sense is a localised matter and that what is considered common sense in one place or at one time is not considered so in another locale or epoch. This putative objection is more of a confirmation, however, of the point being made here about understanding how actions are organised.

## The common-sense attitude

The argument is that:

- it is an inescapable feature of the organisation of actions that their course depends upon what people take for granted;
- among any given set of people there is a vast multitude of things that they will take for granted, that between themselves they treat as obvious, apparent, as going without need of comment or explanation, as transparently and without question plainly the case, and readily known to anyone and everyone, i.e. common sense.

Neither of these contentions says anything about what is treated as common sense in any given case. People are entirely comfortable with the idea that what is common sense in twenty-first-century America will not be the same – certainly not entirely the same – as what was common sense in fourteenth-century China. The reference to 'anyone and everyone' has its own localised applicability: what Californian teenagers of the early 2000s treat as matters that 'anyone and everyone' knows will refer to people like themselves, and these terms are often likely to exclude parents, teachers and other adults.

The dominant element of the natural attitude is its concern with getting things done, its practical character. People in society are not concerned with finding a thing out for its own sake, with accumulating knowledge of how things work in order to have the most organised and comprehensive stock of knowledge possible. Observably they are more concerned with getting certain sorts of things successfully completed by their actions, such as making lunch, getting to work, buying a new coat, filling in forms, checking the stock, and protecting garden plants against frost. Their occasions of doubt arise within the context of such practical enterprises. We do not sit in the living room all day wondering whether water will come out of the tap when we eventually turn it on. The issue only arises when we want some water, and only then if the usual expected flow does not materialise. What people know and take for granted is organised, for them, around the things that they are doing. The question they put to conditions is: are they good enough, can they be relied upon, *for all practical purposes*? The extent to which they doubt, and the degree to which they take measures to resolve doubt, are both characteristically set within practical limits. If water does not come out of the tap, then the kinds of questions that arise pertain to what kinds of causes could interrupt the water supply, and any inquiries into these matters will characteristically terminate the moment that the water supply is restored.

These aspects are not shared with the scientific or theoretical attitude, but, as noted above, we should not conclude that the scientific and the natural (or common-sense) attitudes are entirely distinct. The scientific attitude lies partway between the philosophical method of doubt and the common-sense natural attitude.

## The scientific attitude

Simplistically put, we can say that the scientific attitude is concerned with knowledge rather more than with practicality, wIth finding out as opposed to getting done, and with knowledge for its own sake, rather than with knowledge that enables the fulfilment of a here-and-now practical task.

Further, the scientific attitude is more motivated by the possibility of doubt than is the common-sense attitude, making it closer to the philosophical posture of systematic doubt. Unlike the common-sense attitude, science does tend to doubt things, just to see what doubting them might reveal. However, it cannot doubt upon the global scale of the Cartesian 'method of doubt', since the objective of science is to inquire into the 'world-out-there', and that, of course, means that the existence of that world-out-there cannot be doubted as it can in philosophical reflection. For this reason, science is included within the natural attitude.

Moreover, the working scientist's doubt is much more specific and focused than the philosopher's, for the working scientist doubts that some specific thing is the way it seems, or has been taken to be, in order to investigate and settle this particular doubt. In so doing, scientific inquirers must exclude many things from the (immediate) possibility of doubt and must take for granted very many things as matters of so much common sense, just like ordinary members of society. Similarly, philosophers can (and do) doubt whether words can have meaning, whether it is possible that, if one person says something, another can understand the words at all, but the scientist makes a study with every intention of reporting it to fellow professionals, and therefore cannot enjoy such doubts!

Hence the picture of the scientist as the thoroughgoing and comprehensive sceptic about common-sense understandings unduly makes science out to be like philosophical scepticism, and does not note how selective actual scientific inquiry is and must be about its doubting of common sense. The extent to which it both (and simultaneously) doubts and depends upon common-sense understandings is especially consequential for sociology. The attitude of a real scientific investigator may indeed allow doubting of certain accepted features of the common-sense understandings of the world in which the scientific investigator dwells, e.g. in Copernicus's day the notion was that the earth was at the centre of the universe. Nevertheless, the conduct of the scientific examination itself has to be subordinate, in many respects, to the natural attitude. In fact, the scientific attitude has to take many things for granted and to count upon them as conditions for doing scientific work. It has to treat things as so much common sense for those within the world of science and, in many respects, for those outside the scientific community also.

## Intersubjectivity

The frequent criticism that Schütz makes the social world into something that exists entirely inside the head of the members of society has often led towards the criticism of ethnomethodology as itself an extreme form of subjectivism. Again, this reading of Schütz is far from accurate, since he argues that social reality is an *intersubjective* matter, i.e. the individuals making up a society do not each occupy their own, personal, distinct mental world; instead, they all exist within (allowing for adjustments of perspective) one and the same reality. In short, the social world is a world known in common to its inhabitants.

Schütz thus emphasises the following:

- The extent of each individual's understanding of the world is dependent upon the *social distribution of knowledge*: individuals make sense of the world around them in terms of what they know. Of course, most of what people know is acquired not by learning through or from their own first-hand experience but by learning from others, who, in turn, did not learn most of what they know through or from their own first-hand experience, and so on. For example, we all know, i.e. take it for granted, that the world is round, but we have found it out in school, not by trekking round the globe.
- The individual acts upon the basis of a *stock of knowledge to hand*, which (1) has been built up by being handed down from other members of the society; (2) has been derived from the social stock of knowledge; and (3) has been transferred to the individual through social arrangements such as child rearing in the family, teaching in school, on-the-job training and conversation among peers.

- The individual's rock-bottom assumption is not of living in a unique, private world, perceived entirely differently from the way others perceive it; on the contrary, the world is also known by others, and is known to them – other things being equal – in the same way as it is known to the individual. Of course, things do not appear identical from all points of view, but fundamental to each individual's point of view are assumptions which co-ordinate the differences associated with each individual's specific experience.

Concerning this third point, Schütz identifies two crucial suppositions:

1   the reciprocity of perspectives;
2   the interchangeability of standpoints.

In (1), people simply assume that the way they see things will be matched, reciprocated, by other persons, allowing for their different locations in space and their different places in the course of action. In our familiar example from Chapter 6, motorists driving at high speeds entrust their lives to this assumption: they expect and assume that drivers they can see behind them through their rearview mirror will have a view of their own car in front, and that their perception of the front of the car behind will be matched by the perceptions of those behind of the rear of their own car.

Assumption (2), the interchangeability of standpoints, entails that two or more parties, although in different places, see different but matching things and, vitally, that if they were to change places then they would also exchange perceptions. In effect, if the drivers were to be magically switched between cars, then the driver previously in front would now see exactly what the driver in the rear car had previously been seeing, and vice versa. For example, driver *A* at high speed and intending to change lanes switches on the indicator, and though *A* cannot personally see the rear indicator light flashing, he or she nevertheless assumes that the driver *B* in the car behind can see it and can see what driver *A* would see if positions were to be swapped, thereby receiving adequate warning of the manoeuvre.

For Schütz, it is an analytical problem to understand how people maintain their sense of inhabiting an intersubjective world, how it is the same for you as for me, allowing for various differences of position and background between us. Of course, maintaining this sense of the world known in common can sometimes be a problem for people in society; taking for granted the reciprocity of perspectives and the interchangeability of standpoints, and routinely counting on these assumptions, does not always work out. On occasion people can find themselves confronted with persons who do not behave in ways which accord with these assumptions. Schütz's own example, 'the stranger', is one type of person with whom such expectations are likely to fail.

## Multiple realities

Although Schütz emphasises the extent to which the meaning of events in the social world is routinely shared, with subjective variability being the exception rather than the rule, it might appear from the title of one of his essays in the *Collected Papers* (1962), 'On Multiple Realities', that he does encourage the opposite view. Such a view would stress that the things people understand to be real can and do vary widely among individuals, that each different individual does inhabit a very different reality; but that would once again be an entirely misleading way to read the essay. For Schütz is concerned, in the first instance, with the episodic nature of each individual's experience; over the course of a routine day the quality of our experience is not uniform, but variable, and we are likely to pass through a set of quite different states, all of which are experienced as real at the time they are undergone. For example, there is the contrast between being awake and dreaming while asleep. While we are awake, the events of daily life around us are understood as real, but when we are asleep and dreaming, the events in our dream are also experienced as real: we are frightened by frightening things in our dream, we fear for our life and so on.

These differences are two extremes. Our participation in various spheres of waking life, however, also involves variations in the kinds of things we treat as real and the ways we treat them.

## Finite provinces of meaning

Schütz refers to these different spheres of life as *finite provinces of meaning* in order to indicate the extent to which different (and, in a way, independent) standards of what is real routinely apply in daily life, e.g. in theatricals, science and religion.

Here Schütz is not being a relativist; he is not arguing that reality in any one of these provinces of meaning is just as authentic as reality in any other. Rather, he is attempting to describe the way people understand their own experiences, how they switch (so to speak) from one frame of reference to another within the round of their activities. Nevertheless, within people's experience, they treat one of these provinces of meaning as the paramount reality, namely, the world of daily life. He gives two reasons for this claim:

1   The switch into and out of the other provinces of meaning involves movement into and out of the world of daily life.
2   When events in the different spheres are compared, the standard of reality in daily life characteristically overrides the others.

We illustrate (1) with the example of going to the theatre, parking the car there, getting the ticket, finding the seat and waiting for the lights to go down: all are events in our daily life. After the curtain rises, we may become engrossed in the world – in the reality – projected by the play and, *while watching the play*, treat as real the fact, say, that a Martian visits a human household and exerts various kinds of strange effects on people and events. When the curtain falls, we return to the world of daily life, to the mundane activities of leaving the theatre, finding the car, and so on. We go home, put the cat out, lock the doors, and do other everyday things before going to bed, where we fall asleep and then enter the reality of dreams, where, again, all kinds of strange things (from an everyday point of view) occur and are experienced as real occurrences *while we are dreaming*. In brief, we move from one finite province of meaning to another by way of the world of daily life.

With reference to (2), when we are in the theatre, we are witnessing the presence in an ordinary household of an alien being treated as a real event, but on leaving the theatre we do not immediately phone friends to tell them that there is now proof that Martians are living among us. We know very well that, in the world of daily life, the events on stage are part of a theatrical performance and do not count as real occurrences. Similarly, we know that dreaming that we have divorced our spouse is not going to be recognised in the waking life as having actually gone through a divorce.

Finally, the relationship between science and common sense can also effectively be dealt with in terms of these arguments. Science is another of the finite provinces of meaning accessed from the world of daily life; it too accepts the paramountcy of the world of daily life. Note carefully, however, how we intend this point. It is illustrated by the physicist who starts the day by getting breakfast, reading the mail or the newspaper, driving to work, and chatting around the coffee machine, before entering the world of science, i.e. getting down to serious scientific work. Of course, for the working scientist the world of science is embedded within the world of daily life. This relationship between the world of daily life and the world of science as the working scientist's daily routine is nicely captured in a remark by a professor of physics, quoted by the anthropologist Clifford Geertz:

> Physics is like life; there's no perfection. It's never all sewed up. It's all a question of better, better yet, and how much time and interest do you really have in it? Is the universe really curved? It's not that cut and dried. Theories come and go. A theory isn't right and wrong. A theory has a sort of sociological position that changes as new information comes in. 'Is Einstein's theory correct?' You can take a poll and have a look. Einstein is rather 'in' right now. But who knows if it is 'true'? I think there is a view that physics has a sort of pristineness, rightness, trueness that I don't see in physics at all. To me, physics is the activity you do between breakfast and supper. Nobody said anything about Truth. Perhaps Truth is 'out'. One thinks, 'Well, this idea looks bad or looks good for general relativity.'
>
> (Geertz 1983: 162–63)

When engaged in the serious, scientific work, the scientist may deem irrelevant and may set aside from consideration certain routine matters of daily life: worrying if the pay cheque has come through is not an integral element in physics. While he or she is at serious work, the standards of the science decide what is real and what is not, whether the physicist has found some hitherto unknown particle of matter, or whether the marks on the plotter are merely results of ink leakages in the machine. But notice, even here Geertz's physicist describes how disagreement on these matters is resolved by reference to recognisably ordinary ways of deciding who is right or wrong: such things as taking a poll. At the end of the working day the physicist returns fully to the world of daily life and abides by its standard of reality: e.g. not arguing about needing to have a salary or to pay taxes because the notions of 'salary' and 'taxes' are not recognised as real in physics, and do not even appear in the vocabulary of physics, which is used to define reality when at work.

## Garfinkel: rethinking social order

Though Talcott Parsons (see Chapter 5) and Schütz had corresponded (Grathoff 1978), but mainly to their mutual frustration, it remained to Harold Garfinkel to work out the extent to which Schütz opened up a very different set of problems from those posed by Parsons, albeit the road he took was perhaps not one that Schütz himself did comprehend. In fact, working through the project initiated by Schütz carried Garfinkel far away from the kind of concept advocated by Parsons or any other sociologist and made the doing of sociology itself the main focus of attention. Initially Garfinkel applied to sociology itself the point about the relationship between science and common sense as finite provinces of meaning. Garfinkel wanted to draw out the implications of the sociologist engaging in this back-and-forth movement between the world of science and the world of daily life. Interestingly, the world of daily life for sociology, unlike other disciplines, is also the topic of inquiry for the sociologist and the subject for her or his use of the scientific attitude. Sociology is a research pursuit into the world of daily life, yet its systematic investigations are not only into daily life, but carried out within the world of daily life itself. A dangerously oversimplistic statement of Garfinkel's position is that this back-and-forth movement between the world of science and the world of daily life, i.e. between the scientific and common-sense orientations, leaves sociological thought, particularly its reasoning, in a profoundly ambiguous condition. Clearing up this ambiguity involves giving much more direct and explicit attention to the common-sense elements in sociological reasoning.

A main difference between Schütz and Parsons, who was taken as an exemplar of sociological thought and practice more generally, is in what they regard as analytically problematic. Remember that talk about common sense and communication as problematic entails the *sociologist* wondering about such matters rather than simply taking them for granted; it does not at all suggest that people in society do, or should, find them difficult or impossible to do. Garfinkel says that Parsons just takes it for granted that sociological research can be undertaken within society, that society is available as a world known in common between the members of society, and that the sociological investigator can readily share it with them. The fact that the investigator can assume that the world of daily life is (largely) known in common with those being researched is an essential assumption for communication between the investigator and those being researched, for it is only on the basis of their shared understandings, their mutually knowing what they are talking about, that people can communicate. Communication with those under investigation is not a trivial matter; it is an essential requirement for sociological research, the great bulk of which involves talking to, listening to or reading things by the members of society. Sociological research itself takes place within the world of daily life, and its conduct involves the researcher in finding his or her way around relationships based on everyday understandings. Whereas Parsons took for granted this set of conditions for doing sociological work without the need for further reflection on them, Schütz engendered the idea of making these conditions of sociological work themselves part of the field of study. After all, the sociological investigator making sense of the everyday environment and undertaking mutually intelligible communication with (other) members of society is only a special case of the fact that social life in general is conducted under the natural attitude.

Garfinkel used Schütz to transform the nature of the problem of social order, which was at the heart of sociology for Parsons and others.

## The problem of social order

As he posed it, Parsons intended the problem of order to be set at the deepest, most fundamental level of inquiry. For Garfinkel, however, Parsons's solution to the problem of order – shared values – itself presupposed the prior existence of a social order and so did not go deep enough. Values can only be shared if they can be spread from person to person, if people can make sense to one another, if they share enough understanding to be able to communicate with one another. The attempt to understand the conditions under which people can make sense of one another's activities thus becomes the content of Garfinkel's rethink, in terms of Schütz's notions, of Parsons's problem of order.

Garfinkel was convinced that this repositioning of the problem separated the fledgling venture of ethnomethodology from all other kinds of sociology. These other kinds overwhelmingly took the existence of a world with a common sense for granted. It was a given in their theories and a simple, unexamined presupposition of their research work. His approach, however, would be different in both respects and would not be directed at the same kinds of problems that other sociological theories sought to pose and solve. Whatever ethnomethodology was trying to do, it was not directly continuing the line of argument that stretched from Hobbes to Parsons.

## What is ethnomethodology?

We begin by reverting to the topic of reality. People acting under the auspices of the natural attitude and within the finite provinces of meaning treat many features of their environment as 'real', distinguishing them from other candidate features which are 'not real'. One of the key questions Garfinkel poses for ethnomethodology concerns the basis on which people decide whether something is real or not. For him, it is a topic of study. He is not asking whether people are right to proceed in the ways they do, or whether one way of deciding these things is better than another. He does not evaluate at all the ways people decide what is really going on before their very eyes. His exclusive intent is to describe and analyse the ways people decide 'what is really going on' and 'what has really happened', whatever these may be.

## Ethnomethodology and symbolic interactionism

On the face of it, ethnomethodology seems to be similar to symbolic interactionism. After all, symbolic interactionism shows much concern with the definition of the situation, and the idea of examining how people define the situation might seem almost identical to the conception we are now putting forward. Symbolic interactionism treats the definition of the situation as an interactional matter, emphasising the way definitions – shared meanings – are worked out between people interacting together in a certain setting. Garfinkel's ethnomethodology certainly accepts the focus on interactional matters, but its own programme is to treat them as methodical. The very label 'ethno-methodology' can be simply translated as 'the study of the methods in use among members of the society', or more fully as 'the study of the methods for sense-making and fact-finding in use among the members of the society'.

## Members' methods

Ethnomethodology's attention, then, is focused upon identifying the methods that members of society employ in deciding whether something is real or not, and upon understanding how the methods are employed in doing so.

## Members' methods

In daily life, deciding what is real and what is not amounts to making one or more of an extensive range of distinctions: between the real and the imagined, between fact and fiction, between truth and lies, between correct and incorrect results or conclusions, between true and false accusations, between the possible and the impossible, between what really happened and what was merely a dream.

Ethnomethodology, at its core, involves nothing other than the study of these things. It can obtain access to them by looking at those aspects of an activity which involve the making of such distinctions, i.e. the ways people, in going about their affairs in their daily lives, in their work, leisure, family or other activities, settle whatever questions arise as to what is 'actually the case', 'really so', 'surely a fact', 'unquestionably correct' and so on. The conduct of affairs in daily life is pervaded by the constant need to respond to such questions, to settle them, very much and quite routinely, as a basis for *organising action* – for deciding what to do next. Therefore, it provides us with a way into studying how action is organised in daily life. Clearly, then, the approach does not mean isolating one particular and limited aspect of people's sense-making and fact-finding methods, since these members' methods extensively pervade everyday activities.

These methods are quite ordinary, familiar and unsurprising ways that people inquire into and determine the reality of various things. For example, a very common method is the simple and familiar checking of one source of information against another. If, say, someone tells you about some event that sounds implausible, you might look in the newspaper or watch the TV news to see if it was reported there. If so, that would confirm what you were told. The reverse might work: seeing something reported on TV or in the paper, you might check with someone you knew who would have been involved in the reported matter in order to find out whether what you read in the newspaper was true, exaggerated or mostly made up. Obviously, there are a multitude of such methods, some of which involve considerably more elaborate activity than those we have just outlined, e.g. current work in physics checks out whether postulations about sub-atomic particles are correct and involves the use of machines (accelerators) which are many miles long and staffed by dozens if not hundreds of researchers. More mundanely, deciding the correctness of accusations of legal offences involves a dozen jurors listening to the adversarial presentation of evidence and argument in the courtroom prior to sequestration in a private room where, through perhaps protracted joint discussion, they have to arrive at a conclusion about the accusation.

For ethnomethodology, the definition of the situation and the determination of social reality are just abstract terms which refer to the quite ordinary and, to the members of society, entirely familiar ways of deciding whether something is true or false, correct or inaccurate, objective or prejudiced, factual or just made up. Such questions arise in many different areas of social life and are resolved by methods which have many features specific to the kind of activities about which the decisions are to be made, e.g. the jury operation in courtrooms, the experiment in scientific laboratories, and checking and double-checking the figures can be found in all kinds of financial transactions. Ethnomethodology's central proposal is for the close, detailed examination of the ways the members of society go about defining social reality in their everyday affairs. It aims to identify these ways very specifically. A main rationale for this approach is that much of the stuff of social life is missing from sociological analysis; sociological descriptions of this or that activity characteristically display what Garfinkel has termed a 'missing whatness'. In other words, what makes the affairs carried out within the world of daily life the affairs they are is simply taken for granted. The fact that the people under study are engaged in specific work, e.g. medical treatment, repairing some technological equipment, teaching elementary mathematics, or arguing guilt or innocence, is often taken as the pretext rather than the focus for sociological analysis. For this reason, symbolic interactionism is more interested in similarities between different kinds of work and aims to emphasise the extent to which common social processes are to be found in all or many kinds of seemingly different work, while ethnomethodology is more interested in identifying details of the specific kind of work.

For example, the sociology of science traditionally concerned itself with the structure of the scientific community, the shape of scientists' careers, the prestige hierarchies used to rank disciplines and scientists, and the reward and award systems that motivate and acknowledge scientific achievement. There was very little about scientific *work* in this literature. The fact that working scientists spend immense amounts of their time carrying out observations and experiments in laboratories, observatories and similar places of work was barely noticed until ethnomethodological studies helped to stimulate a now thriving field of sociological studies of laboratory science.

Further, while there may be respects in which the work involved in, say, diagnosing disease or identifying a scientific finding may have similarities in terms of the way the actions involved are organised, the fact remains that gynaecology is sufficiently different from astronomy for workers in each not to be interchangeable. From the point of view of understanding how actions are organised, it is entirely reasonable to suppose that such organisation may be *endogenous*, i.e. specific to the activity under consideration. Consequently, we have to understand how the actions are organised to do that work and not some other kind, in turn requiring us to identify the methods participants use to carry out the work; e.g. how doctors make a provisional diagnosis, confirm it as correct and prescribe further action; or how in an observatory the astronomers suspect, then confirm, that they are on the verge of a major astronomical discovery, i.e. how their work in the observatory establishes the reality of a galactically remote celestial object.

## The situatedness of action

Another key reason for this focus of attention is the concern for the analysis of action as practical action. It is an ineluctable feature of people's actual actions that they are *situated*, i.e. they must be carried out among and through particular circumstances; those performing them cannot adopt a take-it-or-leave-it attitude to these circumstances. For example, potential bank robbers wishing to make use of an escape vehicle face a parking problem. The streets in city centres are crowded and densely parked and it is difficult to find a legal parking space. If one is about to rob a bank, one might not want to draw the attention of the law to a vehicle which is double-parked, or in a prohibited area (see Letkeman 1973). Bank robbers cannot, then, shrug off or set aside as 'trivial', or 'uninteresting', or 'inessential to bank robbery', the need to park their car, and to park it in a way which will not attract undue attention. To be successful, they need to deal with this problem, which, of course, may vary between one city centre and another.

**Situatedness**

Any real course of action involves responding to the specificities of its circumstances; it must be shaped to the particular conditions, which are its environment, and use them as the 'materials' for its accomplishment. In so doing, it must contend with *exigencies* or *contingencies*, i.e. unruly conditions, which arise unexpectedly and even unforeseeably among a given set of circumstances, in order to achieve success.

Thus understanding the organisation of action involves understanding the ways its course is structured by those carrying the action out and under the practical circumstances – the situated conditions – within which the action is to be done.

Recognising the practical situatedness of action brings out the *improvisational* element in even the most routinised, standardised and rigidly prescribed of action sequences. Practical contingencies can afflict even the best-planned arrangement of affairs and, of course, the overwhelmingly large proportion of things people do is far from being rigidly prescribed or highly standardised. On this view, understanding the organisation of action is a matter of understanding how its perpetrators work out the course of the action sequence even as they engage in it, how they work out what to do next over the course of any sequence of activities. Such understanding necessarily involves the sociologist in paying just as close analytical attention as the participants pay practical attention to the specific circumstances of any chosen course of action, for, as noted, those perpetrating the actions have to handle or manage innumerable and assorted features of their acting circumstances in order to produce and succeed in their elected course of action. The attention to particulars may need, then, to be intense and close indeed.

Attending to the immediate situation is also crucial for resolving issues of meaning and sense. One of Garfinkel's most notorious usages is the concept of *indexicality*. This term had been coined by philosophers of language – *not* by Garfinkel – to note the fact that ordinary language contains many terms whose meaning is tied to the particular occasions of their use. An obvious example is the use of pronouns, e.g. 'it', 'that' or 'theirs'. Garfinkel noted that the point could be generalised beyond specific classes of words. Any remark can be taken in different ways according to how it is heard contextually. The question thus becomes precisely how someone hears a remark as having an unambiguous, obvious meaning; precisely how is it understood in relation to the relevant circumstances of the context in which it is produced?

## What is conversation analysis?

A well-known exemplification of these concerns is *conversation analysis*. Originating as an offshoot of ethnomethodology's inquiries, it is now a quite independent venture and occupies a significant position among disciplines concerned with the study of language, albeit – like ethnomethodology itself – currently marginal within sociology.

The motivations for developing conversation analysis were those ethnomethodology proposed for the study of action: to examine action for its practical, endogenous organisation. Conversation is an interactional activity in which participants fit their conduct – in this case their talk – to one another as the activity proceeds. Harvey Sacks, the founder of conversation analysis, saw that conversation must be practically organised, i.e. organised in and over its course by those conducting it.

## How conversation analysis works

The use of audio recordings of people's conversational activities makes it possible to study in close detail the step-by-step organisation of courses of action, since the audio recordings can be played over and over again and the most careful transcriptions of their content made. These transcriptions capture a vast amount of detail about the precise form of the utterances constituting the conversation and the way they fit together, yielding the kind of detail which would simply evade, say, the taker of field notes.

The study of conversation allows, too, for the examination of sense-making operations, for, of course, carrying on a conversation involves making reciprocal sense of each other's contributions, understanding what each is saying. The possession of a retrievable record of the talk allows inspection of utterances to see how, from the form the utterance takes, it can be understood as the parties to the talk understood it. Such sense-making is, of course, an *embedded* affair, done under conversational conditions and in conversational time, i.e. the parties to the exchange have to understand each other and decide what to say on their own behalf while keeping the conversation going, so that virtually an immediate response is required the great bulk of the time. Further, the organisation of conversation has a thoroughly improvised character; it is worked out over its course. Although conversations do have an ordered course, moving from openings through a middle phase to closings, and often involve an orderly progression from topic to topic, it is not decided before the conversation commences what is going to be talked about or how the matters talked about will be spoken of. Although the parties co-ordinate their moves from phase to phase and from topic to topic of the conversation, they do not do so according to any explicitly worked-out procedures decided in advance. At each point in the conversation, they work out what to do next and how to do whatever must be done next in ways that contribute to and achieve an order for the organisation of the talk – not merely its order at this point now reached, but its overall order.

Last, but not least, the formation of a contribution to a conversation is very specifically circumstanced, and the production of a conversation's orderly progression involves managing, during the conversation, the contingencies, the exigencies, which afflict it. The specificities of what has been said and done up to this point in a given conversation are essential to deciding what a current contributor should say and how he or she should say it in order to ensure that it is appropriately understood in the light of all that has been said before. For example, he or she may have to respond to the exigency of being joined by a newcomer when the discussion is in mid-topic. From the point of view of how conversationalists understand the current talk, the analysis proceeds on the assumption that they operate with two central questions:

1 Why that now?
2 What next?

## Conversational turn-taking

From studying conversation in terms of the practical asking and answering of these two questions, conversation analysis came to give pride of place to the *turn-taking* organisation of conversational talk, eventually developing an elaborately systematic account of the way turns at talk are shared out among participants in talk.

> **Turn-taking**
>
> Whatever conversationalists talk about, they do so by each taking turns at talking: one says something, another replies to that, a third comments on the second response, the first speaks again, and so on. Whatever the parties to a conversation are talking about, the way they talk must be done within the framework of such an 'ongoing' distribution of turns.

Consequently, one task for the investigation of talk must be into the allocation of turns with respect to two principal problems in such a distribution:

1 that the person now speaking can complete a turn at speaking; and
2 in such a way that as soon as the first has completed a turn the next can immediately commence a turn.

Thus extensive attention is paid to the ways the form of an utterance (the talk occupying a turn-at-talk) conveys information about when it will be complete. As a simple example, the question (and utterance)

A:   Can I ask you a question?

provides an opportunity for A to speak again. The question format calls upon another speaker, B, to answer and, perhaps, to give permission to ask the question:

B:   Sure.

A can then ask:

A:   Are you married?

'Can I ask you a question?' is characteristically understood as a request preliminary to the asking of a somewhat unusual, delicate or personal question; it would be surprising if the question projected by 'Can I ask you a question?' was 'Do you know today's date?'

   In such a simple sequence the production of information about when an utterance will be complete is interwoven with the *turn-distributing operation*, i.e. the initial question occasions that another person should speak next, e.g. A asks the question, but it also provides him or her with a chance to speak again. After B's response to the initial question, there is the opportunity to ask the question prefigured by it. The recognition of completed turns-at-talk and of opportunity for turns-at-talk involves also the examination of *speaker selection* arrangements, i.e. the ways either the current speaker selects a next speaker, or a next speaker self-selects. 'Can I ask you a question?' selects a specific person as next speaker, while 'Does anybody know where Tom is?' indicates what a next speaker should do – say where Tom is, if she or he knows – but does not indicate which of the persons addressed should answer.

   In this way, the forms for circulating turns among conversationalists can be treated as highly general; they operate regardless of the specific character of the utterances comprising them and of the activities they might be carrying out. Notwithstanding this generality, through a succession of alternating turns-at-talk conversationalists do produce an orderly organisation of talk about whatever they might be talking about. They differentiate the conversation into *episodes*, which they open and close quite naturally. Conversation analysis focuses also upon this episodic organisation of conversations and the ways such episodes are built and bounded. For example, the opening episodes of conversation often involve exchanges of greetings. Again, progressive moves can be made from beginning the conversation to arriving at its first *topic*, involving the way participants to a conversation organise their talk so as to be talking about the same thing, i.e. addressing a common topic. There are also ways for moving towards closing the conversation. For example, careful and extended attention may be paid to an exchange, early in a phone call:

A:   Are you doin' anythin'?
B:   I'm just watchin' *The X Files*.

where the availability of the parties for conversation is dealt with by A's question, indicating that A has called up for a prolonged conversation and is giving B the opportunity to say she is not available for conversation just now. The answer provides that B is indeed doing something – watching a TV show – but that this is nothing much to be doing, and not something that takes priority over conversing with A. Perhaps A has not called up to talk about anything specific, but just to talk; then A and B face the issue of finding something, a topic, to talk about.

Here the fact that B has *The X Files* on the TV provides a possible something to be talked about.

Of course, it is simply not possible, within the few pages we can devote to it, to convey anything of the detail and intricacy with which conversation analysis has examined the finely detailed course of conversation's structure. All of its questions are asked and answered in terms of the portrayal of the ways the conversationalists themselves confront and manage conversation as a practical matter. For example, just how do you say things so as to ask for something without seeming to have rung someone up only to ask a favour? As stressed earlier, conversation has an organisation, which is in use among conversationalists themselves to produce the very conversations that are so ordered. The orderliness correspondingly exhibited is recognisable and intelligible to the conversationalists. Arrangements for turn-taking do not result in successive turns-at-talk which are meticulously alternated, with one beginning immediately upon another's precise completion. There are frequent gaps and overlaps between turns-at-talk. Very commonly, there are either brief pauses between utterances or brief periods when people talk simultaneously. There are occasions when a gap or an overlap itself becomes a topic for conversation analysis, but for the conversationalists the occurrence of such pauses and overlaps is a feature of conversation that is natural, unremarkable and orderly.

In conclusion, the analysis of conversation is that of a *self-organising* system. This brings us to a point at which it is useful to return to the question 'what is ethnomethodology?' and to consider it as the study of the self-organisation of activities.

## Studying activities as self-organising: neglecting the big picture?

The examination of the intricacies of stretches of quite ordinary – even very dull – conversation does not draw the attention or approval of many sociologists.

### Criticism of conversation analysis

The determination of conversation analysis to engage with the minutiae of conversation seems to many to be a matter of taking to a logical extreme the more general position of ethnomethodology, i.e. focusing on the concrete and specific details of localised instances of interaction without attention to the big picture of social life within which they are located.

To many sociologists, it is self-evident that though two people might be having a conversation about what they did on their day off, they will be having it in the context of (say) their daily work for the corporate giant IBM, which is a major international company, part of American society at the beginning of the twenty-first century, and involved in the progressive globalisation of capital.

How can one understand what people are doing in particular cases without reference to this entire complex environment?

We did say that ethnomethodology does not agree to play the game of sociological theory. One of the rules of procedure for ethnomethodology precisely prevents it from adopting such a course of argument, for to adopt it would be to abandon the concept of social scenes as self-organising. From ethnomethodology's point of view, sociological theory has a deeply ambiguous character: the sociological researcher is conceived to be someone who can, apparently, not only inhabit the world of daily life like anyone else, but also step out of this world and observe it from outside, from above. In order to eliminate the latter claim, ethnomethodology treats sociology as done entirely *within the world of daily life*; sociology acquires its materials and its reported observations from within this same world.

Further, it is commonplace for sociological theory to assume that the solution to the problem of social order is to be found outside the immediate social scene or situation. For example, the orderly behaviour of persons is assumed to be due to some prior event, such as socialisation into role expectations, or to some structural condition, such as a hierarchical system of mechanisms controlling the present situation. These ways of conceiving social order, however, tend to result in taking for granted the presently observable orderliness of a social scene, e.g. people waiting to board their holiday flight, seeing people off, waiting for people to arrive at an airport. There is no concern with the way the people involved act in order to make their activities visible to an observer, *any* observer (including one another), as elements in such an orderly arrangement. Given the points we have made above about the exigencies and contingencies of activity, how exactly do those present within a social scene know just what to do in order to fit into its routine, standard organisation?

## Mutual intelligibility

It is not an incidental feature of the organisation of actions that they are produced in ways which exhibit their sense or *intelligibility* to others. It is not an accidental fact about our actions that they are recognisable for what they are to others; much of our activity is directed towards, or conducted for, witnessing by others. Intimately interwoven into our actions is a concern that we perform so that others should be able to identify our actions, to see what we are doing, to understand what we are saying. Since actions are very widely oriented to others and produced in co-ordination and collaboration with them, this concern for the identifiable, intelligible, recognisable character of conduct is a feature not just of utterances, but also of conduct more generally.

The attempt to express this concern has given ethnomethodology one of its 'terms of art', namely, the *accountable organisation of actions*, i.e. the way one aspect of the organisation of courses of actions is a concern to make them observable, intelligible, recognisable, identifiable, and amenable to being talked about and otherwise reportable. To say action-arrangements are accountable is not to say that they are so in the sense in which the term is often used, i.e. subject to, and responsive to, overseeing, as when governments propose to make 'what teachers do in classrooms' accountable to the electorate. Rather, the notion of 'accountable' used here means only 'so organised as to make it possible for those involved in the activities to describe and otherwise report the organisation of these activities'. Describing and otherwise reporting encompasses all imaginable forms: charts, diagrams, tables, brochures, sets of job specifications, remarks in casual conversations, and so interminably on. Accountability *makes visible* the organisation that activities have. Necessarily it involves recognising the circumstantial constraints that impinge upon someone's possible courses of action. How is it, for example, that in producing an activity the person displays awareness that there is a task to be done here and now which cannot be put off until later, that he or she is answerable to others for this task, that doing it adequately means coping with various constraints which are beyond his or her own control, and so forth? Someone's reasoning about these matters is displayed in his or her actions, and it frequently provides for their – the actions' – intelligibility.

This concern with the mutual intelligibility of activities means that attention is paid to what can be called the *visibility arrangements* of social settings, the ways people arrange the environments of their activities, and the activities themselves, to make readily available to others a sense of what is going on, thereby enabling others to understand how the setting works. For example, courtroom hearings of traffic offences in the US are so organised that those waiting for their case to come up can observe and overhear previous cases and, from the way those are dealt with, learn how to behave when their turn to enter a plea comes around. In these ways, ordinary members of the public show themselves to be 'practical sociologists', i.e. they can and do engage in practical sociological reasoning.

## Doing sociology from within

Ethnomethodology's own proposal, then, is to make practical sociological reasoning its main, even exclusive, topic of study.

### Practical sociological reasoning

This is found to inform and organise activity of all kinds and in all areas of life. Regardless of the position of activities within the status and moral ranking of societies, any and all activities in society can be examined as applications of practical sociological reasoning. Of course, the fact that they are looked up to or looked down on itself enters into the practical sociological reasoning.

Not unexpectedly, practical sociological reasoning also pervades professional sociological work, so that the work of those who make their living under the occupational title 'sociologist' can also be examined in the same way as, say, divining water, shoplifting, and the work of ethnomethodologists themselves. The pursuit of this interest defines ethnomethodology's programme and has led to studies of such occupations as those of astrophysicists, musicians, dentists, the police, salespeople, truckdrivers and air-traffic controllers at work; and of such activities as mathematical calculation, plumbing repairs, coping with the effects of blindness, using a metronome to keep time in piano-playing, training in kung fu, telling a story to a class of 6-year-olds, and eliciting a confession from a murder suspect. In addition, studies have been made of professional sociological activities such as interviewing an educational psychologist about his work, and doing ethnography of a half-way house for drug offenders.

## Relativism again, and reflexivity

We now return to the issue of relativism posed at the outset of this chapter. The charge of relativism might seem to be justified by the remarks which we have just been making. After all, water-divining and astrophysics have been mentioned in the same breath and it has been proposed that magical and scientific activities should be studied in the same way. In so doing, we have also transgressed the status rankings by employing putatively crazy or deluded ideas, e.g. equating divination with paradigms of respectability like medical work. In addition, there is the 'disprivileging' of the professional sociologist *vis-à-vis* the other members of society: in comparison with other members of the society, the only distinctive feature of the kind of sociological reasoning done by the professional sociologist is that it is done for a living, whereas everyone else does sociological reasoning as an unreflective part of whatever affairs they carry out in society. According to those who hold a relativist (mis)conception of ethnomethodology, the lessons ostensibly to be drawn are that:

- scientific sociology is no better than common-sense sociology;
- physics is no better than water-divining; and
- therefore, any way of thinking is as good as any other.

Worries about relativism connect with a further problem: *reflexivity*.

### Reflexivity

This point derives from one further element of the above remarks. According to ethnomethodology's logic, the work of professional sociologists (including ethnomethodologists themselves) is amenable to study in ethnomethodological terms. This point is understood in terms of a notion of reflexivity, which means 'applying to itself'.

It is fashionable these days to note that the doing of sociology is itself a social activity and therefore sociology's concepts and theories should be applicable to itself. For example, it is a criticism of, say, functionalist arguments that they do not apply to themselves, that functionalist analysis is not readily provided with reflexive arguments. Ethnomethodology is seen as pioneering this kind of view, i.e. maintaining that its arguments should apply to itself. As understood, however, this notion carries heavier freight, for it is also argued that self-application of arguments all too often results in self-subversion.

### Self-subversion

If functionalist arguments were to be applied to functionalist arguments themselves, they would be discredited. For example, Durkheim's model functionalist account of religion reveals that religion is not really about religion and is not really about God and worship; it is about something else, namely, sustaining social order. Presumably, the application of functionalist arguments to functionalism would show that functionalism is not really about science and knowledge, but really about something else, namely, sustaining social solidarity among sociologists. Hence, in their very application, the arguments would effectively deny their own validity.

In the view of those currently excited by reflexivity, the fact is that, in general, sociological approaches simply cannot afford to apply this principle since it would undermine their very character. The only valid possibility would be to recognise openly that sociological knowledge is impossible because, on the principle of reflexivity, all sociological positions are self-subverting, and a properly reflexive attitude would embrace this unavoidable fact. Reflexivity would bring out the self-subverting tendencies in all other sociological views, while ensuring that it kept to the fore the fact that ethnomethodology itself is no exception to the principle of reflexivity and must therefore undermine itself.

Ethnomethodology is, alas, a disappointment to those who see the potential merits of reflexivity for challenging professional sociology, for it does not seem too keen to develop its full force. As already suggested, however, there are reasons to hesitate in attributing any such notions to ethnomethodology. Garfinkel did give the word 'reflexivity' a prominent place in his initial exposition, 'What Is Ethnomethodology?' – in his *Studies* (1967) – but he quickly came to rue the fact even though he did not himself use the term in the manner others currently use it.

### Garfinkel and reflexivity

Garfinkel used 'reflexivity' to draw attention to the way practical sociological reasoning is embedded in the very activities it concerns, e.g. the way practical sociological reasoning of jurors is done in the jury room, as part of the jury's work and in and through the jury's organisation. Practical sociological reasoning is not done in abstraction from activities, but from their very midst and as an integral part of them. Hence the examination of such reasoning cuts both ways: it considers how the practical sociological reasoning goes into organising, into carrying out, an activity; reciprocally, it considers the way in which the reasoning is itself shaped by the organisation of the activities it is involved in.

Consequently, the *substance* of such practical sociological reasoning will vary from activity to activity. A group of software engineers, meeting to review progress on a software engineering project, reason about the software, while what is reasoned about among jurors is the guilt or innocence of a defendant. What is reasoned about in sociology and also in ethnomethodology is 'social order', but, as we have seen, the terms in which this problem is conceived are very different. There is no discomfort or self-subversion for ethnomethodology in accepting the fact that it too employs practical sociological reasoning to get its work done, thereby providing just another exemplification of the kinds of phenomena it likes to inspect. Of course, ethnomethodology's practical sociological reasoning is itself reflexive to ethnomethodology's own work activities, something embedded, organised in and organising of these activities.

Congruently, the mention of physics and water-divining in the same breath carries no relativistic implications, for the point being made is not epistemological, i.e. about the merits of these activities as bearers of truth; it is simply methodological, i.e. about the way the organisation of these respective activities may be viewed. Each has its ways of practical sociological reasoning and each, along with any other social activity, including sociology (and ethnomethodology) itself, is a candidate for examination in terms of its use of such reasoning in order to organise its daily affairs. At the same time, it must be noted that while physics and water-divining both involve practical sociological reasoning, the substance over which such reasoning is done, the problems that such reasoning confronts, and the ways such reasoning is organised are distinctive in many important respects from the activities of which the reasoning is a constituent part. There is no inclination here either to obliterate the difference between physics and water-divining or to deliver any judgement on their worth. Such judgements figure for ethnomethodology only in so far as they enter into the practical sociological reasoning of the respective activities; perhaps water diviners feel hard done by because their work is regarded as dubious and misguided relative to that of physicists, who are held in high esteem, even though water diviners cannot see why they themselves are denied such status. Ethnomethodology simply does not say that water-divining is as good as physics, or that physics is only as good as water-divining. Since ethnomethodology's concern is with the organisation of activities, such judgements are irrelevant; the only comment it can make is, simply, 'No comment!'

## Small and big pictures (again)

For those who would radicalise sociology towards relativism and self-deconstruction (see Chapter 10), ethnomethodology proves a disappointment. If appropriately deemed a pioneer of relativism and reflexivity, then it has failed to develop further its pioneering moves. Worse, it seems that these attributions might be false, i.e. ethnomethodology has been neither relativist nor reflexive (in the required sense). However, if it is a disappointment on that side, then it has also been a disappointment to those who would continue the 'classical tradition' of sociological theory. Their disappointment is often expressed as a criticism.

### Critics' views of ethnomethodology

Ethnomethodology involves only the study of face-to-face relationships, and has nothing to say about the complex social systems, which have been the main topic of the classical tradition of Marx, Durkheim and Weber. It is not just that ethnomethodology is silent on these matters, but rather that its silence involves (allegedly) a denial of the existence of such structures. Ethnomethodology sets out to be a comprehensive sociology, not just a specialist branch, but assumes (wrongly, say the critics) that the only social reality is face-to-face interaction among individuals. This view denies the existence of real phenomena which provide the causal conditions for the very face-to-face interactions studied by the ethnomethodologist.

For example, ethnomethodology cannot explain why the software engineering business has grown up in the Western world and why computerisation has been so rapidly and widely accepted in business and many other fields. Hence it cannot explain why or how in the first place the software engineers mentioned above are gathering in an engineers' meeting to talk about it. Rather than being a full-scale, fully comprehensive sociology, the best ethnomethodology can hope to be (the argument goes) is a specialism within sociology, which focuses upon small-scale social phenomena and face-to-face situations. For many such critics the logic is: there is a need for a *synthesis* of sociological thought, which will find a place for ethnomethodology that actually complements the theoretical approaches of its ostensible rivals. (See the discussion of synthesising thinkers in Chapter 13.)

However, it is something of a misnomer to talk about face-to-face situations as the situations that ethnomethodologists study, with the attendant suggestion that they are hermetically sealed against the larger social environment. For it is plain that the nature of that larger social environment frequently, and in a multiplicity of ways, enters into the practical sociological reasoning of those engaged in a situated activity.

**Ethnomethodologists' views**

It is in and through face-to-face situations that this social environment is made visible to those involved (and to sociological researchers sitting in). Indeed, the expression 'visibility arrangements' has been coined to identify those aspects of face-to-face situations which serve to display to the participants the relevance and organisation of the larger social complexes within which they are situated, acting and themselves organising.

Finally, what appears to critics as the wilful neglect of the wider social structure is to ethnomethodologists themselves the product of a principled theoretical decision: to treat as the context of social activities the one that is oriented to as such by those they study. Ethnomethodologists have repeatedly explained the connection between their treatment of social order as something done within the local scene and their self-imposed denial, i.e. their self-discipline as they see it, in declining to solve the problem of social order by appealing to facts external to the local scene, e.g. personality, norms and social structures. Nevertheless, the charge of neglecting the wider context refuses to go away. For ethnomethodologists, however, the charge carries no weight, since it amounts to nothing more than a refusal to recognise the difference at the *theoretical* level between ethnomethodology's assumptions and those of other approaches. It amounts to criticising ethnomethodology for not being a more traditional sociology. For ethnomethodology, there simply is no big picture to be had, since there is no standpoint outside the common-sense world of daily life upon which the would-be painter of this picture can rest the canvas. The sociologist's big picture purports to be constructed from outside, but our discussion of Schütz should have made clear that ethnomethodology has no truck with this assumption.

## Conclusion

Ethnomethodology is both credited with and blamed for making one of the most critical contributions to the destabilising of the sociological orthodoxies which had established themselves in Anglo-American sociology. It was taken as presenting a direct challenge to the possibility of any kind of 'objective' understanding of social reality and, consequently, to the realisation of any sociological dreams of grand theory. Ethnomethodology, like symbolic interaction, has been marginalised within sociology and it continues to flourish most extensively in terms of conversation analysis, which is a busy area of work, but one as often as not having ties with linguistics rather than sociology. While marginalised, ethnomethodology none the less remains controversial, something that very commonly has at least to be noticed, to be either commended as a precursor of poststructuralist and postmodern attitudes within sociology, or condemned for playing such a disruptive role within sociological theory. In this latter respect it has intensified many of those oppositions which the 'synthesists' of sociological theory (see Chapter 13) must now attempt to reconcile, with some of ethnomethodology's insights having to be incorporated into the theoretical mix.

## Questions

1 What is the 'natural attitude'? Is it a good description of how you understand and act in the world? In what ways, and when, do you change from this way of being in the world to another?

2 Why does Garfinkel go from the natural attitude to 'members' methods'? Does this move make sense? In what ways is this a solid foundation for sociological studies? Is it more logical than the alternatives, e.g. symbolic interactionism?

3 How does Garfinkel redefine the 'problem of social order'? In what ways is his solution to this different to those of Durkheim or Parsons? Does it make sense to think about this in the way Garfinkel suggests?

4 Why is conversation analysis taken by some to be a way of doing ethnomethodological studies? Why might others disagree? Is it 'about' the everyday world or really a different sort of linguistics?

5 List some of the features of 'practical sociological reasoning'. Are these interesting, trivial, pointless or fascinating (or more than one)? Do they describe how things get done in the social world more effectively than the other social theories you have looked at? Does their 'trivia' mean they are *unimportant*? Why?

6 What does Garfinkel mean by 'reflexivity'? What other understandings of the term might there be? Why have some criticised Garfinkel for his use of this concept? Are they right?

7 Is ethnomethodology a way of doing sociology or an *alternative* to sociology? Why? What makes ethnomethodology look so different to the other theories you have thought about? Does it matter that it is so different?

### Next steps

Wagner (1970) provides a useful collection of Schütz's writings, and Turner (1974) collects an excellent range of the early, classic ethnomethodological studies. Button (1991) is a more advanced text, focusing on how ethnomethodology 'respecifies' fundamental issues in the human sciences.

A short introduction to the perspective is provided by Sharrock and Anderson (1986), and Heritage (1984) is a comprehensive study of the development of Garfinkel's thought and its application by others.

# PART III

# The European tradition

As we saw in Part II, developments in American sociology in the twentieth century tended to work within broadly Weberian and Durkheimian traditions: Parsons tried to integrate the ideas of both thinkers, the symbolic interactionists developed Weber's commitment to methodological individualism, and the ethnomethodologists – at least in part – sought to 'respecify' key ideas about social order apparent in Durkheim's thought. At the same time, however, European sociology was increasingly concerned with developing insights from Marx's work, which was generally speaking neglected in the USA and Canada.

The Marxist tradition in European sociology starts with a dilemma: if Marx was right, then a revolutionary transformation of society should have taken place. The contradictions at the heart of capitalism would have resulted in either the rising up of the working class to destroy it or it collapsing as a consequence of economic shocks (or both). This did not occur. Although 'communist' revolutions did take place in the twentieth century, most notably in Russia, these were unsuccessful or absent in the most advanced economic powers, those which Marx identified as most likely to experience such shocks first.

The Marxian solution to this problem was to rethink the relationship between the economic 'base' and cultural 'superstructure'. The latter must be, it was argued, more important than had previously been thought. Lukács attempted to theorise this relationship in explicitly Hegelian terms: the relationship between our experience of the world and how the world actually is, he argued, is subject to *reification*: we see the world we create as if it were something external that confronts us, and so our understanding of how things are is systematically distorted. Gramsci took these ideas further, construing the realm of understanding as an ongoing struggle for *hegemony*, the dominance of one way of looking at the world over its alternatives: the world, for Gramsci, is ideological through and through. Finally, developing on these approaches, members of the Frankfurt School produced a series of critiques of the contemporary world focusing on the ways in which people are 'bought off', through more permissive governments ('repressive tolerance'), bureaucratic and scientific rationality ('instrumental reason'), popular culture ('the culture industry') and so on. In short, ideology came to be viewed as something so pervasive and powerful that any possibility of social change became questionable.

Parallel to the work of the Frankfurt School, other European scholars in the 1950s and 1960s – in particular in France – were developing new ways of looking at society derived from entirely different sources. The structural linguistics of Saussure and Freud's psychoanalysis provided ways of examining the structures of thought and their social bases. Lévi-Strauss, an anthropologist, attempted to show that the logical structures of the mind – and, indeed, the binary operations of brain cells – were related to the structures of myths, totems, symbols and so on in complex and detailed ways. The 'primitive' and the 'modern' have more in common than is at first apparent, and a correct *structural* analysis of the former can reveal much about the latter. We will use Lévi-Strauss's work *The Jealous Potter* to illustrate how this kind of analysis maps out in practice. Barthes, in his 'Myth Today', attempted to characterise our understanding of the world in similarly structural ways: drinking a glass of wine is totemic in French society, for instance, because it is tied in its meaning to notions of control and sociability – even though the production and distribution of wine requires the operation of capitalist forces that directly contradict such notions. Language and meaning become traps, which systematically prevent us from seeing the world 'as it is'. Barthes's ideas, as we will see, were tremendously influential in the movements that were to follow those outlined in this part of the book. Finally, we will examine the work of Althusser, who took Lévi-Strauss's anti-humanism and anti-individualism and Barthes's notion of meaning as a prison to their furthest conclusions. Maintaining a traditional Marxian economic analysis, Althusser sought to show that ideology – which is *ultimately* derived from the economic base of society, but is *relatively* autonomous in practice – determined the ways we understand the world in far more radical ways than his predecessors in the Western Marxist tradition. Notions of the individual, free will, liberty and so on are all ideological constructs, and their centrality to how we see the world means that ideology may be a trap from which there can be no escape. By combining structuralist analysis and the problematic of the Western Marxist tradition, Althusser appeared to come to more conservative conclusions about the possibility of social change than his alleged 'conservative' predecessors Durkheim and Parsons.

## CHAPTER EIGHT

# Western Marxism

---

### Chapter overview

Just as Parsons, the symbolic interactionists and the ethnomethodologists transformed Weberian and Durkheimian ideas, Marx's work was subjected to a series of transformations over the course of the twentieth century. These were largely organised around the question of why capitalism has persisted, even grown, and nascent revolutionary movements have failed. In this chapter some attempts to address these issues are considered. Lukács's strongly Hegelian interpretation of Marx, focusing on a theory of knowledge and a reconsideration of the Hegelian 'subject', forms the starting point. Gramsci's concept of *hegemony* is introduced and explained. Finally, the ideas of the Frankfurt School (including Horkheimer, Adorno and Marcuse), which attempt to address issues of culture, reason and freedom, are introduced and their relevance for subsequent theorists explained. Increasingly, the work of these thinkers came to focus on a critical engagement with the concept of 'reason' – so central to Weber's thought – with enormous consequences for subsequent developments in sociological theory.

---

## Introduction

Here we will be dealing with the tendency for theorists to give rather Weberian answers to a Marxist question.

This much seems indisputable about Marx's views: societies do not persist forever; they are often transformed into very different kinds of societies, and features leading to such transformations are present in the society as preconditions for its transformation. While essential doctrines for Marxism, these beliefs are not specially distinctive, much less so than the altogether more controversial assumptions that structural transformations involve total transformation in the society's structure, that such transformations must be a result of irreconcilable conflicts within the structure of the existing society, and that some definite social class must be the key vehicle for these transformations. In total, these latter assumptions generate, with respect to capitalism, yet another assumption: the natural course of capitalist development will result in a working-class revolution.

Equally plainly, no such revolution has taken place. The Marxist revolutions that did take place did not occur in advanced capitalist societies, nor were they revolutions of the working class as such (though fractions of the working class might have supported them). The expected working-class revolution did not arise and, in view of these assumptions, the equally natural Marxist question is: why not? What stopped from happening the proletarian insurrection that should have taken place?

Weber argued there was no reason to expect any such revolution. Revolutionary change cannot be ruled out, but, as we indicated, the transformation of a class into an organised political force is the exception rather than the rule, and occurs only under very specific and contingent conditions. The capacity for common consciousness and focused political commitment and organisation is not *inherent* in the nature of a working class, but could result from contingent circumstances. From this point of view, there is nothing to explain.

The Weberian answer to the Marxist question was to be sought in the cultural transformation of societies and, in particular, in those processes of rationalisation which were now interpreted as nullifying the revolutionary potential of the working masses. The working-class revolution was, in the end, *administrated* out of existence. In sloganised Marxist terms the state was conceived as an oppressive agency backed up by 'bodies of armed men', i.e. it used coercive force. In Weberian terms it was reconceived as playing a crucial role in the cultural subordination of the working classes. As we will see, Louis Althusser received much attention for adding an 'ideological apparatus', which did not work repressively, to the traditional Marxist conception of the state as a 'repressive apparatus' (body of armed men).

Some European Marxists were attracted to Freud's ideas about the 'unconscious', since this concept could helpfully contribute to the theoretical management of the increasingly important emphasis on a major problem, namely, the difference between 'the way things in society appear to those who live there', as contrasted to 'how things really are' (when seen from a Marxist perspective). After all, Freud's notion provided psychological content for Marx's insistence on the idea that people do not really understand the reasons for their own actions.

By 'Western Marxism' we mean the tradition of Marxist scholarship originating around the early 1920s, whose central contentions emphasise voluntarism and reading Marx as a humanist thinker. Western Marxism arose from two important sources: (1) divisions within the international communist movement over the proper interpretation of Marx's doctrines; and (2) the failure of the European working class to honour Marxist demands for the international solidarity of the working class against its oppressors in favour of enthusiastically signing up with nationalist armies to kill one another in World War I. Western Marxism gained impetus by opposing 'vulgar' interpretations of Marx such as those given by the then prominent European theorists, e.g. Eduard Bernstein. These interpretations later became associated with the Stalinist orthodoxy that was meant to give the Soviet Union supremacy over Marxism everywhere.

The issue was, from the start, that of the relationship between the economic base and the superstructure of society. What critics found unattractive about vulgar Marxism was its reductive, mechanical character, i.e. reducing social life to nothing more than economic interests, so that all other aspects of social life were seen to follow automatically from the character of the economic structure and the contradictory interests that it generated. Simply put, the way to understand any social phenomenon is to identify the basic economic interests lying behind and animating it. Similarly, the 'vulgar' interpretation took Marx's remarks on the base–superstructure relationship as a rigid, 'one way' formula, stipulating that the 'superstructure' of the institutional, cultural and intellectual life of a society is wholly and directly shaped by the causal power and functional needs of the economic substructure (or 'base'). These cultural and intellectual phenomena are, at best, simply means of dressing up the most unattractive features of human lives, which are seen as exclusively concerned with economic matters. This unsophisticated reading of Marx provoked a reaction among those who argued that, if read correctly, his work allows a more elaborate and flexible interpretation of the base–superstructure relationship.

Western Marxism began with the work of Georg Lukács (1885–1971), a Hungarian philosopher and literary critic, in the early 1920s. It involved a marked shift in interest towards the analysis of cultural phenomena such as literature, art and music, and contrasts with the heavily technical economic analysis that fills Marx's later work, *Capital* (1976). It also attempted to develop a more sophisticated view of politics than was available in vulgar Marxism.

The fact that the working class had not behaved remotely in the way that Marx had 'predicted' it would was seen as itself needing to be interpreted in Marxist terms rather than as disproving Marx, but this could only be done if Marx's work was rethought. Here, a key element was the reflection that the working class had been unable to perceive the true nature of capitalist society and hence its own real interests, which, on Marx's premises, required the overthrow of capitalist society. Marx's basic model held that the development of capitalist society would make its own ruthlessly exploitative and dehumanising character ever more starkly apparent – so stark, indeed, that the working class would effectively have no choice but to recognise that its misery was a direct product of capitalism, and that workers had the power to end this misery for themselves. The improvement of communications as part of the infrastructure would make the formation of a working-class revolutionary consciousness that much easier. The problem was, then, to understand how working-class consciousness had actually been shaped, what had prevented the rise of revolutionary consciousness, and how, if at all, such consciousness could be prompted among the working class.

## Lukács: a Hegelian reinterpretation of Marx

Marx's publishing career suffered many vicissitudes, and a great deal of his work was not published in his lifetime. The manuscripts with the most overtly Hegelian character were written while he was young and not published until after his death, some as late as the 1930s and 1940s. It was, therefore, one of Lukács's achievements to have figured out from the published writings just how much Marx's thought owed to Hegel, and he gave a new interpretation in this light. The context in which Lukács mainly applied this interpretation was literary criticism, for many of his key works were about the history of the novel. However, *History and Class Consciousness* (1971), by far the most influential of Lukács's writings and the one we focus on here, was effectively a contribution to epistemology, i.e. to the theory of knowledge.

## The idea of totality

For Lukács, the key idea in Marxism for the understanding of human life, the object of knowledge, the thing to be known, is the *social totality*.

---

**Social totality**

Lukács saw Marx as essentially teaching that the true identity of things is provided by their relationship to a whole. For example, the individual characteristics of a person do not make that person a slave, and nothing in the constitution of a particular machine makes it an item of capital. These items acquire those identities only as part of a system, as part of an arrangement of slave-holding, or of capitalist production; i.e. they have their identity only in relation to the social whole.

---

In Lukács's view, Marx's most fundamental lesson is that the whole most decisively comes before the parts; the parts cannot be the things they are except in relationship to the whole. In order to spell out the connections making up the complex whole, Lukács introduced the influential notion of *mediations*, which refers to the steps of social relations linking a particular item (in a kind of nested series of larger, more complex units) eventually to the whole; e.g. the child can be linked by the family to the wider world, and the individual can be linked via the political party to the life of the state.

Since the whole is prior to the parts, vulgar Marxism or any simple idea of the causation of consciousness by economic conditions cannot be valid, for it is the system as a whole, the totality, which is the primary cause, and which produces the interrelationship of its constituent parts. The idea of one part of society determining the form of all the others is, on Lukács's interpretation, distinctly un-Marxist. The parts of society (through mediations) determine one another's nature in relation to the totality.

What has this argument to do with knowledge? Marx had shown that we do not understand a particular thing, a given fact, unless we grasp its relationship to the totality. Of course, Marx himself had achieved precisely this, not merely by showing the necessity to understand phenomena in relation to the totality, but also in actually revealing the nature of the totality itself. In order to understand anything, then, we need to understand it in relationship to (in the modern world) the capitalist system as a whole, grasped in Marx's terms. Lukács criticised the prevailing idea of knowledge in society, particularly as embodied in science. He damned it as *empiricism*, which is very close to what is elsewhere in this book called positivism (see Chapter 4); it presupposes that conclusions can fairly straightforwardly be drawn from the observable facts. To Marxism, however, it is important that the conclusions are not so straightforwardly drawn from the way things appear to be, because things *are not* the way they appear to be. The prevailing idea in empiricism lays emphasis upon the importance of facts, i.e. we come to understand reality through the acquisition and accumulation of facts. For Lukács, however, this approach meant that in empiricism facts are treated as merely individual and independent items. Reality is, then, thought of as identified through the addition together of all these facts. But Lukács saw reality as a totality, and so its constituents could not possibly be understood as singular, isolated items. Such treatment would dissociate them from the very things essential to their true identity, namely, their relations to the totality to which they belonged, thereby preventing its proper recognition. Empiricism is not so much a mistake as an ideology, a doctrine that encourages a false understanding of the nature of reality under the impression that we are in possession of a true one. Empiricists think that they establish facts by disconnecting them from the totality, thereby ensuring that reality is presented in a way that will obscure the extent to which singular facts are nonetheless part of an exploitative, oppressive totality. Empiricists are apt, also, to think of facts as things that, once established, are true for ever. But this approach carries the implication that the facts that have been established can never change, thereby denying the truth that, in Lukács's view, Hegel had taught Marx: one does not fully understand anything by identifying its current features. Rather, full understanding comes only when one understands that (1) *everything* must change; and (2) what something is involves understanding what it will become. By suppressing reality's *historical* character, empiricism again functions as an ideology that encourages people to think that the contemporary facts can never be changed and, therefore, social reality itself cannot be altered.

In Lukács's view the fact that only comparatively few subscribed to Marx's ideas shows only that the rest did not truly understand things. The vast mass of the population is subject to what he called *reification*. This concept reinvokes Hegelian terminology and is a term found in early Marx, though one can argue that the idea runs throughout his work.

## Reification

This suggests that people misrepresent the world to themselves: they come to understand the world, which they themselves have made through their own actions, as though it exists and operates according to its own laws quite independently of them and beyond their influence.

For example, Ludwig Feuerbach's critique of religion heavily influenced Marx, who profoundly critiqued it. Feuerbach argued that religious consciousness involves the creation of ideas of God and other supernatural forces, which provide a seriously distorted expression of human powers. In effect, religion displaces these human powers and projects them on to imaginary supernatural beings instead of attributing them to their true source. Having created these ideas, people then use them to understand their own situations and fates, which are then not seen for what they truly are, namely, matters of their own responsibility. Instead, people imagine themselves to be ruled by the wishes, even whims, of deities and other supernatural forces. Comparably, for Marx, the idea of the market provides another example of reification. In so far as people understand the market as something with its own laws and demands, something which decides people's fates, e.g. by throwing them out of work, then they misunderstand its real character as a human product. The market is, after all, no reality in itself, but only the relations of individuals to one another in the producing, selling and buying of goods.

Lukács argues that capitalist society is pervaded by such reifications; they are fundamental to the system, since the mystification of reality disguises the real social (i.e. class) relations of capitalist society. The mark of this process of mystification is that persons are unable to grasp their relation to the totality; they experience reality in a piecemeal fashion. A visual metaphor seems to be implicit in Lukács's argument: the particular location of persons within the system serves to restrict their 'view' of the whole; their position prohibits them from adopting or achieving a holistic perspective, a bird's-eye view of the whole scene. Consequently, even if they have some grasp of the objective character of particular elements, their understanding is seriously distorted by an inability to connect and link them into the whole.

## The working class as the universal subject

Lukács asserts, however, that one group within capitalist society is privileged with respect to understanding the totality, namely, the working class. This assertion is not as arbitrary as it might seem when placed in the context of the Hegelian legacy in terms of which Lukács comprehends Marx.

### The universal subject

Hegel's theory required the *universal subject*, i.e. the one who (in a way) stands for all humanity. By using it, a comprehensive understanding of the whole of human history, from beginning to end, can be achieved. This 'universal subject' was, for Hegel, Western civilisation as expressed in Hegel's own philosophy.

By this device, Hegel seeks to get around what he sees to be a misleading opposition in the theory of knowledge, namely, treating knowledge as a relationship between a subject and an object. In this relationship, subject and object are treated as quite distinct and separate, so that they must be brought into *correspondence*. If knowledge is a relationship between two distinct things, knowing subject and known-about object, then knowledge is only possible if there are indeed two distinct things in this relationship. The effect, though, of this *subject–object dualism* (which, as we noted in discussing Mead in Chapter 6, was enshrined in the Western philosophical tradition by Descartes) is to cut off human beings from 'external reality'. Humans, as subjects of knowledge, stand over against the 'external world' of objects; the idea of the human subject seeking to know the objects which make up external nature is the leading idea of knowledge in this approach.

Against it, Lukács argues that subject and object are not really separate in the case of humanity (or, for Hegel, in the case of nature either); humanity is both subject and object, it is that which seeks to know and that which is to be known. The philosophical tradition following Descartes is therefore another example of reification. Yet the dualism of subject and object is not simply false, for it does reflect in intellectual terms a *historical* reality, the separation of people from the social systems which they themselves have created and perpetuated by their actions. The separation of subject and object, therefore, is at root the social separation of human beings from their world and their separation from each other through their division into antagonistic classes. As a Hegelian Marxist, Lukács argues that history reaches its end point when the opposition of subject and object is overcome, when someone produces the knowledge that is the proper, full self-knowledge of humanity. In Hegel's account, this 'someone' is the philosopher (i.e. Hegel himself). Following the early Marx (see Timothy McCarthy 1978), Lukács identifies this universal subject not with particular individual philosophers but with the working class; it is that class's historic mission to overcome the opposition between subject and object (along with all the other false but persistent oppositions of thought) by overcoming the division of humanity against itself through the abolition of classes.

## The working class as the universal subject

Within capitalist society, the working class is that group which represents humanity as a whole. After the revolution, it will abolish the capitalist class and will then literally constitute all of humanity. Thus the position of the working class in capitalist society is special in virtue of its historical mission to emancipate humankind, thereby enabling it, or at least its intellectual representatives, to comprehend the totality truly. After the revolution, everyone will be in the working class, so there will be no working class.

It is important to note that 'working-class consciousness', as Lukács employs this notion, is not a descriptive concept: it does not describe the outlook of actual workers, but, rather, involves an understanding which is constructed on their behalf and in a way correctly formulates their position and interests in society even though they are mostly not aware of them. Lukács was not the first to propose this idea; it is a cornerstone of Lenin's revolutionary theories. In arguing that Marxism correctly and objectively defines the nature of working class consciousness – that Marxism, properly understood, is this consciousness – Lukács endorses Lenin's doctrine (1963) that the Communist Party is the vanguard of working-class thought and action.

## Gramsci and hegemony

As well as the Hungarian Lukács, Antonio Gramsci (1891–1937), an Italian, was a main figure in the Western Marxist reorientation. In terms of subsequent impact, Gramsci was most influential in maintaining that the struggle of ideas is as important in social life as economic interests. Indeed, the struggle over economic interests is itself conducted through the battle of ideas. Lukács was concerned to combat the idea of Marxism as a science – at least in terms of the conventional view of a science where facts are quite distinct from values. According to this conventional view, e.g. one held by Max Weber, science is capable only of describing, incapable of prescribing; it tells us how things are, but not what we should do in the face of the circumstances. Lukács held this view to be another of the false oppositions which Marxism destroys, for the understanding of the nature of the totality involves an understanding of what it has the capacity to become, of how to bring it about and, thus, of what we ought to do, namely, take the action to realise the potential of the totality, the emancipation of all.

Gramsci argued rather differently: the interest of science in relation to social life is characteristically from the point of view of whether the social life must be understood in science's terms. But this approach is the wrong way round: science as an ensemble of ideas is created in the course of and through human history. Therefore, the real question concerns the role science can have in the perpetual struggles of social life, rather than in seeing it as providing the one true way of understanding reality.

In Gramsci's conception, ideas are effectively weapons whose important role is the part they play in the struggle to change society. Relative to this role, worries about their objectivity and truth are incidental and the crucial issue is *which ideas are winning the struggle*. The essential phenomenon is the struggle for *hegemony*, i.e. domination over the intellectual life of the society and thus over the ideas in terms of which people think about their situation in the society. This domination is just as important as economic power to the persistence or overthrow of a regime, e.g. capitalism. Hence Marxism is of importance not as a scientific economic analysis of capitalism, but most importantly in its role of providing ideas to fight against the current hegemony of capitalism, providing the basis for overthrowing capitalism and installing a new society.

## Hegemony

Gramsci's idea is that cultural and intellectual activities do not merely operate as functions of economic changes, but comprise an arena of social struggle, of domination and resistance. Therefore, the struggle of ideas is a crucial part of the general pattern of struggle, and hegemony is that collection of ideas that prevail over all other ideas.

This conception has been hugely influential upon recent sociology (and especially on the formation of media studies, now a virtually independent area of academic work).

## The Frankfurt School

The next element in the delineation of the Western Marxist legacy is the development of the Frankfurt School. This is the name given to a loosely knit collection of scholars associated with the Institute for Social Research, which originated at the University of Frankfurt in the 1920s, moved to the US in the 1930s and returned to Germany in the 1950s. The main figures associated with the School during its heyday, from the point of view of subsequent effect upon sociology, were Max Horkheimer, Theodor Adorno, Walter Benjamin and Herbert Marcuse; more recently its leading associate is Jürgen Habermas. The School identified its work as *critical theory*, a term we will explain later.

It should be stated at the outset that although it is widely perceived as part of the Western Marxist tradition and will be so treated here, some qualification is needed on this point. The attachment of the School to Marxism was variable from individual to individual, and over the career of different individuals, and the attachment was often to Hegelian (or even religious) forms of thinking – and also to some of Max Weber's – as much as to specifically Marxist ones. All the figures associated with the School were united by a concern to critique capitalist society, and their shared dissatisfaction with capitalism was in terms not so much of the economic injustice and exploitative nature of its relationships as of its psychological and cultural effects. Common threads running through the writings of members of the Frankfurt School concern such issues as the cost to people's psychic lives as a result of reification, the threatening nature of an increasing kind of political gangsterism that they saw with the rise of European Fascism in the 1930s, and – in some ways the most important issue – the increasing decadence of modern culture (here Lukács thought that the Frankfurt School critiques had a rather snobbish motivation). At the heart of the Frankfurt School's critique is the idea that capitalism involves the destruction of the critical thought that is capable of challenging its whole system, resulting in the perversion of human reason.

We noted above that by the 1920s and 1930s Marx's account of capitalism arguably had been outdated by changing events. Capitalism had not immiserated and pauperised its working class, but had given them levels of economic prosperity which, while not always consistently expanding, were generally far in excess of those imaginable in the mid-nineteenth century. Yet if economic developments had the effect of blunting orthodox, 'scientific' Marxist analysis of capitalism, they did so only in so far as capitalism's evils were viewed predominantly in economic terms. In common with Lukács, members of the Frankfurt School placed greater emphasis on ideas than on economics, though, of course, not denying that economic relations are 'fundamental' to society. The shift was one of doctrinal and analytical *emphasis*: the relation between 'base' and 'superstructure' had to be understood in a more complex and altogether less formulaic manner than 'vulgar Marxism' supposed. Whereas orthodox, scientific Marxism concerned itself with the economic foundations of society, the Frankfurt School is more concerned with its dominant cultural forms.

## The Frankfurt School's basic view

Its attitude was, to put it rather crudely, that there is more to life than bread alone; a considerable price had been paid for economic prosperity, for though workers were now economically well catered for, working-class lives remained spiritually and psychologically stunted. The spread of economic well-being may have served to render the working class unavailable for the communist revolution, but it had left workers living lives of a much more impoverished and inferior quality than they need be.

The task, then, was to engage in *Ideologiekritik*, i.e. to understand how the superstructure of society worked to restrict people's lives and reconcile them to their *spiritual* pauperisation. This pauperisation was manifest in many spheres of life, but nowhere more clearly than in politics. Throughout Western Europe the rise of democratic parliamentary structures during the late nineteenth and early twentieth centuries had transformed the political landscape, rendering obsolete the orthodox Marxist view that the industrial working class could not possibly achieve power through parliamentary processes. Far from being excluded from the political process, the working classes, by virtue of the introduction of the universal franchise and the growth of mass, popular parties, seemed to have a genuine possibility of taking political power without need for revolution. Yet, across Europe, the working classes seemed unwilling or unable to avail themselves of this possibility. Not only were they uninterested in revolutionary political action in being the basis for the advancement of humanity through participation in a revolutionary Marxist movement, but they seemed equally unwilling to sign up in support of parliamentary Marxist parties. In so far as they were available for political activity, they were just as likely to be recruited to the movements of demagogues such as Hitler. Such developments as the rise of Fascism only served to confirm the urgency of the task of understanding how and why the working class had become reconciled to, and included in, capitalist society, since it seemed to many as though European societies were entering a new age of darkness, in which irrational and immoral forces had been unleashed. Far from opposing such forces, the working class had been mobilised in their support.

## Capitalism and Enlightenment reason

The key to the Frankfurt School's understanding of the origins of this situation was their analysis of the link between capitalism and a particular historical version (or perversion) of human reason. In essence, their view was that 'Reason' had been captured by capitalism; both reason and human lives were significantly reduced as a result. Thus their conception of modern capitalism owes almost as much to Weber (with his notions of rationalisation, disenchantment and 'the iron cage') as to Marx. Like Weber, they looked upon it as, in many ways, a puritanically repressive regime within which human relations and affairs were conceived in terms of – were reified into – the kind of calculated, impersonal, instrumental connections that are characteristic of bureaucracies. It is conceivable that human lives could be richly fulfilling and have a free and sensual relationship to the world around them, in which people would recognise themselves as natural beings, as belonging to nature. However, the capacity for such a life is denied under capitalism. It is within the capacity of reason (a Hegelian element) to provide this kind of existence, to reveal to humanity its unity with nature, and to enable people to develop their full, enriched sensual existence. However, capitalism has defeated reason's ability to do so. In part, under the name of *Enlightenment*, reason has taken a wrong turn. Indeed, it is the role of the critical theorist to act as a last bastion of critical reason – a critical reason of the sort that Hegel envisaged, i.e. dedicated to revealing the way in which misunderstanding of existing conditions obstructed the capacity of people to fulfil their true nature. It is used to criticise existing society in order to reveal the idea that truly free existence was impossible, was only an illusion, and to show how this illusion is created and preserved by capitalism and its culture.

### Reason and the Enlightenment project

The position of the Frankfurt School can be summed up in two principal points:

- The *Enlightenment project*, while ostensibly aimed towards delivering human freedom, had in fact served as a vehicle for repression of human potential, even (metaphorically) its enslavement.
- Reason, rather than playing a sovereign part in the evaluation and reorganisation of society for human betterment, had been co-opted into serving the purposes and defending the interests of one particular form of society, namely, industrial capitalism.

## The illusion of freedom

In order to make their case, the Frankfurt School were necessarily involved in showing that many of the features of modern society, which seem to embody, express or enable freedom, do not, in fact, really do so. The highlight of this kind of demonstration is a relatively late (1964) product of the School's work, *One Dimensional Man*. It was written by one of its affiliates, Herbert Marcuse (1898–1979), and had a strong effect on the intellectual climate of the late 1960s. In it Marcuse coined the expression 'repressive tolerance' to exploit precisely the apparently contradictory nature of the conjunction of its two terms.

### Repressive tolerance

Modern industrial societies are claimed to have a much-vaunted tolerance and freedom of expression, allowing the formation and communication of all kinds of ideas and the acceptance of a widening diversity of lifestyles. All these apparently amount to a massive liberation, a truly extensive realisation of freedom and the very opposite of repression. On the contrary, Marcuse argued, this tolerance is one of the forms of repression; it is one of the ways in which the system inhibits the possibility of change by effectively drawing the teeth of any challenges to it.

Thus to tolerate diversity is not to tolerate real revolutionary determination, since no *real* revolutionary threat is allowed; instead, it is defused, and dissent is regularised into merely another and inconsequential activity within the system ('bought off', in a way). Dissenting ideas are turned into commodities, into commercialised products of the system: they can be harmlessly (and profitably) disseminated as books, television programmes and films. Critical, even revolutionary, thought is reduced to a kind of leisure activity.

Marcuse's book was an expression of the Frankfurt School's attachment to a Hegelian interpretation of Marx's ideas, which emphasised the dialectical element in this thought, especially its negative character. Here 'negative' is not used as any derogatory characterisation. To talk about 'negative thinking' can be to emphasise something virtuous, since the point about dialectics is their initial assumption that things are to be identified not only as what they are, but also as what they are not. To say what something *is* also says what it *is not*, e.g. to say that a number is the number 'nine' is equivalent to saying it is not 'eight' or 'ten', and so on. In this way, dialectics attempt a massive break with classical logic as the basis for thought, providing a profoundly different mode of thought. For our purposes, classical logic can be thought of as resting upon the *law of identity*: a thing is itself and nothing else (in formulaic terms, $A = A$). In this logic, it would be a contradiction to say that $A = $ not $A$, but this is just what Hegel's dialectic does say: a thing is what it is not or, more precisely, a thing contains its own opposite. This is not a contradiction or a paradox, but Hegel's way of attempting to come to terms with the idea that change is inherent in the nature of things, i.e. something is both itself and its own opposite, in the sense that it is in the process of becoming that 'other' thing. For example, a seed is and is not a plant: it is not now a plant, but a seed, but it will become a plant, will cease to be a seed and change into a plant, i.e. something becomes what it is not. Hence Hegel is offering a drastically different conception of logic and of thought.

From the vantage point of the Frankfurt School, then, it is a defining feature of thought to think not only about what is, but also about what is not but *might* be. In this alternative logic, Marcuse (1955) and other Frankfurt School theorists see the opportunity for thought bursting out of the narrow range of considerations set by the 'empiricist' mentality with its unquestioning acceptance of the status quo, questioning the givenness and inevitability of 'what is', and contemplating the possibility of radical changes in the nature of 'what is' as it becomes 'what is not'. In short, they value dialectics as a source of *oppositional thinking*. In Adorno's late *Negative Dialectics* (1973), the 'negative' role of critical theory was recognised to have been rendered politically impotent, more or less reduced to revealing the necessary incapacity of other schemes of thought to attain the comprehensive grasp of reality to which they aspired, but unable to point out directions in which suppressed potential could be released.

At the heart of the School's critique of Enlightenment reason is the claim that it has nullified all forms of oppositional thinking, that it has remained within the limits set by classical logic and thus within the limits set by bourgeois capitalist society. Even Marx had remained partially captive, as evidenced by his concern to provide an analysis of the 'scientific' economic laws governing the workings of the capitalist system. Only by thoroughly freeing oneself from the assumptions inherent in the orthodox conception of reason and logic can one hope to restore the power of critical thought, with its possibility of genuine freedom, but social conditions no longer favour this possibility.

## Science as control

For many, and certainly for 'the Enlightenment', the development of science is taken to be equivalent to the development of reason *per se*, and the progress of science is seen to promise a truly rational basis for the conduct of social life, allowing humanity to achieve, for the first time, full control over its affairs and thus to enjoy authentic freedom, i.e. it is finally exempt from political tyranny, religious delusion and blind prejudice. So much for the ideal; but the School alleges that the reality is somewhat different. The Enlightenment took up rather than originated the idea that nature and humanity are in opposition, i.e. existence is a struggle between the two, and that the condition for humanity's well-being is the control of nature. Hence, even the natural sciences, for the Frankfurt School, are an expression of the determination to dominate and exploit, because their role is to make nature subordinate to humans, so it is hardly surprising if the same impulses run through social thought as well.

In practice, the most important of human ends has proved to be economic productivity. In consequence, the achievements of the natural sciences have resulted not only in the domination of nature, but also in the domination of some human beings over others. The practical realisation of natural scientific knowledge in the form of technology has given humankind control over nature by means of creating organised forms of labour in which the many are dominated by the few. Furthermore, the tools of logical thought and mathematical calculation, so effective in developing laws of nature, have been transformed into the basis for a whole 'worldview'. This view is a general way of thinking which includes an emphasis upon uniformity, leading in turn to further domination and the impoverishment of many people's existence because of efforts to impose regularity and predictability on human activity. The tools of logical thought and calculation have been adapted from their successful development in scientific inquiry into the means for the administration of society, throughout the whole of life and not just in work situations, thereby attesting to the rise and prevalence of what Weber identified as bureaucratic forms. Far from delivering freedom, the development of reason provided people only with the illusion of the greater freedom of seeming to be able to indulge individual preferences, while subjecting them to ever more rigorous and thoroughly disciplined administrative regulation. In short, these preferences can only be formed within the limits of choice that the administered structure can accommodate. In reality, they are very restrictive.

Consequently, the actual role of science has been a rather one-sided application of reason for practical purposes such as economic production; rather than serving as the basis for true human self-understanding and the development of full human potential, it has sought to understand people in terms that will make them most useful for business and administration. Science exemplifies what the School characterises as 'instrumental reason', to which the full promise of 'reason' has been entirely reduced as a consequence of the Enlightenment.

## Instrumental reason

Reason is devoted to figuring out the most efficient ways to achieve practical ends and considered therefore only as a means to practical purposes, to making the existing system more effective, rather than as a way of rethinking it. Within such a view, human beings also are seen only in terms of their use in efficiently achieving practical objectives; they are almost reduced to being mere objects.

Such instrumental reason is incapable of questioning the way things are, of seriously challenging the social order; it essentially takes the way things are as simple givens within which it must formulate its inquiries and set its tasks. Perhaps we can see why the Frankfurt School had a considerable resurgence of popularity in the 1960s among student radicals who challenged the role of scientists working for the military. Such scientists were seen to be in the grip of instrumental reason; they could not – on the basis of their science – raise vital questions, e.g. should humanity be producing weapons capable of its self-destruction? Should it be providing the tools for the competitive self-aggrandisement of nation states? As a part of the 'military-industrial complex', the scientists were incapable of doing other than taking the military objectives of producing bigger, more destructive weapons for granted.

A *critical theory* was necessary to grasp the big picture and challenge the idea that science should be in servitude to politicians. Science was condemned not only as the plaything of politicians, but also as a means of manipulating and controlling people rather than contributing to human welfare. Similarly, the social sciences were also critiqued, since they too were seen to be involved in seeking to control people, to make them into happy, passive and manipulable beings. A leading example was the type of studies of industrial work which took over the management assumption that the objective is to increase efficiency. Hence the social sciences showed their perversion by capitalism and their lack of independent critical inquiry by the way they applied knowledge in the form of their input into managerial control, advertising and other propagandistic media.

The struggle to master nature had been largely successful, but not as a struggle on behalf of human freedom. On the contrary, it had required the continued and increased domination of some people by others, as well as the imposition of a rigorous ordinance of self-denial on individuals. Science had contributed to the status quo, and its mind-set had been immensely helpful to the advancement of what Weber had termed the 'rationalisation of social relations', i.e. their reconstruction as shaped by the kind of law-like, predictable, controllable regularities of the natural sciences. According to science of this kind, the image of the world of strict, remorseless regularity had also been impressed upon and demanded of individuals as a condition of their participation in the so-called progress of society and of reason. People had been induced into thinking of themselves in terms of, and imitating the ways of, law-like regularities, and into existing as mere mechanical cogs in a great social machine.

To satisfy the demands of such a restrictive existence, it is necessary for people to renounce essential elements of their nature, to forgo their individuality, spontaneity and sensuality, and to act as interchangeable, utterly predictable, entirely impersonal entities. However, while people can to some extent suppress aspects of their own nature, their real human needs are not diminished; the frustration of these needs generates unsatisfied yearnings and a fund of undirected ('free-floating') but aggressive resentment. The widespread distribution of such unhappy individual minds ensures fertile fields of recruitment for *gangster-politicians*, who can vent these resentments by providing a sense of power and destiny to individual lives which have otherwise been reduced to the meaninglessness of small cogs in vast machines, as well as pointing them at targets, e.g. they can take their frustrations out on ethnic, religious or political minorities, intellectuals and so on. These gangster-politicians can offer something of greater significance through (at least the illusion of) involvement in something greater, in a movement with large political significance.

## Instrumental reason

The Frankfurt School's account of industrial society links two classical sociological analyses: Weber's account of rationalisation and a Hegelian-Marxist reading of capitalist development. Marx's own thought is faulted in so far as he too places prime emphasis upon the use of knowledge for domination; his economic theories unquestionably favour the unlimited expansion of productive powers in the exploitation – the domination – of labour. Weber's emphasis on the spiritually debilitating effects of rationalisation was picked up and his critique taken further by Frankfurt School writers. Philosophies inspired by and derived from natural science (such as empiricism and positivism) attempt to reduce all phenomena to the physical and are therefore seen to express the extent to which reason has been debased. Their application has subjected people to oppressive administration and, in so far as their influence permeates every aspect of social life, people's very existence is devalued, their position in the world diminished and their experience impoverished.

The Frankfurt School accepted Weber's idea of the 'disenchantment of the world' and also agreed with him that, *pace* claims about the beneficial effects of the Enlightenment, reason does not in fact result in progress towards a true understanding of things. Instead, the process divests human life of meaning, and all relationships are reduced to the merely instrumental. Human relations with nature and with one another come to be nothing more than means to some (materialistic) end. Enlightenment reason has become instrumental reason. It is not defined by a radical and questioning confrontation with the world 'as it is', setting out to show that the world could and must be otherwise. Instead, it accepts the way things are as if this is how they must inevitably be. It is compliant in the service of the needs of that world 'as it is'.

Ironically, then, Enlightenment reason was self-deluding, was much less of an embodiment of reason than it thought itself to be. Setting itself up as the unrelenting debunker of myths, it was itself the avid perpetrator of one such myth, i.e. that of man as the God-like being, which was at the root of the will to domination. With the secularisation of industrial society, the myth of God who was master over everything had superficially been abolished, but only in so far as the notion of God had been displaced by that of 'Man', the essence of whose being was to achieve total domination of the world (through reason and its application in technology). The dialectical result of Enlightenment's self-realisation was in finding its greatest fulfilment in the regimes whose drive towards total domination over their populations endowed them with the title *totalitarian*, rather than in societies of emancipated human beings. The Frankfurt School saw a clear link between the development of Enlightenment reason and the twentieth-century emergence of totalitarian regimes in Europe, as exemplified by the fascist Nazi Germany and the communist Soviet Union, both of which had risen to prominence in the 1920s and 1930s – in the formative years of the Institute for Social Research.

## The culture of capitalism

Reason had been captured by capitalism. This was one cause for despair. Another was that reason had served to capture and tame the working class. A main task which the Frankfurt School set itself was to understand the way in which the working class, especially the industrial working class, had been rendered content with capitalism. The analysis of this phenomenon had several facets. One concerned psychological conformity: how people could develop personalities of the sort that would put them loyally at the disposal of totalitarian regimes. *The*

*Authoritarian Personality*, published in 1950 and based on collaboration between Theodor Adorno (1903–69) and a group of social psychologists at the University of California, was a major study of this topic. This theme is less relevant, however, to the flow of our discussion than a second one, the role of the culture industry in promoting mass culture.

Modern society has become *mass society*.

## Mass society

This concept was widely employed in American social science during the 1940s and 1950s in order to emphasise once again how individualised industrial society has become. In many ways this idea accords with the condition of egoism described by Durkheim, i.e. individuals have become isolated from one another, separated from social ties and the support of relatively intimate groups; instead of making up an organised society, they are simply an undifferentiated mass, in which each individual stands in direct and lone relationship to the large political, administrative and economic structures of the society and is cut off from social ties provided by communities, which should mediate between the individual and the powers that tried to shape and direct him or her. In the view of the Frankfurt School, this relationship is increasingly one of regulation; more and more aspects of individual lives are subject to direct or indirect control by centralised administrative bureaucracies, with the result that the difference between 'private' and 'public' life is largely obliterated. The increasing power of the mass media to speak directly to and act manipulatively (possibly in the interest of demagogues) upon the lone, vulnerable, persuadable individual was greatly to be featured.

(As we shall see in Chapter 11, this theme is taken up by Michel Foucault.)

In addition to regulatory bureaucracy, the other key institutional feature of mass society is the *culture industry*.

## The culture industry

Whereas administrative bureaucracies enforce control over people's lives, there remains also the need to pacify people, and the culture industry provides people's lives with (superficial) meaning. Since, again, there are no intermediary groupings to command individuals' allegiance and provide their lives with meaning, the institutions of the culture industry, or, more appropriately, the mass media, fill this gap; individuals, being without strong ties and social supports, readily turn to the mass media for their ideas.

The Frankfurt School did not condemn all aspects of culture as conformist, e.g. they regarded 'high culture' favourably, although, in the end, they came to view only the most generally inaccessible, formally abstracted and technically impenetrable forms of art (e.g. Schoenberg's musical compositions) as the last outpost of critical thinking. For them, mass culture was 'low' culture, a 'mockery of what had been striven after in the great bourgeois works of art' (Adorno and Horkheimer 1979: 126). Mass culture effectively masquerades as Enlightenment but actually operates as mass deception. In sum, their critique is that in popular culture art has been replaced by entertainment, imagination by technology and technique.

## Components of mass culture

First of all, mass culture is made up of commodities; it is produced to be marketed. As such, its character is derived from the calculations of its producers as to what its consumers can be induced to want: production is governed by the kind of calculation associated with marketing and comprises a kind of manipulation of consumers into wanting things that they would not 'naturally' want. Mass culture is antithetical to high art. It is produced by organisations which are weak and dependent relative to the major economic and political structures. Consequently, the culture industry must appease the more powerful industries and services that provide it with its technology and finance. It is a kind of lowest common denominator operation; its products are homogenised, sharing predictable, undemanding formats, which themselves are effectively calculated, showing that the culture industry is thoroughly commercialised and pervaded (and perverted) by the spirit of business. The audience's imagination is suppressed, and no independent thought is demanded (or allowed). The mass media seek to convey an image which accords with their audience's notion of ordinariness, i.e. the audience's understanding is not stretched or challenged, and things are presented as if they could not imaginably be otherwise. The critical spirit is everywhere eliminated in favour of reinforcement of the passive, compliant attitude that the pressures of life in the society have already instilled in consumers.

Of course, the reproduction of the obvious, familiar world within the products of the culture industry confirms the ordinary world of the audience's experience as *the real world*. It is the only world there possibly can be, with no tension – let alone confrontation – between the outlook expressed in the product and that which is general in the society. At the same time, the culture industry flatters its victims with illusions, not least that they are capable of free and independent choice, even though the consumables they are presented with are ready-made, mass-produced and allow only the bare semblance of choice. For example, the packed and varied shelves of the supermarket with their innumerable brands give the impression of a huge range of choice, though in important respects the brands are basically the same. An exaggeration of difference in service gives the illusion of choice. Spurious individuality is also conveyed, with the superficial differentiation of physical appearance or stylistic quirk in, say, designer clothing, but within the context of a (contradictory) message that (again crudely) happiness is to be found in conformity. Indeed, mass culture is not even escapist, though its initial attraction may be that it appears to be so. For though it may even promise to be escapist, Adorno and Horkheimer note that 'in front of the appetite stimulated by all those brilliant names [of stars, etc.] and images there is finally set no more than a commendation of the depressing everyday world it sought to escape' (1979: 139). This kind of argument will be given an ironic turn some sixty years later, when it is applied to the embracing of just this line of thought by the intellectual culture which arises out of the turbulence of the 1960s. It is partly developed under the influence of Marcuse, where 'the counterculture' is analysed as a form of differentiating consumerist identity (see Heath and Potter 2005).

In support of the Frankfurt School analysis, Walter Benjamin (1892–1940), another German scholar of the 1930s (loosely allied with the School), stressed that the capacity of modern technologies to reproduce visible and audible 'realities' appears to authenticate the representations projected in media images, i.e. the technology effectively disguises from the viewer the fact that these images are selections or artificial creations. It enables images to be presented in such a way as to convey the impression that reality is being neutrally reproduced rather than artificially simulated. In this way a particular cast is given to the portrayal of reality; it is effected through clichés and stereotypes which – inevitably – conform to the prevailing ideology.

In reality, then, the Frankfurt School's critique is not actually of the *individualism* of modern society, but of its *false* individualism, i.e. the creation of fantasies of independence, choice and autonomy in a society that actually is uniform, thoroughly regulated, conformist and often strongly authoritarian.

## Conclusion: defrauded by history?

Although the main writings of the Frankfurt School were produced in the period between the late 1920s and early 1960s, their *direct* influence was at its peak from the early 1960s to the early 1980s, and is now ingrained in much intellectual/academic culture. As we indicated in Chapter 2, with the recent waning of interest in Marxist ideas in sociology, the critique of industrial society and its intellectual foundations in Enlightenment reason has moved on. The mantle of critique has now passed to the poststructuralists, whom we discuss later, but whose thought often strongly matches and therefore continues Frankfurt School themes (see Chapter 10).

We have mentioned the Frankfurt School's doubts about the realisation of Enlightenment ideals, but in key respects the position the School took was ambivalent. The idea of reason enshrined in the institutions of industrial society is critiqued because these realisations amount to *perversions* and *debasements* of reason, rather than because any appeal to reason is suspect. The School was pessimistic about the prospect of a revolutionary overthrow of capitalism in accordance with orthodox Marxist doctrine, but nevertheless its approach is essentially optimistic: if only some effective means could be found with which to oppose the prevailing institutions of industrial society and expose the falsity of their intellectual foundations, then there would be at least the prospect of reconstructing society along different lines, i.e. on the basis of genuine rationality and freedom.

We stated at the outset of this chapter that Western Marxism set itself the task of identifying the reasons for the incorporation of the working class into capitalist society. It wanted, however, to do more: it wanted to resuscitate the prospect of fundamental societal change and locate the source from which a transformation of the system might come. As Marcuse recognised, the crucial problem is in finding the vehicle for such a reconstruction once the revolutionary impotence of the working class is acknowledged. It might be argued that the 'failure' of the Frankfurt School was the inability to identify this alternative vehicle convincingly and, more profoundly, even to conceptualise the basis upon which its claim to rationality would stand.

## Questions

1 What does Lukács mean by 'totality'? How does this relate back to Marx's ideas? Is this really different to the concept of ideology? Why? What contemporary social phenomena can be understood using this term?

2 Why does Lukács refer to the working class as the 'universal subject'? How does this develop Marx's critique of Hegel? Is Lukács right? Does his argument make sense in the context of Lenin's arguments about the role of the Party? How are the two positions reconciled?

3 What does Gramsci mean by 'hegemony'? How is this different to Marx's concept of ideology? How is it different to Lukács's approach to class consciousness? Are his arguments theoretical or political in origin? Does this matter?

4 Which elements of the Frankfurt School's ideas come from Weber in your opinion? Do they develop these ideas beyond what Weber made of them? Which of the Frankfurt School's ideas are original and which are already covered by Weber under the term 'rationalisation'? How do these questions relate to the concept of the Enlightenment?

5 How might tolerance and freedom serve the purposes of repression? Could this not be said of any form of tolerance? Is freedom therefore impossible? What kinds of 'freedoms' are the Frankfurt School's theorists talking about? What contemporary examples of these things can you think of?

6 What is 'mass society'? Why is this concept important? How does it relate to class consciousness? How does it relate to Weber's notion of disenchantment? Is the Frankfurt School's use of this concept correct? Can you think of any modern examples of how this might operate today?

7 What is the 'culture industry'? Why do the Frankfurt School criticise it? Are they right? Is this really different to previous forms of culture? Have things moved on? Are new technologies inevitably used to maintain control or can they be liberatory? Is the argument too pessimistic? Does it rule out the possibility of social change?

## Next steps

Bronner and Kellner (1989) and Connerton (1976) provide useful selections of many of this tradition's key texts.

Bottomore (1984) is a good, short, introduction to the work of the Frankfurt School as a whole, and Held (1990) provides a longer, more advanced, account. The final volume of Kołakowski (2008, three volumes collected as one) still provides the most coherent critique of the twentieth-century Marxist tradition.

## CHAPTER NINE

# Structuralism

## Chapter overview

Just as the symbolic interactionists and ethnomethodologists emphasised the neglect of language and meaning in American and British sociology, the structuralists focused on how these phenomena were underplayed in French social thought. Bringing Saussure's linguistics and Freud's psychology to bear on social theory allowed thinkers like Lévi-Strauss, Barthes and Althusser to radically reframe understandings of what 'the social' might consist in. Lévi-Strauss sought to demonstrate that the mind and the social are *systems*, organised in the same ways language is organised: the analysis of myths allows this organisation to be made explicit and described. Barthes's *semiology* provided a methodology and approach for applying structuralist ideas more broadly, showing how 'natural' representations of the world are really ideological and distorting: we are prisoners of our language. Althusser's radical reading of Marx allowed such ideas to be reframed in the context of *ideology*, showing how the 'normal, natural' way the world appears shores up capitalist social relations and prevents the development of effective opposition to them. The critical examination of 'reason' undertaken by the Western Marxists (introduced in Chapter 8) was deepened and radicalised by these thinkers, opening up the space for the poststructuralists and postmodernists who were to follow them.

## Introduction: the linguistic model

It is common in the social sciences for an approach in one discipline or field to adapt its inspiration and most basic assumptions from another discipline. 'Structuralism' has its origins in linguistics as a model for social and cultural analysis, drawing upon what was, until the 1950s, one of the most successful strands in linguistics. In fact, structural linguistics was itself deemed in certain respects the most successful of the human and social sciences.

In the first instance, a language is a system of words, i.e. in this approach a system of *signs*. In the traditional, i.e. pre-structuralist, view, the meaning of words is thought to result from the fact that they stand for other things, e.g. the names of things stand for the concrete objects themselves, or for the ideas in a speaker's head. Stable relations between words and their *referents* (i.e. the things or ideas that the words refer to) enable people to identify certain objects as the things the words stand for. Understanding a language is, then, understanding the ways the signs in the language can be combined to state new ideas and/or refer to complex things. However, Saussure's bold proposal was to dispense with this view in favour of considering signs entirely in terms of the (internal) relations between them.

## Saussure's structural linguistics

The structuralist approach in linguistics originated in the work of Ferdinand de Saussure (1857–1913), somewhat under the influence of Durkheim's ideas. Writing at a time when the study of language was in its infancy, Saussure sought to define a subject matter for linguistics (just as Durkheim had done for sociology) and comparably sought it in a supra-individual phenomenon, the language system (which he termed *langue*), rather than in the individual one of speech (in his terminology, *parole*). His approach treated the act of speaking very much as a secondary phenomenon; order in language was to be explained in the systemic relations between words (or 'signs') which pre-exist any particular act of speaking, and not in terms of the ways individuals put words together to say things. Furthermore, the language system was to be understood as a *system of differences*, of contrasts, i.e. quite differently to previous accounts.

Saussure's strategy can be seen as akin to Durkheim's treatment of totemism. Prior to Durkheim, writers on totemism characteristically had sought to understand the meaning of the totemic object in terms of its own properties, to figure out how people could see something especially valuable or awesome in the natural phenomenon (animal, plant, place, etc.) that was their totem. Against such accounts of totemism in terms of the practical or psychological importance of the totems, Durkheim argued that their meaning could not be accounted for in terms of their objective properties. All instrumentalist explanations fail, since there is nothing particularly practically useful or awesome about totemic objects. Instead, the totemic object is a sign and stands for something. Its specific nature is itself arbitrary; it does not really matter what the particular totem is, any more than the sacredness of the national flag depends upon its design.

The role of the totem was to bind people together; it stood for the social group from which it derived its potency. For Durkheim, unifying the social group involves differentiating between sets of people. The role of the totem is to bind some people together in separation from others, therefore the totem must differ between groups; i.e. someone claiming to be a member of the emu clan is at the same time saying he or she is not a member of the parakeet (and vice versa). What is important about the totemic objects, then, is that they should be different from one another. The system of totemic symbols is crucial.

Similarly, for Saussure, the meaning of a sign is only arbitrarily linked to the sign itself; there is no reason why we should use a particular configuration of sound, such as 'totem', to mean what it does. The same goes for any other word in the language: some other sound could have been used to carry the meaning. Language is about communication, about the conveyance of information from one person to another. The capacity of a system to convey information derives from contrastive relations built into the system itself. Thus the *whole system* is important, not any single unit within it. The meaning of a word does not derive from the word itself, nor from the thing it stands for. The important feature of a word is that it should differ from other words, that it should contrast with them, e.g. saying something is 'red' is to say it is 'not green', 'not yellow' and so on. Saussure viewed language as just one *semiotic system* (i.e. system of signs) among many. His larger project, never realised, was to locate language within the broader set of communication systems. Although Saussure never completed his project, it was taken up again after World War II as the goal of the structuralist movement.

## Freud: the workings of the unconscious

A second source of inspiration for structuralism can be found in the writings of Sigmund Freud (1856–1939), the founder of psychoanalysis. The ideas of Freud are honoured – in conjunction with those of Marx (see Chapter 2) and Friedrich Nietzsche (see Chapter 10) – both by structuralists and by their poststructuralist successors for contributing to the idea of the *unconscious* as a source of the determination of human conduct.

### The unconscious and structuralism

The idea of the unconscious is important to structuralism since it proposes to discover the very structures that govern the nature of human thought generally and, at the same time, to be making an original discovery. In short, it proposes to find out things of which all people have been previously unaware. Structuralism is interested in the deeper, unconscious structures that operate within the mind. Individual thinkers are quite unaware of them, yet they shape the organisation of whatever individuals do consciously think.

Freud's ideas about the unconscious, especially when mediated by the influence of a Parisian psychoanalyst, Jacques Lacan (1901–81), were immensely influential on French theoretical ideas in the post-1945 period. By arguing that the unconscious was constructed like a language, Lacan offered the irresistible prospect of combining Freudian notions with the linguistic and semiotic ideas that also captivated theorists at that time.

Freud himself claimed to give a general account of the human mind. He maintained that it included two main parts, the conscious and the unconscious.

The conscious is those workings of the mind of which we are aware and which we can control. It is accompanied by thoughts of which we are not aware, of which we are not conscious; they take place in the unconscious. The *unconscious* is – and here the connection with Nietzsche is apparent – the direct expression of our organic, biological, animal natures, of what Freud regarded as the basic, instinctual drives that demand satisfaction – drives for food, for sex and so forth. The animal nature of human beings has an indiscriminate, insatiable desire for immediate pleasure, an unreasoning, uncontrolled demand for the easing of the unpleasant tensions which build up in us when our desire for food or sex is frustrated. Such a nature would be self-destructive if left to itself. Sheer, blind striving for immediate satisfaction would result in damaging, eventually fatal, contact with the environment, because although human beings have instinctual needs, they have no instinctual ways of satisfying them. Therefore, it is necessary that the drives at the basis of human personality be controlled and directed, but this requires that the organism must:

1  learn to postpone the demand for instant satisfaction in favour of less imme-diately but more safely gratifying responses; and
2  learn about its environment in order to grasp practically effective ways of achieving gratifications.

Thus the human being learns to regulate its drives, and to adapt its reactions to its circumstances, something which it does through the development of its basic personality. This development takes place first within the family relation-ship and later within the larger society. The individual must learn not only how to relate to its natural environment – what it can safely eat, etc. – but also to its social one.

As part of developing its social nature, the individual will learn that certain of its reactions are not allowed, that they are not acceptable to others. The urge to be aggressive to other people, even the wish to see them dead, is a natural, ata-vistic reaction, but it is not acceptable within society. The developing individual will come to share this general social attitude, although, at the same time, these natural, unacceptable responses will continue to occur. However, the individual will be unable to admit that it has such wishes, and will deny them to itself by suppressing and forgetting them – in Freud's terms, will repress them. The indi-vidual will drive those thoughts out of the (conscious) mind, but not from the mind altogether. Instead, they are exiled to the unconscious, where they persist, and where they will continue to seek expression. If these unacceptable thoughts are to be expressed, it cannot be done directly, in plain and open form, but must happen in some other way, in a form which does not look at all like the original thoughts and which misrepresents, and therefore conceals, their socially unac-ceptable nature. Thus Freud accounts for dreams as the way in which uncon-scious thoughts gain expression in the mind; the dream is a way of trying to express and fulfil a wish which cannot be expressed and fulfilled in an explicit way. However, seeing what wish it is that a dream expresses and fulfils is rather akin to breaking a complex code; only the trained psychoanalyst, who can see that the events in dreams are symbolic, and who understands what the symbols stand for, can do it.

## Self-deception and the normality of neurosis

Freud's view was that many of the milder mental illnesses were the results of unresolved tensions retained in individual unconscious minds, tensions involving thoughts which could not be consciously admitted by their individual owners, and which individuals therefore consciously deny. These thoughts continue to be expressed in the form of *seeming*, e.g. a seeming physical paralysis for which there is no physical basis. The explanation given by Freud would point to this paralysis as really psychological, not physical; as the result of inner tensions, in which, say, very strait-laced individuals experience incestuous sexual desires, but are unable to tolerate the idea that they could possibly have such feelings. Such a psychological conflict could take the form of physical expression, with the distress caused by the paralysis being a kind of self-imposed punishment for having those forbidden feelings. The purpose of Freud's psychoanalytic clinical operation is to enable the patient to become aware of, to become conscious of, these inner, unconscious, suppressed conflicts. Awareness provides the capacity to sort out the feelings and to overcome the conflict, which means that the physical symptom will evaporate.

Thus Freud argues that people are often unaware of the true psychological causes of their behaviour, of the unconscious impulses which can compel it. When they seek to explain things that have such unconscious causes, they give explanations which they think are true, but are, in fact, false. Because the unconscious impulses are ones which they – after the fashion of their culture and of the standards they have come to share – cannot regard as acceptable or admissible, the explanations that they give seek to present these 'low', unacceptable motivations in improved, 'higher', generally acceptable terms; they therefore seek to explain behaviour as the product of the rational deliberations of the conscious mind rather than in terms of the irrational, impulsive unconscious drives in which it actually originates.

In Freud's account, the discipline of the instinctive impulses and their subordination to conscious control is essential for the healthy development of the individual into someone capable of achieving satisfactions in a civilised way. Being reared within the family, and then the wider society, individuals learn to restrain their unconscious impulses. The self-denial of immediate satisfactions and the acceptance of a socially imposed discipline is the price of civilisation. Some individuals, however, can have their lives severely disrupted by psychological afflictions arising from the unresolved conflicts in their unconscious. The operation of science – the application of the scientifically derived doctrines of psychoanalysis – will enable reason to emancipate individuals from such afflictions, offering relief by providing people with rational, conscious understanding of the conflicts underlying their symptoms. Nevertheless, Freud does argue that the existence of civilisation involves a cost to the expression and satisfaction of human instinctual drives, though, as indicated, he himself thought the price well worth paying. As we will show, poststructuralist thinkers have particularly seized on Freud's point about the extent to which civilisation is antithetical to free self-expression, but they do not accept his view on the acceptability of this cost.

## Lévi-Strauss on 'the savage mind'

Movements of thought are often associated with specific locations. Just as symbolic interactionism was associated with Chicago (see Chapter 6), so the structuralist movement in social science was centred in Paris after 1945. The first major thinker in this movement was the anthropologist Claude Lévi-Strauss (1908–2009), who, in fact, developed many of his ideas during his stay in New York during the 1939–45 war, often through contact with other Europeans also exiled there. His writings brought together the structuralist model of language – with notions about the mind inspired by the Freudian idea of the unconscious – set against the background of Marx's distinction between base and superstructure, and his ideas about the nature of ideological thought.

After Saussure, subsequent thinkers developed the idea of contrast as the basis for systems of meaning into a powerful and sophisticated linguistic scheme. On the basis of these successes, Saussure's ideas were re-imported into the social sciences, initially through the anthropology of Lévi-Strauss, who aimed to give an account of the system of unconsciously operating rules of thought built into the human mind. One of his first (short) works was on the subject of totemism. It reviewed the development of thought about totemism since Durkheim's time, to some extent turning the structuralist argument against Durkheim himself. This book, *Totemism* (1962), and another early work, *The Savage Mind* (1972), form a pair and we will consider them together.

Lévi-Strauss's concern with totemism has to be understood against the background of the long-standing anthropological argument over whether 'primitive' people think differently from people in 'advanced' societies, and his entire work is a demonstration that *fundamentally* they do not, though superficially there are very significant differences. For some contributors to this debate, the presence of totemism and similar thought systems in tribal societies reveals that 'primitives' are incapable of truly logical thought on the grounds that they cannot distinguish between practical thought, which can be used to act on the world, and magical thought, which *they imagine* can be used to change the material world. Lévi-Strauss refuses to regard totemism as something special and unique to tribal societies; it is only a small part of a more general phenomenon which has to do with the organisation of human thought and, particularly, with the way human and other natural phenomena are interrelated in thought.

### Totemism

Against Durkheim, Lévi-Strauss argues that the key to totemism has to do with the organisation of thinking, with the operation of the intellect, and not with social organisation. He goes on to claim that studies of totemism show that so-called 'primitive societies' use natural phenomena to think with.

According to Lévi-Strauss, the possession of totemism by tribal, 'primitive' peoples and its absence from our 'advanced' societies does not indicate a true division in the nature of the minds; it is only a superficial difference. The human mind works always in basically the same way, and the difference between the 'primitive' and 'advanced' societies is due only to the conditions under which the mind has to operate. The 'advanced' societies are marked by the development of a historical accumulation of complex apparatuses for the expression of abstract thought, e.g. writing and mathematics. Such systems enable the expression, preservation and communication of thought, facilitating complex and abstract intellectual operations. The inhabitants of 'primitive' societies do not possess such systems, but are no less capable of sophisticated intellectual operations. Like us, they engage in abstract, rigorously logical and sophisticated thinking, but they have to express and communicate it without access to the means available to us, which means that they have to express their thought in a very different way. This is what we meant by summarising Lévi-Strauss as thinking that there are superficial differences in the way 'we' and 'they' think, for the means for the expression of logical thought are different in each case. Our thought is often published in long, learned and technical tracts, but theirs is shared through the oral narration of mythical stories. *Fundamentally*, we and they think the same, for both forms of expression are the bearers of formally intricate logical reflection.

In *The Savage Mind*, Lévi-Strauss employs what has now become a widely used expression, *bricoleur*, as an analogy to characterise the form of thought characteristic of tribal peoples. *Bricoleur* is French for a kind of handyperson, who will do a job with whatever materials there are to hand. A *bricoleur* has an accumulation of tools and materials collected up over time, and access to whatever useful things are present on the scene where the job must be done – a contrast with, say, the auto-mechanic, who has a collection of dedicated tools. The *bricoleur*'s task is to find, to improvise, a way of doing the repair job with whatever materials happen to be to hand, whereas the auto-mechanic is applying a set of pre-developed procedures, and can only work on problems that fit the toolkit. In Lévi-Strauss's account the situation of the 'savage mind' is comparable. When it wants to think about a problem, it does not have access to specialised tools for the work of thought – such as writing and mathematics – and if it is to do the work of thinking then it must use whatever resources are to hand. The materials are those of nature – plants, animals and natural phenomena. For, unlike us, in the tribes Lévi-Strauss is talking about, every individual shares in a hugely detailed knowledge of the natural environment.

The attempt to understand the totemic system must recognise, first of all, that the use of natural phenomena to represent social relations is only a small part of the general pattern of using natural phenomena as the medium for intellectual operations, an approach that 'we' also share, e.g. when naming sporting teams after animals – bulls, rhinos, lions – to signify their role as courageous and aggressive groupings. To understand the totemic system and the other cultural forms of such societies is to see how complex and universal intellectual problems are posed and tackled in ways expressed through a particular content derived from the natural world.

Although Lévi-Strauss's approach owes much to Durkheim's emphasis upon the nature of the totemic object as a sign, he none the less turns his argument against Durkheim's fundamental ambition. Lévi-Strauss says that Durkheim 'affirms the primacy of the social over the intellect' (Lévi-Strauss 1962: 97), but though he, Durkheim, aimed at and stood by this overriding ambition, he was a scholar of integrity and he was on occasion forced to admit things which were not consistent with it, e.g. when he admits that 'all social life, even elementary, presupposes an intellectual activity in man of which the formal properties, consequently, cannot be a reflection of the concrete organisation of the society' (1962: 96–97). Lévi-Strauss agrees with this observation of Durkheim's that the basic forms of thought are not derived from the social order. Instead, he insists that they reflect very general forms of operation, which are socially and culturally invariant because they derive from universal characteristics of the human mind.

In Lévi-Strauss's view it is hardly surprising that there are universal processes of the mind since the operation of the mind is dependent upon the operation of the brain, which itself operates in terms of *binary oppositions*, i.e. electrical pulses which go on and off.

## Binary oppositions

These are simply paired terms which directly exclude each other, and starkly and sharply contrast, say, 'on' and 'off', 'up' and 'down', 'left' and 'right', 'man' and 'woman'. Lévi-Strauss is a firm advocate of what philosophers call the *mind–brain identity thesis*, i.e. knowing the workings of the brain reveals the nature of the mind. Accordingly, he can assert that the human mind operates fundamentally in terms of such binary oppositions.

Therefore, the way to properly understand totemism and other products of 'primitive cultures' is to analyse them in terms of this universal principle of operation.

## The structural study of myth

Lévi-Strauss dedicated his subsequent career to this task. His work was dominated by the structural study of myth. The structuralist approach is worked out in and through detailed examination of a very large corpus of myths taken from 'primitive' – mainly South American – societies, climaxing in the production of four large volumes comprising *Mythologiques*, translated as *An Introduction to a Science of Mythology* (1970, 1973, 1978, 1981).

These myths tell stories in which people, for example, pay visits to heaven, go on quests, are assisted by animals (which may talk to them), and sometimes the people even turn into animals. From our point of view, these stories seem quite hard to understand, involving a rather arbitrary series of events.

## Myths as a system

Lévi-Strauss argues that if we were enabled to detect the underlying structure of the narrative, to discern its constituent elements and the way these are arranged, then we would see that these stories are not arbitrary, meaningless sequences of events. Through his structural analysis we would see that they are (1) concerned with deep, profound intellectual problems; and (2) rigorously logical in their underlying structures.

Concerning what myths are actually about as opposed to their surface content, Lévi-Strauss argues that there are things in human life that deeply and persistently trouble us, for which it is difficult to obtain satisfactory, stable solutions. For example – and something which matters a great deal in his work – the problem of the relationship between nature and culture is a matter of considerable ambiguity in human thought, since we sometimes starkly contrast 'nature' and 'culture'. We think of ourselves as creatures of culture *rather than* nature, contrasting ourselves with other creatures, which are part of nature only, i.e. merely animals. Yet we too are part of nature, we too are animals, and our capacity to develop culture could be said to be natural to us. Thus as human beings we both are and are not part of nature, and culture is both natural and unnatural: an unsatisfactory position from the point of view of logical consistency and symmetry. Lévi-Strauss holds that myths are often quite sophisticated attempts to resolve this unstable logical position and, indeed, other, similar kinds of logical problems.

As for the organisation of myths, Lévi-Strauss insists that they only seem to consist of randomly sequenced occurrences; properly analysed, they can be seen to be highly and complexly structured. At one point (1963: 213) Lévi-Strauss compares our reading of the myth with attempting to read an orchestral score in which all the notes have been placed on the same line. We would not see much musical structure in such a document until the notes were redistributed on to different lines in order to separate the various instruments. Similarly, to read myths as just a linear succession of incidents will not reveal the logical structure that they embody. Structure is detected by redistributing the events in the story among the various patterns of *contrast* (or binary opposition) which fundamentally make them up. In doing so, we find the myths embody structures of intellectual thought which are so rigorous that they are rather like mathematics in character.

As an illustration of his method, Lévi-Strauss takes the Greek myth of Oedipus. He first decomposes the events into several collections of elements. Some events instantiate the 'overrating' of blood relations, e.g. Oedipus's marriage to his mother. Several events instantiate the opposite, namely the 'underrating' of blood relations, e.g. Oedipus slaying his father. Hence he produces a contrast: overrating and underrating blood relations. A third set of elements consists of incidents in which monsters are slain by humans: a dragon has to be slain in order that humankind can be born from the earth. A fourth set pertains to the names of major characters in the myth; they are all names with meanings associated with difficulties in walking straight and standing upright, e.g. Oedipus's own name means 'swollen foot'.

Lévi-Strauss then attends to the way these collections of elements relate to one another. For him, the key is the autochthonous origin in the third set of elements above ('autochthonous' means 'born from the earth'). The myth is an attempt to think through the contradiction found in a culture with (1) a belief in the autochthonous origin of man; and also (2) the knowledge that we are born from man and woman. In Lévi-Strauss's own summary:

> The myth has to do with the inability, for a culture which holds the belief that mankind is autochthonous, to find a satisfactory transition between this theory and the knowledge that human beings are actually born from the union of man and woman. Although the problem obviously cannot be solved, the Oedipus myth provides a kind of logical tool which relates the original problem – born from one or born from two? – to the derivative problem: born from different or born from same? By a correlation of this type, the overrating of blood relations is to the underrating of blood relations as the attempt to escape autochthony is to the impossibility to succeed in it. Although experience contradicts theory, social life validates cosmology by its similarity of structure. Hence cosmology is true.
>
> (1963: 216)

In this way Lévi-Strauss has rearranged the elements in the myth, breaking up the narrative structure. He extracts from the story various elements of different kinds that stand in logically contrastive relations to one another, namely, overrating is the logical opposite of underrating. He can then seek to show further logical relations between these initial logical relations after the fashion of the algebraic formulation

$$a : b :: c : d \text{ (i.e. a is to b as c is to d).}$$

With the Oedipus myth, this formulation shows that underrating of blood relations is to overrating them as attempting to escape from autochthony is to the likelihood (nil) of succeeding. Through this mythic representation, thought is able to achieve the reconciliation of an impossibility: to provide an intellectual bypassing of a tension within the culture from which the myth is taken, i.e. the tension between the cultural belief that humankind springs from the earth and the plain everyday fact that we come from the womb, thereby allowing the preservation of the cultural belief in the face of that practical knowledge.

In Lévi-Strauss's work the basic pattern of intellectual operations takes the form of binary oppositions, although they are often involved in a triadic nexus, i.e. two opposing terms have another mediating between them, bridging the gap between them, or standing part-way between them, thereby providing a transition point from one to the other, e.g. rain can connect the earth and the sky, above and below; or a man climbing a cliff can be between 'above' and 'below', and at any given point, perhaps closer to one extreme than the other.

## An illustration: *The Jealous Potter*

Obviously, some two thousand cumulating pages of incredibly detailed analysis of myths taken mainly from the cultures of Latin American (and, less frequently, North American) tribes provide a much more intricate and complex structure than our brief illustrative reconstruction of the Oedipus myth can even suggest, but we will attempt to give some flavour of the major work by considering Lévi-Strauss's comparatively short study *The Jealous Potter* (1988).

*The Jealous Potter* follows his major, four-volume work *An Introduction to a Science of Mythology*, in which he dealt with one of his major themes, namely, the demarcation of nature from culture, as reflecting a preoccupation of human thought, which is apparent in some of the myths concerning the acquisition of cooking fire. In the myths, human beings had to strive for the possession of fire. Fire is the focus of a cosmic struggle between the people of the above – celestial beings – and those of the below – creatures living on the earth, including humans. Human beings were successful in their efforts and attained secure possession of cooking fire. In the shorter study he deals with the fact that the origins of pottery are also a topic of myth, for pottery is one of two great – cultural – arts which the most basic human societies have, the other being weaving. The origin of pottery, however, must be a secondary or dependent matter, to the extent that it presupposes the possession of cooking fire (for pots must themselves be 'cooked' by fire), and the pattern in such myths is therefore rather different from those analysed in myths about cooking foodstuffs. In the myths, humans do not acquire pottery by effort, but incidentally, as a beneficial by-product of another unending cosmic struggle between celestial beings (represented by birds) and aquatic creatures (represented by snakes). Unlike the possession of fire, the art of pottery is not permanently assured, but constantly endangered; great care needs to be taken, otherwise it can very easily be lost.

Lévi-Strauss begins from the way in which associations are often assumed between a craft and the character of its practitioners, noting that one such connection commonly made is a tendency for potters to be viewed as jealous. Here 'jealousy' is more than just sexual jealousy; it is also 'professional jealousy', possessiveness and secretiveness about one's professional knowledge and skills; so the jealous potter is protective of the art. What, Lévi-Strauss wonders, could be the basis for this association? By an elaborate, often roundabout, series of steps, he seeks to understand the connection between pottery and jealousy: how is it made by, how does it fit into, the pattern of interrelationship among the elements of mythic tales? Much of the fascination of one of Lévi-Strauss's accounts of myth lies in following the seemingly tortuous argument by which he draws out complex roundabout connections between things that seem, initially, unrelated. (Note here the similarity with psychoanalytic method.) In this case, he is going to connect – at least – pottery, jealousy, the goatsucker (a species of bird), the sloth, the howler monkey, opossums, subterranean dwarfs, heavenly bodies (including meteors, the sun and the moon), and the relationship between life on earth and the after-life. Further, he is going to connect these different elements across considerable geographical distances, for one of his key arguments is that the mythical thought of the Americas was essentially unified. Even this short work encompasses myths drawn from tribes from Latin America, the North American plains and Californian region, and the west coast of Canada.

Consequently, he must face, for example, this question: since the sloth is a creature confined to Latin America, what creatures could fulfil its signifying function in the myths of North America? Although the fascination of the work may lie in following its convoluted unfolding, our brief exposition is best served by first revealing the ending. The analysis in *The Jealous Potter* reveals that the structure of the constellation of myths involved is basically built around the treatment of the living body as a kind of pipe; things pass through a pipe, and the extent to which they can do so defines the elements which provide the key contrasts in the myths. The openings in a pipe provide means of entry and of exit, therefore it is through openings in the body/pipe that things enter and are ejected from the body. He notes that 'these openings can be at the front or back, above or below: mouth, nose, ears, vagina and anus. Each can perform three different functions: closed; open to receive; open to eject. The myths under study here illustrate only a few of these combinations' (1988: 163). For example, laughing, vomiting, eating, farting and excreting are among the bodily functions that figure prominently in the tapestry of the pottery myths.

Lévi-Strauss summarises the main lineaments of the stories told by the myths:

> Plots primarily motivated by marital jealousy chose a Goatsucker for a hero or a heroine and connected this Goatsucker physically or logically with the Sloth, who 'originated in jealousy' and was also jealous of his excrement. Through the Sloth we were introduced to the image of the comet or meteor. In South America it issued from excrement over which the Sloth had lost his jealous control. For the Iroquois, the comet or the meteor was the immediate cause of the jealousy that prompted a husband to eject his wife through a hole as if she were his excrement. Jealousy can be defined as a feeling emanating from the desire to hold on to something that is being taken away from you, or as the desire for something or someone you do not possess. We can say, then, that jealousy tends to support a state of conjunction whenever there is a state of threat or disjunction. All subsequent developments, however varied their themes, pertain to different modalities of disjunction, whose immutable nature is to break up formerly united terms by putting distance between them – a distance sometimes large, sometimes relatively small.
>
> (1988: 173)

Furthermore:

> The lesson taught in these myths is that earth must no longer be what men eat but must instead be cooked, like food, in order to enable men to cook what they eat. In the state of nature, earth was food; in its cooked form it becomes a vessel – that is to say, a cultural product

and

> [As] the function of fire becomes double (it cooks food or cooks pots in which food will be cooked) there emerges a dialectic of internal and external, of

inside and outside: clay, congruent to excrement *contained* in the body, is used to make pots *containing* food, which will be *contained* in the body, until the body, relieving itself, ceases to be the *container* of excrement.

(1988: 176, 177)

The way Lévi-Strauss works towards these conclusions is not as arbitrary as this bald summation might suggest. After all, his mode of analysis is meant to treat connections made in the myths as themselves intelligible rather than arbitrary. At its heart, *The Jealous Potter* seeks to trace the elaborate logic which links jealousy, excrement and meteors because these things *are* connected in the narratives given in the myths, e.g. in some stories the excrement of particular animals turns into meteors. He asks how such connections can be made.

Recognising the symbolic significance of pottery provides another key to Lévi-Strauss's analysis of this case. At the root of all thought is the contrast between shape and shapelessness; pottery involves imposing shape on the shapeless, giving form to clay. The activity of pottery itself is risky; its operations can be very delicate and its objectives are easily frustrated if things are not done just so. Of course, the transforming of the shapeless into the ordered is involved in the very creation of the world (we might note here the role of humankind as 'clay' in biblical symbolism); that pottery reproduces this imposition of order marks it out as a special kind of activity.

In the myths, pottery is connected with jealousy in three ways: (1) the art of pottery is jealously guarded by those who possess it; (2) the art itself is a jealous one, i.e. it imposes strict requirements upon its practitioners if it is not to desert them; (3) it is specifically connected to marital jealousy: in one myth, clay, the material of pottery, originates from a woman who is the object of struggle between rival husbands. In South American myths, marital jealousy is often connected with the goatsucker, a bird with a wide mouth and voracious habits that stands for greed. For example, in myths of marital discord (which arises in some cases from the jealousy between wife and mother-in-law over sons who do not really want to leave their mothers) one of the parties involved in the relationship turns into a goatsucker. The goatsucker is associated with another characteristic: splitting. There are both physical and social separations. On the physical side, in some myths the goatsucker dismembers other birds and smashes rocks; on the social side, it is linked with domestic separation brought about by 'jealousy among men over the same woman, the jealousy of the rejected lover (man or woman), the inability of two lovers to be together or marital discord' (Lévi-Strauss 1988: 52).

The mythical system is relational, and the association of the goatsucker with other things is to be understood in terms of the way in which that creature stands to other creatures used in the myths: a prominent opposition of the goatsucker is with the sloth. Why opposition? Lévi-Strauss points out that the two creatures exhibit paired opposed characteristics: oral versus anal, continent versus incontinent. Remember, the goatsucker's trait is greediness in its eating habits, so in the myth it stands for incontinence connected with the mouth, i.e. for orality. On the other hand, the sloth is noted for the fact that it infrequently excretes and is possessive about its faeces; it even collects up its own droppings, exemplifying anal continence. Just as the goatsucker is associated with pottery, the sloth is associated with weaving, another of the great arts. As a small eater and infrequent and tidy defecator, the sloth is seen as naturally well bred and therefore a suitable natural model for a culturally well-bred, technically refined activity such as weaving.

Lévi-Strauss insists that the myths of peoples far-flung across the Americas are interconnected, yet the sloth does not exist outside a delimited area of Latin America. Since it is associated in myth with subterranean dwarf people who have no anus, then, where the sloth is not available as a character, the way to find a connection is to search myths for dwarfish subterranean people. Finding some such people, the next step is to ask what kind of animals they are associated with, e.g. the squirrel and the opossum in North American tribes.

Lévi-Strauss then notes that the creatures associated with the subterranean dwarfs are tree-dwelling, thereby evoking for him a three-tiered world: those who dwell above (in the trees), those who dwell on the earth and those who dwell beneath it. This model for the relationship between super-humans and humans is conceived in terms of the problems that arise in respect of creatures living one on top of another, e.g. gods above people. Those who live up above are apt to make a dump and sewer of the space of those living below; of course, humans treat the world beneath them in the same callous way. Hence defecation provides a connection between different levels of reality, as excreta are typically passed down to a lower level.

This connection now evokes another animal contrast, this time between the sloth and the howler monkey. Again, the contrast is in terms of the orifices of the body, the mouth and the anus: the howler monkey is both anally and orally incontinent; it is a noisy animal, and also defecates frequently from high up in trees, unlike the sloth, which does its infrequent excreting close to the ground. In the myth, the sloth's care about excretion is connected with a concern for the preservation of the earth and life on it; if it were to defecate freely and incautiously from high up, its excreta would be transformed into a meteor, wreaking destruction.

To sum up, Lévi-Strauss uses the examples of cooking and pottery to show how lessons about the relationship between nature and culture are conveyed in myth. He makes connections between the structure of the cosmos and the excreting behaviour of animals through drawing on the pattern of orifices and their open/closed states. Excreta are treated as a (no pun intended) fundamental metaphor for separation, domestic separation being one form (humankind and the gods are another), and as a mechanism for interconnection between the different strata of reality.

## Lévi-Strauss's anti-humanism

Clearly, Lévi-Strauss's approach is uncompromisingly intellectual, yet there is more to it than intellectual puzzle-solving. The operations of the intellect are concerned with social matters, for the logical problems that the mind addresses arise from the contradictions within the life of the society, with the fact that social relations cannot themselves be organised with thoroughgoing logical consistency. In these respects, we can discern – as previously mentioned – Marx's background influence, especially his use of the Hegelian idea of insoluble contradictions as internal to a social system. Myth confronts these contradictions and draws out patterns of relationship in the form of the mythic analogies, which make it appear that these logical difficulties can be overcome, that their reconciliation is possible. Since, however, these contradictions in social life *are* contradictions, it remains the fact that they cannot be reconciled in real life. Myth creates the illusion that they can, making them easier to live with. Thus Lévi-Strauss's analysis of myth is not very far from Marx's concept of ideology and its functions, i.e. to appear to overcome in thought contradictions that cannot be resolved in reality; in the end Lévi-Strauss presents myth as a form of collective self-delusion.

However, we must be careful here not to take too 'humanistic' a view of Lévi-Strauss's work. A strong *anti-humanist* perspective informs his structuralist approach; it was massively influential in promoting the *subject-decentring* movement, which has been such an important unifying element in recent theoretical developments (see below). Lévi-Strauss's analyses of myth are not designed to provide us with an appreciation of the ingenuity of individual tellers of these myths and their ability to conjure up such elaborate constructions, for the meaning structures of the myth are not the conscious contrivance of the teller at all. Rather, they are the product of unconscious operations of the mind, of which the teller is not aware. Lévi-Strauss sometimes sees himself as akin to a scientific observer of some natural phenomenon; its actual and law-like order is just not discoverable to naive participants in its observable, surface detail. Only through complex analytic reconstruction of the phenomena can this order be found – compare the way laboratory scientists tear things apart in order to discover their true (inner) nature.

In fact, the individual tellings of the myths are only instances of the operation of the general, unconsciously operating pattern of the human mind. The individual tellers of the myths are therefore providing only partial realisations of a complex system of pattern possibilities. The individual teller does not create the basic pattern for producing the narrative of the particular myth. Consequently, we can only understand this basic pattern properly by seeing the way it is worked out across the whole range of myths.

Below we shall talk about 'the death of the author' and 'the abolition of the subject', explaining more fully what such expressions mean, but in these arguments of Lévi-Strauss's we can find some important contributions to the formation of these ideas. Note, for example, that Lévi-Strauss does not collect myths on the basis that we collect stories in our society, i.e. that they are the product of the same teller, the creations of the same author. Nor does he seek to understand them by making any reference to the lives or circumstances of those who tell the myths. Lévi-Strauss does not look for a pattern in some myths, which results from their being the productions of one and the same creative individual, nor does he have the slightest interest in attempting to trace the cultural history of particular myths. Instead, he looks for a pattern that is present in *all* myths, regardless of who created them or from what geographical region they originate. His crucial question is whether logical connections such as opposition, inversion and mediation can be found between the structural components of the myths.

From Lévi-Strauss's standpoint, then, the 'authors' of the myths, i.e. their tellers, are unwitting operators of the structure of thought underlying the individual myths; they tell the myths as they do because of the nature of that structure. In this respect, the underlying structure can be seen to be in control of the telling of the myth and, thus, of the teller of the myth, rather than the teller being in control of his or her own conduct. The true meaning of the myth, then, is created not by the individual teller, but by the system, which shapes the teller's behaviour. Further, the 'author' of the myth does not provide the principle of unity among them. The 'author' is not 'a centre' from which each myth singularly and distinctively originates and derives its meanings; nor is the individual author the focus around which the myths are assembled into unified collections, i.e. in our society the *oeuvre* of an author is assembled into a 'collected works'. Neither the pattern in the myths nor the principle which connects them together originates in any single focus or centre, for the pattern is distributed across the whole of humanity, and the meaning of any one myth is only to be detected, as *The Jealous Potter* has illustrated, through tracing interconnections across a wide range of other myths. Myths are connected with one another across considerable distance of time and space since they represent the elaboration, the working out, of different, perhaps complementary, possibilities within the general pattern.

Thus meaning originates from the *system*, not from the individual. The 'author' is anonymous and even unknown, an irrelevance from the point of view of understanding the meaning of the myth; we need to know more details about other myths in order to understand this one, not further detail about the lives and intentions of the 'author'. Among structuralist and poststructuralist thinkers this notion in part is what is meant by talk of the *death of the author* and the *decentring of the subject*. In summary:

1  Reference to the figure of 'the author' is not essential to the understanding of writings and may, indeed, be obstructive to true understanding of the meaning of writings.
2  The individual (in the form of 'the author' in connection with writing) is not the centre from which the meaning of meaningful phenomena originates. The meaning of the phenomenon does not, perhaps, derive from any centre.
3  The individual's mind is not a unity, but is divided into two mutually unaware components, the conscious and the unconscious – an idea inherited especially from Freud. Telling and listening to myths is a conscious affair, but the rules which structure the myths operate unconsciously – like the rules of language.

Thus the anti-humanist element is large in Lévi-Strauss's treatment of myth.

## Reconfiguring the human sciences

Lévi-Strauss's appeal went far beyond the boundaries of social anthropology, his nominal discipline. Methodologically, his work seemed to many to prefigure a new approach to the social sciences, one that promised to realise the goal of a rigorously formal, generalised methodology and even point the way towards the often longed-for mathematisation of social analysis. The equations and diagrams which littered his texts projected an image of a discipline in which formal, algebraic-type mathematics could be widely used, rather than the measurement-oriented quantitative maths which was more usually entertained as the key to making a genuine science of sociology – though Lévi-Strauss is at pains to point out that his formulae and diagrams are not true mathematical ones. On a more substantive plane, Lévi-Strauss seemed to offer an approach to the analysis of cultural phenomena that could be applied to all the cultural products of humankind, including those of our own society and, for example, all artistic creations. For example, disciplines such as (indeed, particularly) literary criticism could apply his methods to the examination of poems and novels, and social scientists could – if they wanted – apply it to horse racing, pet ownership, gardening, or one or other of the scientific disciplines, among a huge host of other conceivable topics. Lévi-Strauss might not himself entirely approve of this next suggestion, but it was none the less quite natural to think that if the underlying structures of culture were universal, the outgrowth of one and the same human mind/brain, then the methods of structuralist analysis should be generally applicable. At the same time, Lévi-Strauss retained Marxist elements in his thought and was willing to think of his analyses of myth and other aspects of culture as contributions to the theory of the superstructure. An important element of his thought about myth was a direct borrowing from Marx, namely, the idea that ideology attempts to overcome, in thought and in theory, contradictions in the organisation of social life which cannot be overcome in reality, in practice.

Though Lévi-Strauss's own studies were directed towards analysis of rather esoteric phenomena, there was no reason in principle why the self-same methods could not be applied to looking at everyday cultural phenomena of our own societies. For example, things as diverse as food, fashion, wrestling or a newspaper photograph could be analysed *semiologically*, i.e. purely as a form of communication and as a system of signs. Thus Lévi-Strauss's structuralism initiated tendencies that were to lead eventually to the formation of what nowadays are known as cultural studies. Interestingly, however, despite presentation as a potentially very general method, this kind of structuralism has tended to remain the sole possession of its founder, much as, say, Goffman's supposedly general schemes are rarely successfully imitated. Still, semiological ideas have had a major impact in this field, albeit in ways now quite far removed from Lévi-Strauss's original scheme. The leading figure in such a development of semiology – towards critical theory and social analysis – was another French intellectual, Roland Barthes.

## Barthes: semiology and contemporary culture

The work of Roland Barthes (1915–86) is broadly divisible into two phases, an early structuralist one and a later 'poststructuralist' one. In this chapter we focus upon the first, leaving his later works for the next chapter, where we discuss poststructuralism. Even in his early writings, however, there are indications that Barthes himself was never wholly comfortable with the commitment to structuralist ideas; he displays a somewhat ambivalent attitude, being at once drawn to the idea of a remorselessly all-encompassing science but also showing an apparent repulsion at the thought of it. There is a strong contrast between writings with a theoretical, systematic, scientific cast to them, such as *Elements of Semiology* (1967), and other, more fragmentary and essayist works, such as *Mythologies* (1973). Barthes's later writings (see the next chapter) become progressively more literary, allusive and self-consciously experimental, e.g. *A Lover's Discourse* (1978), or *Roland Barthes by Roland Barthes* (1977).

In his early, anthropological phase, Barthes brings structuralism home to the analysis of contemporary Western, particularly French, culture. For Barthes, as for Lévi-Strauss too, Marxist assumptions are importantly presupposed in the whole picture of what he is doing, though whether he was, strictly speaking, a Marxist is one of the many questions about his work that remain unsettled. The Marxist influence is, if anything, more pronounced than in Lévi-Strauss, in that Barthes's early studies are devoted to the analysis of French bourgeois culture in a manner very much akin to that of *Ideologiekritik* as developed by, for example, the Frankfurt School, as we discussed in Chapter 8.

Also like Lévi-Strauss, Barthes draws his major inspiration from Saussure, who, as we noted earlier, had envisaged linguistics as a part of semiology, the general science of signs. In *Elements of Semiology* Barthes presents his programme for such a science, based on the idea – which originates in Saussure – that the words of language are not the only things that comprise systems of signs. For example, the various activities of eating, wearing clothes, and owning and driving a car can all be conceived of as such systems. Barthes argues, however, that it is impossible to think of cultural systems such as dress, dining, motoring and so forth independently of language (certainly in Western society). For example, part of the point of fashion – a topic to which Barthes eventually devoted a whole book (1985) – is to be talked and written about; therefore, the account of language must be at its most general and inclusive. Accordingly, Barthes proposed to develop the science of semiology to give central emphasis to language in accordance with the general *linguistic turn*, i.e. the emphasis on the importance, indeed centrality, of language that is such a strong feature of post-war Western thought, and certainly crucial for subsequent poststructuralist developments. Language is not the only sign system, but it is the one on which other systems tend to be dependent.

## Mythologies of culture

The investigation of semiology was interwoven with the considerations of ideology. A significant difference between Barthes and Lévi-Strauss is marked by their very different uses of the notion of myth. As we have seen, Lévi-Strauss was concerned with myth as a distinctive feature of so-called primitive societies; for him, myths are means by which pre-literate peoples utilise the world around them, thereby building complex structures of thought which are concerned with universal human problems and with the technical inconsistencies of their culture. While retaining the idea of myths as constructs, Barthes employs myth in more concretely Marxian-oriented terms which treat ideology as being more about providing justification for the existing system.

## Barthes and myth

Myths are patterns of cultural activities and ideas that have a fundamentally ideological character in that their function (in part, at least) is to obscure reality by conveying a sense of naturalness about things which are integral to one particular cultural configuration, namely, modern bourgeois society.

Barthes's starting point was a

feeling of impatience at the sight of the 'naturalness' with which newspapers, art and common sense constantly dress up a reality which, even though it is the one we live in, is undoubtedly determined by history...I resented seeing Nature and History confused at every turn, and I wanted to track down, in the decorative display of *what-goes-without-saying*, the ideological abuse which, in my view, is hidden there.

(1973: 11)

His purpose, then, was to reveal the extent to which things presented by the culture as purely natural were instead – or at least, were also – cultural phenomena: their representation as natural was, in important part, *mis*representation. For example, something as seemingly natural as eating and drinking was not to be seen as that alone, for eating and drinking are also meaningful, with the eating and drinking of certain kinds of things functioning as a sign. Thus one can examine eating and drinking (or the wearing of clothes) not only from its practical point of view, but also as a process of communication, and therefore as the functioning of a system of signs along the lines of the dichotomously contrastive mode stemming from Saussure. For example, Barthes emphasised the extent to which the drinking of wine is, in the first instance, associated with French identity. He described wine as 'the totem drink' (1973: 58) which provides the basis for the morality of French sociality, in the sense that knowing how to drink wine is the mark of an admirable, controlled and sociable individual; it is integral to all the ceremonial activities of French life, large and small. At the same time, however, he points out that the admirable and agreeable features attributed to wine are also the product of French capitalism and its exploitative nature, involving, for example, the appropriation of Muslim lands in North Africa for a product for which the Muslims themselves have no use. As for steak and chips, the steak is a prestige food associated with strength, the eating of which can, for example, 'redeem' the effete character of intellectuals, making them seem more earthy and worthy people; the eating of steak and chips is (or was) associated with French 'national glamour'.

According to Barthes, the role of myth is to naturalise, to make things which are contingent and historical seem necessary and eternal, to make things which could have been different and which may have their roots in dubious circumstances seem as though they could not be otherwise, as though they are entirely innocent, i.e. entirely beneficent and harmless in their nature. Remember, the emphasis upon the character of wine, its fine and improving nature, makes people forget – in the sense of disregard – the fact that the wine itself is created through unequal and exploitative relations. In more of Barthes's own words, myth

> abolishes the complexity of human acts, it gives them the simplicity of essences, it does away with all dialectics, with any going back beyond what was immediately visible, it organises a world without depth, a world wide open and wallowing in the evident, it establishes a blissful clarity: things appear to mean something by themselves.
>
> (1973: 143)

In modern societies, then, the role of myth is to depoliticise, to present things in a way which can be taken for granted, simply and naively accepted as the way they must be, obscuring the fact that these things might be recognised, if seen in their full, complex and historical character, to be more equivocal and contested than they are seen to be. In this way, Barthes connects structuralism with themes that had been developed as part of *Ideologiekritik* (see Chapter 8); they have now become staple elements in cultural analysis across a whole range of social scientific disciplines.

## Prisoners of language

In subsequent works, one of Barthes's principal targets was the literary style of realism, which seeks to present itself as though it is not a style at all but simply a natural way of writing.

### Realism as ideological

Realism is essentially ideological in that it seems to portray how things really are in the world, merely providing a window on the world; i.e. the written text is like the pane of glass in the window, something which is looked through and disregarded for the purpose of seeing something beyond it. Realist writings are thus apt to deny that their own status involves employing a style. Style is thought of as ornamental and decorative, to be attended to in reading for its own sake. Hence realist writers insist that the writing is of no interest in itself, that it is merely a functional vehicle for the relating of the facts. On the contrary, Barthes counters that realism is as much a style of writing as any other, there is no such thing as prose which purely states the facts, and supposedly realist texts are, in fact, complex composites of literary style.

The grand master of realism in nineteenth-century French literature was Honoré de Balzac, so that it is certainly no coincidence that, in his book *S/Z* (1975a), Barthes subjects one of Balzac's short stories (which concerns two main characters, Sarrasine and Zambinella – hence Barthes's title) to a most detailed and extensive literary analysis, the intention being to reveal that this ostensibly realist tale is, in fact, constituted out of no fewer than five stylistic codes, which serve to structure the story and to create suspense in the reader. For example, they enable the invocation of references to locations in ways that make those references not merely the names of places but also the symbols of certain sorts of things, e.g. today 'Hollywood' is much more than the mere mention of the name of a place. The codes enable the building up of a thematic pattern in the story and the episodic structuring of the story into different sequences. Finally, the code which draws upon what is known in common, the common sense of the culture, serves to anchor – to secure – the story's conviction, attaining the reader's consent to aspects of the telling which hinge upon being known to be so because everyone knows that they are so. Hence far from being a neutral medium through which reality is portrayed, the story is a complex contrivance, which achieves its character as a transparent, style-free portrayal of 'reality as it is' through being a dense and elaborate construction out of stylistic elements.

In a less literary context, namely, the case of media coverage of the Tour de France, which is ostensibly the simple reporting of an actual event, Barthes argues that the coverage is in fact shaped by the way it draws upon a quite traditional literary form – the epic. For Barthes, then, the difference is not between those writings which are without style and merely report the facts, a feature often attributed to 'realist' writing, which is meant to be plainly descriptive and devoid of 'literary' ornamentation, and those which involve an eye-catching, attention-attracting style, which are replete with 'literary' features. The real contrast is not between those with and those without style but, rather, between two different styles, which Barthes terms 'the readerly' and 'the writerly'. The prime difference is in the relation the text has to its readership, whether – in the former case – it is written to be easy to read, making the reader into someone passive, a mere recipient of the message that the text delivers to him or her (many popular novels are obvious examples of this style), or whether the text is written in a way which demands a contribution of the reader, making the reader into an active participant in the reading and virtually transforming the reader into a writer, i.e. the reader has to put a lot of effort into reading, into figuring out what the text is saying, what the story is and so on. In short, the reader in the 'writerly' case has to make a contribution in determining how the text is to be read. Equally plainly, this characteristic pertains to many so-called literary novels. For a simple example, the British writer B. S. Johnson published one of his novels (1969) in a box as a collection of separately printed chapters, with no indication of an order in which to read them; it was necessary for the reader to make a decision about the order, to work out for himself or herself whether there was any correct order for reading. Barthes, of course, approves of the writerly kind of writing, for it means that the text draws attention to itself, provides a perpetual reminder of the fact that it is a contrivance, thereby inhibiting any falling back into the illusion that one is looking through a window on to an external reality.

Barthes is arguing, in respect of literature (and, by implication, of all other kinds of texts, however non-literary they may be regarded as being), that there is no such thing as an authentically realist writing which provides unvarnished reports of 'the facts'. For all writing carries with it, and is made out of, the cultural codes under which it is produced. It therefore inevitably absorbs the real world into these codes in ways that cannot be extricated from one another. More generally, then, Barthes is sounding the theme of 'prisoners of language'.

### Prisoners of language

This is the suggestion that we can never know reality in itself, for our only access to it is through the cultural schemes (particularly the codes) that we have, and which are, because of their ideological character, *distorting prisms*. It is impossible to represent (describe or otherwise portray) reality independently of these codes, for any representation must be done in terms of them.

Hence Barthes needs to subvert these modes of representation – which are not merely written, but also take the form of activities or artefacts, such as wrestling or the Eiffel Tower – which seek to present themselves as natural, as simply reproducing what is given in reality. After all, he argues, there is no other way in which we can make contact with what is 'out there' at all except through one cultural code or another.

This theme of 'prisoners of language' is an important element in the epistemological/methodological travails of recent sociology. In shifting towards the critique of language and the idea of representation associated with language, Barthes was moving in the direction of poststructuralism; therefore, we will take up his work again in that context in the next chapter.

### Althusser: Marxism as science

The third major figure in the structuralist period was Louis Althusser (1918–90). However, Althusser was not really connected with structuralism in the sense in which Lévi-Strauss and Barthes were, i.e. engaged in applying the underlying idea of structural linguistics to the analysis of social forms. In his writings, Althusser was much more concerned with redefining the contemporary understanding of Marx. He did share the anti-humanist perspective displayed by Lévi-Strauss and Barthes whose work was meant to signify 'the death of the author', but his primary concern was to establish and explicate the correctness of the theories to be found in Marx's late writings.

Althusser's work is essentially centred upon the problem of the relation between base and superstructure in Marx, involving him in two main, though interrelated, operations. One is establishing *the* correct reading of Marx, making an identification of what, in Marx's own writings, are ideas essential to Marxism, as well as what is properly Marxist in the writings of his successors. The other is to amplify the properly Marxist things that Marx had said, particularly in respect of how economic and ideological elements figure in society.

Unlike in Barthes, there are no equivocations in Althusser's commitment to the idea of science. His work depends on his assumption that Marxism (whatever it is) is a correct – indeed, is the first and paramount – science of *social formations*, i.e. of societies. However, although Marx may have created this science, he had not perhaps always been fully aware of what he was doing, and his writings, both early and late, are admixtures of scientific and ideological elements. For Althusser, there is a complete break between science and ideology; they are two distinct things. We can only establish a science (something which is true) by entirely breaking with ideology. It cannot be the case, therefore, that we can create a science by continuing and developing something with an ideological nature.

Consequently, Marx could not have developed his science on the basis of Hegel's philosophy at the time, as many have increasingly argued. Hegel's philosophy is ideology whereas Marx had made the transition to science. Since his early writings were very much a continuation of Hegelian themes, Marx must have broken completely with his own early writings.

## The break between early and late Marx

The break does not involve rejecting the kinds of answers that a Hegelian would give to Hegel's problems and substituting a different kind of answer. The break must be complete and it must, therefore, involve rejecting even the questions that Hegel asked – to use Althusser's own word, installing a completely new *problematic*. The key to the nature of any science is its problematic.

On this basis, Althusser devotes much effort to locating the point in Marx's career at which the break was made, but the intricacies of this operation need not concern us here; it is sufficient to say that he found the scientific content of Marx's thought in the late writings, particularly in the volumes of *Capital*. Indeed, Althusser eventually came to the point at which the only writings of Marx he could find to be *totally and definitively exempt* from any trace of Hegelian influence were two very short and, otherwise, comparatively minor pieces: the *Critique of the Gotha Programme* and *Marginal Notes on Wagner* (Althusser 1971: 90).

Two aspects in particular about the Hegelian tradition were anathema to Althusser: (1) its humanism, and (2) its notion of the social whole as an expressive totality. Althusser's objection to both can be seen to originate in his opposition to *essentialism*, i.e. the idea that there is a specific nature to an object (or phenomenon), an essence. The essence of a thing is the basis on which the object is to be explained and is an assumption crucial in Hegel. For example, the

Hegelian account of historical development treated the mind as the essence of human beings, and therefore treated the history of human thought as the development, the realisation, of that human essence. This view is the very paradigm of 'humanism'. Relatedly, Hegel held the idea of the 'expressive totality', that is, he treated any given period of history, and the organisation of a society, as a complex but internally unified thing made up of distinct parts, each of which was, however, an expression of some central theme or element. In Hegel's case, of course, a given historical period was an expression of the stage of development that the human mind (or spirit, as he would term it) had achieved, so that all aspects of life and thought were pervaded by the same kind of self-awareness. The level of self-awareness reached by the human mind, together with the intellectual dilemmas in which it was necessarily entrapped, provided the basic principle (or centre) around which the whole historical epoch and its societies were organised.

Althusser's position was a reaction to the extensive attachment of much of twentieth-century European Marxism to a Hegelian interpretation of Marx, which insisted on interpreting all his thought in terms of the (Hegelian-inspired) humanism so fully expressed in Marx's early writings. This interpretation of Marx emphasised and celebrated certain of his remarks, such as that human beings were the creators of their own history albeit not in circumstances of their own choosing. On this assertion, the history that people make is to be understood as the development or realisation of human potential through the material transformation – by means of productive activity – of their world.

Also in accord with Hegelian conceptions, Marx's view of society and its development was conceived as an expressive totality, unified throughout by the *single* principle of economic determinism, by the idea that the rest of society was shaped by the influence/need of its economic structure. Apparently, this assumption was the basis for Marx's base–superstructure theory and relatedly the notion of ideology. Althusser's counter to this Hegelian interpretation involved reconsidering the nature of the relationship between base and superstructure and formulating a conception of ideology certainly very different to that usually attributed to Marx.

The notion of base and superstructure as it is often interpreted in Marx is an instance of the conception of expressive totality. Society is a complex, differentiated structure, but it is organised around one unifying principle, i.e. the determination of other forms of social organisation by the need for the optimal development of the particular form of economy (agricultural, industrial, etc.). Although a society involves not just economic institutions, but also political, religious, educational and other ones, they are all to be understood as subordinate to and expressions of the needs of the economy. They arise in response to the requirements of the economic structure to perpetuate itself and thus serve to create and recreate the legal, political and other conditions essential to its continued operation. For example, religious doctrines, political beliefs and legal conceptions come to be understood as ideological in the sense that they are false conceptions, which play the role of justifying or otherwise facilitating the operations of the economy, of reconciling those within the society to its ways, which they would have occasion to question and perhaps overthrow if they were not misled about their true character.

For Althusser, this conception of the social whole (or, in his terms, 'formation') is much too simplifying. It goes against obvious facts about society such as the features of the superstructure being not only, and certainly not simply and directly, functions of the organisation of the economy. The notion that the economic base determines the superstructure involves an excessively coherent conception of the society. Society is indeed a unity of some kind, but it is not unified with all of the parts being an expression of a single basic principle or influence. It cannot be so, because historical events such as the transformation of a social formation, e.g. from feudalism to capitalism, do not derive from one single cause but require many different causes – what Althusser terms an '*over-determination*'. That the Russian Revolution took place was in important part due to the weakened and disaffected state of the army after prolonged warfare – among other causes – and not due to the nascent development of the capitalist economy alone.

## Althusser's key concepts

In developing this argument, Althusser attempts a delicate balancing act between relaxing the principle that the economy determines the rest of the social whole, on the one hand, and yet retaining the idea that the economy does exercise more than just a contingently causal role, on the other, since to abandon the economy's critical role would destroy virtually everything distinctive to Marx's thought. He attempts this balancing act through three notions:

1   the economy as *determinant in the last instance*;
2   the social formation as a *structure in dominance*;
3   the relation between parts of the society as being one of *relative autonomy*.

Together, these ideas constitute the core of Althusser's theoretical stance.

Althusser maintains that a general truth about the shape of societies is indeed their dependence upon the development of the economic base (point 1 above): if production in a given society were not organised in that way, then it would not be the same society, and the whole would not be structured like that. Consequently, the role of the economy is to be considered fundamental in fixing the nature of the other parts; it is more than just one part of society among others. However, there is no simple formula for deriving the organisation of the rest of society from the nature of the economy, or for deriving or explaining most, let alone all, features of the other structures in the society by the influence of the economy. Neither should it be supposed that within any given society the economy would necessarily be the dominating segment of its organisation. The idea of structure in dominance (point 2 above) refers to the tendency in any given society for one element to dominate, one set of institutions to prevail over and control other sectors of the society. The social formation is a complex interplay of structures, but it has a dominant element at the level of practical affairs, which is not necessarily – is not, in fact, even commonly – the economy. For example, in many societies in Western Europe, and for a long time, religion was the dominant force in society, and the church was the institution that prevailed over all others, even over monarchs.

The social whole is a complex structure, as it is composed of different elements – economic structure, political structure and so on – each having its own different requirements and its own history and rate of development. These different sectors change, but they do not automatically change together in close conjunction and at the same pace. The recognition of this fact is termed the 'relative autonomy' of structures within the social formation (point 3 above).

## Relative autonomy

This allows that, say, parliamentary arrangements can arise in different ways and develop according to their own 'laws', so to speak; their development has its own kinds of preconditions, which have nothing specifically to do with the nature of the economic structure of the society, but are, rather, in the nature of parliamentary arrangements themselves. Thus each arrangement – legal, political, administrative, religious, etc. – has a measure of independence from the others, manifests a degree of autonomy. However, the autonomy is *relative*. It should be contrasted with the simplistic idea (in Althusser's assessment) that the structure of the society as a whole is a straightforward function of the economy's own development. But the autonomy can only be relative, given the notion that in an indirect way the economy is a decisively shaping influence on the configuration of the whole complex. In short, the economy does not play the role of the immediate shaper of the social formation, but has the role of determinant in the last instance.

This point is anything but the minor quibble it might seem to anyone without a stake in the fate of Marx's legacy. Without this idea Althusser's Marxism would hardly qualify as Marxist at all. If he were saying only that the different structures of society interact with one another, each possibly, and certainly occasionally, exercising causal influence on the others, with causal effects between them being frequently reciprocal, then his position would amount to a version of Marxism which would differ not at all from the platitudes of sociology generally, and certainly would differ only in points of subject detail from Parsonian systems analysis. Hence his insistence that the economy is more than just one structure among others distances him from existing versions, against which Althusser argues for the economy as *primus inter pares* (first among equals). Thus Althusser differs from those he criticises by arguing that the economy does not directly determine the form of other structures within society; their form depends in part upon the nature of their own internal development and upon the ways they interact with one another, i.e. they have autonomy from economic determination. He does, however, set limits to its extent and to the conditions that determine how independent of the economy some other structures can be. In this way, the nature of the economy can determine the dominant element in a social formation; it may be the economy that is to be dominant or it may be some other component.

The development and workings of the social formation are to be understood in terms of *structural causality*.

## Structural causality

This was meant to emphasise that the determination of the form and development of a social formation and its constituent parts was a phenomenon in its own right; it could not be understood in (so to speak) a bottom-up way, i.e. arising from the intentions and actions of individuals.

Althusser's anti-humanism was resolute: the minimal constituents of social structures were positions and relationships, e.g. the positions of worker and manager and the relation of employer–employee, prescribed by the structure, in this case the economy. Actual individuals are of no significance in Althusser's theory; they merely play the part of occupants of these positions, the bearers of their responsibilities. Althusser would argue that he is not displaying his own theoretical predilection in respect of capitalism; it is capitalism itself which has reduced people to the merely incidental occupants of the positions and relations it prescribes, effectively making individuals interchangeable in terms of economic functions, ensuring that it makes no difference to *the structure of positions* whether one person rather than another occupies and fulfils the requirements of any given position; all that matters is that someone does.

Rather than the structures of the social formation being created by individuals, it is the other way around: the individuals are mere by-products of the society.

## Individualism as ideology

In the argument we have met often before in the French tradition, once again the idea of 'the individual', so often the foundation for attempts at social theory, can be seen as an ideological construction, the product of a specific period and its culture. As signalled at the outset of this section, Althusser declares this idea to be a part of bourgeois ideology. The reciprocal of this argument is, of course, that ideology (bourgeois or otherwise) cannot be a creation of individuals.

## Ideology as structure

Althusser generates a revisionist – what he would call 'authentically Marxist' – account of ideology. Ideology is often thought of as created by particular individuals or groups, and serves as a means of communication and persuasion whereby those individuals or groups induce others to believe certain things, thereby duping them into accepting otherwise unacceptable conditions. On Althusser's terms, this account cannot be correct, for it underestimates the extent to which ideology is structured; ideology does not consist in what individuals think; rather, it is in fixing the framework within which individuals think, thereby setting the limits to what they can think. Language provides a model here. Individuals communicate with one another in a language and may persuade one another through such communication, yet we do not suppose that they contrive the language that they speak. In the same way, though individuals may think in an ideology, they do not contrive it. Furthermore, actual individuals are not aware of the extent to which their own existence as 'individuals' is drawn from ideology.

Althusser shares the standard Marxist view that ideology and science are contraposed and Marxist science is a critique of ideology, but he does not draw the usual conclusion, namely, that science can help to deliver the abolition of ideology. It cannot do so, because science is not an adequate basis on which practical life can be conducted. Science is a purely specialised pursuit with an entirely impersonal point of view; it cannot, therefore, be used as the basis for any one individual's personal view of her or his situation and of its practical requirements. There is no room *in science* for a personal point of view. Further, science is purely concerned with the pursuit of knowledge, but a person's conduct in society also has many practical concerns; what is required for the person to get on with his or her life cannot be derived from the theories of science. Since the only alternative to science is ideology, then life in society must necessarily be based on it. As Althusser suggests, in every society people must be mentally shaped, reshaped and equipped to respond to the demands of their conditions of existence (in plainer terms, 'enculturated'). Since this demand cannot be met by scientific theory it must be fulfilled by ideology. However, under conditions of relative autonomy the particular forms which individuality will take vary across the different structures of the social formation.

On the other hand, while there may be varying ways for individuality to develop (because of relative autonomy), none the less, in a capitalist society ideology must serve to ensure the reproduction of the conditions of capitalist economic production (because of determination, in the last instance). Thus ideology is structured, albeit in different ways and to different degrees, around the general requirements of the economy. Althusser argues that, in a modern society, the structuring and reproduction of ideology is achieved through *ideological state apparatuses* (ISAs).

As mentioned above, in traditional Marxist theory the state has treated ideology as a means of achieving domination for a given, ruling class within the society, as an instrument of class power and, therefore, as a repressive agency primarily, capable of resort to violence in order to back up the control of the ruling class if necessary. However, the conditions for the reproduction of capitalist conditions of production require that the subordinate classes be equipped with the skills requisite to their work, and also with the attitudes and outlook that will make them well-behaved and compliant participants in the productive process. Consequently, control of the society cannot be simply on the basis of the threat – and sometimes the actual use – of physical coercion alone. It must involve control of the mind, i.e. hegemony, as Gramsci termed it. Althusser's distinctive move is to propose that the *state* is the mechanism of hegemony, which it achieves by two means: through coercion but also through ideological control. The state consists in two distinct (though, of course, related) apparatuses: the *repressive apparatus* (the police and armed forces particularly, under the single, central direction of the political authorities) and the *ideological apparatus* (a heterogeneous assortment of social forms not united under any central direction).

## Ideological state apparatuses (ISAs)

The list of ISAs which Althusser provides is:

- the educational system;
- the family;
- the legal system;
- the political system;
- the trade unions;
- the mass media;
- the cultural domain and leisure spheres.

They are clearly a mixed bag, involving very varied activities, and there is certainly autonomy among them, i.e. they have their own independent, internal developmental tendencies. However, Althusser makes two general points about them:

1  The autonomy is, again, only relative, and the heterogeneity of the assorted ISAs is quite superficial, for they all operate under and emanate from a single ideology, that of the ruling class.
2  These seemingly independent spheres of social life have in common the crucial fact that they are all part of the state apparatus.

Claim (2) might seem odd: while we readily count the government, its police and army, and its civil service bureaucracy as part of the state, we would not normally count the family or the trade unions as such. For Althusser, this shows how perfectly we have been captured by the ruling – the bourgeois – ideology. After all, this separation of the state and these other spheres is founded on the distinction between public and private sectors, which is internal to bourgeois ideology and therefore dispensable from any genuine Marxist theory which must purge itself of all elements of ideology, especially bourgeois ones.

Not only does relative autonomy figure in Althusser's formulation of the ISAs but so, too, does the notion of dominance. Not all ISAs are equal. In a given social formation, there will be some ISAs – in the cases he discusses, a pair – which are dominant. In the Middle Ages the church and family were the dominant ISAs, and in capitalist society the education and family pairing has replaced them. If we take the governmental arrangements of democratic parliamentarianism to be the dominant ISA, we might not accept this latter point, but we would be wrong. Modern history has shown that democratic parliamentarianism is by no means essential to capitalism, which has proved itself to be compatible with quite other types of governmental arrangement. Althusser briefly states the essence of his argument on behalf of the dominant position of 'the school' over the other ISAs, which also instil the appropriate capitalistic attitudes: 'no other ideological State apparatus has the obligatory (and not least free) audience of the totality of the children in the capitalist social formation, eight hours a day for five or six days out of seven' (1971: 148). And, of course, schools work with the family.

For Althusser, then, ideology shapes who and what we are as members of society. Our whole existence in society, lived as it is in and through participation in the various ideological apparatuses, is permeated with ideology. In Althusser's conception, ideology is equivalent to what in other, non-Marxist traditions would be called *socialisation*. Little wonder, then, that capitalism has proven so resilient as a system. It is built into each of us at an early age and reinforced in all (quite detailed) aspects of our daily existence. Such an all-encompassing view of ideology inevitably led to complaints that Althusser's conception left no space to develop opposition to the status quo. If ideology is built so deeply and intricately into the structures of social existence, if, indeed, it underpins them, if it is itself the foundational structure, then what has become of the idea of resistance? These concerns, perhaps more than other more philosophical objections to Althusser's structuralism, had the effect of creating disenchantment and paving the way to poststructuralism (see next chapter). If this was what Marxism had come to, arguably its usefulness as a critique of society was outlived.

## Conclusion

Structuralism played a powerful part in reorienting Anglo-American sociology towards European social thought. It also broke down disciplinary barriers, in so far as the structuralist method, originating in anthropology and linguistics, appeared to be a means of analysing cultural phenomena generally. It had an especially strong influence on literary work, where 'theory' was to become a key term as a result. Combined with the influence of Western Marxism's concern with cultural hegemony, structuralism's nature as a form of cultural analysis heavily shifted interests towards the analysis of what were, in Marxist terms, superstructural phenomena. A little like Talcott Parsons, however, structuralism will, perhaps, be more influential in terms of the effects of the reaction against it, rather than through its positive achievements. Poststructuralism's name reflects the fact that it does follow from, and owe some of its ideas to, structuralism, so much so that Manfred Frank, for example, preferred to term it 'neo-structuralism'. It now exercises a much greater and more far-reaching influence on contemporary thought than structuralism proper ever attained, and while there are continuities between them, these are outweighed by the differences.

## Questions

1  What do you understand by the term 'structuralism'? How does it relate to the ideas of Saussure? How does it relate to the ideas of Freud?

2  Why does Lévi-Strauss think Durkheim's concept of *totemism* is so important? Is he right? What does he add to the concept? Does his account make more sense than Durkheim's own?

3  Lévi-Strauss believed that Freud's ideas about the unconscious meant social theory had to be transformed. Was he right? Do other theorists offer more effective alternatives? Does it make any difference whether or not people are conscious of the real nature of myth? Why?

4  What does Barthes mean by 'myth'? How does this develop the ideas of Lévi-Strauss? How does it relate to Durkheim's ideas about religion? How does it relate to, or differ from, Marx's notion of ideology?

5  Why does Barthes argue we are prisoners of language? Is he right? If he is, what implications does this have for social change and political opposition? What logical problems might there be with his position? Is Barthes's argument the same as that of Peter Winch?

6  What does Althusser mean when he says the economic base has 'relative autonomy'? How is this different to Marx's arguments? Is Althusser's reading of Marx something you agree with? Why? If Marx is read as a humanist or a Hegelian would that mean Althusser's argument could no longer apply?

7  Althusser argues that 'the individual' is an ideological construct. How does that view differ from those of Marx, Weber and Durkheim? Which is right? Why?

## Next steps

The clearest starting points for the key structuralist thinkers are Lévi-Strauss's (1962) *Totemism*, Barthes's (1973) *Mythologies*, and Althusser's (1971) *Lenin and Philosophy*.

The range of structuralist texts is best approached through an overview. Harland (1987) provides a clear, short account of structuralist thought and its aftermath, while Glucksmann (1974) offers a more detailed, critical, narrative, focusing on Lévi-Strauss and Althusser.

# PART IV

# Post-sociological perspectives?

The Western Marxist and structuralist approaches outlined in the previous part ended pessimistically: both the Frankfurt School and Althusser seemed to indicate that social change was unlikely, to say the least, and perhaps impossible. Perhaps more than for their philosophical and theoretical weaknesses, this pessimism motivated subsequent thinkers to try to move beyond their constraints. The 'post' perspectives – poststructuralism and postmodernism – came to dominate sociological thought in the 1980s and 1990s, in both America and Europe, either by being appropriated or by being fiercely opposed. In this part of the book we will examine these approaches, and, separately, the work of Michel Foucault, the most sociologically influential figure associated with them.

The poststructuralists took as their starting point Barthes's notion that language is a prison and Althusser's idea that the ways we see the world are irredeemably ideological. If these arguments are correct, they posited, then the very bases of Western Marxism and structuralism are themselves open to question. If Barthes is right, there can be no 'gap' between thought and reality, because 'reality' can never be grasped separate to thought, to language. If Althusser is right, language and thought are themselves ideological in nature and, as such, must be the sole subjects of sociological examination: the relationships between thought and power thus become the core concern for social investigation. Abandoning 'scientific' pretensions, taking pleasure in the examination of 'discourse' for its own sake, and replacing Marxian understandings of the nature of the world with anarchist concerns about domination and regulation, the poststructuralist turn was a radical break with its structuralist forebears. Roland Barthes's later work will be used to illustrate these developments as his movement from structuralist analysis of myth to his increasing concern with 'the Text' is emblematic of the shift from one to the other.

Michel Foucault was the most influential structuralist/poststructuralist thinker for sociological purposes, and his works have become core texts in criminology (*Discipline and Punish*), medical sociology (*The Birth of the Clinic*) and studies of deviance (*Madness and Civilisation*). His theoretical positions reflected the slipperiness of both the structuralist and poststructuralist perspectives, but his concern with 'discourse' provided a more solid footing for more conventional sociological approaches than the works of Barthes or Althusser. In particular, Foucault's recognition that certain ways of thinking are historically specific – they cannot emerge at the 'wrong' time, and are tied to the events that precede them – allowed for a more nuanced view of language and thought than Barthes's joyful playing with 'the Text'. Furthermore, Foucault advanced a novel conceptualisation of how power operates in the world, permeating all social relations from top to bottom. In many respects, we argue, Foucault's appropriation by sociology was made easier by the fact that, although deriving from the same kinds of concerns pursued by the structuralists and poststructuralists, his thought is strongly congruent with many aspects of Weberian and Durkheimian scholarship.

For a more radical – perhaps, according to its adherents, the most radical – 'post' perspective, in the final chapter in this part we turn to the postmodernists. Taking a similar starting point to the poststructuralists, the postmodernists embraced the ideas of chance and randomness in meaning. Derrida, in particular, argued that language is always something that can be understood in multiple ways, something potentially chaotic, and that 'meaning' is itself a form of ideological closure, taking one particular linguistic possibility and making it *the* fixed point for understanding. Rather than seeking out definitive meanings, therefore, Derrida's 'deconstruction' was meant to reveal the arbitrary and paradoxical nature of a text, demonstrating that its 'meaning' is actually something that could be very different. The postmodernists proper – Baudrillard and Lyotard in particular – took Derrida's analysis further, arguing that the world itself had lost its meaning. 'Grand narratives' of progress, liberalism, socialism and the rest are no longer applicable: the world has become fragmented and diverse, and seeking to make a single coherent sense out of this diversity is no longer appropriate. The world, in short, has itself become postmodern, and modernity is finished. If poststructuralism embraced anarchist ideas, postmodern theory turned to an explicit nihilism.

## CHAPTER TEN

# Poststructuralism: abandoning the certainties of meaning

---

**Chapter overview**

The apparent failure of the Western Marxist and structuralist projects led to a great deal of soul-searching and self-criticism among Western sociologists, in particular those working within the Continental traditions. Incorporating ideas from the philosopher Nietzsche, the poststructuralists developed Althusser's ideas about ideology and Barthes's notion that language is a prison to question the bases of Marxian and structuralist thought. The idea that there could be gaps between reality and ideology was abandoned – as no such non-ideological reality could exist – and the scientific pretensions of structuralist thought were left behind. Language itself, modified into the concept of *discourse*, was to be the sole subject of sociological analysis, with its relationship to power and its imperfect nature particular areas of analytical interest. The later work of Barthes, in which texts are not analysed in their own right but rather treated as the means of joyfully dissolving meaning and the self, provides the starting point for this. Ultimately, poststructuralist thought led to a reframing of concepts of power and domination, which came to be understood as apparent throughout all social activity, incapable of being evaded: the Marxian idea of revolutionary change was abandoned.

---

## Introduction: background and some provisos

In this and the next chapter we remain in Paris. Lévi-Strauss began to develop his main ideas in the 1940s; Althusser's most influential work involved a collaborative seminar held in the early 1960s devoted to his *Reading Capital* or, rather, explaining Althusser's way of reading capital. The considerable standing that the seminar won for him in Parisian intellectual life was soon lost when, perhaps compromised by his position as almost the official philosopher of the French Communist Party, which did not like revolutionary movements that it did not control, Althusser failed to make a strong public and supportive response to 'the events' of May 1968. These 'events' were short-lived (lasting only a few days, though obviously casting a very long historical shadow), and revolutionary activity was curtailed, but their occurrence, and the disappointment with the Marxist response, as epitomised by the Communist Party, ensured that there was a commitment to developing intellectual opposition to capitalism, but doing so by means of providing a non-Marxist critical way of thinking.

Owing to the delay of translation, Althusser's impact upon British sociology was also delayed, and the heyday of its influence was in the early 1970s when 'structuralist Marxism' was a key phrase, and was used by theorists such as Barry Hindess and Paul Hirst (in collaboration) as a springboard for a drastic (though rapidly evolving/shifting) critique of the epistemological foundations of sociological understanding. The assertion of a structuralist Marxism was a welcome occurrence, no doubt because the vigour with which the arguments for the 'interactionist' approaches such as symbolic interaction and ethnomethodology were being pursued seemed to pose the threat of elimination for 'structuralist' theories (by which was meant, theories such as Durkheim's and Marx's, which affirmed the reality of 'objective social structures' above and beyond the level of individuals). The 'interactionists' were understood as individualists who denied there were any such realities, and Althusser's difficult, technical and, unquestionably, ingenious ideas were seized upon as a reassertion of the continuing viability of the older 'structuralist' project. The idea that the universities might be 'red bases' of the sort that Marcuse had imagined could substitute for the absence of a militant working class did not last beyond a few modest exercises in the occupation of university buildings in the UK, and talk of revolution also soon abated, although concern with preserving the *theoretical* possibility of the revolution remained intense. There was much argument to make the case that, in one respect or another, meliorating approaches to social justice were necessarily ineffective and attempts to moderate the inequities of a capitalist society within its framework would be inhibited by the counter-active forces of the capitalist system itself. In other words, significant social change must involve the transformation of the system as a whole.

While Althusser's influence reinvigorated confidence in the importance of 'objective structures', it seemed to perhaps go too far in that direction, especially in respect of its anti-humanism, its reduction of individuals to place-fillers within the social formation. Edward Thompson, a historian of the English working class, conducted a notably strong polemic against the Althusserian over-exaggeration of structural determination (*The Poverty of Theory and Other Essays*, 1978). These uncertainties, along with other considerations, had much to do with creating the idea that the relationship between structure and agency, between structural causation and independent individual action, was the key theoretical problem facing sociology.

However, the extensive radicalising of the UK university population in the wake of the American countercultural movements and the events of May, having prepared the ground for a warm reception for Althusser's provocative work, also opened the way for much more attentiveness to 'European' – especially French – social thought, and developments in Paris were much more closely followed. The result was that the poststructuralist theorists began to have their (very different) influence. The introduction of the idea of 'the social' into numerous disciplines played a key role that would intensify the weakening of disciplinary distinctions, if not so much of academic boundaries.

In Chapter 8 we mentioned the way the critique of capitalism gave way to a critique of the culture of modern society and, eventually, to a condemnation of one particular but very prominent and influential aspect of it, the so-called Enlightenment project, i.e. the aspiration of bringing people to freedom through the use of reason. Poststructuralism has put the challenge to the Enlightenment at the centre of contemporary debate, and stated a most thoroughgoing scepticism about reason.

Previously we mentioned the Frankfurt School's doubts about the legacy of the Enlightenment, pointing out that its position is ambivalent. It critiques the idea of reason enshrined in the institutions of industrial society because these realisations amount to perversions and corruptions of reason, rather than because any appeal to reason is intrinsically suspect. Thus its position has an optimistic aspect, in the sense that if only some effective means can be found to expose the falsity of the intellectual foundations of the prevailing institutions, then there is at least the prospect of reconstructing society along different lines, i.e. on the basis of genuine rationality and freedom. With the poststructuralists, however, the critique of the Enlightenment is radicalised; they replace the ambivalence towards reason displayed by the Frankfurt School with outright rejection. Poststructuralism expunges all traces of such optimism.

In order to understand the character of this scepticism we need to examine the intellectual foundations of poststructuralism, in particular its relationship with structuralism, out of which it developed and in relation to which its view of language was forged. Before we do so, however, a few words of caution are necessary. To give any general characterisation of poststructuralism is problematic for two reasons. First, the poststructuralist movement is anything but unified. Indeed, several of those most prominently associated with it, whose ideas we discuss below, have – as symbolic interactionists did before them – expressed their reluctance to accept the label. They have complained of being lumped together with other thinkers with whose thought they see no strong affinity. For example, Michel Foucault was uneasy about the classification of his early work as 'structuralist' and also his later work as 'poststructuralist', and he and Jacques Derrida, 'another poststructuralist', by no means always see eye to eye. These complaints alert us to the fact that there are significant differences among the positions of those conventionally assigned the label 'poststructuralist', and that in giving a general characterisation of poststructuralism we can do little more than identify a set of themes, some broadly shared, but others understood quite differently by different thinkers.

Second, more difficulties stem from the complex, unconventional and often elusive nature of poststructuralist arguments themselves. Poststructuralists often defy the usual conventions of academic/scientific discourse, intending their work directly to challenge these, but there can be much – even calculated – ambiguity about the extent to which they have withdrawn from these conventions. Just how radical poststructuralist positions actually are is also ambiguous, since they are sometimes presented as though they are quite extreme, and at other times are set out in a much more moderate way. Among poststructuralists themselves, ambiguities and inconsistencies in their own ideas do not necessarily count against them. They are disdainful of scientific aspiration and academic convention altogether. After all, they are engaged in a profound critique of 'Western reason' with its demands for logic and system; rather than comply with those demands, they resist them, embracing, even cultivating, ambiguity, contradiction and paradox. In this way, poststructuralism disarms – often utterly frustrates – its critics by celebrating inconclusiveness and even inconsistency.

With these provisos to the fore, we sketch the origins of the poststructuralist movement. It was another predominantly Parisian development, which both reacted against structuralism and also, in important respects, grew out of it. In the earlier part of their careers, two prominent poststructuralist thinkers, Roland Barthes and Michel Foucault, had structuralist allegiances, seeking in some ways to take the structuralist arguments to their extreme. That is not to say that they were taken to their logical conclusions, since taking them to that extreme involves going beyond their logical limits, even into paradox. Henry Miller attached to his *Black Spring* the aphorism, 'the French have a passion for logic, as have the insane'; we can see its reflection in the poststructuralist combination of a determination to pursue the process of logical systematisation to its utter extreme in a way that reveals the unreasonable nature of an excessive attachment to reason itself.

## The debt to Nietzsche

As mentioned in Chapter 9, the failure of Marxists such as Althusser to give a positive lead in the disturbances of 1968 led thinkers like Foucault and Derrida to repudiate Marx's work as a basis for their own efforts. (Derrida pointed out, in response to criticisms of his work as apolitical in nature, that he had always had an affinity with Marx's views.) Despite the emphasis upon the determination of people's conduct by social forces of which they were not aware (through the workings of ideology), Marx had remained an Enlightenment-minded figure in that he had retained his faith in the value of conscious, rational thought to overcome the domination of these unconscious determinants. Reason alone could not emancipate humankind – Marx's rejection of Hegel was in no small part due to Hegel's assumption that it could – but reason could guide effective class action to deliver this result. Though acclaimed for his contribution to the discovery of unconscious forces in human life, Marx was now being criticised for underestimating the extent to which these forces pervaded it and could not be overcome.

The rejection of Marx, however, did not represent a step towards the reduction in the dependence of contemporary social thought upon nineteenth-century theory. Another nineteenth-century thinker, Friedrich Nietzsche (1844–1900), was assigned the tutelary role which Marx had previously occupied. Nietzsche had much more profound doubts than Marx about the nature and capacities of reason and the significance of modern civilisation.

Nietzsche's primary importance in relation to poststructuralism is in terms of his attack upon the spirit of modern civilisation, i.e. that of the nineteenth century in Western Europe. Nietzsche referred to his work as 'philosophy with a hammer' to indicate that the task he had set himself was substantially destructive: to tear down the two 'false gods' of religion and reason. In Nietzsche's opinion the culture of Western civilisation had become sterile and oppressive, making individuals living under it timid, unadventurous and repressed creatures. Nietzsche blamed Christianity for teaching people to be meek, compliant and dependent. Human nature had two conflicting sides. One, the wilder, uncivilised side, is instinctive, impulsive and undisciplined, but also vigorous and strong. Nietzsche termed it the *Dionysian* element, naming it after the Greek god of drunkenness. The other, contrasting side of human nature, however, is the *Apollonian* (after Apollo, a Greek sun god of great beauty); it is concerned with discipline, control, order and form, but, also, it has become insipid and constricting, an expression of bourgeois conformism, rather than of the boldly adventurous soul. One of these sides – the Apollonian – had markedly gained the upper hand in the nineteenth-century West, an unhealthy situation for civilisation and culture.

For Nietzsche, the great prestige accorded to reason at that time and in that place was a perfect symptom of the dominance of the Apollonian outlook; reason was conceived of as the apogee of discipline, control, restraint, and neat and tidy order, yet it was neither so valuable nor so beneficial as it was made out to be. Rather than being the fullest and most extensive fulfilment of the capacities of the human mind, reason obstructed its most adventurous, creative, imaginative and powerful uses, which could only be released if the Dionysian side were to be given much greater rein. Within modern society, the representative figures were businesspeople and scientists, who were dull, uninspiring and pallid creatures in comparison with the great and heroic achievers of earlier civilisations.

In short, the vaunting of reason was a matter of self-deception. The point about the predominance of the Apollonian mode was not merely that it sought to bound the impulsive, Dionysian side, whose anarchic spirit would threaten to destroy the structures of order and discipline that had been developed, but that it also sought to suppress and deny the very existence of this element of human nature. It would not admit that human beings have these two sides, and that the expression of the Dionysian qualities is essential to a healthy situation. The mind was elevated over the body, and the culture of nineteenth-century Western Europe would not allow that people have a more physical, earthy, animal existence, which also needs satisfaction, as well as the need to satisfy their 'higher' intellectual powers. The picture of human beings painted in the culture was one-sided in concealing the existence of the Dionysian aspect. However, the fact that the culture would not admit to its existence did not mean it had ceased to exist, for human beings continued to have the same two-sided nature. It did mean, though, that the outlet for the impulsive, wayward side of individuals could not be open and direct.

## The will to power

For Nietzsche, the roots of individual motivation were in what he termed '*the will to power*', i.e. in the instinctive human drives to grow, to develop in strength and potency, and to be increasingly powerful and dominant. This will to power was the natural, biologically rooted source of all human activity and achievements – including those of reason itself – but its nature made it the sort of thing that contemporary culture could not acknowledge or approve.

The modern Western mind, i.e. that of Nietzsche's time, could not think of itself as driven by instinctual urges and was, therefore, unable to admit to itself the true nature of the underlying forces which propelled it. Therefore, the culture had to misrepresent itself as the product solely of the 'higher' mental powers, entirely dissociated from those 'lower' drives rooted in the animal nature of human beings (including, of course, the will to power). As a result, the culture it had created could, in more modern terms, be said to act as a rationalisation, i.e. explaining the nature of human beings, the ways their minds work and the reasons for their activities in a way which makes them seem better, more high-minded, objective and public-spirited than in truth they actually are or could possibly be. A rationalisation is sincerely given, but is false because the mind is divided against itself. In a situation in which the Apollonian inclination is so dominant, the suggestion that Dionysian tendencies have any contribution cannot be accepted, cannot be allowed to enter into conscious deliberation, cannot even be thought.

Thus reason commonly sets itself up as the pure product of its own operations, something created entirely out of the impartial, reflective and dispassionate desire to know, thereby setting itself out as entirely in opposition to passion and impulse. It was Nietzsche's intention to dispute this opposition and question this self-portrait of reason.

Nietzsche's scepticism about the source and nature of reason as an expression of the will to power and as something which has been applied to achieve the subjugation of the more Dionysian side of human existence greatly influenced the poststructuralists. Far from regarding science as enabling the triumph of reason over unreason, of rational thought over unconscious processes, Nietzsche's approach encouraged the view that science is itself only one more manifestation of the unconscious, just another product of the will to power. Rather than being a vehicle for the emancipation of humanity, science, along with the heritage of Christianity, played the part of forming the docile, sheep-like character of people in modern society. This Nietzschean idea can be clearly seen in Michel Foucault's concern with the way social arrangements in Western Europe progressively marginalise and eradicate 'Dionysian' aspects of social life and engender a passive, dependent, manipulable individual (see the next chapter). Foucault adopts this view in stressing the extent to which social life involves the disciplining and suppression of the wilder, more disorderly aspects of human existence. In particular, his later work immensely emphasises how the growth of social scientific fields (such as psychiatry and criminology) has been interwoven with the development of complex administrative structures designed to make people easily controlled through the creation of an elaborate and detailed set of techniques of social organisation.

Max Weber had certainly incorporated Nietzschean elements in his thought, and partially prefigured the shift that was about to take place. Modern society appeared paradoxical to Weber, in so far as it provided a life of unprecedented material satisfaction for an equally unprecedented proportion of its inhabitants, and yet people were not happy. This was because the economically and administratively rationalised structure of those societies, combined with the scientifically rationalised character of their worldview, had become spiritually desolating.

This was the theme of the 'disenchantment' of the modern world. The shift that we mention is away from the critique of capitalism as a society which denies people their humanity by reducing the working class to a materially impoverished, almost animal existence, towards the critique of bourgeois culture, seen as the dominant, and spiritually impoverishing, culture.

## Differences between structuralism and poststructuralism

The difference between structuralism and poststructuralism can be (crudely) reduced to the following point:

Poststructuralism abandons the scientific aspirations of its structuralist forebears.

It does so because it sees an insuperable paradox in providing a critique of the inescapable ideological contamination of language by means of that same ideologically contaminated language; with Althusser it sees (virtually) no means of escaping ideology.

Poststructuralism adopts a conception of language as a species of power; its use inherently involves domination, which we may term the 'prison house of language' (see Jameson 1972). This expression is often used to convey the idea that people are unable to get outside language in order to encounter and truly comprehend reality in itself and independently of all human preconceptions, but can only perceive it through the medium of language, with its inbuilt preconceptions. This is certainly the case made by poststructuralists, but to this conception they add the idea that language is a vehicle of social control, i.e. the way it regulates people's thought serves the social purposes of regulation and domination.

Consequently, poststructuralism develops an anarchist, rather than a Marxist, politics.

## Everything is political

Politics is at the top of the poststructuralist agenda. As mentioned in Chapter 9, it involves the attempt to find an alternative way of criticising bourgeois culture from that provided from a Marxist basis. The difficulty the poststructuralists see (in parallel with the Frankfurt School: see Chapter 8) is that the relentless following out of structuralist arguments disables the prospects of oppositional thinking. At its core, the poststructuralist rejection of structuralism asserts the political character of everything, language most of all. By contrast, structuralism is perceived as having a comparatively apolitical stance. This stance arises directly out of structuralism's view of language. Poststructuralists like Barthes sought to solve the problem of how to retain structuralism's *anti-representational* view of language without succumbing to political quietude.

## Representationalism

This is the label given to a traditional theory of language, as we noted in the previous chapter, which understands that the function of words is to name, or stand for, things. In this traditional view, language is understood quite literally to re-present things, to enable us to make absent objects present to us, to enable us to speak of and relate to things even though they are not actually physically there. On this theory, at the basis of language exists a connection between the linguistic (words) and the external to language (things).

The poststructuralists understand Saussure to have severed the tie between language and any world outside language. His account features the signifier and the signified as only elements of the sign. The *signified* is the idea in the mind of the speaker, i.e. the concept associated with the *signifier*, which is the physical (aural or graphical) vehicle, e.g. a sound or letter. Some words do stand for things, but the relationship between the word and the thing it stands for is an arbitrary and conventional one. Hence, the relationship between words cannot reflect anything essential about the nature of external reality, and about the relations of the things that comprise it. Of course, philosophers have (fruitlessly) sought to capture through language the inherently essential nature of things. Regrettably for this enterprise, the meaning of words is given through the organisation of the language itself, through the pattern of contrasts that makes up the system, and not by the relationship of words to physical things; words do not stand as names for things. Consequently, the nature of signs – which we will largely treat as words – is determined internally within the system of language; it has nothing to do with any external world outside language. From this view the poststructuralists draw an epistemological conclusion: since language is not a vehicle of representation (there is no room for a representational function in Saussure's account) then it cannot be used to represent the external world. Hence it cannot be a basis for knowing the external world, for saying things about how the world truly is.

The problem with which poststructuralists grappled can be briefly stated as follows. If social reality is entirely constituted out of sign systems then the idea that there can be any 'outside' to those sign systems ceases to have any meaning. Consequently, the idea that there can be any tension between the sign systems and reality itself disappears. By definition, sign systems cannot misrepresent reality, if reality consists in these sign systems. Nor can these sign systems operate repressively if there is nothing outside them to be repressed. Yet much criticism of capitalist society is based on the discrepancies between reality and its representation, between people's true needs and the ideologically instilled ones. The structuralists Lévi-Strauss and the early Barthes had many Marxist elements in their general social thought and were certainly inclined to criticise capitalist society, yet in terms of thoroughgoing structuralism, it seems that they were not entitled to do so. Persistence with the logic of structuralism seems to take away what was regarded as its point, namely, to critique bourgeois culture. After all, from this critical standpoint there is no place outside society from which to criticise it.

## Abandoning aspirations to science

Poststructuralists part company with the legacy of structuralism on another key point: the aspiration to scientific status. Like their structuralist forebears, post-structuralists reject humanism, insisting that the system of language operates independently of speakers' intent. Speakers may appear to be in control of the meaning of language, but in fact they are quite unconscious of the system of language within which their speaking takes place. Therefore, they are essentially unaware of much that is going on when they speak. Hence language operates according to its own ways, beyond the conscious control of speakers.

The structuralists were certainly keen to deny significance to the *subject*, and talked about the structure of language operating according to its own laws, thereby emphasising their own allegiance to the project of achieving a scientific understanding of language and culture. Here the poststructuralists discerned a dilemma.

### The dilemma over science

By continuing to aim to be scientists, the structuralists operate in defiance of Saussure's idea that language is not a vehicle of repre-sentation, yet the very idea of science is representationalist, i.e. it manifests the conviction that language can be used to re-present things outside itself. In short, the structuralists aim to talk about the external world, which is inaccessible through language.

The poststructuralists resolve this paradox at the heart of structuralism by giving up on the idea of trying to be scientists. They regard the scientific pre-tensions of structuralism as yet another manifestation of the Enlightenment project; making a clean break with it involves abandoning such pretensions entirely.

The critique of representationalism and the rejection of scientism are linked moves. Structuralism failed to think through rigorously the ideological connec-tions between language, representationalism and science. From its standpoint, representationalism was treated simply as an incorrect theory, which would be replaced by a more adequately scientific understanding of language. Poststruc-turalism asserts a much stronger connection between language, representation-alism and ideology. Representationalism is not just an incorrect theory but also a master ideology that pervades language and shapes its use. The idea of represen-tation, i.e. that language speaks about the external world, is so deeply rooted in language – and so interwoven with relationships of domination in society – that it is virtually inconceivable that its control can be entirely or even substantially evaded. Thus the ideology of representation is built into the whole way Western society is organised, so that people pick it up without its ever being explicitly or deliberately taught; it is not formulated or advanced by any group within society, and it is not a position espoused by any party as a political cause. Language is so entirely saturated with this ideology, not merely contaminated by it, that purging it of ideological elements is simply not conceivable. Consequently, while it is essential to expose the falsity of representationalism wherever possible, it is hard to conceive how ideology could be thoroughly eliminated. Ideology is the framework within which the individual thinks; it is imposed upon the individual through language. This view is much akin to Althusser's conception (see Chapter 9), though not necessarily in explicit alliance with it. Although his concept of ideology moves away from the traditional one in this respect, it was none the less used as part of the quite traditional contrast between ideology and science, which has now collapsed.

Far from being in stark contrast, science must be seen as a prime instance of ideology – indeed, the leading exponent of the ideology of representation. The whole notion of science as capable of giving genuine knowledge of the nature of the external world, e.g. telling us how things are at the further end of the universe, or down at the most inconceivably minute levels of matter, is entirely at odds with the idea that the external world is inaccessible to us, i.e. that words can really and categorically not capture reality. On this argument, science itself is one of the central candidates to be exposed as falsely presenting itself as representational. By the same token, those who make it their business to expose this falsity must themselves eschew any conception that what they do is any kind of scientific enterprise; despite continuities with structuralism, they must distance themselves from it. As Barthes put it:

precisely because all thought about the historically intelligible is also a participation in that intelligibility, structural man is scarcely concerned to last; he knows that structuralism, too, is a certain form of the world, which will change with the world.

(1972: 219–20)

The point, then, is to turn the arguments of structuralism against structuralism itself and to subject to analysis not only what are patently mythologies, but also what is ostensibly knowledge, including science.

The rejection of science is related to two other points on which poststructuralism differs from its structuralist parent. First, structuralism inclines too much towards one side of the traditional body–mind dichotomy, being mentalistic; it is an approach concerned with tracking the abstract, immaterial operations of the mind, and thereby excluding from its attention the physical, bodily existence of human beings and the material conditions of living. Second, structuralism has a problematical relationship to history, arising from its natural focus on identifying the general and unvarying principles of the structure. For example, in Lévi-Strauss's approach these principles result from the universal physical structure of the human brain. Consequently, structuralism did not develop a way of dealing with the historical character of social existence. On both points the poststructuralists adopt a more radical stance. For them, the separation of language and thought from the body and its life in a practical world was a product of structuralism's failure to free itself entirely from the legacy of Cartesian dualism (see Chapter 6). Here the poststructuralist concept of *discourse* crucially refers to ways of speaking and thinking that are patterned and socially accepted.

### Discourse

For the poststructuralists, discourses are conceived historically; they are not fixed and universal, but rather emerge at certain points in history; the relationship between discourses is not predetermined but historically contingent.

The concept of discourse is not reconcilable with that of science since the very notion of science as conventionally understood is itself a cornerstone of one particular discourse, namely, the one established in the seventeenth- and eighteenth-century Enlightenment. Therefore, there cannot be a science of discourse.

## The unruliness of language

Another general element crucial to understanding the broad poststructuralist position is its emphasis on the *unruly* nature of language.

### Unruly language

Although language is put to the service of social ends, it never can be identified with such ends and should never be regarded as *straightforwardly* ideological. Similarly, while language is socially controlled and used as an instrument for the conduct and organisation of day-to-day affairs within society, and while it is almost by definition, in the poststructuralist scheme of things, an instrument of domination, none the less it has the potential for disruption; i.e. it tends to escape from and/or subvert the arrangements which seek to contain it.

This view gives us a picture of a struggle between language and social arrangements. Existing social arrangements strive, so to speak, to straitjacket the language, to regulate, control and discipline its operations, and, to a very significant measure, succeed. Eventually, however, they exhaust their capacity for control and reach a point when their schemes for the control of language break down. Better put, the schemes of control reach their limits: the whole system of control does not break down; rather, there are limits at its borders and peripheries, beyond which enforcement cannot extend. Now, in this case, the energies and potentialities of language itself exceed what is allowed for within the socially imposed scheme. The conception of the sign perhaps brings out most starkly this contrast between structuralism and poststructuralism. For structuralism, the sign is well behaved in terms of the requirements of the orderly, structured schemes of scientific categorisation; it can be described in terms of elegant, formal, almost mathematical systems of generalities. For poststructuralism, it is a most unruly element, whose nature is only superficially captured by such neat and tidy – Apollonian – structuralist schemes. Moreover, its potential cannot be contained within them, or any other such schemes. In the poststructuralist view, the notable consequence for method involves recognising the ultimately uncontrollable nature of the sign and, therefore, doing everything that will allow it full rein and let it run free.

For poststructuralists, then, the structuralist account of the system of signs is partial rather than wrong. It emphasises the extent to which meaning is socially imposed and controlled and how it is produced through *conformity*. This structuralist approach is certainly acceptable, but at the same time it is necessary to recognise that the system of signs is not entirely controlled and that there is the potential to evade and resist social regulation. The system of signs is two-sided, i.e. it has a socially regulated aspect and also an undisciplined, uncontrollable side. The undisciplined aspect of the sign system is not to be thought of as involving individuals resisting social regulations which are imposed upon them, for this notion brings back the very idea of the subject as a centre, and the poststructuralist tendency is towards the thoroughgoing decentring of social phenomena. Consequently, the poststructuralist account is still as anti-humanist as the structuralist – if anything even more so. The ambivalent nature of meaning has nothing to do with individuals and individual intention. The undisciplined behaviour of meaning is an expression of its nature, i.e. its true nature. While meaning is systemic, it is also inherently unstable, motile and multifarious; it is too fluid to be captured in any fixed, stabilised and rigid arrangement. This undisciplined character is, so to speak, the true nature of the sign system. The socially organised, conformist government of the system goes against its nature and, therefore, is only problematically (and often unsuccessfully) dominant over its unruly potential. The crucial element for the poststructuralist position is, then, to demonstrate the disruptive potential within the sign systems, with the purpose of highlighting the dogmatic, repressive, even dictatorial character of the conventional side.

Here the notion of language as unruly owes much to Nietzsche's ideas, especially his discussion of the conflict between the Dionysian and Apollonian elements in human life to which we referred earlier. Although abandoning Nietzsche's terminology, poststructuralists retain the contrast it expressed, together with his tone of strong disapproval for the way the vigour of exuberant, inchoate, erratic energy is stifled by the imposition of lifeless, impersonal, restrictive order. Order is conceived as involving the suppression – but not the elimination – of this energy, which retains the potential of transgressing the boundaries set out to contain (and constrain) it.

Deleuze and Guattari, a pair of poststructuralists with a position built out of their own distinctive mix of the common elements of Nietzsche, Marx and Freud, provide a nice way of making the contrast between the structures of thought imposed by the structure of capitalism, which contain and shape individual desire in 'productive' ways, and the alternative possible forms of thought that cannot, by their nature, be contained within the bounds that capitalism must set (1987). The contrast uses a vegetable analogy: the 'arboraceous' model is identified as one that is presumed in much of Western thought. Knowledge is like a tree, secured by deep, stable, unchanging roots, and developing in a unified manner from its origin (or centre) into a hierarchical structure (the trunk grows from the roots, the branches from the trunk, one branch from another, leaves from the branch and so on). Against this conception, Deleuze and Guattari call for 'rhizomatic' thinking, the kind of growth that the strawberry plant exhibits, where it spreads out in all directions. These plants generate new branches, which, in spreading out in all directions, make many new connections. Best and Kellner eloquently summarise their aim – and, effectively, the whole poststructuralist legacy – as being to

> extirpate roots and foundations, to thwart unities and break dichotomies, and to spread out roots and branches, thereby pluralizing and disseminating, producing differences and multiplicities, making new connections. Rhizomatics affirms the principles excluded from Western thought and reinterprets reality as dynamic, heterogeneous, and non-dichotomous. A rhizome method decentres information and languages into multiple semiotic dimensions.
>
> (1991: 99)

Poststructuralists aim to bring out how much the ways we talk and think consist in (effective) attempts to coerce language, to exercise violence on and against it, to force it into patterns that will not fit. The approach involves identifying those points where this control breaks down and drawing out the ways the actuality of language cannot fit within the restrictions being imposed upon it. Further, these points threaten the structure of the whole, i.e. they do not just occur at the limits of the system, but reflect back (and reflect negatively) on the principles underpinning the whole system. The boundaries or margins of both language and society – in poststructuralism these are often the same – are sites of crucial significance, places where the tension between the straitjacketed forms of language comes under strain and where the straitjacketing of meaning becomes manifest. *Transgression* is another key word in poststructuralist discourse; it refers to the refusal to fit within conventional classifications and divisions or to respect prohibitions on the crossing of boundaries.

### Barthes as a poststructuralist

Thus Barthes in his later phase viewed language and reading as repressive, as means for imposing upon readers the conventions of the society (and of language, and the institution of literature itself). In fact, readers were often only too willing to subordinate themselves: language, he remarked at one point, is fascist. Barthes's efforts at exposing the ideological and repressive character of the meanings of French bourgeois society had, however, themselves been conducted within that same language and in compliance with the conventions of science. The thorough logic of Barthes's later position meant, of course, that his own analytical efforts could not be exempted from his critique. Therefore, the structuralist attempt to develop a science of culture and a scientifically based literary criticism was futile.

Looked at in this way, structuralism appeared more like an operation inimical to the nature of literature than a method for grasping its true nature. Barthes now came to feel that structuralism was seeking to assert uniformity over diversity and plurality, and attempting to make the vast multiplicity of all the stories there have ever been into mere variants of one and the same basic story, i.e. it was reducing them all to one single, underlying basic and general form. There was need, then, for a reversal of strategy: rather than seeking to reduce diversity and ambiguity, the purpose became, instead, to defy this structuralist proclivity by not merely emphasising diversity and ambiguity, but increasing and intensifying them – indeed, proliferating them. The role of the reader must be transformed from that of the passive recipient of a pre-formed and delivered message into that of an active, creative participant in literature.

Barthes's later poststructuralist stance was criticised by those who wished to defend the view that creativity is in the hands of the author of the text, and the literary critic, for example, is merely someone whose role is to understand and appreciate the creativity of the author. His critics could not accept Barthes's implication that literary criticism is just as creative as the production of literary works; the reader is on a par with the writer – in a way, the reader is a writer. Accepting this view undercuts the possibility of objective standards of literary criticism and therefore any basis of agreement on a canon of works of recognised literary worth. Rejection of such a canon was indeed Barthes's point. Given his attitude that conventions and passively received forms repress and inhibit the spontaneity and creativity of individuals, it is not surprising that he argues in this way.

As we outlined in Chapter 9, a key work in Barthes's transition from structuralism to poststructuralism is his book *S/Z* (1975a), in which he analyses a Balzac tale of tragedy resulting from gender stereotypes. Barthes's treatment retains some structuralist features. He claims to identify five *codes* at work in the text. These are:

1 *the hermeneutic*, which deals in the puzzles posed by the narrative;
2 *the seme*, which regulates the metaphors and allusion;
3 *the symbolic*, which deals with symbolic oppositions such as 'indoors/ outdoors' and 'dreaming/waking';
4 *the action*, which deals with the actions of characters in the story and provides them with a logic of events;
5 *the reference*, which involves all the references to the culture and draws upon the common knowledge of the reader.

However, if Barthes is using structuralist ideas such as 'codes', i.e. underlying, generative rules, he is using them in a less than systematic way: the book itself is made up of ninety-three short commentaries – albeit variable in length and rather arbitrarily assorted – on parts of the text, some including criticisms of structuralist ideas. The problem of reading is spelled out as more of a moral than a scientific one. It confronts the reader with the choice of either being a merely passive dupe of the text, ingesting from it a (for Barthes, nauseating) diet of received conceptions and spurious, illusory solutions to the problems of life, or adopting an active, creative approach which effectively recreates the text being read. See how Barthes's commentary on 'Sarrasine' recreates the story so that the reader is becoming a writer. To live by convention is to lead an inauthentic life. The challenge is: do you want to live authentically? The aspiration to the creation of coherent, integrated, logically structured works is common to classic literature and to structural analysis. When found, it is to be attacked and disrupted. Barthes hereafter – in, for example, *The Pleasures of the Text* (1975b) – champions what he calls 'the Text'.

Barthes's conviction that the institutions and conventions of society are antithetical to the true, free, spontaneous nature of the individual means that to be confronted by the Text the reader must be non-social, i.e. he or she has to operate outside the social realm with all its laws, rules, structures and other orderly, regular, coherent divisions that make up its hierarchical, authoritarian and regulatory structures. The satisfactions for such a reader will derive more from physical and sensual responses than through any meanings of the text, since meaning is too intensely interwoven with convention. Thus the words themselves will be the object of attention, rather than their meanings and any purportedly guiding authorial intentions and schemes; the reader can revel in a babel of language. What the reader seeks is a state surpassing pleasure, which Barthes terms '*jouissance*'. It is translated as 'bliss' or 'ecstasy' and is a sensual, not an intellectual, experience. The Text that offers the opportunity of such ecstasy, such a sensual, heady and vertiginous experience, cannot be found in the easy pleasures of reading provided by the transparent, smooth and comfortably engrossing bestseller type of story, which draws upon and reconfirms our stereotypes and prejudices.

Literature, however, does provide one of the places where it is possible to evade the burden and pressure of social conventions. Text will offer us the language itself as an object of our attention, rather than as a medium for the thoughtless presentation of our culturally given comforts, and in such a way that it will not be our familiar, taken-for-granted tongue. It will be so presented as to be disturbing, challenging and unsettling, provoking us to linger on the Text, to brood intensely over it and to relish our responses to it. The bliss engendered by such poring over the Text will, of course, be a personal and incommunicable response, for such bliss itself takes place through transgression of, i.e. moving outside, the settled conventions of language. It cannot, therefore, be reabsorbed into language for expression to others. To be in the state of bliss entails the patterns and segregations shaped by the culture losing their hold over the individual, who is thereby deprived of the conventional supports of self and security. The self, in any conventional sense, is disintegrated (which is to border upon madness, in conventional terms) and the blissfulness derives from the extremity of this condition. In summary, Barthes has displaced literature from being an object of analytical, scientific work to being a source of self-absorbed hedonism.

In his last works, Barthes practised what he had previously preached, producing, for example, an 'autobiography', *Roland Barthes by Roland Barthes* (1977). The autobiographical form is a personal one, but in this case the form of the genre is tampered with, the demarcation between the true and the fictional is muddied and confused, and the requirements of an orderly structure are displaced by a string of separate thoughts arbitrarily arranged, i.e. set out in an approximately alphabetical manner. It is playful and humorous in style; it declines to be assertive or argumentative, rejecting these moods as forms of violence, of imposition on the other; and it refuses also to locate itself within the dualistic oppositions which are the points of reference of conventional thought, e.g. 'self' and 'other', 'subject' and 'object'. The real Roland Barthes is not the character who is the (often obliquely approached) topic of the book, but the one encountered in and through the writing, which ensures that any suggestion that the identity of Roland Barthes is fixed, stable and continuous is constantly unsettled, e.g. by switching between the first and third person terms, i.e. 'I' and 'he' are both used to refer to 'Roland Barthes'.

This account of Barthes should readily convey how he conceives language as the leading instance of social convention, and how he regards convention as inimical to individual well-being. In these respects Barthes is representative, and reflective, of the general poststructuralist position, for he was influenced in the formation of his later views by the work of Foucault and Derrida, whose ideas will be discussed in Chapters 11 and 12.

## Poststructuralist ambiguity

### Representational writing

The notion of language as inherently unruly connects with the intellectual unruliness of poststructuralism itself. As noted above, poststructuralist ideas do not comprise a straightforward and consistent body of propositions; ambiguity and even contradiction are its characteristic features. Indeed, they can be seen as essential, given its antagonism to the classical, linear, logical modes of thinking identified as part of the Enlightenment legacy. We should not be surprised, then, to find ourselves faced repeatedly with ideas that seem to run counter to one another; for the poststructuralist, such outcomes are not only inevitable – they are to be celebrated.

A first ambiguity relates to representationalist forms of writing. Poststructuralists explicitly forswear such writing and seek to foster a new attitude towards a language that is concentrated on the sensual pleasures inherent in its uses, regardless of meaning or communicative function. Even so, and even though they might not claim any scientific status for what they do, none the less poststructuralists frequently write in ways that are apparently representational. For example, Michel Foucault, as we shall see in the next chapter, writes about previous historical periods and subsequent changes with respect to the formation of modern penology, or the development of the contemporary Western treatment of sexuality. His critics and defenders debate whether or not his historical studies are sound and they do so in quite conventional ways, arguing over the extent to which the facts correspond to Foucault's assertions. However, Foucault himself is (at least sometimes) prepared to disown any representationalism, to deny that he has written anything other than fictions, works that have no representational ambitions. Yet his own occasional disclaimers do not resolve the question of how far his actual practice is consistent with these declarations; certainly, the merits of his work are widely understood in traditional academic terms as being in substantial part representational. Moreover, they are even advocated and opposed in much the same ways as some purportedly scientific theory.

Other poststructuralists, such as Barthes and Derrida, make a much more obvious attempt to break with the conventions of representationalism. A thorough and consistent rejection of representationalism must involve undermining these tendencies in one's own writing, not only in the work of others. Similarly, in contemporary fiction it is commonplace to find that many aspects of a novel are designed to remind the reader that the work is fiction, i.e. an artificial contrivance, which must not be mistaken for some kind of factual report. The idea of admiring a novel for its realism, i.e. its attempt at a faithful portrayal of the nature of life as actually lived, has been completely rejected by many contemporary novelists. Instead of realism, their novels are presented as objects to be admired as works in and of language, to be relished for the pleasures that can be derived from the ways the words are assembled. This kind of writing tends to be approved – and emulated – by poststructuralists.

Barthes's disruptive play with the conventions of the autobiographical genre has been mentioned above. Jacques Derrida (1930–2004) continued to write scholarly pieces, albeit often in forms which disrupt conventional expectations. For example, a book called *Jacques Derrida*, jointly authored with Geoffrey Bennington (Bennington and Derrida 1993), has a quite unusual format. Bennington attempts, in his commentary on the top half of the page, to give a systematic account of Derrida's thought, while Derrida's comments, at the bottom of the page, are specifically constructed to frustrate Bennington's effort to encapsulate Derrida's thought in a system. Another work, *Glas* (Derrida 1986), has its pages divided into two columns: in one, Derrida discusses Hegel's writing, in the other that of Jean Genet (see Chapter 12 for more on this).

We hasten to note that the rejection of representationalism is not meant to suggest that scholars should write fiction rather than fact or novels rather than reports, since the rejection abolishes the difference between fact and fictions. Alternatively put, it asserts that there are (and can be) only fictions. Foucault's contention that he had written only fictions does not reflect some decision on his part but, rather, only his acceptance of a necessary situation, i.e. he wrote only fiction because that is all that anyone can write. All writings are fictions; there is no other kind. Works that look as though they are factual reports, the results of researches, findings about the real world, i.e. works that take themselves seriously in this respect, are only prisoners of the ideology of representation.

## Critical consciousness

A second area of ambiguity or contradiction, bringing us back on to the territory of the Frankfurt School (see Chapter 8), concerns the issue of critical consciousness. The contemporary vogue for poststructuralism in sociology undoubtedly has much to do with the fact that it is perceived by many as offering a critical stance towards society distinct from a Marxist tradition which was once strongly associated with the critical theory of the Frankfurt School and is now widely discredited.

Poststructuralists themselves seem to be ambivalent on such questions as the following: can they provide the basis for an oppositional politics? Is their approach any longer consistent with a critical stance towards the status quo? What are the grounds for such a critique? Here poststructuralist thought owes much to Durkheimian conceptions, albeit reproducing them in a rather inverted fashion. Durkheim has a strong claim to being the pioneer anti-humanist in sociology. His writings show individualism as a social product; processes of inclusion and exclusion create a sense of oneself as belonging to a society. Individualism involves recognition of common membership among some, while at the same time other people are treated as excluded from the society or group. For example, as we saw in Chapter 4, the basis of his account of crime is that the moral community of society can only exist because there is a difference between those who do and those who do not belong within it; the existence of society demands the existence of criminals, i.e. those who fall outside society's moral limits.

The poststructuralists concur that identities are defined contrastively. They use the expression 'the Other'.

## The Other

This term is used to convey the message that any given form of existence requires its Other. For example, we can only be a superior people if there is an inferior one and can only be sane if there are mad people.

But whereas Durkheim looks at the necessity of this Other from the point of view of society, as a kind of sacrifice of some people on behalf of the existence and solidarity of society and, thus, of the well-being of those within the society's boundaries, the poststructuralists are apt to look at things from the other point of view. They concur with the idea of the exclusion of individuals as a kind of sacrifice on behalf of social solidarity, but in taking things from the Other's point of view, they are not inclined to see the making of such sacrifices as a satisfactory solution. Instead, these are viewed as an infliction, an imposition upon the Others; their position on or outside the boundaries of conventional society is coercively endowed and punitively enforced. The poststructuralists do not see why some individuals should pay the price of other people's comfortable and comforting sense of themselves; they do not see any justice in the sacrificing of one set of individuals on behalf of the psychic well-being of others.

Yet in some ways, rather than continuing Durkheim's arguments, the post-structuralists fulfil his prophecies about the development of an extreme cult of the individual in modern society, whereby each individual becomes a sacred object. Despite its denunciation of the subject, poststructuralism has such a strongly individualistic cast to it that it can reasonably be interpreted as expressing, or at least implying, not only an anarchistic moral and political theory which is rigorously and thoroughly anti-hierarchical, but even an extreme form of it. Anarchists characteristically oppose the existence of government, supposing that if individuals were left freely to conduct their affairs, a more beneficent situation would develop. However, poststructuralists see life in society as oppressive not merely because of the existence of a governmental apparatus, but because of the pervasively coercive nature of social relations in general. They often write as though the attempt of one person to influence or affect another involves violence and terror. Here, then, coercion simply means imposition, the making of demands by some persons on others, rather than any overt force or compulsion. For example, they sometimes dub as 'theoretical terrorism' the demand for logical consistency, a demand that can result in criticism of people for their inconsistencies in intellectual argument. In poststructuralist arguments, then, coercion is given such a wide definition that virtually all social relationships, even the most localised and transient such as conversational exchanges, are seen as involving the use of power, i.e. the attempted coercive imposition of one person's will – and, through it, of social conventions – upon another. From this point of view, asking someone a question involves attempting to compel her or him to honour and abide by the (socially established and enforced) conventions of the language. Having so widened the coverage of terms like 'power' and 'terror', they have, of course, at the same time intensified the problem of how it can ever be possible to achieve truly non-hierarchical, non-coercive relations, since domination and coercion are now seen as pervasive of social relations.

For example, Foucault has been characterised as holding a Hobbesian conception of social life (for Hobbes, see Chapter 5), involving an eternal and universal struggle of all against all, the very conception that Durkheim sought to eliminate conclusively. Whether this characterisation is true or not, Foucault certainly did see even the finest details of social existence as permeated by the workings of domination, and expressed this idea in talk of the *capillary actions of power* (capillaries are the innumerable small tubes of which plants are made and through which move the substances that they metabolise). Similarly, Barthes held to the ideal of a language which could operate independently of the exercise of power, yet came to the despairing conclusion that it could only be utopian, i.e. unobtainable; what little non-coercive contact could be sought between human beings was only attainable outside language altogether, e.g. in literary form, only through the sensual contact with the voices of another as embodied in the Text. The poststructuralists, then, seem to accept an anarchistic individualism in so far as they treat all conventional social relations as coercive, restrictive and essentially as an unnecessary imposition upon the individual. But they are not hopeful anarchists, for they see little prospect of lifting the overall burden of oppression, save at marginal points and to marginal degrees. The Marxist idea of a full-scale confrontation with and shattering of the status quo has been left behind.

## Conclusion

Critics of poststructuralism often warn that its acceptance is associated with the rejection of belief in science and in the superiority of our scientifically based, technologically supported civilisation. They argue that such notions threaten to unleash irrationalist forces which will hasten the end of civilisation as we know it. Rather than seeking to counter such objections, at least some poststructuralists seem to delight in them, revelling in the idea that by their writings they could bring the massive edifice of Western civilisation crashing down. As for its replacement, they might perhaps welcome the collapse into anarchy as for the better rather than the worse, but they do not count on it. After all, ranged against them is the vast, deeply entrenched and all-pervading network of oppressive forces which, for the great bulk of the time, succeed in portraying themselves as improving, progressive, liberating influences; they cannot be confronted or overturned on a general scale, for they are thoroughly interwoven with even the details of life in the society (remember the capillary metaphor), but can only be challenged at particular points and in fairly specific ways. Poststructuralists have to seek victories at the margins, sometimes through direct political action by particular groups, e.g. Foucault himself was associated with a prisoners' organisation agitating for reform. Usually, however, they work through intellectual activity to expose the pretensions of the dominant forces and to violate and subvert their conventions and divisions.

The result is ambiguity: however opposed poststructuralists might be to the idea of a political programme, all talk of oppression and control seems only to make sense in relation to some vision of freedom, some idea of what human life could be like in the absence of the repressive forces of language, reason and power. A worked-out version of this alternative, or even a clear statement of its possibility, is no more forthcoming in poststructuralist writings than in the work of the Frankfurt School. The difference is that whereas the Frankfurt School believed in this possibility – it was their *raison d'être* – the poststructuralists are more cynical. Indeed, a generalised and deep attitude of cynicism might plausibly be said to be their defining outlook, the crux of their anti-Enlightenment stance. But without some commitment to at least the possibility of an alternative, positive vision of social life, what sense can there be to the notion of critical consciousness? What point can there be to political action if its likely outcome is a Hobbesian (non-)society? However, we are jumping the gun somewhat; before developing this conclusion, we need to consider in more detail the work of the leading poststructuralists, beginning with the writer who has been most influential in sociology, Michel Foucault.

## Questions

1. What is Nietzsche's role in poststructuralist thought? Why is he important in this respect? Is he right? In what ways is Nietzsche's role in poststructuralism similar to, and different from, Freud's in structuralist thought?

2. What are the similarities and differences between structuralism and poststructuralism? Which, if either, is right? Was structuralism 'wrong' if poststructuralism is 'right'?

3. Why might language be understood as 'representational'? What other understandings of language – e.g. from symbolic interactionism or ethnomethodology – might there be? Which, if any, are right? Why does a rejection of representationalism lead the poststructuralists to also reject science? Does this make sense?

4. What is an 'unruly sign'? How does it differ from other kinds of signs? In what ways does it develop ideas from Saussure, Lévi-Strauss or the early Barthes? What are its implications for individuals? What are its implications for 'social systems'?

5. Why does Barthes argue that the author is 'dead'? What are the implications of this position? Was the author ever alive? Is poststructuralism a development from earlier forms of social thought or is it something new? If the poststructuralists are right, are they right *now* or have they *always* been right?

6. What is the 'Other' and why is it important in poststructuralist thought? Is the 'Other' good or bad? What contemporary examples can you think of? In what ways does the analysis of the Other move beyond the 'underdog bias' of, for instance, labelling theory? What are the arguments for and against sociologists having an opinion on these kinds of issues?

7. Is poststructuralism an abandonment of critical social thought? Is it apolitical? Is it the result of disappointment with the development of earlier theories or a new development in its own right?

## Next steps

Barthes's (1991) *The Grain of the Voice* provides a clear, informal, expression of his changing views. His *The Pleasures of the Text* (1975b) remains the most succinct expression of his later thought.

Harland's (1987) *Superstructuralism* is as good a basic introduction to poststructuralism as it is to structuralism itself. Best and Kellner's (1991) *Postmodern Theory* is a more detailed and comprehensive overview of the debates about the poststructuralist turn. Norris (1990) is an excellent critique of the relativist tendencies in poststructuralist thought.

## CHAPTER ELEVEN

# Michel Foucault: abandoning the certainties of reason

---

**Chapter overview**

Michel Foucault, like Barthes, was a key figure in the movement from structuralism to poststructuralism. His influence on sociology has, however, been far greater. Foucault acknowledged that only certain kinds of thoughts are possible in any era, but stressed the contingent and relative nature of ideas: ideas do not develop logically (as Hegel argued) towards 'progress'. In any period, 'discourses' dominate and shape the extent to which only certain things can be said in only particular settings. Foucault's work on madness and the development of medicine provided empirical examples of the workings of discourse. Foucault's later work, in particular on prisons and sexuality, developed these ideas by integrating a novel conceptualisation of power (as 'power/knowledge' and 'biopower') as something present in all social relations. Much of Foucault's work strongly parallels aspects of the Western Marxist and structuralist schools, but is strongly compatible with the ideas of Durkheim and Weber.

---

## Introduction: Foucault's first phase

Michel Foucault (1926–84), like Barthes, made a transition from initially structuralist to eventually poststructuralist ideas. Throughout, he was exclusively concerned with historical investigations, centring on the changing nature of knowledge and the creation of categories of outsiders in society. His studies counter the regular accusation that structuralism cannot comprehend history and change. In this first section we consider his first four major books, which together make up what might – and against his objections – be called his structuralist phase: *Madness and Civilisation* (1967), *The Birth of the Clinic* (1973), *The Order of Things* (1970) and *The Archaeology of Knowledge* (1972). They form a kind of quartet centred mainly upon fundamental changes in the nature of thought in Western Europe in the period leading up to present times. They deal with the way the order of the world is conceived and how thought makes connections between the things in the world. However, a note of caution: it is possible to exaggerate the continuity between these studies. It is worth noting that Foucault's own attempts at linking them were made retrospectively and in a manner that suggests this unification was somewhat sardonic rather than fully serious. In the fourth, methodology volume, *The Archaeology of Knowledge*, the systematic formulation is something of a self-caricature; perhaps it is an at least partially parodic exercise in the vein of systematic, abstract theorising, an approach eschewed in the other three volumes. Ostensibly, the three preceding historical studies depend on certain key concepts, particularly 'archaeology', 'episteme' and 'discursive formation', but these ideas enter into the historical analysis progressively, and the notion of discursive formation in particular is only developed in any thorough way in the retrospective *Archaeology*. None the less, for ease of presentation, we will begin with the last book of the four and consider the set of abstract concepts presented there. The central question concerns their relationship to Foucault's largely debunking purposes, which mainly aim to provide a new, structuralist way of writing the history of ideas.

## Unearthing epistemes

In Foucault's view the development of structuralism marked a new point in the history of systems of thought. Its appearance around 1950 marked the beginning of the end for the period of modern thought and the start of a postmodern period (see the next chapter). For Foucault, the key feature of structuralism was that it decisively decentred the subject, especially through the contention that unconscious structures rather than the conscious mind of the subject explain conduct (see Chapter 9). The intriguing question arose: how could one write a history of ideas if there were no subjects? Foucault rose to this challenge by applying the notion of the unconscious on a collective level, proposing that for any given historical period there is a kind of unconscious structure to the whole organisation of thought generally, i.e. thinkers are very much of – are captives of – their age. Attention is directed to the unconscious forces which guide and direct the explicit theories and other ideas thinkers come up with, and not to the thoughts which individual thinkers consciously form. There is an underlying matrix of presuppositions which confines the mind in a given period and makes only certain kinds of thoughts thinkable. This matrix is what Foucault terms the *episteme*.

### The episteme

Foucault presents the episteme as a common structure within which the various, sometimes conflicting, ideas of individual thinkers, their schools and disciplines are formed. Furthermore, these epistemes are socio-historically situated: the development of any given set of ideas can take place only in certain highly specific conditions which involve a combination of features of the episteme with other socio-historical conditions.

If a particular conjuncture of conditions does not hold, then the ideas will not form, indeed *cannot* form, because the conditions are not ones under which it is possible to think them.

Foucault aims to *historicise* the history of ideas thoroughly.

## Historicism

The development of ideas is socially and historically situated. Alternative versions of historicism emphasise (a) contingency, i.e. there are no underlying laws, no general pattern to history; or (b) laws, which give history a determined path and pattern.

Two vital elements distinguish Foucault's argument from previous approaches: he divests the development of ideas of any notion of (1) necessary, pre-destined development; (2) progressive movement. The history of ideas seems naturally inclined to trace a continuing succession of ideas, one set leading to others, preferably as part of a logical, cumulative sequence. Foucault rejects this view: epistemes do succeed one another, but they are discontinuous, i.e. one episteme abruptly displaces another, with no continuities between them. He also rejects any notion of a progression that would enable us to look back upon the less enlightened conceptions of our predecessors. Consequently, his work is strongly relativist. He shared with the English historian E. P. Thompson, himself no relativist, the ambition to rescue people of the past from 'the enormous condescension of posterity' (Thompson 1968: 13). Ideas from the past often seem bizarre, misguided or unnatural to us, and we may flatter ourselves that this is because we now understand things better. On the contrary, we only think this way because we do *not* understand things better than our predecessors. Indeed, to assume the necessary superiority of our ideas shows that we understand these Others (and ourselves) hardly at all. We are not really aware of the successive epistemes within which our European forebears lived. The extent to which we can be aware of them is problematic but, if we were attuned to them, then we should see that things which seem strange to us were, for those inhabiting the episteme, every bit as natural, comfortable and right as our certainties are to us. Foucault inclines towards portraying people within an episteme as being its prisoners. Yet they are not conscious of their confinement; they think within the episteme, not about it. Therefore, they cannot consciously comprehend the episteme. Persons in a later episteme are no better placed; those in a successor will not be aware of the previous episteme. After all, they are not conscious of their own, let alone of that of a previous age, given that the episteme does not figure explicitly in the thought it enables. Hence people from a later age are not really able to understand the previous one or even themselves.

One consequence of this approach is an element of paradox, since Foucault attempts to get us to understand ourselves through understanding previous ages and their epistemes. One of the ambiguities of Foucault's work is its purposes: are his studies intended as genuine histories or as fables, for want of a better term, albeit fables of a complex, sophisticated and documented kind? In fact, the title 'archaeology' suggests that a purpose is to dig up the buried layers of preconceptions underlying previous periods of thought, i.e. the widespread, unconscious structures not explicitly held by individual subjects but framing the possibilities of what those individuals can think/say (since thinking is done in and through language). Foucault's continuity with structuralism is apparent here; it provides the basis for referring to his early works as his structuralist phase. In contrast with Lévi-Straussian structuralism, however, Foucault's studies do not seek to identify any universal unconscious structures; rather, they are concerned with very specific configurations, historically localised to an age and a region. This historical proclivity provides one reason why Foucault would not affiliate himself to structuralism, despite his affinities with it.

## The structure of discourses

We have coined the expression think/say to bring out Foucault's notion of *discursive formation*, which emphasises that sets of ideas cannot be divorced from language. In line with structuralism, Foucault regards thought and language as two sides of a coin. He does not want to treat ideas and thought as mental phenomena, occurring in the privacy of the individual consciousness, for to do so would put the subject back in the position from which Foucault strives to displace it. Therefore, he attends to what is explicit and public, that is, what is said (or, more accurately for historical studies, what has been written).

---

**Discourses**

Discourses are ways of speaking/writing and operate according to rules, and these rules articulate with socio-historical arrangements and circumstances.

---

*The Archaeology of Knowledge* attempts to spell out the general dimensions of the rules of discourse.

Foucault provides a battery of concepts for analysing the constitutive features of discourses. A discursive formation consists in the first instance of objects, the things that can be talked about. For example, 'mental patient' is an object of the discursive formation of modern psychiatry, something that can now be talked about and acted towards in various ways, e.g. identified, treated therapeutically and so forth. Prior to the development of the formation, this object could not be talked about; the persons nowadays identified as 'patients' could only be spoken of in the prior discourse of madness, i.e. as 'madmen' or 'madwomen'. Additionally, the discourse has certain concepts for talking about the properties of the object, e.g. the mental patient may be spoken of in terms of various 'mental illnesses', such as paranoia or manic depression. Further, Foucault's *enunciative modalities* (explained in point 2 of the list below) are the ways of discursively marking the cognitive worth of what is said. Finally, *themes* can develop within these enunciative modalities; they are expressed in these concepts and talk about these objects; they are strands of thought relating to some given conception, e.g. the idea of evolution is a theme of biological discourse. Foucault insists that a discursive formation is not to be thought of as an internally coherent unity. He uses the notion of *field* to emphasise that a discourse is open to various possibilities and elements, which are *dispersed*. His whole point is that the kinds of positions which seem to set individual thinkers at odds with one another are none the less contained within the same discursive formation and operate under the formative influence of a common episteme. Thus the discursive formation of psychiatry involves many different conceptions of the basis of mental illness and different notions of how mental illness should be treated; they are often at odds, if not in open warfare.

In more detail, then, Foucault identifies four processes that determine the distribution of the 'field' of a discursive formation:

1 *The formation of objects*, i.e. what things can be talked about within the formation, what kind of objects can be introduced into it, who controls such admission. Here *grids of specification* provide the criteria for recognising, classifying and relating these objects, and also for differentiating them from other kinds of objects. For example, within the discourse of psychiatry they involve the symptoms that manifest particular types of illness such as schizophrenia, and the specific syndromes or illness sub-types which are medically recognised, such as catatonic schizophrenia and paranoid schizophrenia.

2 *The formation of enunciative modalities*. Just as not anything can be said, so not anyone can say particular things; they can be said only in certain sorts of settings, under certain conditions by certain kinds of people. For example, psychiatry involves the giving of diagnoses, which are only properly given within the context of a professional relationship by people who are qualified on the basis of their observation of the patients' behaviour. These rules also govern the formation of concepts regulating the relationship between statements, and whether or not the statements are accepted, excluded or awaiting definitive assessment. For instance, the statements of the psychiatric patient are often treated as symptoms, as expressions of the patient's illness, and not as potentially true statements about actualities.

3 *Procedures of intervention*. These regulate the way new statements can be produced or the ways they can be transformed, as when verbal statements are converted into mathematical symbolism, or spoken statements are transcribed into written form. For example, in psychiatric medicine there are professional rules about who is qualified to describe and record a patient's symptoms in reports which count as medically authoritative.

4 *Strategies*. These are the development of themes, the selection and development of certain lines of possibility, e.g. the formation and development of treating mental illness through talk or, alternatively, through drug regimes.

The dispersion of statements across the field of the discursive formation can obviously be a complex matter, further compounded by (1) the interaction of one discursive formation with another; and (2) the interaction of the formation with non-discursive constraints. In forming the concepts of one discursive formation, people frequently draw upon another, e.g. the idea of psychotherapy through talk drew upon the religious model of the confession. Of course, discourses are socially regulated; they are subject to constraints of authority, or normative restriction, in respect of what they can say.

These general ideas – archaeology, episteme and discursive formation – notionally underlie Foucault's three early studies of madness, medicine and classification. We say 'notionally' since these ideas are more prominent in *Archaeology* than in the previous three books, and because the details of these studies are not necessarily explicitly arranged around them. Nevertheless, these studies certainly exemplify the broad directions indicated by these abstractions. They do have some theoretical linkage and, taken together, they present an analysis of some of the main elements of the Enlightenment transformation of Western thought. As one commentator remarks:

> Foucault maintains that his histories of madness (disorder), disease (orderly disorder) and epistemic fields (order) in the classical period together expose the 'deepest strata of Western culture', the strata that mark the threshold of modern thought and the emergence of the concept of Man.
>
> (Poetzl 1983: 153)

Further, though Foucault may be said to be delving into the archaeology of thought systems, his work from *Madness and Civilisation* onwards is underpinned by a conception of the pattern of social change from the sixteenth to the twentieth century. It shows a development which conforms broadly to Weber's story about the progressive disenchantment and rationalisation of the modern world (see Chapter 3), leading to the development of what the Frankfurt School calls the 'administered society' (see Chapter 8). As we shall see later, this theme provides the main connecting link between Foucault's early studies and his later ones.

## The discourse of the asylum

*Madness and Civilisation* (1967) is an ironic comment upon the way the formation of the modern notion of reason, which contraposes itself to coercion and repression, has itself contributed to these. If this is the abstract story that Foucault seeks to tell, the concrete one concerns the transformation of what was defined as madness in the Renaissance into what has become mental illness in the modern world.

In the fifteenth century, madness was conceived in two disparate ways (remember, epistemes are not internally uniform or coherent). The first was in cosmic terms: when human animality breaks out of social control, it places an individual in communication with awesome, tragic forces which drive towards destruction, yet also give the mad person special and secret knowledge. The second was satirical: madness was conceived as a kind of comment on reason, making mock of human fallibility and frailty. In this period the mad were outcast from regular society, but they were left free to wander, and they remained in connection with society in so far as they deserved to be listened to. The cosmically mad could give voice to wisdom, and the satirical form of madness could have its own wisdom: there was the idea of 'the wise fool'.

With the change from the Renaissance to what Foucault calls 'the classical age' (beginning in the later part of the eighteenth century) there is a profound alteration in the conception of madness, which ceases to be something authentic in its own right. Now it is defined as entirely outside reason and is rejected as antithetical and dangerous to it. No longer a fate befalling the individual, madness now is thought of as chosen by the individual; thus mad people reject the standard of reason. Consequently, they are not open to rational persuasion, so that the only mode of treatment to which they might respond and through which they can be controlled is physical confinement and coercion through brutal treatment. At the same time as the mad were being rejected from social life, the attempt was being made to conceive madness in terms of science, i.e. to bring it within the reach of reason. Hence madness could not be treated as entirely devoid of reason (otherwise it would defy comprehension in terms of reason); instead, it was represented as a *perversion* of reason. In this way the concept of madness developed as a misapplication of reason; the mad have the power to reason, to develop logically ordered thought, but they apply it on the basis of falsehood, misconception and delusion. They are incapable of comprehending the world correctly not because they have turned their back upon reason but, rather, because they have faced it too fully and been dazzled by its light.

These changes were interrelated with other changes in the society of the time. First, there was the 'great confinement', a period early in the classical age when all kinds of socially troublesome individuals – the poor, the sick, the vagrant, the criminal and the mad – were indiscriminately locked up. This development in part was an opportunistic response to the fact that lazar houses (buildings designed to house lepers) had become superfluous with the disappearance of leprosy from Europe, thereby creating the opportunity to confine all those who might threaten social order. Subsequent changes in social values, however, produced pressures for the separation of the mad from other inmates, e.g. the growing belief in the need to make productive use of all possible labour and, associatedly, a conception that poverty and unemployment were not necessarily the choice or fault of the poor and unemployed. Hence there was more discrimination between those confined, separating those who could be returned to gainful work from those who, like the mad, could not. In a moment delicately poised between two possible directions for confinement of the mad – prisons or hospitals – it so happened, though by no means inevitably, that the hospital was deemed the appropriate option.

The differentiation of the mad from the general population of the undesirable and their relocation to the hospital context is widely advertised as a progressive development, involving both more humane and better-informed treatment. The mad person was becoming the patient, and the patient was no longer treated through brutal discipline but through medical regimes based upon scientific knowledge. Foucault maintains that this appealing image is not true.

## The treatment of the mad

This image conceals the fact that the change was no improvement; if anything, it was a continuation of the deterioration in the situation of the mad. Since the Renaissance they had lost their freedom and dignity and had been reduced to silence: nothing they had to say was worth listening to. Further, the treatment was not truly medical in nature and was not based upon genuine scientific knowledge. The doctor controlled inmates with power, not expert knowledge. The hospital was an intensely moralised environment for compelling the inmates back into conformity with social rules through the manipulation of their guilt.

## The origins of the clinical gaze

With respect to physical disease, Foucault argues that again the conjunction between developments in fundamental concepts and social currents gave rise to the discourse of modern medicine and to its site of operation, the clinic. *The Birth of the Clinic* (1973) holds that the French Revolution with its associated wars was a major precipitant of medical reorganisation. The involvement of all experienced doctors in military medicine left a vacuum in civilian medical treatment which was rapidly filled by quacks, in turn giving rise to demands for administrative measures for ensuring good medical treatment. These measures set medical competence based on observation of actual disease as the standard. The provision of the clinic, i.e. a site where doctors could acquire experience of illness and study it systematically, was another contingent development, going rather against the grain of the prevalent idea that illness should desirably be treated at home. Nevertheless, the charity hospital did develop, gaining the necessary financial support from the wealthy because they considered it a worthwhile investment in their own self-protection. The poor gained medical treatment and, through studying them, doctors could develop a better knowledge of disease from which, eventually, their sponsors could themselves benefit.

On the epistemic level the development of modern medicine involved the displacement of the classical conception of disease. Put simply, Foucault's case is that the classical conception is only incidentally connected to the human body, i.e. disease manifests itself in the body, but the fact that it occurs in one place or another in the body is not relevant. Indeed, the true nature of disease is only to be grasped by abstracting its essential nature from surrounding, accidental circumstances, which may be concealing this essence rather than revealing it. Moreover, the idea of treating disease in hospital makes no sense either, for the hospital is an artificial context further complicating the business of abstracting the disease itself from the setting in which it is incidentally located. As a first step, then, this classical conception of disease as a hidden essence is displaced as a result of a wider shift in ideas about the nature of the sign at that time. Instead of differentiating between signs of the disease, which are not essentially connected with it, and symptoms, which are part of its essence, the change involved the abolition of this distinction of symptom and sign; now all the observable occurrences associated with the disease were a part of it.

However, the observable occurrences of disease remained those which were on the surface of the skin, and the second step in shifting from the classical to the modern concept of disease was to adopt the dissection of corpses as a method of inquiry into disease. This method was far from being the most obvious way to learn: those who studied disease could not have seen any sense in dissecting corpses prior to a certain point in the development of ideas. Here Foucault argues against the more accepted view that the adoption of dissection was delayed beyond a point at which it might have been introduced due to popular (religiously inspired) prejudice against the use of corpses in this way.

## The clinical gaze

In the eighteenth century there was no problem in obtaining corpses, but medical practitioners needed a change in their concepts to see any relevance in the practice. It required a change in ideas to bring dissection into conjunction with the investigation of disease, since prevailing conceptions saw diseases as occurring on the surface of the bodies of living creatures – quite a difference from the inspection of corpses! An extension of the idea of 'surface' made possible the introduction of dissection because it now came to be conceived as an examination of surfaces, i.e. the surfaces of the body's inner organs. This conception involved a new way of looking at the body, the *clinical gaze*.

In its turn, the clinical gaze made possible a profound shift in the conception of disease, for disease was no longer considered as only incidentally related to the body on which it was manifest; rather, it was now conceived as originating in the body's own nature, as part of life itself.

## Words and things

The third and by far the most complex and demanding of this trio of studies examines general conceptions of knowledge, again tracing development from a Renaissance conception, through a classical phase, to a modern one and beyond. The title was translated as *The Order of Things* (1970) to avoid conflict with an already published book entitled *Words and Things*, which would have been more literal and more accurate. A main element in the study of changing concepts of knowledge is the role of language and the topic of representation, which will predominate in our summary of the story of Foucault.

The Renaissance was dominated by the idea of resemblance. The whole universe was seen as filled with and interrelated by resemblances; it was possible to pursue an endless chain between one thing and another, understanding one set of resemblances as a product of yet further resemblances. Thus the medieval 'doctrine of signatures' held that 'every herb was stamped with a more or less clear sign of its uses; so that, for example, a yellow blossom indicated a likely cure for jaundice, or a root shaped like a foot became a remedy for gout' (Thomas 1973: 224). Language was unproblematically part of this world, for all things within it, including linguistic signs themselves, were part of the ubiquitous pattern of resemblances and were themselves to be understood in terms of relations of resemblance to the things that they spoke of. Therefore, language did not present any special sort of problem; it was to be understood in the same terms as anything else. Further, the tracing out of the resemblances was a matter of finding the relationships that had been inserted and assured by God. The business of such tracing out was a putatively endless matter; it did not lend itself to systematic structuring, so knowledge did not show the kind of cumulatively structured character it has now acquired.

With respect to language, the change from the classical episteme involved the change from resemblance to representation. Rather than language being understood to be simply a God-given part of the pattern of creation and integrated into the all-pervading pattern of resemblance, it began to be conceived as something that existed within the human mind. Words stand in a relationship of representation to things. The conception of knowledge also shifted: now it was a pattern of strict similarities and differences rather than a notion of reality consisting in a set of (vague) resemblances. Language, too, was part of this reality, itself to be understood as such a pattern. The form which the depiction of such a reality could take was the tabular arrangement, the distribution of elements within a grid mapping the characteristics they did and did not share, thereby permitting the abstraction of the essence of a given phenomenon (see the classical concept of disease above). The grid brought in a crucial element of systematisation to the organisation of knowledge. At the same time, this approach engendered the possibility of – in the ideal case, at least – an exhaustive description, i.e. one could notionally enumerate all the similarities and differences for a particular phenomenon.

The further change from the classical to the modern episteme, however, places language not in the mind but in history, along with life in general and human beings in particular. Phenomena are no longer to be understood as consisting in an abstract, timeless essence, which can be arranged in a static tabular display, but as existing in time. This change is most vividly exhibited in the change from natural history to biology, from the portrayal in tabular classifications of natural history to the evolutionary conception championed by Darwin. Humankind and language, conceived as historical phenomena, can now become topics of scientific knowledge. They can be both the subject, i.e. creator, and the object, i.e. thing to be known, of knowledge and representations. However, the situation has become destabilised, because the effectiveness of representation is no longer assured and the link between the capacity of words and the things they purportedly stand for is no longer guaranteed by the nature of reality itself, but has become problematic. In the Renaissance, God forged the connection of words with things, and in the classical age it was assured by the nature of things and by language itself. In the modern period there is nothing to provide such assurance.

Thus the modern period of thought prominently features two tensions:

1  People seek to reconcile the fact that they are both subject and object of knowledge.
2  They seek to secure the connection between words and things in the light of an awareness that this relationship can no longer be viewed as a necessary one.

How can people know themselves with any (scientific) certainty while at the same time recognising their own contingency? What language can secure such knowledge if language itself is a human product? For Foucault, it is impossible to resolve or reconcile these tensions; the consequence is a fateful instability at the heart of modern thought.

These tensions are the background to Foucault's remarks about 'the end of Man'. These remarks may seem obscure and tendentious, but they merely refer – in the jargon of *The Archaeology of Knowledge* – to the formation of a particular *object*, Man. (Note that 'Man' here refers to humanity, not just to males.)

### From subject to object

Within modern discourse, people are integrally identified as something that can be talked about as a potential object of knowledge; this way of talking was simply not possible within the Renaissance and classical discourses. These tensions within the modern discourse have been unresolved and the modern episteme is (perhaps) disintegrating. If so, then perhaps this notion of people will not even figure in the new discourse, i.e. since structures are becoming the objects of knowledge in human studies, the notion of 'Man' will not be employed in this emerging episteme.

Moreover, the notion of representation as well as that of 'Man' is losing its hold. In its place has arisen the realisation that language is an autonomous reality, which creates and runs the *subject*, rather than the other way about: language is an end in itself, rather than being looked upon as an instrument to be used to gain knowledge of an extra-linguistic reality. These notions mark Foucault's shift towards his later, poststructuralist phase.

## Later studies: genealogies of power/knowledge

No sooner had Foucault provided the account of his (supposed) methods of analysing discursive formations than he made a shift in his project which led him to subordinate the idea of archaeology to that of *genealogy*. The discontinuity, however, did not require the prior studies to be jettisoned entirely; rather, something implicit and subordinate in them was brought to the fore.

### Genealogy

Derived from Nietzsche, the concept of genealogy was concerned again with developing the buried history of thought, but this time with the specific objective of revealing a link between *knowledge* and *power.*

Foucault himself observed that he had paid attention to the connection between the different knowledges and the operations of power, e.g. in his work on psychiatry. Of course, he had been much concerned with the way people were marginalised within society, and with how discursive formations had been shaped by authority relations and changes in dominant ideologies. Nevertheless, the connection had not been fully explicit or central. Now his genealogical investigations were to be used to develop a new conception of power.

Foucault's historical perspective, his story of the development of the administered society or, as he preferred to call it, the *carceral society*, henceforth focused upon the way activities are brought under regulation. This process involves the development of bodies of professional and administrative functionaries equipped with a supposedly scientific body of knowledge on the basis of which activities are transformed into rational objects. The task of such functionaries is twofold:

1   to implement a process of redefinition whereby activities are turned into something that can be thought about rationally within the categories of a science;
2   to reorganise conduct along these purportedly more rational and efficient lines.

The task does not end there, since thereafter these redefined activities require continual management – in the sense of administration – in order to sustain and enhance their efficient organisation, thereby providing further rationalisation.

However, it is not the activities of professional and administrative functionaries themselves that are Foucault's main focus, but rather the nature of their *disciplinary power.* The creation of the various bodies of supposedly scientific knowledge that serve as the basis of professional and administrative practice has involved the formation and deployment of the idea of the normal phenomenon (here 'the normal' has more of a moral rather than a scientific force). The administrative arrangements are devoted to the maintenance and development of the normal phenomenon. Of course, the notion of the normal involves its Other; the application of this idea across different activities serves to create more categories of deviants. For example, the formation of an idea of normal sex goes along with, is inseparable from, the idea of other, abnormal sexual practices. The attempt to manage activities (and even the whole population) so as to enforce and sustain what is conceived as normal, and to seek to regulate, if not eliminate, that which is conceived as abnormal, in its turn requires monitoring of the activity – '*surveillance*' is Foucault's term (which can include all kinds of monitoring of people's activities, such as policing, or administrative supervision).

Consequently, activity is reorganised in ways that seek to make things more visible, more readily amenable to observation, investigation and supervision. Thus surveillance extends into more and more areas of society; it is itself increasingly rationalised.

As in the early studies, so in the later ones, Foucault's account of modern society is making a case about the formation of the modern subject. The term 'subject' now has very much the sense of one subjected, i.e. dominated and controlled. The theme is comparable with the argument about mental illness, i.e. the change towards modern society has replaced physical brutality as a means of discipline. Effectively, it has produced individuals who are self-controlling and can think for themselves. They can live in the delusion that they are free, autonomous beings because they are not aware of the extent to which they have been shaped by the detailed, intricate and elaborate mechanisms of power.

The earlier studies sought to reveal the buried past underlying the formative stages in the development of the modern age, but the explicit use of the notion of power was not a central element in them, although it is not, after all, that difficult to see power at work in the incarceration of the mad and, later, their subordination to moralising control. In genealogical studies, however, Foucault directly speaks of power and seeks to trace the way bodies of knowledge – such as the human (social and psychological) sciences – have grown up in conjunction with, and as servants of, power.

## Power/knowledge

In the modern world, the development of power and knowledge are so intimately interwoven that they cannot properly be spoken of separately, and the display of their interconnection requires the formation of a special mode of expression, namely *power/knowledge*.

The two develop together, and modern society involves new forms of power, whose recognition requires a new conception, i.e. power without a subject.

Previous conceptions have seen power as something in the hands of either individuals or groups, e.g. exercised by a ruler or by a ruling class – a conception of power *with* a subject. The point about power in modern society is that it is diffused throughout the affairs and activities of the society, not exercised on behalf of any individual or group in particular. Rather, the operation of power has become internal to the organisation of activities. This internality contrasts with sovereign power, the kind of power a ruler has over her or his subjects. This power is over their activities but is external to them, i.e. the sovereign is not concerned with or involved in the organisation of the day-to-day affairs of the society. In the spirit of efficiency, power is more effective if it does not regulate activities from a distance – as the sovereign does – but is interwoven into the very activities it is to regulate, for it can then operate closely and intensely upon these activities, e.g. a teacher can oversee, regulate and direct the detailed organisation of a small class of pupils. The spread of administrative arrangements throughout modern society has extended this kind of power in all directions, making it part of innumerable domains of life. All the different administrative domains of society do not connect up with one another and, even within each administrative domain, there is no extensively co-ordinated and unified direction. So although power pervades these environments, it does not serve any single purpose, nor is it in the hands of one or even a few individuals. It is everywhere, and/but it is undirected. It is disciplinary power not only in the sense that it involves punitive, disciplining measures, but more so in that it develops well-disciplined individuals who are prompt and obedient.

## The carceral society

In his later studies, Foucault develops this analysis in relation to two fields of activity in modern society: the development of the prison, and the emergence of modern sexuality. The themes of surveillance and discipline are manifest in Foucault's next book, *Discipline and Punish* (1977). Foucault's account of the prison and of penology as a form of power/knowledge is best known for its reproduction of Jeremy Bentham's idea of the panopticon, a design for an ideal prison – at least in Bentham's eyes. It is a circular arrangement of individual cells dominated by a central observation tower.

### Carceral society

Foucault treats the panopticon as a metaphor for modern society, the carceral or imprisoning society, an expression reminiscent of Weber's 'iron cage'. For this metaphor, Bentham's model has the relevant features of:

- being purportedly a completely rational plan for the treatment of prisoners, thus reflecting the extent to which thought is devoted to devising ways of controlling people;
- emphasising the extent to which the system is designed to encourage people to control themselves through reflection on their own conduct;
- conceiving the thoroughly constant and pervasive supervision of the inmate: the model represents the ideal of a totally administered society.

Foucault notes the value which the model places upon the purportedly rational, planned scheme as a basis for organisation, and the manifestation in the plan of the idea of all-encompassing surveillance; the central tower means that everything that the inmate does can be constantly and exhaustively overlooked. He also notes the idea of individual responsibility: the prisoner is an isolated individual left alone with his or her thoughts and given the opportunity to reflect upon his or her sins and to see the merits of better ways.

Foucault charts the development of penology in terms of a transformation in the notion of punishment. We have commented previously (see Chapter 4) on the strong Durkheimian threads in Foucault's work, and they are apparent here. In the pre-modern era, punishment was premised upon the idea that crime is an assault upon the collective body of society, as represented by the sovereign. Punishment, therefore, primarily consisted in some kind of retributive assault upon the (literal) body of the criminal, the nature and extent of which depended on the magnitude of the crime. Physical mutilation, torture and violent forms of execution, all normally conducted in public, were the legally required and socially accepted responses to various types of criminal actions, from theft to murder. Imprisonment was not viewed as a form of punishment, but simply as a means of ensuring that a criminal would be available for punishment, i.e. criminals were confined prior to their trial and while awaiting the carrying out of the sentence. Confinement did not have a unique connection with crime, many types of non-criminals being kept in prison in order to remove them from society, e.g. the poor and the mad.

With the development of penology in the eighteenth and nineteenth centuries, public ceremonies of trial and punishment gave way to administrative rituals conducted by specialised legal professionals, and incarceration came to replace physical mutilation as the normal form of punishment. This change involved a shift to a different conception of crime and of the relationship of the criminal to society. In brief, the logic of punishment became associated with the idea of control, i.e. control of the criminal by the authorities and of the individual by himself. The prisoner was required to conform to a disciplined regime of daily life in which everything he or she did was subject to monitoring and regulation.

As in the earlier studies, Foucault's account in *Discipline and Punish* is guided by the idea that, contrary to Enlightenment propaganda, the great shift in the nature of Western societies has *not* been towards the replacement of arbitrary power by rational organisation and the displacement of authority by knowledge. Instead, it has involved only a reorganisation of the way power is exercised. Very crudely, far-ranging, deeply penetrating and complex networks of regulation, including the self-regulation of individuals, have replaced control by the royal ruler through the occasional administration of brutal punishment. Foucault refers to the change from sovereign power, where the locus of control is external to the activities and relations controlled, to *disciplinary power*, where activities and relations are, so to speak, controlled from within themselves. We have exchanged the loosely supervised existence of pre-modern society for a most closely, extensively and intensively supervised existence. As for its rationality, the purpose of many of the human sciences has been to contribute to the development of this network of supervision, to provide ways of more effectively controlling individuals. Foucault's linkage of power/knowledge refers to the way (often self-styled) scientific knowledge combines and collaborates with administration in the formation of new, refined and improved ways of keeping people under control.

As this last remark implies, it is important to note that *Discipline and Punish* is not simply a study of the origins of the modern prison. Foucault regards the penal regime as a model for the organisation of modern society generally; the prison is merely one institution of carceral society, in which individuals and their behaviour are subjected to – and subject themselves to – surveillance. Other, similar institutions include the school, the hospital and the business organisation. Nevertheless, even though disciplinary power has been dispersed throughout the society, power is still focused on, if not concentrated in the hands of, the state. This *biopower* has resulted from the changing nature of the state's power, which derives from its total population – large, healthy, educated and trained – and not from its military strength alone. The idea of the population as a whole as an asset of the state has given rise to efforts to manage and cultivate it, to enhance (so to speak) its asset value, to provide for the general welfare of the population.

### Biopower

Biopower is the power involved in the management of the population.

In his series of books on sexuality, Foucault connects the development of modern sexuality to biopower, and also seeks to elaborate another aspect of power – what he calls its 'productive' side.

## Sexuality as discourse

The volumes on the history of sexuality were Foucault's final and incomplete work. They usefully clarify the way discourse creates its object, since sexuality seems to be one of the most natural, innately human and, therefore, invariable facts. Foucault does not doubt that human biology is pretty uniform, or that people everywhere engage in acts of sexual contact, but he does argue that sexuality is a socio-cultural creation. Sexuality as we know it is the production of a particular set of historical circumstances and obtains only within the terms of a discourse developed relatively recently, i.e. since the seventeenth century.

The nub of Foucault's argument can be explicated with reference to a paradox. We in the UK often tell ourselves we are (or were until relatively recently, with the coming of 'sexual liberation') a sexually repressed civilisation. The high point of this repression was the Victorian era, and we are still living with the legacy of that time. Sex is, therefore, something that we are not allowed to speak of; its expression in discourse is inhibited and was then entirely forbidden. Note, then, that we are already talking (in Foucault's terms) about a discourse. The story of repression is not told (only) about the prevention of sexual activity itself, but also about what we are allowed to say about sex. The story is not just about behaviour, but also about silence, about limits on language. The paradox is that we continue to tell this story, to put into discourse the complaint about this suppression of discourse. In other words, we keep on speaking about that which we are (supposedly) forbidden to speak about.

The paradox is somewhat fuller since we not only speak of the fact that we are (supposedly) forbidden to speak of sex, but we constantly speak of sex itself. Accordingly, the story of repression is simply not true; what is true is that there has been a change in the way we can speak of sex. There has not been an inhibition about speaking of sex at all.

Sex has become a particular type of discourse. The essence is that (1) the way sex can be spoken of has changed; under the Victorians, there was certainly an inhibition upon the free expression of sexual feelings and reactions; but (2) there was an efflorescence of attempts to speak about sex in scientific and therapeutic ways, which (3) were intimately interwoven with, and constitutive of, efforts to make sex amenable and subject to regulation in order to create a healthy, flourishing and productive population. In the end, then, the very opposite of the traditional story of repression is true, for the whole development of the discourse of sexuality has been to get people to speak of sex, to incite – Foucault uses this word – them to talk about it.

The development of the discourse of sexuality builds upon the deeply entrenched Western practice of confession, an area in which talking about sex was already established. Confession has developed from a practice distinct to religion into one widespread in society and often employed by science, e.g. in psychotherapy. There is a change in its nature, though, in that originally confession was concerned merely with the fact of bodily transgressions, i.e. the sinful sexual acts performed; now the confessional relation has been psychologised, has come to attend to the thoughts, feelings, intentions and other mental concerns involved with sexual acts. Foucault's account here parallels his argument in *Madness and Civilisation* (1967) about the way control shifts from regulation of the body's activities towards manipulation of the mind. Another parallel is the medicalisation of sexual matters, which, in his own words, meant

first of all that the sexual domain was no longer accounted for by the notions of error or sin, excess or transgression, but was placed under the rule of the normal and the pathological (which for that matter were the transposition of the former categories; a characteristic sexual morbidity was defined for the first time; sex appeared as an extremely unstable pathological field...). This implied furthermore that sex would derive its meaning and its necessity from medical interventions; it [confession] would be required by the doctors, necessary for diagnoses, and effective by nature in the cure.

(1967: 67)

Hence the new medical vocabulary is entirely continuous with the old moral vocabulary of sin, transgression and guilt, so patently associated with social control. The medicalisation of sexual discourse simply involves substituting newly coined, scientific-sounding words for previous, moralising terms; the concerns of social control are retained, but now less overtly as they are concealed in a vocabulary which is seemingly, but only seemingly, technical/scientific.

The development of the modern discourse of sex, formed in concepts of heredity and racial purity, originated out of a concern to ensure the thriving well-being of the bloodlines of bourgeois groups and not as a means of suppressing the sexuality and fertility of the 'lower orders'. It was only later (and in adjusted form) that the practices forming around such concerns were exported to the subordinate classes. Foucault characteristically notes that these developments placed a general moral obligation on people to subject their sexual conduct to surveillance so as to ensure that it would not detract from the purity or strength of the physical inheritance. These developments became fused with the formation of the idea of the state as a matter of population rather than of sovereignty, e.g. modern wars are fought on behalf of the population, not on behalf of the sovereign. In major part, the state's job has become the management of a population. Consequently, it requires administrative mechanisms to ensure the reproduction, health and longevity of the population, and to provide social welfare measures such as education and training to shape the population in response to the needs of the society's disciplined pursuits, such as participation in the military and in industry. Foucault draws an ironic contrast between those cultures in which knowledge of sex takes the form of a mastery of erotic arts and the modern Western one, where knowledge of sex is identified with medical and scientific information.

For Foucault, in this instance power was not repressive but *productive*; it did not inhibit either sexual activity or sexual expression, but created something entirely new, giving rise to a whole new discourse of sexuality and an associated set of new practices. While this discourse was very much rationalised around the requirements of biopower, it did not entirely ruin sex – as Drury (1994) puts it – by turning it into an instrumental activity to be overseen and regulated by medical and other bureaucracies. For the discourse also engendered new sexual pleasures and developed new sources of resistance to power. This resistance is important; the point conforms to Foucault's general claim that disciplinary power and resistance to it go together. The development of specific disciplines provides the opportunity for reactions against them, e.g. prison discipline creates inmate subcultures and prison riots.

To illustrate more fully, in the field of sexuality much effort has been devoted to the repression, even elimination, of homosexuality. Medical discourse has contributed massively towards a conception of 'the homosexual' as a type of person suffering from an illness with certain characteristic symptoms and causes, and amenable to certain modes of curative treatment. This development is just what Foucault means when he talks of discourses as creating their object. Of course, prior to the formation of the contemporary medical discourse people engaged in same-sex relations, but 'the homosexual' as a conception of a person *did not exist*; it came into being with, was created by, the formation of that discourse. While the formation of the concept of 'the homosexual' was developed with the aim of repressing homosexual activity, it also produced counter-action, creating a basis on which homosexuals can think of themselves as people with something in common, as people who are badly treated, who should organise to achieve the acceptance and legitimacy of their sexual practices. An outcome of the medical discourse of homosexuality, therefore, is something unintended and unexpected: homosexuals have been able to think of themselves as a social category united by common interests. On this basis they have formed groups to oppose the stereotypical image of themselves and to fight for civil rights.

## Summarising Foucault

Although Foucault may be seen as someone who moved away from an early structuralist towards a poststructuralist position, from the beginning his work was also importantly different from that of Lévi-Strauss and Barthes. Foucault did begin by seeking to isolate structures, but they are not the universal structures of the human mind; rather, they are the general structures of thought – epistemes – that dominate and are tied to a particular epoch. These historically and socially situated structures are subject to displacement by quite different, successor structures. From the start, therefore, his thought was thoroughly relativistic; the transformation in Western society after the seventeenth century represents not any kind of progress or improvement but merely a change, a reorganisation. The Enlightenment's self-evaluation as a progressive force is directly challenged in an attempt to expose the human sciences, on which the Enlightenment set such store, as offering only a delusory prospect of progress. Indeed, the main platform of Foucault's arguments is consistently that knowledge does not entail liberation and does not contrast with power, or, more importantly, does not necessarily or automatically oppose it. Knowledge is complicit in power relations to the extent that in his later work Foucault routinely refers to 'power/knowledge' to indicate the fact that the two are – not in every case, but in the great preponderance – inseparably related to each other.

Foucault's work changed quite significantly over its course, but the notion of discourse is one element that plays a central part throughout. The increasing role that this concept played in his writings is perhaps the clearest index of his shift away from structuralism and towards a poststructuralist position. His studies are much concerned with language, albeit not as a general system of signs. Rather, language contains particular, self-subsistent sectors, each developing in connection with particular forms of social organisation, and each arising along with, and as part of, the reorganisation of activities and the elaboration of new social practices. In many ways, Foucault's investigations are into how the conditions necessary for *the very idea of something* to develop. They involve the development of a discourse, i.e. a way of speaking, constituent vocabularies, the rules regulating what it is possible to say, who can say things, under what conditions, and with what consequences. Only within such a discourse can the idea even be formed.

Foucault's main studies, then, are all focused upon the way some institution, with which we are now familiar and which we take for granted, could come into being. Further, it is important to notice that the development of a discourse is itself decentred: it does not arise from the efforts of one or two individuals, or even from any concerted effort to bring it into being. Rather, it emerges without anyone foreseeing it, from a variety of dispersed and frequently independent developments, interacting with one another to engender, as their entirely unintended end result, the organisation of activity with which we are now familiar, e.g. the visit to the doctor's clinic for a medical examination. Foucault is apt to remark that discourses create (or produce) their objects, which may seem to imply that the development of language can of itself bring actual things into being. This perceived implication can enrage many sociologists for its apparent absurdity. However, his inclination to speak in this way does not create any real problems; there is nothing to strain at in the suggestion that only through the development of a discourse is it possible to have a particular phenomenon. For example, there have been sick people throughout history, and people from remote times may well have suffered from many of the illnesses, diseases and afflictions that sick people now suffer from, but sick people were not always and everywhere patients. Only comparatively recently has the idea of 'the patient', as we now know it, come into being, i.e. as a person whose health is to be administered through participation in a clinic. This idea has arisen with the conjoint development of a physical site for the medical consultation, and of a professional grouping to regulate and manage such consultations. In this sense, 'the patient' can only exist through, is only thinkable in terms of, the discourse that has grown up along with, and out of, these organisational and occupational restructurings.

Foucault's diagnosis of modern society is akin to the mass society envisaged by the Frankfurt School (see Chapter 8), albeit emphasising much more strongly the extent to which individuals are subject to a regime of rationalised administration, making them into passive, acquiescent subjects who even co-operate in their own subordination. Modern society seeks to instil in each individual the disciplined self-control of his or her activities, combined with the elaboration of an ever more encompassing system of monitoring. In this way, things that might seem benign – such as the medical and caring professions – are to be revaluated as malign, part of the network of supervision and regulation. The medical and social services have ever-expanding mandates to investigate areas of social life, to find out more and more about people in society, to obtain inquiring entry into more and more formerly private areas of life, to accumulate records on them, to intervene in these areas of life, to acquire powers to reorganise people's private affairs and to subject them to disciplines, i.e. rules of, and prescriptions for, behaviour intended to bring their conduct into line with the general standard. In short, these services work to normalise people, i.e. to align them with the norm. Normalising in matters of physical health, mental outlook or practical conduct might superficially seem to be done to benefit the individual, but the ways these practices are built up derive very commonly out of a conception of the necessity for the authorities to manage the population; these normalising practices are ways of rendering the population tractable to the managerial activities of the (characteristically state) authorities. It is not what the individual wants, but what the system is deemed to need, that is the decisive consideration.

Despite the way these arguments may sound, there is another important difference between Foucault and the Frankfurt School. His notion of power is anything but a rerun of the (Marxist) idea of a ruling class or stratum using power – or power/knowledge – in order to maintain control over subordinate groups. To think in this way supposes a centre to the operation of power/knowledge in society. This is anathema to Foucault's way of thinking, since he argues that power is not possessed by individuals and groups and exercised by one set over another. Rather, he holds that power is the milieu in which individuals and groups operate; the workings of power are not centred in any one group or source, they do not arise from any given location in the social structure, they do not all operate from any singular site. For him, power is everywhere, it comes from everywhere – recall the all-pervading capillary connections. The network of surveillance, the patterns of discipline and the knowledges that service them have all grown up outside anyone's control. The arrangements they have were formed quite independently of anyone's purposes; they just cannot be understood as being created in order to permit one group of people to control others.

The consequences for politics are significant. On this conception the idea of confronting power is absurd, for such an idea requires that there be a place within society where power resides. Since power is all-pervading, there cannot be any focused, united assault upon it. In so far as modern society is portrayed as being almost exhaustively pervaded by supervision and regulation, there seems to be every reason to draw a conclusion, reached by some members of the Frankfurt School, that the possibility of extensive revolutionary activity within the society has been rendered nugatory. Certainly Foucault rejects the idea of any wholesale uprising of the sort that Marxists envisage. Is *all* point to political activity ruled out? Foucault produces, somewhat like a rabbit from a hat, the contention that power generates resistance, that there are reactions against supervision and regulation almost as an inherent response to them, though these are only localised and peripheral within the society as a whole. For example, prisoners oppose in many ways the dominance of the prison system, through minor acts of disobedience, sometimes through prison riots, and through organising pressure groups to fight for their interests. In place of revolutionary activity the most that one can do politically is to align oneself with such struggles; Foucault himself devoted his political efforts almost entirely to agitating for prisoners' rights.

## Conclusion

A final point: our discussion perhaps has shown that, notwithstanding its structuralist predispositions, Foucault's work involves a blend of Durkheimian and Weberian ideas (see Chapters 3 and 4). We have noted the similarities with Weber's preoccupation with the process of rationalisation and the development of what we might call the totally administered society. Durkheim's later writings on the social nature of knowledge and the origins of the categories of thought are other vital components in Foucault's work and clearly inform his investigation of the way the categories of (particularly) the sciences can originate. The significance of these classical sociological legacies shows Foucault in some respects making a sociologically comfortable adaptation of structuralism, consistent with dominant themes in the classical tradition. He goes some way towards a radicalisation of structuralism. Yet his depiction of modern society as a disciplinary society dominated by rationalist discourses of professionalised knowledge/power seems overwhelmingly to be characterised by coherence, system and order, despite his caveats about internal inconsistencies and sites of resistance. Consequently, for a fully radical, genuinely poststructuralist stance, we have to look elsewhere, principally to the writings of Jacques Derrida (see next chapter).

## Questions

1 What do you understand by Foucault's concepts *episteme*, *discourse* and *archaeology*? What empirical examples does Foucault use to explain these terms? What contemporary examples could you use to illustrate them?

2 To what extent is Foucault's treatment of madness original? In what ways is it similar to, and different from, Goffman's work on asylums and the symbolic interactionist approach to deviance?

3 Summarise Foucault's argument that modern discourse shifts the 'individual' from subject to object. What examples does Foucault give, and what others can you think of? Now summarise Weber's arguments about rationalisation and disenchantment, again providing Weber's examples and contemporary ones of your own. How do the ideas of these two theorists differ from one another? In what ways are they similar?

4 What does Foucault mean by the 'clinical gaze'? What examples does he give, and what others can you think of? Is this the same thing as thinking about modern medicine as an ideology? How might it relate to Weber's ideas about rationalisation?

5 What is 'carceral society'? How do 'discipline' and 'punishment' relate to this? In what ways is it connected with the concept of discourses? How do prisons and sexuality instantiate this concept? What contemporary examples can you think of that would illustrate this idea?

6 What is Foucault's concept of the 'individual'? How does it differ from Durkheim's? How does it differ from those offered by Western Marxist thinkers? In what ways is it similar to and different from Althusser's rejection of the concept?

7 Are contemporary societies 'administered'? What does this mean? In what ways might Foucault's 'power/knowledge' allow us to show aspects of this administration? Is this a better concept to use than those of either Marx or Weber? How might this be compared to Parsons's arguments about the relationships between systems?

## Next steps

Rabinow (1986) compiles a useful selection of Foucault's writings. Foucault's own writings are generally lucid and well translated: his *Madness and Civilisation* (1967), *The Birth of the Clinic* (1973) and *Discipline and Punish* (1977) demonstrate his approach, and the more difficult *The Order of Things* (1970) and *The Archaeology of Knowledge* (1972) provide a theoretical and methodological rationale.

McNay (1994) is an excellent short introduction to Foucault's thought, and the less sympathetic introduction by Merquior (1991) acts as a more sceptical counterpart. Major-Poetzl (1983) is a difficult but comprehensive overview of Foucault's earlier writings.

## CHAPTER TWELVE

# Postmodernity: abandoning grand theory

## Chapter overview

Postmodern theory starts with the same roots as poststructuralism, but uses them to generate different emphases, claims and policies. Derrida's work is foundational for these theoretical moves: it is similar to that of the structuralists and poststructuralists in many ways (he emphasises the contrastive nature of meaning in language, takes that language to be a trap, and argues the 'author' is irrelevant) but crucially inverts Saussure's approach to language. Instead of language being a structured system of signs to be analysed and classified, Derrida argues that language is random and chaotic, making 'meaning' a form of ideological closure. The point of analysis – *deconstruction* – is to reveal the contradictions, incongruities and paradoxes in any text: to show that sense is always built on arbitrary and fallible ground. Such ideas were central to the subsequent *postmodern* theorists, who took ideas like Derrida's to indicate a breach not only with previous ways of thinking but also with all previous forms of social organisation: the world itself, they argue, has ceased to be modern and is now postmodern. Central to these ideas was Lyotard's argument about *grand narratives*: theories of the world. In a fragmented, diverse contemporary world such theories are incoherent and redundant. Ideas like a shared set of values, the class struggle, historical progress, and so on, simply do not make sense any more. Baudrillard took these arguments further by arguing that signs have replaced objects, and appearances have become more 'real' than the things they are supposed to 'represent'.

## Introduction: Derrida – the project of deconstruction

Like those of Foucault, Jacques Derrida's arguments are also primarily about language. Derrida not only rejects representationalism, but also comprehensively abandons any notion of meaning as systematic and of language as providing a handle upon the world. Meaning is *imposed*, thereby committing an act of closure, which is a form of *violence* against language. Meaning always appears coherent and systematic, but this appearance is chimerical. Once set free from the violence of closure, language will show itself to be wild and unpredictable, magnificent in its disorderliness. Derrida's project, therefore, is to rescue language from the violence of ordering, to oppose closure by *deconstructing* meaning and thereby restoring openness to language.

These are exciting-sounding ambitions, but what precisely do they amount to? Derrida is a philosopher by training and occupation and his writings are primarily intended as an attack upon philosophical positions. His arguments are essentially pitched against the dominant philosophical tradition, i.e. Western metaphysics, which aspires towards an ultimate or final knowledge of reality. Derrida holds that it is impossible to fulfil this ambition, which is counter-productive and oppressive. Derrida's arguments can be taken to be directed against Western thought more generally, against a worldview shared by many more than a few philosophers, but having the same characteristics as his particular target in philosophy. Although distinctive, in its specific development Derrida's critique essentially involves many of the same points we have already considered in Barthes and Foucault (see Chapters 10 and 11), namely that the Western way of thought, expressed through language, is basically repressive: it seeks, particularly, to formulate a straitjacketing conception of language; it seeks to inhibit the unruly ways of language as part of a generally repressive orientation. It is to be countered (at least in part) by a practice that exposes this repressive dimension and cultivates the wayward nature of words. For Derrida, exposing some of the key assumptions underpinning metaphysics (even Western thought generally) contributes to undermining its credibility and contributes to its subversion. One such key assumption is the attainability of *presence*.

## Opposing the metaphysics of presence

For Derrida, the search of Western metaphysics for ultimate, final knowledge comes down to the issue of the relationship between speech and writing. Such philosophers as René Descartes (see Chapter 6) and Edmund Husserl (see Chapter 7) have sought ultimate, certain knowledge in the idea that it must be founded in the self-evident.

> **Presence**
>
> The self-evident is what is absolutely true beyond all possibility of doubt. Therefore, it must be patently true immediately, and merely on presentation. Certain knowledge must therefore be experienced directly without anything intervening between it and the perceiver.

For Derrida, the search for the presence of absolute certainty proved elusive because it is not to be had. It is a chimera.

He alleges that the idea of presence has found one of its expressions in the way the spoken voice is regarded – at least as far back as Plato – as more authentic than the written word simply because the one producing the words is present when they are produced. Our spoken words are immediately tied to our presence, to our being there to utter them. Similarly, for our interlocutors they are tied to our presence; they must be with us for them to hear our words, and they can then and there debate our meanings with us, getting from our mouths our personal authority for what we mean by our words. With writing we may not be present to accompany our words, to clarify and elaborate upon them if that is required in order for them to be understood; indeed, we may even be long dead when someone reads our words and wonders what we really meant by them. According to Derrida, on this basis many philosophers take speech to express the essential nature of language, i.e. speech is a matter of immediate contact between speaker and hearer and the speaker has the capacity to control the meaning of her or his own words.

Derrida seeks to reverse this relationship and thereby make his conclusive demonstration of the illusory nature of presence. A true understanding of the nature of language comes from writing, rather than speech. Here Derrida agrees with the post-Saussureans (such as the structuralists and his fellow poststructuralists) in rejecting the idea that the presence of the speaker guarantees security of meaning. This idea expresses the classic conception that it is the individual – the subject – who is the source or centre of meaning. Instead, the language system itself and not the individual speaker is the source of meaning. The notion that the speaker originates meaning and ensures it through being present at its production and in control of its interpretation must be rejected.

## The subject decentred

The presence of the speaker (the author) is not necessary to the production of meaning.

Writing makes plain that we do not – cannot possibly in the case of dead authors – have access to the presence of the author, yet we are not prevented from reading or from satisfying ourselves that we have understood what was written. For us, 'Homer' and 'Shakespeare' are not actual persons who could enter into our presence; rather, they are collections of writings. A better term is texts; 'writings' suggests the activity of someone who is doing the writing, whereas 'texts' suggests the ensemble of words on the page and so does not put into the foreground this connection with an individual producer. After all, anything we say about Homer or Shakespeare as individuals arises primarily from the texts and not the other way around. When people try to decide whether Homer was a single, individual poet, or whether the *Odyssey* and the *Iliad* are ensembles of different works, possibly by several authors, or when people argue about whether Shakespeare was the author of the plays under his name, the primary basis for their efforts is the reading of the poems, the epics and the plays, in ways which look for stylistic unities and breaks as part of a search for clues, allusions and hidden messages.

## The text as source of meaning

Homer and Shakespeare as individuals emerge from the texts, though the way people commonly talk might make it seem that they hold the opposite view and that the text arises from the individual.

For Derrida, that the individual author is not essential to the meaning of his or her written words establishes a general point about language, i.e. the subject does not guarantee the source of meaning. He then applies this idea to speech situations and concludes that the presence of the actual speaker is no more relevant than in the case of the written word. Consequently, the situation taken by metaphysical philosophers as the paradigm of presence is denied; for them, the phenomenon of presence ensures meaning, but presence is shown to be illusory.

## Différance

Derrida has another main argument – again deriving from Saussurean origins (see Chapter 9) – against Western metaphysics. It is often assumed that the true nature of things is to be found in their origins, that a grasp on their essence is to be gained by tracing them to their beginnings. The idea of the presence of the speaker as the guarantor of meaning is one example of this conception: to find out what the words really mean, we must have access to the place whence they initially came, the mouth of the speaker.

However, such an idea is contrary in at least two ways to post-Saussurean views, views which identify two axes to language, the *paradigmatic* and the *syntagmatic*.

## The paradigmatic

This refers to the fact that on any occasion of speech the meaning of spoken words is due to their relationship to words which are not themselves spoken, i.e. the contrastive element which we have noted before (in Chapter 9).

When we choose a particular word in a sentence, we do not use many other words that could have gone in that same position. For example, in developing the sentence 'the cat sat on the mat', in the position where we put 'cat' we have a choice of many other words that could have gone in the same place – 'dog', for example. The word 'cat' is chosen because of the way it *differs* from those other words.

## The syntagmatic

This refers to the selection of words in sequence. A sentence is built up in a temporal sequence, and the meaning of a word in a sentence depends not only upon the words that come before it, but also on those which come after it. We have to wait to see what other words come after to see what a particular word does mean.

For example, if we have a sentence which begins 'The man ate', we shall have to listen (or read on) to see what follows; if the sentence goes 'The man ate his words' rather than 'The man ate the fish', we shall see that 'ate' is very different in the two cases. In other words, we ascertain the meaning of a word by moving further away from its point of origin. The point applies not just to words, but also to sentences. We find what a prior sentence means by hearing/reading what follows it.

In Derrida's hands, however, these arguments are taken further. We have spoken as if waiting for further words and sentences does enable us to decide what is meant, but Derrida wants to argue that we can never arrive at an absolutely definitive, final meaning, for the chain of words and sentences is never-ending. We seek to establish what the earlier words mean by listening to or reading what comes later, but there will always be more signs, i.e. more words and more sentences. We can never be sure that the words will not take on a quite different sense by events occurring later.

For example, in Francis Ford Coppola's film *The Conversation*, words to the effect 'He would kill us if he could' are replayed many times, and are understood to express the fear the couple have that the woman's husband would revenge himself upon them if possible. Then, in the closing sequences of the film, the way the situation is set up leads us to hear the words not as an expression of fear for the lovers' own lives, but as their justification for their decision to murder the husband. They now have the sense, 'We must kill him first, because he would kill us if he could.' Of course, we conclude that this meaning of the words is final, that we now know what they meant all along, but we do so only because Coppola's film draws to a close. There was nothing to stop Coppola prolonging the film and making other twists on this meaning. The chain of signs is endless, and since its elements can work retroactively, there is no point at which we can say utterly conclusively, absolutely finally, what a given string of words means. Thus the desire to establish the actual meaning of a word leads us not in the direction it is commonly supposed to, i.e. back to their initial minting, but in the opposite direction, further away from that point of origin, as we seek to ascertain what was meant by seeing what comes afterwards, with the point of origin receding ever further in time.

Derrida coins the expression '*différance*' in a play on two relevant French terms.

> **Différance**
>
> Convenient for translation, this item pertains to the paradigmatic and syntagmatic axes of language: to the importance of *differing* (i.e. of contrasting) and of *deferring* (i.e. of postponing any final conclusions).

Neither at the beginning nor at the end is there a point at which the definitive, unequivocal meaning can be found, since, in a way, there is neither a beginning nor an end. In so far as the location of such a point is essential to being able to ascertain meaning, and as there is no such point of origin or conclusion, then meaning cannot be ascertained.

Derrida's work has been immensely influential in literary criticism, which has very often given interpretative primacy to the author, seeking to understand literary materials better by assuming that she or he is the source of their meaning. For example, the meaning is to be found by investigating the biographical circumstances of the author, reading the author's letters, interviewing people who knew the author, sometimes interviewing the author in person if available. For Derrida, this approach does not ascertain the meaning of a text by means of other materials such as the life or opinions of the individual. Rather, it attempts to ascertain the meaning of one text by reference to other texts. These texts can be written or spoken (remember, spoken words are also texts; they are a form of writing, not the other way around). The whole operation proceeds at the level of texts, of relating elements within a text to other elements in the same text, and of relating one text to other texts, and for this reason followers of Derrida speak of *intertextuality*. Thus traditional approaches to literary studies depend for their methods upon the assumption that writings are centred, i.e. their meaning originates with a subject, whereas acceptance of Derrida's line of reasoning involves a comprehensive decentring of texts.

## 'There is nothing outside the text'

Almost as important as his rejection of the subject is the fact that Derrida, like Barthes and Foucault, emphasised the (so to speak) opacity of language, i.e. the extent to which it is important to respond to it for its own sake, rather than to treat it as a means to an end, as in the representationalist tradition. This tradition does so in effect by conceiving language as a window on the world, something we use to access the world outside. Equally, the literary critical tradition has been concerned with the meaning of the text as its message, i.e. what it intends to tell us about the world outside itself, the information or advice that it seeks to convey about how things are or what to do. Derrida, again, is attached to the common poststructuralist conviction that the understanding of language is not to be looked for through conceptions of it which are dominated by the idea that language is essentially a medium through which other things (such as the nature of reality or the intentions and purposes of individuals) are to be sought. The aim is, rather, to examine language as a phenomenon in its own right as found in texts, assemblies of written or spoken words, and indeed to examine any other phenomena that function as signs in human life.

## 'Nothing outside the text'

Derrida, no doubt provocatively, once made the notorious remark that 'There is nothing outside the text', which many have understood as some kind of denial that anything exists except words (signs), i.e. there is a language but no external world.

*Perhaps* Derrida might have meant that, from the point of view of understanding texts, the appropriate thing to do is to examine the texts themselves, to see what they are like and how they work, without supposing that the key to what a text is saying/doing is to be found somewhere else (such as in the mind of the author).

Another *possible* way of understanding the suggestion that 'There is nothing outside the text' might be to suppose that Derrida is trying to problematise the distinction between what we say or write on the one hand, and what we talk or write about on the other; to show that what are treated (in philosophy at least) as clear-cut, categorical distinctions, sharply separating different realms of phenomena, are anything but. In short, 'words' and 'things' are not as sound, sharp and stable as they are there presented. On this reading, Derrida is not trying to demolish these distinctions, to do away with them altogether. He is no less impressed than Hegel by the fact that philosophy is preoccupied with seemingly irreconcilable oppositions. Hegel sought to show that they could be overcome through reconciliation over the full expanse of history (see Chapter 2), but, if we may put it this way, Derrida is determined to destabilise those oppositions (at least as they have been philosophically construed) and to show that what they attempt to demarcate cannot be contained within the boundaries laid out by the oppositional categories. As mentioned, with respect to the opposition of speech and writing, Derrida sought to show that the philosophers' criteria for contrasting the two did not really distinguish them. Indeed, in terms of these same criteria, writing, not speech, seemed best to embody the general character of language.

Hence he stands the previous contrast on its head: speech seems now to be a derivative of, and dependent on, writing, rather than the other way around. Thus, saying that 'There is nothing outside the text' might also be a way of problematising the language/reality distinction, which is a major staple of philosophical dichotomising. Here, the point would be to suggest that the distinction is more complex and much less clear-cut than it sounds; separating out the world in itself from our ways of talking about it is easier said than done. If so, Derrida is not therefore doing away with the distinction altogether. After all, the attempt to make the separation (by way of distinctions and contrast) will itself have to be undertaken in language, and subject to all the problems which afflict the attempt to set up stable, categorical distinctions.

On Derrida's own account of the nature of language, the exercise will be ultimately frustrated. In the same way, Derrida does not set out to demolish the difference between literary and philosophical texts, thereby denying any difference between philosophy and literary theory. Alternatively, he does not set out to deny that there are any differences between literary and factual documents; rather, as part of his programme of destabilising dichotomies, he would want to challenge any claim that this distinction comprises a set of simple, pure, clear-cut and uncomplicated differences which can be given in any sweeping and general way.

To illustrate further, we have mentioned Derrida's *Glas* (1986), in which the page is divided into double columns, each column being devoted to a different figure (see Chapter 10). The first is on Hegel, the great philosopher, the other on Jean Genet, a French literary figure of the 1950s and 1960s with an 'outlaw' past and identity as homosexual, thief and prisoner. Derrida's comments are intermixed with materials from the two figures he is commenting upon, and he draws their writings from diverse sources, including personal documents as well as their formally published work. The text is meant to induce uncertainties, both in the sense of doubts and questionings, and also in the sense of things that cannot be resolved or settled. The first is how to read it, for there is no right way of deciding how to alternate between the two columns. Further, the intermixing of the texts raises doubts about authorship: who is to count as author of an assortment like this? There are doubts about its character as literature and/or philosophy. Hegel is a philosopher, but are his contributions to this book to be read as philosophy? Genet is a literary figure, but could his work be read philosophically in relation to Hegel's? And is *Glas* itself to be seen as philosophy, or as a work of literary art, or as a practical joke in the surrealist mode? And what about the relationship of literature to philosophy? Might Genet's writings have something to say to the philosophy of Hegel?

*Glas* can thus bring out doubts about truth and its connection to authority. For example, perhaps Genet's 'outlaw' attitudes informing his own search for truth are a denial of the association that Hegel makes between truth and social authorities, such as the father as the figure of authority in the family, or the state as the authority within society. Is, then, philosophy's traditional idea of its search for truth merely another expression of patriarchal domination? In these ways, *Glas* displays the sense in which deconstruction (see below) is not an attempt to depict or analyse any given text with a view to bringing out its coherent meaning. Rather, it performs on texts operations which are disruptive of the quest for coherence, and uses texts to create further and different texts which generate, perpetuate and proliferate ambiguities, keeping things unsettled and uncertain, and crossing and recrossing boundaries in ways which show that they cannot stably and unequivocally contain things within their limits.

Philosophical work and factual reports may have many literary aspects to them and many fictional elements in them; yet to say that there is no principled difference between literary and other kinds of texts is not necessarily the same as saying that there are no differences between a piece of fiction and a factual report.

## Redrawing the boundaries

The denial of a principled distinction between literary and other texts has an important methodological consequence: it offers the prospect of an extensive redrawing of boundaries within the social sciences and humanities and also makes a tremendous impact on the practice of literary studies themselves. It suggests a fundamental shift in the definition of subject matter, i.e. opening up the boundaries of textual analysis to incorporate many other ('non-literary') kinds of texts. Indeed, since every use of language is a text, there can be no principled grounds for drawing definitive boundaries between any of the disciplines concerned with language and its uses. Derrida's arguments have as a by-product the most profound disciplinary implications: it is no longer possible to treat literary criticism, history, sociology or any other of the human studies as discrete domains on the basis that they deal with different phenomena, have different intellectual concerns and characteristically work with different forms of data; e.g. literary studies addresses fictional and poetic writings; history studies historical documents; sociology works mainly with interview materials. From the standpoint provided by Derridian arguments about texts and intertextuality, such differences obscure a more profound truth.

### Disciplines as convention

Since no text, and no (so-called) type of text, has inherent meaning, no distinctions between texts (or text types) can be treated as authoritative; they are nothing more than conveniences, impositions of arbitrary (and ultimately groundless) convention. We will consider this point in more detail later.

As already mentioned, Derrida argues against the tradition in philosophy as well as literary criticism. This tradition (perhaps) dominates the broader culture, the general way of thought in the Western world. He is protesting against the effort to straitjacket thought within the confines of unity through logical consistency. His concern is not just to confront or to complain about the dominance of such traditions, but to undermine them and to contribute to the liberation (the free play) of the sign, i.e. to escape from these straitjacketing inclinations and to *empower* (so to speak) the discipline-resistant, uncontrollable nature of language.

Derrida's arguments also have significant methodological implications. As mentioned, the level of operation is, he insists, entirely at the level of the text. We are irreducibly dealing (in literary and philosophical work, and in other intellectual operations) with texts, either written or spoken. If anything is to be done about the straitjacketing of language, it must be done in and through texts. Consequently, his argument requires the development of a way of working on texts which undermines the illusion of control over them and over meaning, releases the boundless, uncontrollable capacity of signs, disintegrates the apparent centres and structures in texts and, finally, proliferates the diversity of meanings. The methods developed by Derrida (and also independently by the critic Paul de Man) comprise strategies for dismantling accepted meanings and interpretations, aptly named *deconstruction*.

The policy of deconstruction can be intensely offensive – certainly to the project of the Enlightenment with its emphasis on reason – since it sets no store on logical consistency, usually considered the essence of reason. For Derrida, the unrelenting demand for logical consistency is merely so much dogma, an exercise of power through the attempt to create a structuring grid within which texts can be contained, into which they will be coerced. There seems to be a great deal at stake: the continuing pre-eminence of a whole way of thinking, and not merely disagreement about the policies of literary criticism. One way this thinking is exhibited in Western philosophy is in its dualisms, the oppositional pairing of terms, on which it focuses, e.g. 'truth/falsity', 'speech/writing', 'mind/ body', 'philosophy/literature'. As we saw in Chapter 2, Hegel had also noted this usage, making it the basis for his own philosophical scheme, thinking that he could resolve these dualisms. For Derrida, however, they are not stable; the separations they make cannot be sustained. Furthermore, the dualisms are not just oppositions, they are characteristically inequalities; one element of the pair is considered the basic, more profound, or otherwise dominant element. Take Derrida's own argumentative starting point: not only are speech and writing contraposed, but also writing is invariably the inferior element – a view that arouses his animosity.

## Deconstruction

The operation of deconstruction works in the opposite way to conventional attempts to identify a coherently structured text, unified under its title and the name of the author. The conventional direction seeks out as much internal consistency as possible, trying to bring all aspects of the text within the scheme. Its obverse, deconstruction, cultivates incongruities and paradoxes, highlighting the ways texts are internally divided within themselves, showing how one part of the text counteracts the effect ostensibly sought in another, and revealing especially where aspects of the text resist, confound and unravel the order which seeks to impose itself upon the text.

Some of the operation of deconstruction can be very simply understood as showing that a crucial dualism, an opposition between two categories, cannot be sustained as an opposition. It also claims to demonstrate that the supposed priority of one element over the other cannot be defended and the usual hierarchy can be reversed. For example, the opposition of speech to writing is attacked as an opposition, since Derrida treats speech as a kind of writing (so speech and writing are no longer opposed but are the same thing); yet he also promotes writing above speech, since writing, not speech, most perspicuously exhibits the essential nature of language.

## Towards postmodernity

In so far as poststructuralism involves the abandonment of the idea that there is an overall, rationalised order to social thought and progress in social development, it moves beyond modernity and becomes *postmodernity*. The terms 'poststructuralist' and 'postmodern' are often used interchangeably, but we have separated them here, at least (though not only) for presentational reasons. The poststructuralists have been concerned to provide arguments as to why the modernist conception, or the Enlightenment project, as they prefer to call it, cannot be sustained, to show how it is unsustainable relative to the historical developments of the modern period, and to formulate alternative conceptions. However, it would contradict their own arguments to suppose that the critique of the Enlightenment project was thinkable at any time, that the shift beyond modernity had taken place entirely as a result of the free development of the logic of thought and of discussion.

### Postmodernity

If we are moving beyond modernity, we are not merely moving beyond a particular intellectual outlook. Rather, we must be moving beyond the particular historical period (or epoch) in which the notions of modernity were thinkable into one in which those notions are no longer thinkable, i.e. a postmodern age.

We have chosen, then, to discuss under the heading of 'postmodernity' those thinkers who have rather more to say than Barthes, Foucault and Derrida about the specific character of contemporary society, about the extant or emerging postmodern world.

## Lyotard on the postmodern era

However much those who argue for a postmodern approach may eschew Marxist influences in favour (usually) of Nietzschean ones, we cannot help but notice that their argument remains persistently Marxist in its mode. For both Lyotard and Baudrillard, the two key figures in the postmodern analysis, the legacy of Marxist thought – specifically, Marx's base–superstructure distinction – infuses their work, albeit in somewhat different ways.

Jean-François Lyotard (1924–98) begins his analysis of contemporary post-World War II society from observations about the way the changing structure of economic production has transformed the position of knowledge, especially as a result of the rise of the computer. Here we have the idea of the information age, in which knowledge will itself become a productive force, perhaps the predominant productive force. There have been corresponding changes in the nature of science and technology, which have become particularly focused upon problems of language (as was illustrated in the trajectory from Lévi-Strauss to Derrida: see Chapters 9 and 10), and we note that the information industries involve technologies of communication.

## Knowledge as a commodity

Not only does knowledge become a productive force, it also increasingly becomes a commodity, i.e. something produced for the purpose of sale. Knowledge as something to be instilled in the human mind is being displaced by the idea that it is something to be sold.

Consequently, the whole place of the production and dissemination of knowledge within contemporary society is being reorganised.

In the contemporary world, economies are increasingly globalised; economic activity is now beyond the directive control of individual nation states. At the same time, the production and control of knowledge have become an economic phenomenon and, as such, an increasingly political (i.e. governmental) question in so far as issues of control over the economy, including knowledge, increasingly arise. What possibility is there of rational control of these developments? Lyotard maintains that the thought that there might be any sense to these developments has become untenable; they are driven only by what Weber (see Chapter 3) called means-ends rationality, what Lyotard himself terms *performativity*.

## Performativity

Essentially this is the standard of practical (particularly economic) efficiency.

The expansion of the economy has become an end in itself, quite independent of any of the standards by which we might otherwise seek to judge things. Usually we do not desire to judge things only by standards of efficiency; there are other standards such as moral goodness, beauty and fairness. Science, however, knows nothing of these things, and scientific knowledge is, of course, a driving force of the economy.

On this argument, it follows that if there is to be knowledge of what is good, beautiful and fair, it cannot be scientific knowledge. If such knowledge is to be found, it cannot be within the forms that scientific knowledge can take. It must take a different form, which Lyotard dubs *narrative*.

Lyotard thus provides yet another version of the transition from traditional to modern society, involving in this case the increasing displacement of narrative by science, making for fragmentation and the loss of wholeness. It is, again, a recounting of the triumph (the empty triumph) of rationalism.

### Narrative

In traditional societies, narrative is the common, predominant form within which knowledge is conveyed. Lyotard asserts that knowledge of different kinds can be transmitted through stories. In these traditional societies the role of narrative is functional; it subserves and contributes to the needs of social solidarity.

By contrast, the modern or postmodern form of contemporary society is made up of isolated, atomistic, instrumentally connected individuals. It results from the dissolution of the social solidarity of traditional societies, a process which, in Lyotard's telling, is effected through the rise of the way of thought characteristically dubbed rationalist and pre-eminently embodied in science, i.e. it requires logical, formal demonstrative reasoning sustained by empirical truth. In short, it requires theoretical structures, not stories. Narrative does not traffic in argument and proof and cannot therefore satisfy scientific standards. Rather than recognising narrative as signifying a different kind of knowledge, however, those enamoured of scientific standards disvalue it, denouncing it as a form of archaic or impoverished thought, e.g. as primitive thought or mere opinion.

## Grand narratives

Paradoxically, scientific standards are not, and cannot be, self-justifying with respect to such qualities as moral goodness, beauty and fairness because scientific discourse explicitly excludes narrative discourse, the only form of language that can provide such justifications. Any legitimisation for scientific discourse must, however, be drawn from narrative forms; indeed, they illicitly and surreptitiously (but inevitably) must intrude. Ironically, then, science cannot do without stories; the task of stories is to provide justification and legitimisation to science. For Lyotard, the modern age has been marked by a number of *grand narratives*.

### Grand narratives

These have attempted to provide overarching, comprehensive stories of the development of science, thereby endowing the development of science with sense, with a guiding and worthy purpose.

For example, Marx provided a grand narrative of science which placed it within the framework of the total history of the human species and attributed to it the purpose of contributing to the progressive freeing of individuals, on the way to the emancipation of humankind as a whole. Another grand narrative, usually referred to as positivism (see Chapter 4), tells of the advance of scientific knowledge, of a continuous movement towards the achievement of final, comprehensive and unified knowledge.

Such myths are often intertwined with the development and justification of the nation state. Lyotard argues that these grand narratives are themselves myths, which have lost their hold. Now science has moved away from acquiring knowledge for such high-minded purposes and for its own sake, towards knowledge merely being bought and sold by business and the state. Knowledge is acquired for its practical (political or economic) use, and not for its own sake or its improving or emancipatory value. Further, the capacity to justify scientific activity by integrating it into judgements of goodness and beauty through narrative has diminished as the spheres of science, morality and art have been progressively differentiated out in 'modern-into-postmodern' societies. The possibility for artistic and ethical commentary upon science is drastically undermined as these spheres of social life become ever more separated from each other and from the direct, day-to-day experience of people in society; such matters are made over into the business of experts.

## The redundancy of grand narrative

The modern outlook, with its hope in the all-commanding, all-comprehending power of reason, has been obviated. It is not now possible for people to place credence in grand narratives, for such attempts at overarching and unifying schemes simply cannot encompass the diversity, the fragmentation, of society today. Since this condition is not temporary, then the day of the grand narrative is over.

### Signs in and out of control: Baudrillard

Jean Baudrillard (1924–2007) started as a sociologist operating within a Marxist perspective. Later, by his own account, he turned against Marx and sociology, asserting both to be outmoded and irrelevant. Nevertheless, despite these assertions we will suggest that his work remains in many ways quite continuous with both. Baudrillard's announcements of the end of things – 'reality' and 'the social' being only two (but main) examples – on inspection prove to be hyperbolic expressions of somewhat less exceptionable points. In a way, one could summarise – somewhat unfairly, we admit – Baudrillard's main claim as being that contemporary society is dominated by television and advertising (and electronic media more generally), and this domination involves a dehumanisation reminiscent of the emphasis upon, and condemnation of, alienation found in Marx's early analysis of capitalism (see Chapter 2). Indeed, Baudrillard's claim appears to be that media dehumanisation *is* the contemporary form of alienation. Although Baudrillard does attempt an upturning of the fundamentals of Marx's thought by reversing the base–superstructure relationship, thereby making the production of culture the defining characteristic of contemporary society, Marx's concept of capitalism as a dehumanising force principally drives his arguments.

Similarly, the later Baudrillard professes intense hostility to sociology and categorically dismisses it, yet a central element of his picture of modern society amounts to the recovery of a central preoccupation of both the Frankfurt School and 1950s American sociology: the mass society (see Chapter 8). It was commonly held among both that mass society was marked by cultural superficiality and the political inactivity of the great majority of the population. Baudrillard's assertion of the *death of the social* refers precisely to the political and cultural indifference and unresponsiveness of people; correspondingly, the death of sociology follows only in so far as it involves a conception of sociology as consisting in theorisation of the dynamic and historical role of the masses (in the old Marxist sense). So understood, sociology is justified as a pursuit only so long as a case can plausibly be made for the imminent overthrow of the system by those it oppresses. Since Baudrillard (along with most contemporary sociologists) cannot find plausible grounds of this sort, sociology is dead. Baudrillard's notion of the mass into which society has collapsed (and therefore ceased to be) means that any source of organised opposition or challenge to the status quo has disappeared. In its place there can be, at best, nothing more than a quasi-dormant sullenness: an inert resistance to the persuasion of politics, the blandishments of advertising, and the solicitations of the media. It is true that Baudrillard's later work is often more a series of cryptic aphorisms than an explicitly developed argument, but its preoccupations and insistences remain continuous with those of his more traditionally argumentative stances.

There are good reasons, therefore, for not taking too literally Baudrillard's pronouncements concerning the death of this or that. For example, Baudrillard proposes that a perfect crime has been committed, that reality has been disposed of without anyone (except, of course, our Baudrillardian detective) noticing.

## The death of reality

How is the claim to be understood that reality has been done away with? Not, we think, as the denial that anything ever really happens, but, rather, much more as a denial that what does happen comprises real (in the sense of authentic) instances of things. For example, when people say that junk food is not 'real food', they do not mean that you do not get anything to eat, but that you do not get anything with the proper qualities and nutritional values that real food is supposed to have.

For instance, when Baudrillard argues that the first Gulf War did not take place (Baudrillard 1995), he is not denying that there was military activity in the deserts of Kuwait and Iraq, but is rather saying that this military activity did not represent a real war, i.e. amount to a war in the sense which has been traditionally understood. It was not, for example, a contest between two military forces, but between one side with awesome military power, and another side hardly well-enough organised or equipped to amount to an army. It is a bit more complicated because Baudrillard uses 'real' to make a slightly different contrast, which is the kind that is used in computing with terms like 'real time' and 'virtual reality'. Much of the military activity which took place in the Gulf War was not real, in the sense that much of it did not involve first-hand military activity on the part of human beings, but, rather, was done through electronic, virtual media. So pilots never faced their enemies in reality but only through their virtual representations on electronic displays.

Reality has thus been disposed of in the sense that our actual experience of the world around us is now thoroughly interwoven with and overlaid by virtual representations. We 'watch Grand Prix motor racing' from our couches, on TV screens, and never go near the actual races, and we may well think that the television picture is better because we see more of the race, get replays of the action and so on.

Lastly, as a fourth element, Baudrillard is arguing that there is (may we use the word?) really a reversal of the relationship between the supposed media of representation and the reality those media purportedly represent. Far from what is shown on the television, cinema screen or video display being a representation of a pre-given reality, it is, rather, increasingly the case that what happens in reality forms itself in terms of, after the fashion of, its representation in the media. For example, actual, on-the-street police get their own idea of how the police, and therefore they themselves, do/should behave from watching cop shows on TV; the virtual has become the model (or *code*) for the actual.

Similarly, while Baudrillard began with Marxist suppositions, which he subsequently denounced, showing that his career has been one of movement, the idea that this shift involves a decisive renunciation would be misleading. There is much continuity in his career, and the changes frequently consist in taking further his previous positions, even pushing them to extremes.

Baudrillard is centrally taken with the idea of modern society as *consumer society*, and the terms in which consumer society is depicted are what evolve through his work.

## Consumer society

The cumulative picture he paints of consumer society is one in which an extreme (possibly even the ultimate) form of dehumanisation has occurred and the objects have taken over. The response of people is to make themselves as much like these objects as possible.

The evolution of this view involves adopting the idea that objects themselves have become signs, and so it is no contradiction to say that Baudrillard both:

• sees society as being dominated by objects; and
• sees society as pervaded by signs.

In characteristic Marxist vein, Baudrillard sees the consumer society, with its apparently prosperous, comfortable and enriched lives for many, as a snare and a delusion, as a continuation of the traditionally exploitative nature of capitalism. People are not consuming because they want the things that they are consuming, because these things fulfil their needs. Rather, they are consuming because they are being made to. Were consumption an expression of human needs, then it would (at least on Baudrillard's estimate) result in the satiation of those needs; but they are not satiated and consumption continues to change and grow, following the familiar expansionist dynamic of capitalism. In the age of consumer society, human relationships are becoming more and more at one with objects – one's house, car, television, wardrobe, etc. – rather than with people. The importance of objects in people's lives, however, has less to do with the use those objects have than with their meaning. Here is another aspect of the dehumanising effect of capitalism, which Baudrillard's later work will emphasise: the essential meaninglessness of life in consumer society.

## The turn against Marxism

Given these strong Marxist themes in his work, how is it that Baudrillard came so vehemently to reject the Marxist tradition? Two main elements are important in understanding Baudrillard's turn against Marxism:

1  Baudrillard attaches himself to a nostalgic picture of 'primitive' society involving symbolic exchange, a situation that denies the use value of objects.
2  He regards Marx as a perpetrator of bourgeois morality, particularly the work ethic, which is simply outmoded in a consumer age.

Marx's idea was, of course, that capitalism was a system that perverted the treatment of objects. In Marx's terms, objects have a *use value*.

### Use value

This refers to the things one can actually use objects for, e.g. eating in the case of a banana, knocking in nails in the case of a hammer.

Under capitalism, objects are produced not for their use value, but for their *exchange value*.

### Exchange value

This is their capacity for being bought and sold in capitalist markets.

Exchange value, rather than use value, decided whether objects were produced, how they were distributed and so on. Furthermore, as we saw in Chapter 2, part of Marx's conception of human nature was that the essence of human existence is work. In work, true human fulfilment may be found, albeit not under the degrading working conditions of capitalism.

Confronting these two points, Baudrillard turns Marx's own concepts against him.

### The rejection of Marxism

Baudrillard argues that the idea of work as a fulfilment of human essence is nothing more than acceptance of the bourgeoisie's own ideology; the idea that production and accumulation are natural features of human life is refuted by life in 'primitive society'.

Baudrillard takes his picture of this type of society partially from Durkheim's collaborator, the anthropologist Marcel Mauss (see Chapter 4). In such societies it is often the high spot of people's lives to engage in the wasteful destruction of property. For example, among the native peoples of British Columbia (as it now is) a ceremony called the potlatch involves the wealthier members of the tribe attempting to impress others in a competition by giving away and destroying their possessions. Mauss sought to explain such behaviour in terms of the symbolic meaning of possessions: what possessions signify about the possessor is important, not their material utility. Another element is also taken from Mauss: an emphasis upon the gift. The exchange of gifts in an elaborate and widely extending circle of relationships is a prominent feature of some so-called primitive societies. Such networks of reciprocal gift-giving show, for Baudrillard, that the objects which are exchanged play a symbolic role: the giving of gifts requires exchange, with the object playing the role of making a connection – one of mutual recognition – between people. The objects themselves have this symbolic significance; they are not exchanged to be used, i.e. they are not valued for their capacity in use. Thus Marx's use value is not a necessary foundation for understanding objects, but is itself a creation of certain social conditions.

In these arguments against the foundational status of the material character of objects, we can see how Baudrillard is led to the claim that now people carry a sense of a loss of the authentic human contact that can be found in symbolic exchange. In Western societies, even if objects were not part of a process of symbolic exchange, they once were embedded in social relationships, but now they have been extricated from them; objects now form systems in their own right. For example, in more traditional Western societies, objects were closely linked with social stratification; whether or not people could possess certain sorts of things depended upon where the people stood in the social hierarchy; the significance of objects was entirely dependent upon the structure of social relationships. However, objects have now been abstracted from such contexts and have an autonomous standing. What matters now is how objects stand in relation to other objects, not how they fit into and facilitate human social relations.

## Objects and social relations

The basic charge that Baudrillard makes against contemporary society is that objects and their meaning determine social relations, rather than the other way around.

## The consumption of sign-objects

What does it mean to say that objects relate to one another rather than reflecting social relations? Baudrillard employs the example of interior decorating to indicate how a particular object is conceived as part of a system, how it is to fit in with other objects according to various principles, e.g. colour and textural matching. He makes use of a notion of the *code*, which many commentators find obscure, but these kinds of principles, which articulate objects into patterns, can perhaps be seen as one kind of exemplification. Another is a computer, which operates according to binary code. The idea of things as increasingly operating according to (one or another) code makes an analogy with the Saussurean view of language and fits with Baudrillard's contention that objects are operating as signs.

## Objects as signs

The production of capitalism is now a production of signs, superficially seen quite literally in the way the productive resources of capitalism are increasingly devoted not to the production of physical objects, but to signs (words and images), e.g. television, computer supplies and so forth. However, Baudrillard's point is that physical objects are also signs. This is the point at which his inversion of Marx takes place, when he insists that the nature of objects as signs is more basic, more fundamental, than their nature as objects with a use value.

Consequently, what is needed to displace Marxism is a political economy of signs.

People have themselves been, so to speak, absorbed into the system of objects. They have been removed from a society in which their sense of themselves was rooted in spatial and social location and are now governed by the codes, which produce and circulate signs (including objects). Consuming them is governed by fashion. The possession of things is relative to the images they carry or convey, rather than to their use value. The fact that the images of things change means that new things are desired; the laws of fashion play a strong part in driving consumer behaviour. Consumer goods are being used as a way of forming social difference, not distributed as a consequence of it. In this sense, objects produce (kinds of) people, not the other way around. Thus social identities amount to nothing more substantial than a collection of signifying objects, e.g. wearing spiky hair, chains, safety pins and so forth marked someone out as a punk in the late 1970s.

If production is not the fulfilment of human essence (as it was for Marx), then consumption is certainly not its fulfilment either. Though Baudrillard might deny it, his intent, certainly the nature of his characterisation of consumer society, conveys an impression that a loss of true meaning and an increasing shallowness of existence are involved. We have already referred to the nostalgic contrast implicit in his writings; for him, pre-capitalist and earlier forms of capitalist society placed people in more stable and authentic structures of existence. We have not yet mentioned the way Baudrillard indicts consumer society for bringing about the loss of reality itself.

## Baudrillard on hyperreality

We have seen that one key element of the Marxist scheme, and one that Baudrillard certainly retains, is the role of ideology, though the term he uses is 'alibis', by which he refers to ideological justifications of the system.

> **Alibis**
>
> The idea that an object is wanted/possessed for its use value is an alibi, i.e. a misleading justification, for the object's real role is as a sign in circulation.

Comparably, the alibi for signs themselves – whose whole point is just to proliferate and circulate – is that they have a use, namely, to refer to reality. Baudrillard goes along with numerous other poststructuralists in casting doubt on the idea that signs refer to anything outside themselves, that their role is to identify a pre-existing reality. Rather, it is the other way around, with the sign projecting the reality of which it speaks, a projection that already contains marked ideological elements. We cannot speak of nature, for example, in a way that is not deeply implicated with ideology. In many mouths the notion of nature is permeated with the conception of the unspoiled, though it might in other mouths carry the connotation of the raw and the ruthless (as in 'nature red in tooth and claw'). The central application of this element of *Ideologiekritik* (see Chapter 8) in Baudrillard involves the argument that the operation of culture (of signs) in consumer capitalism is such as to convey the impression (the alibi) that signs do refer to an external reality, when in fact that external reality has been lost by being displaced.

Baudrillard's main targets, and the institutions which principally exemplify these matters, are television and advertising. In both cases a similar alibi obtains: the impression is given that a broadcast or an advert is referring to something real, i.e. a newsworthy event or the use value of the advertised commodity. In fact, the broadcast and the advert have become ends in themselves, things which are consumed for their own sake, not for what they talk about. To fill out the example a little further, consider the way politics has shifted on to television, with television reporting of politics displacing the politics – reporting itself becoming the politics.

As we illustrated earlier, Baudrillard made himself notorious with his argument concerning the first Gulf War. During the build-up to it, he asserted that it existed solely as a sign and not at all as a real world event, a real war. What was occurring was only a media phenomenon, not a war that was taking place in the desert. It was simply something shown on television, for everyone to see. Even when the Gulf War did 'take place', Baudrillard persisted. The war had not taken place, for the role of any actual fighting was merely to contribute to the virtual struggle taking place on television screens. The battle scenes were produced (in the desert) merely to be reproduced, i.e. to provide things to show on television in order to give the image of American supremacy and victory.

## Signs as reality and hyperreality

In the modern world, the world as given in signs (especially as images on television and computer screens) is the reality. This reality has not only displaced the original reality but has transcended it, has become more real than real, has become, in Baudrillard's term, *hyperreal.*

Examples are the attempt to make video games more exciting than the racing or fighting activities that provide their materials, and the aspiration to develop virtual reality to a point at which it will give ever more intense and convincing experiences.

In a way, though, we are being a little bit false to Baudrillard's ideas by talking about the reality and the sign since, for him, they have imploded. They have become so involved with each other that it is no longer possible to separate what is real from what is, say, fictional; though, of course, it is a feature of the ideological nature of the system of signs that it functions to project and protect the impression that there is a difference between the image and reality, that the reality exists beyond the image, thereby concealing the fact that the reality has disappeared. Witness how the emphasis in television coverage of the Gulf War is on eyewitness reports, pictures from near the front and so forth.

## The simulacrum and the death of the social

According to Baudrillard, we live in the time of the *simulacrum.*

## The simulacrum

This is an image without an original.

The current era of hyperreality is the product of a historical progression in which the relationship between reality and sign has gone through various forms to arrive at this point. This four-stage sequence began with the traditional society, in which signs were installed within and governed by the social order, and where there is no problem about the relationship of signs to reality. The Renaissance was the time of the *first order* of simulacra, when the sign was independent of reality and produced a change with the loosening of social control over social position and concomitantly over signs. People could be socially mobile (unlike in traditional society) and thus they could use signs in the competition for, and confirmation of, rises in status. The competition for signs inevitably gave rise to counterfeiting, ways of using signs to convey a reality to which they do not actually correspond. The *second order* of simulacra comes with the industrial age and the mechanical reproduction of images. Now that images can be bought and sold freely, the difference between an original and a repro-duction ceases to matter, and many industrial products are mechanical repro-ductions, but not of any original. For example, the mechanical line produces many motorcars, each reproducing the same design, but not reproducing some first, original, copied car. The *third* stage, in which we currently live, is increas-ingly dominated by digital technology, a prominent instantiation of the rule of code. In the age of the hyperreal, signs now generate reality rather than reflect or distort it.

Baudrillard is not wholly fatalistic; he does find some limited grounds for opposition to this state of affairs. However, it is not an active form of resistance; rather, 'the mass' exhibits an inert, sullen resentfulness. Mass communication contrasts with symbolic exchange. In the latter case both parties are active; a message is exchanged and the action of each is a response to the other. Mass communication, however, is a one-way process, with no real recognition of, or response to or from, the other; in Baudrillard's view 'the mass' in contemporary society has not absorbed the messages sent out through the mass media. It is resistant to them since, being only one-way, they are not truly communicating. Hence the mass neither absorbs nor responds to them. Somewhat as happens with the astronomical phenomenon of black holes (into which light is drawn but from which it cannot then escape) the output of the media is directed at and into the mass but nothing is returned. The mass as such has no active part to play in the politics of the society, refusing to respond to the blandishments of the media, or to let itself be known through its own political actions. Hence it can be known only through research, e.g. opinion polls, which it may entertain itself by deceiv-ing. The unresponsiveness of the mass does not show contentment, but rather discontent and resentment.

## The death of the social

This change of the majority of the population into a television audience, and the audience into a privatised, non-communicative people, comprises the formation of 'the mass' or, alternatively, the *death of the social*.

Incidentally, this death of the social signifies in its turn the end for sociology. Here Baudrillard echoes Durkheim since, without the social, sociology has no subject matter and no *raison d'être*.

As we said, Baudrillard's argument is about the meaninglessness of lives in contemporary societies, where all sorts of boundaries are collapsing, e.g. between fiction and reality, between science and art, between the sexes, between work and leisure, etc. A social order structured around differences has given way to a society in which characteristics are freely purchasable in the consumer culture. It is a society in which the point of differentiation is not to mark real differences, but to attempt to recreate differences which have disappeared or are disappearing, to produce boundaries that are no longer necessitated by the order of social affairs. There is a shallow nostalgia for what has been putatively lost, such as nature, but the nature that is yearned for has never really existed. Instead, it is an ideologically loaded conception of nature, a nature whose recapture is attempted through simulations, e.g. through wilderness parks, nature conservancies and the devotion of television time to images of animals in the wild.

Whatever might be said about Baudrillard being fascinated by and even relishing many of the characteristics of contemporary society, it is hard to read most of his writings as other than highly critical of such a society. He depicts its culture as essentially aimless and enfeebled, in which the point of many activities has been lost, displaced or confused; it is a stagnant, shallow and dispirited culture. Its tone is distinctly hysterical and many of its tendencies are out of control, as seen in *fatal strategies*.

## Fatal strategies

These stem from their own logic of development, which will take them progressively to extremes and ultimately to self-devastation; e.g. the enthusiasm for the car has brought us to the point at which the roads are clogged by cars.

The culture cannot resist the capacity of digitally encoded materials to proliferate across, and eventually to obliterate, all lines of separation, and to reduce things to the lowest common denominator. It is a culture devoid of real creativity; many of its strongest reactions are simply panic reactions. There is frantic pursuit of ephemeral fashion, the re-creation of what has gone before; the mere and unimaginative recombination of available elements is the main base of further productivity. Such a 'culture' can hardly be credited with this title, since it is without real meaning, foundation or purpose. The great majority are alienated from a culture which, through its media of mass communications, seeks to maintain the great illusion, namely that the reality principle is still in operation, even though that reality has been displaced entirely by the burgeoning of simulations.

## Conclusion

The work we have been reviewing in this chapter is often characterised as nihilistic, meaning that it rejects all established beliefs and values. The long-established and well-entrenched convictions bequeathed by the Enlightenment are certainly open to dismissal. In the context of theory, the very notion of discipline begins to sound inappropriate, with its suggestion of a well-demarcated, distinct and independent field of activity, and the further suggestion of regulation and self-regulation through subordination to controlling methods of inquiry. Thus the approaches reviewed in Part IV are often accused of bringing the academy into both intellectual and political disarray. At the least, the critique of the Enlightenment means, in respect of theory, the drastic redrawing of intellectual boundaries, and the abandonment of the traditional theoretical and methodological ambitions of the social sciences, especially the ambitions for rigorous and thoroughly standardised methods of inquiry and all-embracing, universal theoretical schemes. The desire to assemble growing bodies of positive knowledge is now confronted with approaches that are devoted, rather, to continual confrontation with, and subversion and dissolution of, all attempts to develop and promote supposedly 'rational' schemes and 'rationally' based social arrangements.

In recent years, however, there has been a general move away from the conclusions reached by the postmodernist 'turn'. The 'autonomist' Marxism of, amongst others, Hardt and Negri – while indebted to the work of, amongst others, Foucault, Deleuze and Guattari – asserts the existence of the social, and reinstates a sense of conflict underpinning social relations (see Chapter 14). Philosophers like Alan Badiou and Slavoj Žižek, who locate themselves in the Marxian/Freudian traditions, are more popular than their explicitly postmodern counterparts. Finally, as we argued in the introduction to this book, there is a greater public interest in issues central to mainstream sociology than in the past: the events of the 2000s – from terrorist attacks, through wars of dubious legality or use, to global financial crises – call for explanation, and the explanations being offered bear a strong resemblance to those provided by the thinkers described in the first two parts of this book.

There is also evidence that there is a more general sociological backlash against the nihilism of 'pure' postmodernism. Michael Burawoy's increasing influence in American sociology is testament to this. Burawoy, in his Presidential Address to the American Sociological Association in 2004, argued:

> If the standpoint of economics is the market and its expansion, and the standpoint of political science is the state and the guarantee of political stability, then the standpoint of sociology is civil society and the defense of the social. In times of market tyranny and state despotism, sociology – and in particular its public face – defends the interests of humanity.
>
> (2005: 24)

While seeking to embed sociological work in the concerns and orientations of a broader public (and, subtly, to change the emphasis of what sociology constitutes), Burawoy's argument can most clearly be understood as an explicit rejection of all the key tenets of the poststructuralist and postmodernist movements. Society exists, and it is the job of sociology to defend it, intellectually and (more controversially) practically. Although many sociologists have criticised Burawoy's 'public sociology', it is telling that these criticisms have not tended to be defences of the 'post-sociological' positions. Viewed from the perspective of such 'engaged' sociologists, changes in the world necessitate a change in intellectual orientation. Viewed from the perspective of postmodernism, it seems that its own development and rise to influence may itself have been a fatal strategy.

**Questions**

1  Summarise and provide examples of Barthes's argument that the author is 'dead'. Is he right? Summarise Derrida's argument about the irrelevance, the disappearance of the author. In what ways does Derrida's account move beyond Barthes's? What aspects do they have in common? How do they differ? Which makes more sense to you and why?

2  What are the *sociological* implications of Derrida's argument that there is 'nothing outside the text'? Is he right? In what ways does this argument move beyond Marxian notions of ideology and hegemony, or structuralist and poststructuralist arguments about language as a prison? Does Derrida take a logical next step beyond these arguments? Has someone, somewhere along the way from Marx and Durkheim to Derrida and the postmodernists, made a silly mistake?

3  What does Derrida mean by 'deconstruction'? Is this a way of understanding the world? Is it a research method? What is the *point* in deconstructing the meaning of a text? If there is nothing beyond the text, and all texts can be shown to be incoherent, why bother analysing them?

4  What is a grand narrative? Can you show how the arguments of social theorists dealt with earlier in this book have the character of grand narratives? Why does Lyotard argue that grand narratives are impossible in a postmodern age? Is he right? Are there still ethical, legal or other principles that apply everywhere (or should apply everywhere)? Is the statement 'grand narratives are no longer possible' itself a grand narrative?

5  Lyotard has a particular view of what a postmodern *society* looks like. Outline the main features of this view. Can you think of any contemporary examples of the world that seem to prove Lyotard's point? Can you find any counter-examples? Why does Lyotard argue the social world has developed in this way? Is he right?

6  What is Baudrillard's view of a postmodern *society*? In what ways is this view the same as Lyotard's? How does it differ? How does each relate to Marxian notions of ideology? How does each go further?

7  Baudrillard argues that signs have replaced physical and social phenomena as 'reality', and that 'what really happened' is no longer that important. What examples does he give to back up this argument? What contemporary examples can you think of that would support his position?

**Next steps**

Kamuf (1991) collects Derrida's key writings, and Poster (2001) Baudrillard's. Lyotard's position is stated in his rather difficult *The Postmodern Condition* (1984).

Bennington's contributions to Bennington and Derrida (1993) are probably the clearest expositions of Derrida's ideas. The best overview of the perspective as a whole remains Jameson's *Postmodernism* (1991), and a shorter version can be found in his 1984 paper.

# PART V

# Contemporary trends

The 'post' theories covered in the previous part have not been without their critics. In parallel with their development, therefore, new directions in more conventional social (or sociological) theorising have been sought. This final part illustrates where those directions have led, and what kinds of developments their passage has allowed.

First, developments beyond the Anglophone tradition outlined in Part II have been underway. Just as Parsons attempted to show that Weber and Durkheim have as much in common (when viewed in a particular way) as they do to differentiate them, many of the contemporary trends in 'conventional' social theory are attempts to show that the differences between Parsons's systems theory on the one hand, and the empiricism of the symbolic interactionists and ethnomethodologists on the other, are matters that can be resolved theoretically. In practice, however, such theorists tend to hew to Parsons's ideas. Mouzelis, Giddens, Bourdieu and Habermas are the central figures in these movements. Mouzelis argued that the legitimate criticisms made of Parsons's social theory must be addressed, but that this can be done within the broad framework of functionalism: 'neofunctionalist' theory, therefore, seeks to render Parsons's arguments in a manner that allows them to be more open to possibilities of conflict, inequality and social change. Giddens's 'structuration' theory takes interactionist concerns more seriously: he argues that social structure and human agency are mutually constitutive. Social theory has to overcome the (false) dualisms that disagreements between Parsons and the interactionists opened up in the form of a new synthesis. Bourdieu's theory follows similar lines, but is influenced more strongly by phenomenology, taking the subject/object dualism (rather than structure/agency) as its starting problematic. Finally, the work of Habermas is considered. Broader in scope than the other theorists, but less coherent, Habermas sought to use alternative concepts from phenomenology (in particular the 'lifeworld') to generate a theory that simultaneously allows for a critique of ideology and permits the more stable and functional analyses of Parsons: reconciling the ideas of the Frankfurt School and structural functionalism.

As one might expect, these approaches have not been without their critics. Changes in the nature of the social world – in particular, the end of the Cold War, the rapid development of globalisation, and the growth of the service sector in the West – have led some to argue that synthesising old theories is no longer appropriate. The world has changed, and theory has to keep up. In Chapter 14 we examine these claims, and consider the ways in which the criticisms of earlier social theorists (in particular Parsons) have been used to warrant the development of new theoretical models.

Finally, we will consider the ways in which these criticisms have played out in the development of new theory. In Chapter 15 we will examine the claims of 'emancipatory sociology', taking feminist approaches to sociological study, queer theory and postcolonial theory as perspicuous examples of the trend. While the recognition that class is not the only form of stratification is welcome (although clearly not a new idea), we will argue that these forms of sociology offer little new theoretically. As the topic of inquiry – women, LGBTQ people, the 'subaltern' – has shifted, the tools being used to investigate those topics have remained stubbornly familiar, despite the claims made for freshness and innovation.

## CHAPTER THIRTEEN

# Back to sociological theory?
# Reconciling theoretical oppositions

## Chapter overview

The 'post' theories outlined in the previous section have proved unsatisfying to most sociologists. A return to more conventional theory has therefore been underway over the last thirty years, although this has not been without its critics. Such theory is based on the overcoming of 'dualisms' in social thought: subject versus object, structure versus culture, individual versus social-structural, and so on. It is Parsonian in form, as it tries to conceive of society as comprising stable structural arrangements, and thus sidelines the parallel and competing arguments about social order offered by symbolic interactionists and ethnomethodologists. Mouzelis's arguments are central to this: he argues that the future for *sociological* (rather than social) theory depends on finding an accommodation between Parsons's system building and the legitimate criticisms made of Parsons's work. Mouzelis's arguments, like those of others such as Alexander and Turner, suggest that the 'best' way to understand society is through a moderated form of functionalism, more open to the possibilities of disruption and social change, and more sensitive to the hierarchical and stratified nature of social organisation. Giddens's *structuration* theory follows a parallel course: he argues that Parsons's overemphasis on the systemic and social-structural (over social action and individual agency) requires correction. Giddens argues that, over time, individuals (re)produce the social structures that constrain and contain their actions: structure and agency *generate one another*. Bourdieu's work follows the same course as Giddens's, but taking the object–subject dualism (rather than structure–agency) as its starting point. His concepts of *habitus*, *practice*, *field* and *capital* form the elements of a systemic sociological theory, with some phenomenological influences, which claims to overcome the dualistic nature of its predecessors. Habermas, similarly, uses some phenomenological concepts – in particular the 'lifeworld' – as elements of a theory that promises to integrate critical theory's systematic analysis of ideology and critique of 'reason' with Parsons's more optimistic analysis of contemporary society and the liberatory aspects of Marx's thought. All these theorists have been the objects of severe criticisms, with two lines of argument being particularly important: (1) their theories do not integrate in any meaningful way with studies of the social world; and (2) they simultaneously fail to engage with the problems of earlier social theories and reproduce the 'dualisms' they claim to have found in their own arguments.

## Introduction: back to sociological theory

The previous three chapters have been reviewing efforts at sabotage, attempts to derail the intellectual project of attaining a definitive comprehension of reality in all its dimensions, natural and social, that has provided the structure for intellectual life in the West for three hundred years and more (as well as the rationale for the worldwide hegemony that this intellectual tradition has had with respect to the definition of knowledge). Key to the sabotage has been the purported revelation that the intellectual project was and is part of a wider political project, and one very different from that with which it might have imagined itself associated. The political project *has* achieved the overwhelming rationalisation of modern societies, but it does *not* coincide with the dissemination of sovereign individual reason, a mistake that intellectuals have often made. The centralised, disciplined structures of modern society, as most graphically embodied in industrial mass production, have been disintegrating as the nature of the Western societies shifts toward the decentralised and fluid forms of a 'consumer society'. As a result, the structures of 'modern' thought too have folded in upon themselves. Intellectual resistance to dominant arrangements is no longer conceivable as an association between an intellectual vanguard and a potentially revolutionary mass.

This outcome is what Baudrillard is talking about when he announces the passing of sociology as a result of the death of the social ('the social' being – effectively – the traditional working class). Opposition does not, because it cannot, involve the setting up of a confrontational alternative to the existing way of things in the milieu of organised politics. Instead, it becomes a species of guerrilla campaign against the prevalent structures of thought, with occasional limited and localised association with identifiable dissident groups (as Foucault sought to unite with prisoner organisations). The ideals of rationality and their 'grand narrative' ambitions are associated with those prevalent structures, and their forms are, therefore, everywhere to be eschewed as residual of a discredited rationality.

Those prevalent structures do not collapse just because they have been declared anathema by poststructuralist theorists, for, of course, the latter's arguments are strongly resisted and (sometimes) intensely reviled in other intellectual circles. The authenticity and indispensability of a notion of rationality, much associated with and vindicated by the *success* of the natural sciences, is vigorously defended, with postmodernism and poststructuralism being even more vigorously denounced as a misguided and dangerous brand of irrationalism, itself a corruption of reason. The temperature of these exchanges has moderated across all disciplines in recent years but the issues involved have not yet, by any means, gone away. In this part of the book we deal with the attempt of a more classical idea of reason and of the 'grand narrative' to reassert itself, an occurrence welcomingly proclaimed (in the title of one book) as 'The Return of Grand Theory' (Skinner 1985).

This renewed enthusiasm for the possibility of a 'grand narrative' in the form of a general sociological theory was meant to be a stabilising response to the poststructuralists. One of the luminaries of 'The Return of Grand Theory', Jürgen Habermas, forcefully speaks up for a more traditional, Enlightenment conception of reason, and argues for the need to attempt to complete 'the unfinished project of modernity'. Such enthusiasm is not universally shared, however, even among those who have reservations about the claims of the postmodernists. For example, Frederick Crews (1986) complains of the way theorising in the social sciences has virtually run away with itself and become *theoreticism*.

> **Theoreticism**
>
> Crews's complaint was that theorising had become an end in itself, dissociated from its original purpose and detached from empirical inquiry and evidence.

Such theorising very largely involved the theorists using recombinations of elements of one another's schemes. Crews's complaint was against the way theorising seemed to have dissociated itself from the business of informing and organising empirical inquiry (and its results). In losing sight of the connection to empirical work, it had also loosened itself from the constraint and discipline which such a connection entails. In short, the need to relate the constructions of theory to (evidence of) the real world can provide a check upon the excesses of theory. Consequently, our original thought was to title this chapter 'The synthesists' in order to reflect the extent to which the theorists we shall look at – Nicos Mouzelis, Randall Collins, Jeffrey Alexander, Anthony Giddens, Pierre Bourdieu and Jürgen Habermas – contribute few new theoretical ideas to the schemes they propound. Their schemes are constituted by selectively cannibalising ideas from previous and diverse sociological theories and traditions. To this extent, our treatment confirms Crews's complaint about theoreticism.

## Dualisms and their resolution

In many ways, however, the resurgence of sociological (grand) theory was motivated less by the developments that we have outlined in the past three chapters than by the issues developing in Chapters 6 and 7. After all, the intellectual careers of the prominent new 'grand theorists' began in the period when the reaction against Parsons was the dominant mode, and their conception of the problematic was formed by the possibilities of that time, especially the risk to the idea of an independent 'social reality', one that consisted of something more than a collection of individuals each with their own subjectivity. The critiques offered by ethnomethodology and symbolic interaction were perceived to have made such inroads into the traditional, structuralist views that it was felt that they would go so far that, if unchecked, they would invalidate structuralist views altogether.

The contestations over these issues highlighted the fact that there were – or could be supposed to be – two main and different sociological traditions: one taking Max Weber and his idea of social action, the other having Durkheim and Marx, and their focus on objective structures, as the iconic figures. The struggles were between the recent protagonists of these lineages, but the struggles were unnecessary if the two traditions could be recognised as complementary, the dispute between them involving not rival claims about the essential nature of social reality, but different respective emphases on the importance of one undeniable aspect of a two-sided social reality. According to this view, the recent disputes had been a (rather less numerous) version of the six blind men and the elephant, where people each seize on one feature of something and mistake it for the definitive feature of the whole.

The point was not to go back on the critiques of (especially Parsonian) structuralism, but to prevent those critiques from eliminating structuralism altogether, i.e. how to dissociate the idea of 'social structure' from Parsons's version of it, and how to accomplish a merger of the two traditions. In other words, we are talking about the origin of 'structure and agency' as the dominant problematic. It redefines a general sociological theory in terms of a balanced incorporation of both 'structure' and 'agency', where agency is conceived as the legacy of the interactionist/ethnomethodological approaches. Society, it is to be emphasised, is

- *both* a matter of spontaneous individual actions *and* of the structural direction of conduct;
- *both* an organisation of 'macro structures', of large-scale time- and space-spanning arrangements encompassing millions of individuals who know nothing of each other individually, *and* one of 'micro situations', of immediate personal encounters between individuals;
- *both* an objective and a subjective reality; indeed, it exists independently of individual will and awareness, transcends the individual point of view *and* is a subjective reality, i.e. is also the object of experience for its individual members, something that they encounter through their common-sense understandings;
- a *composite* of both 'structure' and 'culture', which combine, and the two interact with each other so that there can be no question of the simple primacy of structure over culture; and
- *both* the product of individual actions *and* the setting for those actions.

We note, however, that this attempt at a programme for blending a balanced accommodation of the alleged two traditions adopts a canonically Parsonian conception of their actual problematic, namely, how to account for 'social order' understood as politically stabilised arrangements. The reconceiving of social order in terms of 'sense making' (in the interactionist and ethnomethodological tradition) is barely acknowledged, let alone represented, in the numerous schemes that attempt such a blend.

W. G. Baldamus, in his *The Structure of Sociological Inference* (1976), observed, perhaps ironically, that sociology has thrived on dualisms, even providing a list of some of the most prominent ones. The attempt to conceive society as two-sided goes back, in recent sociological thought, to the late 1950s, when Ralf Dahrendorf (1958) argued that society was 'Janus faced'; he was trying to balance the two traditions of (Parsonian) consensus theory with conflict theory, by arguing that society is both consensus and conflict. Alan Dawe (1970) spoke of two sociologies, oriented towards the problems of 'order' and 'control' respectively, again to weigh constraint against spontaneity, but one of the key efforts towards synthesis was made in *The Social Construction of Reality* (1967) where Peter Berger and Thomas Luckmann pitched their effort in terms of an argument that society is both objective and subjective realities by combining Mead – society as subjective – with Marx – society as objective. They achieved an account that can hardly be discriminated from Parsons's portrayal of the relationship between socialisation and institutionalisation. Quite how the weight is to be distributed between structure and agency within the scheme is the question on which the various syntheses differentiate themselves from each other (and very often, purportedly, though equally often, questionably, from Parsons). Equally, the theorists vary with respect to the ideas that they draw from the different traditions to make up the particular mix that their theory defines. Thus, both Giddens and Bourdieu appropriate the notion of 'structure' from the Lévi-Straussian tradition, but on the 'agency' side Giddens is much more derivative from Goffman and ethnomethodology than Bourdieu.

### Mouzelis and the synthesisers

In 1990 Nicos P. Mouzelis published *Back to Sociological Theory*, which was followed in 1995 by another book, *Sociological Theory: What Went Wrong*. These were only one author's contribution to a number of books expressing concern about the state and identity of sociology – by which is meant, primarily, sociological theory – to appear in recent years. Running through these books is a clear sense that sociology has lost its way, with its very disciplinary identity being under threat, its defining issues being no longer addressed in any systematic way and its central task of constructing an analysis of the nature of society being effectively abandoned.

The attempt by Mouzelis and others to reassert the importance of sociological theory against social theory is to seek to pursue – in principle perhaps rather more than in practice – the very project which has been dismissed as *demodé* by social theory, i.e. by proponents of poststructuralism and postmodernity. For Mouzelis, one source of the difficulties which need to be corrected by the reassertion of sociological theory resides in the overreaction to Talcott Parsons, and we share, at least, his view that the critical response to Parsons was commonly misinformed and misguided (see Chapter 5). In this respect, Jeffrey Alexander and the neo-functionalist tendency (see below) are mainly devoted to a rehabilitation of Parsons's thought in response to *some* of the criticism. Mouzelis himself is critical of Parsons yet none the less wishes to see a resuscitation of the kind of theorising in which Parsons engaged. Mouzelis seeks to present it as a modest enough ambition, i.e. to provide a generalised conceptual apparatus for assisting empirical investigators, enabling them to give a systematic co-ordination of their work by means of a shared frame of reference within which to compare their results. At the same time, however, we also know that the idea of theory that derives from Parsons is of an all-embracing scheme, one which smacks of a would-be grand narrative of the sort that Lyotard tells us can no longer be credible (see

Chapter 12). Moreover, it also retains the idea of sociology as a theoretically governed science. This idea is to defy (though not perhaps to defuse) social theory, which denies the possibility of grand narratives, of general, all-encompassing schemes. And, of course, social theory also rejects the concomitant notion that abstract generality can be a successful form of understanding.

Mouzelis and those he discusses have been struggling, then, against the tide of intellectual fashion, i.e. social theory, which sees itself as having largely left behind the concerns of sociological theory (see also Chapter 15). The concerns of the synthesists remain much the same as those provoked by Parsons and the reaction against him – indeed, inevitably so, in so far as the synthesists attempt to construct theories which will overcome what they see as divisions within sociological thought. That is, they appreciate that sociological thought has been riven with dispute, and that the various factions identify themselves in intellectually oppositional ways. Hence there are recriminations between determinists and voluntarists, between realists/objectivists and idealists/subjectivists, between macro or structural and micro or interactionist, between (methodological) individualist and holist, and between consensus and conflict sociologies, to name some of the main divisions. The theorists we discuss in this chapter have sought to put an end to this internal division and to construct unified theoretical schemes for sociology. We call them 'synthesists', however, because their efforts at theory construction have not involved any attempt at a fundamental reworking of sociology's problematics and basic ideas; they do not seek to bypass the previous oppositions altogether.

## Synthesis

A main objective of the synthesists' respective theories has been to achieve comprehensiveness by including the main disputing positions within their proposed new, single, unified theory in an attempt to incorporate and reconcile the ostensibly divided positions. Expressing this point in the simplest terms, the theory-building technique has been to replace 'either/or' with 'both/and'.

Thus it can be seen how the previous 'either/or' situation – *either* society as conflict *or* society as consensus, *either* society as objective *or* society as subjective reality – is replaced by 'both/and', i.e. society as *both* conflict *and* consensus, society as *both* objective *and* subjective reality. Seemingly opposed views were to be reconciled within a single scheme, whereas both Dahrendorf and Berger and Luckmann had merely offered indications of axes along which the combination of these views was to be attempted, without much effort at elaborating the scheme that could result. The attempt to spell out rather more elaborate schemes singles out most of the theorists we are dealing with here. Their schemes seek to reconcile and combine some (or even all) of the above-mentioned sociological oppositions. Nevertheless, we should perhaps note in all these theorists one characteristic which brings them into some correspondence with thinkers in social theory: their response to power.

## Power

> In the case of the sociological theorists, this characteristic lays an emphasis upon power and domination as key phenomena which any general theory must treat as of central concern, and represents a common reaction against Talcott Parsons. If anything, they are convinced that social cohesion and consensus originate in power rather than, as Parsons proposed, the other way around. Thus any empirical consensus is only an imposition.

As already suggested, Mouzelis himself diagnoses a key source of post-Parsonian difficulties as resulting from the (over)reaction against Parsons, an overreaction which had, however, correctly recognised two of the failings of Parsons's theory: (1) underplaying the voluntaristic aspect of social life; and, relatedly, (2) overconcentrating on the *macro* (large-scale), whole-system level of analysis at the expense of the *micro* level (face-to-face interaction between individuals). Mouzelis can therefore welcome, for example, the appearance of interactionist sociologies such as those detailed in Chapters 6 and 7 (symbolic interaction and ethnomethodology). These sociologies, however, are accused of going to the other extreme: in Mouzelis's account they insist on treating face-to-face interaction as completely detached from the macro level, if they do not altogether deny reality to the latter. If we were to accept Mouzelis's own characterisations of Parsons, of interactionist sociologies, of his criticism of Parsons's failings, and of overreaction to them, then a middle road would be called for. Such a road would recognise that society has both macro and micro levels of structure; these levels are not independent, since micro levels of interaction are not between individuals considered as isolated entities, but between individuals considered as bearers (to use Weber's terms: see Chapter 3) of the affairs of larger social units, such as churches and schools. Mouzelis endorses Randall Collins's (1981) formulation of this position as *situationalism*, as opposed to individualism.

## Situationalism

> Collins argues that individuals act in terms of social situations, so that one acts within the context of a bank, a church, a scientific laboratory or some other socially organised environment, and that, therefore, micro and macro analysis can be connected by analysing the way activities, connected in chains of interactions, realise the organisation of larger social structures (as the relation of teller and customer enacts the affairs of a bank, the monetary system and so on).

The approaches of macro analysis should be combined with the methods of micro analysis, for the study of the latter should proceed through the use of audio and video recording and be examined through the kinds of techniques that have developed for analysing such materials in, for example, ethnomethodology, and not through, say, social survey methods.

Mouzelis's own agenda is to combine such observations about micro-sociology and the formulation of this position as situationalism with a view of society as a complex, differentiated, articulated but, above all, hierarchical structure. He is convinced (falsely, as we have tried to show in Chapters 6 and 7) that the above interactionist approaches have denied, neglected or understated the extent and importance of the fact that social life takes place within hierarchically structured arrangements. His objection to poststructuralist and postmodernist approaches is that they have overestimated the extent to which there is a demise of boundaries in their emphasis on the way contemporary society changes, i.e. in their focus on the disintegration of traditional social forms, the collapse of an overall organisation for society, and the concomitant evaporation of many of the established lines of social division. At the same time, by overestimating these changes, they have underestimated the extent to which reality can still be comprehended in terms of the traditional categories of sociological analysis. Indeed, Mouzelis insists upon the relevance of these categories; the social theorists have not done away with distinctions between, say, macro and micro any more than they have really liquidated the boundaries between disciplines. Mouzelis cannot accept the poststructuralist idea that society as a centralised and differentiated structure of hierarchical relationships no longer exists. For him, an alternative picture of society as a plurality of diversified, independent discourses or language games (to use Lyotard's adaptation of Wittgenstein's phraseology), which are not arranged in any stably hierarchical pattern, is quite unacceptable.

Mouzelis wants to maintain that society continues to exist in this traditional conception, and that it is within the hierarchical structure of social relations that discourses are formed and implemented. He suggests that the poststructuralists are less than consistent; while they disavow this traditional conception of society, at the same time it is at work in their actual analyses. The ultimate recommendation from Mouzelis is for a moderated functionalism.

## Moderated functionalism

This respects the view of society as a structured whole, but employs this conception in a heuristic, not a dogmatic, manner, i.e. it is used as a tool for provoking questions about the sustaining conditions for particular institutions or practices in relation to the requirements of the society as a whole.

This conception of the social whole, the system, emphasises the systemic properties to a lesser degree than does (perhaps) Parsons, and recognises that the various levels of social organisation, macro, meso (i.e. middling) and micro, are themselves interrelated within a hierarchically structured order. Mouzelis's efforts, then, are primarily akin to those of the neo-functionalists, who have sought, within their broadly Parsonian standpoint, to accommodate objections to Parsons's (supposed) underemphasis on disintegration and conflict within society. They also resemble Louis Althusser's attempts to relax the systemic conception of Marxism, through notions of relative autonomy (see Chapter 9). Mouzelis's moderated functionalism brings him close to the grouping of post-Parsonians known as neo-functionalists, perhaps most prominently represented by Jeffrey Alexander (1985).

## Neo-functionalism

The neo-functionalists allow that Parsons's work is not entirely exempt from conservatism, from idealism (in the sense of giving too great an emphasis to the role of ideas/culture) and from excessive theoretical abstraction, though less so than many critics have alleged. Neo-functionalists follow a broadly Parsonian line, with the following guiding principles:

- Functionalism provides a descriptive portrayal of society as a relatively self-contained system, which is organised through the interaction of its parts, but without any suggestion that there is any overriding principle or force directing the system as a whole.
- Ideas of system equilibrium and system integration are analytical tools to help describe society, though without assuming that members of society are attempting to achieve these conditions. Alexander (1985) says that integration is a possibility and that deviance and social control are facts, thereby making it quite clear that there is no naive assumption that actual societies are fully integrated.
- It is assumed that there must be some degree of integration of culture, personality and social system. Naive assumptions about complete integration within culture, personality and social system respectively, as well as between them, must be avoided; within and between these elements there are tensions which create strain and provoke change.
- Change is not only a product of strain and tensions. Indeed, change can often produce strain and tension. There is a long-term evolution of Western societies through the progressive differentiation of previously undifferentiated features of the cultural, social and personality systems. These changes have moved the society as a whole from one relatively integrated level to another, and have become reintegrated at a higher level of adaptability.

But does this form of functionalism represent its final denaturing? As we noted with Althusser (see Chapter 9), the idea that society is made up of a set of parts which interact with and affect one another is a general sociological idea, and certainly not distinctive to functionalism. Turner and Maryanski (1979) argue that what was both distinctive and also problematic about functionalism was the idea of explaining features of the society in terms of the needs of the whole system. This idea is absent from neo-functionalism.

There was also argument as to whether Marxism is a form of functionalism.

## Marxism and functionalism

On the one hand, Jon Elster (1985) argued that the greater part of Marxist analysis was actually functionalist in nature. For example, Marx does analyse the organisation of capitalism in relation to meeting the needs for reproducing the capitalist system. For Elster, this part of Marx's work was invalid and needed to be reworked on the basis of an individualist approach. On the other hand, G. A. Cohen (1978) agreed that Marx's core theory did use functionalist analysis (of the kind which recognised that parts of the society could contribute to the maintenance of the whole) but, for him, it was a perfectly valid form of analysis.

## Giddens: the theory of structuration

A critique of the shortcomings of functionalism was the starting point for one of the most notable attempts at theoretical synthesis in contemporary sociology, contained in the writings of Anthony Giddens. The work of Giddens is impossible to summarise in its totality, since it ranges across many different kinds of writings. There is Giddens the commentator, who has written essays on just about every major figure in the history of sociology (and many minor ones). There is also Giddens the substantive social theorist, who, over his career, has written on an immense variety of topics and problems, from suicide to social class in industrial capitalism, and from violence and the nation state to modern identity. There is also Giddens the textbook writer, author of several of the most popular introductory works on general sociology and classical sociological theory. Since none of these is directly relevant here we shall pass over them and concentrate on the Giddens most relevant to our purposes, and also the most controversial in contemporary sociology, i.e. Giddens the general theorist. In a linked series of books from the mid-1970s onwards, and culminating in *The Constitution of Society* in 1984, Giddens put forward a theory intended to provide a unifying framework for sociology.

Giddens's critique of functionalism centred on its failure to provide a convincing overarching framework for sociological analysis. His principal target was Parsons. His criticisms of Parsons followed the lines with which we are now familiar (and which, we have suggested, are not necessarily to be accepted as accurate, even if they are in general circulation): an overemphasis on the unifying structures of society and neglect of centrifugal forces; an unjustified assumption that normative consensus is the principal underpinning of social structure; and a failure to take adequate account of the interpretative dimension in human action. Notwithstanding these basic shortcomings, however, Giddens recognised the importance of Parsons's project in attempting to formulate an integrated set of concepts which would solve the basic problems of sociological theorising. The problem was not that Parsons had set himself this goal but that he had failed to accomplish it. Giddens took up this same challenge, i.e. to show how the divergences and inconsistencies of sociological theorising could be overcome by building a systematic theoretical scheme that would bring together apparently different – even opposed – sociological ideas. Later we will bring out important differences between Giddens's and Parsons's projects, not least in terms of how the projects are brought off and the success with which they bridge the gap between abstract theory and substantive analysis. First, however, we consider the main lines of Giddens's theory.

## Structuration theory

Giddens was in accord with a then contemporary mood in arguing that the turbulent disputation between the diverse sociological traditions was unnecessary, and that the dualistic confrontation between these either/or choices should be recognised as the misrepresentation of a fact about society itself, a series of commitments to one-sided pictures of a society that was itself two-sided. The points of disputation did not mark out the lines of a true dualism, but only the features of a *duality*.

Giddens's own theoretical contribution, then, was to show how the superficially contrasting emphases of the rival theories could be combined within a single coherent scheme that provided, then, a rounded picture of the elephant (society) that the blind men had grasped only by one part or another. Giddens's scheme is identified as *structuration theory* after its key move of linking together and reconciling what Giddens takes to divide sociological approaches: the master dichotomy between *action* and *structure*. It is now to be displayed as two aspects of a single social process, namely, 'structuration'. In Giddens's view, sociological theorising falls into two broad types.

### Action and structure

On the one hand, action theories emphasise the individual actor as the creator of society; actors possess consciousness and therefore have agency, the capacity to plan and reflect upon their conduct. They give meaning to their circumstances and act towards one another on the basis of these meanings. The outcome of these actions is the formation of relationships and patterns of action that ultimately make up what we refer to as a society. Action theories thus take a bottom-up view of social life; they do not deny that it is structured but regard structures as products of action and interaction. Structural theories, on the other hand, take a top-down view. In Durkheimian fashion, they characterise society in terms of patterns and forms which (1) are independent of individual actors and their intentions; and (2) constrain the possibilities of action.

For Giddens, both viewpoints express a partial truth. Giddens aims to show that these two broad perspectives are not incommensurable but complementary and mutually interdependent; we misunderstand the nature of social life if we imagine that one must be correct and the other one wrong. To say that they are two sides of a coin is a bad analogy, since we can only see one side of a coin at a time. It is better to say that they are connected in the manner of the axes that define a two-dimensional geometric space, e.g. a graph. Of course, if we insist on looking in a one-dimensional way – if we turn the social object into a one-dimensional figure by, say, only looking along its length – then the other dimension disappears and society seems to be purely action or purely structure. Giddens's task, then, is to show how we can see both dimensions at once without going cross-eyed.

Giddens refers to this two-dimensionality of social life as *duality of structure*.

## Duality of structure

Social structures seem to have a fixed, object-like character only as long as we observe them from a point of view that leaves aside the dynamic processes of action in and through which structures are continuously sustained and recreated.

Here we note two important points:

1 Parsons himself emphasised that 'structure' was a relative matter; what looks like a fixed, given, object-like thing at an abstract level will, upon closer examination, be seen to be a series of ongoing processes, of individual activities – there isn't any *real*, substantial difference between structure and process.
2 These processes are what Giddens refers to by the term 'structuration'.

## Structuration

This is a generic term to emphasise that society is both produced and reproduced. Society is indeed produced by the actions of individuals; the effects of these individual actions accumulate into stable arrangements that then provide the conditions for further individual actions. Actions, shaped by these given conditions, will then tend towards perpetuating established patterns, i.e. *reproducing* that society. Thus action and society are involved in a two-way relationship, each involved in producing the other.

Giddens is apt to proclaim 'space–time distanciation' as his major theoretical contribution. In his estimation, it involves a significant rupture with the classical tradition, which did not acknowledge this, for Giddens, utterly profound phenomenon – but for a sceptical view of the originality of this move and its distance from classical theory, see Rosenberg (2000). Time–space distanciation really involves the changing forms in which social relations can be extended across time and space, i.e. they facilitate the building of communities widely distributed across space, involve large numbers of individuals, and also enable the development of social arrangements that are capable of considerable longevity, a span which can extend far beyond that of a human lifetime, e.g. the traditional Chinese empire covered vast and populous territory and endured for centuries. Time and space are 'bound' into social relations through such forms as literacy, which makes possible the formation of bureaucratic organisation that, in turn, makes possible the influence of otherwise remote individuals upon one another. Through such influence, the regulation, standardisation and integration of their activities into large complexes of interaction, which can also organise to reinforce their own continuity, are achieved.

In Giddens's conception, 'structures' do not in themselves exist in time and space. Giddens owes to Lévi-Strauss this idea of structure having a 'virtual' character. It is a kind of matrix which delimits the possible forms of activity in the way in which the 'structure' of a language provides a vast repertoire of possible grammatically formed sentences. But the structure of the language as such does not exist anywhere – you cannot go out and find it, will never meet it on the street. It has only a kind of abstract existence, *except* in so far as it is reproduced in the minds of individuals, i.e. it is learned by them.

As a consequence, Giddens is very close to the methodological individualists since he wants to affirm that within time and space there are only individual human beings, their actions, and the unintended consequences of those actions. Structures, in the Giddens sense, play their part in empirical social life through the actions of individuals, actions that both produce and reproduce stable social relations, i.e. 'structuration'. Structure plays its part *through* individuals, and it does so because its forms are internalised in the individual mind, where it provides the framework within which individuals form their thoughts and their actions. Again, then, as with Berger and Luckmann, and so too, as we will see, with Bourdieu, and as with Parsons before them, the key to the relationship between action and structure turns out to be socialisation.

The historically accumulated organisation of a society, then, is to be understood in terms of its 'structure', which crystallises the abstract, general principles that are axes of conduct within that society. The society, thus, is the condition for individual action, and it provides a given and, to a large extent, unchangeable setting for the individual's actions. Here we are close to Durkheim's idea of the objective nature of society, i.e. its large collective arrangements and accumulated cultural apparatus confront the single individual as something that is irresistibly there so that an unaided individual's effort can make barely any impact upon it, let alone induce significant modification in it. And, indeed, as we shall see in a moment, Giddens thematises this aspect of his structuration story by emphasising the very Durkheimian significance of *constraint* by the social order on the individual's action. Thinking, however, that the result of the Durkheimian legacy has been to overemphasise the 'constraint' aspect, he calls up the corrective of a stress on the 'enabling' role of structures. For example, the grammar of a language constrains what we can acceptably say, but, at the same time, mastery of it provides us with a capacity to say an indefinitely large number of things.

However, both the enabling and the constraining aspects of the structure really come through its *cultural* transmission, through its being learned by individuals, so that, as we said, the effects of structure very much work through *socialisation*. Again in a very Durkheimian mode, and one shared with Parsons, the individual is constrained by 'external' or 'objective' circumstances that will be encountered as the given ways of doing things in society. In the main, however, they will not be *experienced as constraints* by the socialised individual, who will, through internalisation of those same given, socially required ways, have no inclination to act in other than the way 'appropriate' to those circumstances.

Of course, Giddens does not want to suggest that society is produced by individuals, in the sense that the nation state or the agricultural arrangements of feudalism are the design or achievement of some single individual or even some few coordinated ones. The production of the social order *in the first place* was no individual's aim; rather, it was the product of the actions of very many distributed, uncoordinated individuals. There are only individuals, though, and so the production of social order must take place through their actions, and it must, then, be produced through the unintended consequences of those actions. Here the affinity with methodological individualism is strong, and identifies a line of thought to be found also in Habermas. Once established, and 'crystallised' into 'structures', the social order is also *reproduced* through the unintended, rather than the intended, consequences of individual actions. If the structure of the language consists in the conventions governing the formation of sentences, then socialising children into these conventions will perpetuate the language. Children are taught the language not to perpetuate the language, but to use the language to say and do things necessary to their practical lives. Ensuring that the language will not basically change for three hundred years is no part of anyone's intent, but that will be the effect of passing on the language through continuous practice, for, of course, it is by practising the language that children are socialised into it.

Structures are very much akin to, or are indeed nothing other than, *rules*, which, together with *resources*, play a major role in Giddens's scheme. In his discussion of rules Giddens draws heavily on the linguistic turn in sociology, which we have commented upon extensively in earlier chapters. For example, from the writings of Winch (see Chapter 6) he draws the point that actions are rule-following; recognising some piece of behaviour as a kind of action involves seeing it in terms of a rule or set of rules.

## Rules

Rules are constitutive as well as normative, i.e. rules make actions recognisable as the actions they are as well as defining what should and should not be done in a given set of circumstances.

From the structuralist/semiological tradition of Saussure, Giddens draws the idea that rules form systems which pre-exist any particular instantiation they have in a given item of behaviour (speech). But whereas in Saussure the distinction is drawn between speech (*parole*) and language (*langue*), Giddens distinguishes between *action* and *practices*. Practices are the organised forms of action to which sets of rules apply and which they define. Thus practices mediate between the two dimensions of action and structure; practices are the organised forms or contexts of action (i.e. what Wittgenstein referred to as 'games') and the patterned components of social systems. Giddens defines resources as the following:

### Resources

These are 'the structured properties of social systems, drawn upon and reproduced by knowledgeable agents in the course of interaction' (Giddens 1984: 15). Thus 'resource' refers to anything which provides the actor with power, i.e. with some means for realising his or her ends.

Resources may take a variety of forms, including material (wealth, property, etc.), symbolic (personal prestige, the trappings of office, etc.) and biological and cognitive (physical strength, skill, knowledge, etc.). In performing any action, the actor draws upon and utilises some of these resources; an action uses up some resources, though Giddens is quick to emphasise that one must not assume a zero-sum conception of resources, i.e. that a resource is necessarily finite and therefore is limited in its distribution and diminished in its use. While this may be true of some kinds of resources in some uses (as when someone uses up their prestige by making improper requests, thereby imposing upon another's deference or goodwill), it is by no means always true. For example, my knowledge is not diminished in its use, nor does my knowledge about something preclude your knowing it also. In fact, the zero-sum situation is the exception rather than the rule in social life, contrary to much sociological theorising about power. Here Giddens is reiterating the very argument on power that Parsons had used.

Drawing attention to 'resources' is one of the means by which Giddens intends to distance himself from Parsons, and, thereby, to align himself rather with the 'conflict theory' tradition. Here the point is to argue that resources are unevenly distributed so that even though people may be governed by the same social rules, their capacities to act in accord with those rules may be differentially affected by whether they have the practical resources required to carry out that course of action. For example, the rule is that any American-born citizen can run for President, but in practice several million dollars are needed just to get into the contest. (We might remember, here, Merton's functionalist account of anomie (see Chapter 5), on the divergence between a uniformly internalised culture and unevenly distributed means – or resources, in Giddens's language.)

Giddens asserts that 'one of the main propositions of structuration theory is that the rules and resources drawn upon in the production and reproduction of social action are at the same time the means of system reproduction' (1984: 19). Again, this is the idea of duality of structure.

## Structure, rules and resources

Structure consists in the organised pattern of rules and resources that actors utilise and, in using, reproduce. A further feature of structure, therefore, is that it persists in time and space.

Giddens claims that sociological theory has tended to neglect the significance of temporality and spatiality in analysing social life. Rules and resources are structural precisely because they transcend the particular temporal and spatial location tied to any given occasion of their use. Therefore, what crucially is reproduced in action and interaction is this temporal and spatial transcendence. Of course, the form that such reproduction takes is a matter for empirical investigation.

A further element in Giddens's analysis of structuration involves identifying three *modalities* of structure.

## Modalities of structure

These are three general forms which structure can take and which are produced and reproduced in action and interaction. These three forms are referred to as *signification, domination* and *legitimation*.

By *signification*, Giddens means language and other symbolic orders, i.e. all those ways for human beings to express themselves and communicate with others. The organised forms of communication both make possible particular communicative acts and, at the same time, reproduce the system of rules, the codes. Members of society share these codes, which makes it possible for them to understand one another.

By *domination*, he refers to all the organised ways in which humans are related to one another in structures of hierarchy and control. Once again, at the same time these structures make possible certain kinds of actions and interactions between persons and also reinforce and reproduce the hierarchies which these actions presuppose.

By *legitimation*, he means the normative aspect of social systems, the sets of moral beliefs that are shared by some or all of a society's members. All actions are subject to normative appraisal, to judgement about whether they are proper, acceptable, desirable and so on. Giddens emphasises that, while such judgements are informed by socially shared assumptions, it may not be the case that all members of society accept the same moral standpoints. Indeed, in the kind of complex and differentiated society we live in, such consensus is highly unlikely (as Durkheim had made the platform argument of his *Division of Labour in Society*).

Clearly, these structural modalities are abstractly conceived, but each constitutes a locus around which the various concrete institutions of a society cluster. Thus, again, Giddens's idea has something in common with Parsons's notion of the functional prerequisites of society (i.e. the AGIL framework: see Chapter 5). This is somewhat strange, since, as we have indicated, Giddens is highly critical, not to say dismissive, of functionalist thinking in sociology: in fact, Giddens refers to structuration theory as a 'nonfunctionalist manifesto' (1979: 7). The major difference is, perhaps, in the tone of the observations. In Parsons, domination and legitimation are conceived as, so to speak, positively functional for the social system, for they are the ways in which the co-ordination and direction of collective action are made possible. Unless some people comply with the directives of others, then no large-scale collective projects can be organised, and compliance with directives cannot be achieved by force alone. Unless many people accept the right of others to demand that they act in a certain way, unless they regard the demand for compliance as legitimate, then they will not act in ways that will effect the mobilisation of large numbers in a united cause. In many ways, Giddens does not differ in the substance of the argument, but, in tune with a more contemporary mood, perhaps conveys the impression that domination and legitimation are rather more negative features of society than Parsons contends. Of course, they are often experienced as oppressive by those who are subject to them.

Giddens does not want to integrate only the structure–agency pairing, which we identified as the master contrast. He also wants to integrate other aspects, e.g. 'macro' and 'micro' sociology. Thus he draws heavily upon Erving Goffman and ethnomethodology to emphasise, in Goffman's case, the extent to which face-to-face social interaction is, so to speak, the empirical scene of social life, the place where direct social relations take place. He insists, however, that society cannot be reduced to such face-to-face interactions, and, as noted above, what crucially is reproduced in action and interaction is this temporal and spatial transcendence, such that arrangements of social relations are constructed which extend far beyond the immediate, localised moment.

## Giddens's synthesis

Much of the controversy surrounding Giddens's structuration theory has centred on what kind of theory it is and whether it successfully synthesises the action–structure dualism. A common criticism is that it fails to do so, merely reproducing and confirming dualism by favouring one side of the dichotomy over the other. Which side the theory of structuration favours seems to depend on where the critic is coming from: critics from the structuralist side (e.g. Sica 1991; Craib 1992) accuse Giddens of attempting to reduce structure to action, and of failing to give sufficient weight to the determining social forces which constrain actors' choices. Conversely, interpretative sociologists (e.g. Thrift 1985) have tended to view structuration theory as an ultimately self-defeating exercise in building an interpretative dimension into what is essentially a structuralist, systematising framework.

What these criticisms are really raising is the question of whether Giddens actually succeeds in synthesising the duality of structure and action. Is the theory of structuration a genuine synthesis or merely an eclectic collection of ideas that are conceptually and methodologically distinct? Giddens draws on such a wide range of sources that it is hard to resist the sense that the main purpose of structuration theory is to find a place for just about every socio-logical idea, regardless of the compatibility of the assumptions that inform them. The problem, of course, is that detaching ideas from their intellectual origins carries the risk of destroying their intellectual integrity and rendering them sociologically toothless. The most damaging criticism that can be lev-elled against Giddens is that structuration theory has no real bite; it is bland, contributing no truly distinctive solution to any significant sociological prob-lem. This question of what difference structuration theory might make to the studies that sociologists conduct is more significant than the kind of position-ing critique referred to above, i.e. interactionist or structuralist. If the point of the theory is to make possible studies which can grasp the duality of structure that supposedly constitutes social life, how does structuration theory translate into such studies?

Two things are notable here. First, Giddens's own substantive work does little to develop and apply structuration theory, unlike that of Parsons, whose substantive writings were exemplary in applying his theoretical approach to the analysis of a wide range of empirical issues. Second, in arguing for the empirical relevance of structuration theory, Giddens frequently cites as studies exemplifying its approach work which was not actually informed by it. For example, Paul Willis's well-known study *Learning to Labour* (1977) is discussed extensively by Giddens (1984) and judged to be exemplary in its theoretical approach, for showing how structural constraint and actors' con-sciousness are to be reconciled and the reproduction of structure empirically described. Yet Willis was inspired by quite other ideas; his work was writ-ten without any reliance on the main concepts of Giddens's theory, such as structuration and duality of structure. If the empirical insights to be derived from structuration theory turn out to be nothing more than new labels for familiar forms of sociological analysis, what does Giddens's achievement amount to?

## Bourdieu: reconciling objectivity and subjectivity

Another notable contemporary synthesist is Pierre Bourdieu (1930–2002). Like Giddens, Bourdieu is centrally concerned with the reconciling of sociological dualisms. Perhaps because of his early background in philosophy, the dualism which occupies centre stage in Bourdieu's thought is the classic epistemological one between objectivism and subjectivism.

### Objectivism and subjectivism

Put at its most simple, the question is whether knowledge is inde-pendent of the situation of the knower or a product of it.

Bourdieu holds to what is often referred to – though he does not use the term himself – as a social constructionist view of knowledge. He holds that all knowledge is the product of social conditions and therefore is socially determined. A classic criticism of this view – one we have encountered before (see Chapter 7) – is that if applied universally, it raises a problem about the status of sociological knowledge and thus about itself as a claim about the world. If all claims to knowledge are social constructions, why should we accept sociology's claims as anything more than yet another social construction? At the heart of Bourdieu's sociology is an attempt to resolve this problem.

Bourdieu does not believe that what we have called the social constructionist argument means that knowledge is unattached to the world. In particular, the knowledge which sociology itself creates is more than just a product of the professional ideology of sociologists; it is genuine knowledge which tells us something about the world. In other words, Bourdieu's position is that both subjectivism and objectivism express partial truths. Bourdieu advocates a resolution of this dualism that involves building a reflexive sociology – in a particular sense of that nowadays overused term.

To understand what the notion of reflexivity means to Bourdieu, we need to consider his account of the contrast between the subjective and the objective points of view, which are associated with the actor, on the one hand, and the scientist on the other. We have come across this dualism before in earlier chapters, and Bourdieu's version resembles other versions we have encountered. The distinction is between how the social world appears to those acting within it, and thus the kind of knowledge they can possibly have of it, and how it appears to those who seek to study it from the standpoint of science. The subjective point of view is characterised by two features:

1   It is a partial point of view in the sense that the location of the actor within society means that only certain things are available to him or her; only a certain amount of the whole can be seen or comprehended.
2   It is also an interested viewpoint; the actor sees things from a stance shaped by his or her practical concerns, which change over time, sometimes from moment to moment.

The objective point of view, by contrast, is distinguished by comprehensiveness and permanence. The scientist sees things – or attempts to do so – from a 'God's-eye' position above the level of practical involvement and the fleeting impressions of momentary change.

In Bourdieu's view, this dualism gives rise to a paradox which sociology has never adequately resolved. Since the task of the social scientist is to understand, from the standpoint of science, events which are constituted by the way social actors perceive and respond to their experience, it is not sufficient for the social scientist simply to adopt the objective stance and ignore the subjective one. Yet, on the other hand, embracing the subjective point of view would seem to make scientific objectivity untenable. As with Giddens's contrast between action and structure, but perhaps even more sharply, one is faced with the problem of reconciling opposites. Needless to say, like Giddens, Bourdieu has what he believes to be a solution.

## Bourdieu and phenomenology

The solution involves taking a further step back. For Bourdieu, it is not that the sociologist is too far removed from lived social life to study it, but that in a certain sense he or she is not removed far enough. To understand sociology itself and its relation to what it studies, the sociologist needs to take another step back. Just as the sociologist initially distances himself or herself from the social actors under study, so the possibility of reflecting on the doing of sociology means recognising that the sociologist also takes up a stance which is socially constructed.

The sociologist creates the social world as an objective reality, objectifies it. To understand how the sociologist's process of objectivisation works, it is necessary to objectivise that in its turn, to stand back from it. In Bourdieu's own words, the goal is 'to uncover all the presuppositions inherent in the *theoretical* posture as an external, remote, distant or, quite simply, non-practical, non-committed, non-involved vision' (1990: 60).

Thus Bourdieu sought to apply to the doing of sociology the same perspective as sociology applied to those it studied. It is only from the scientific, objectivist standpoint that the partiality, the subjectivity, of the actors' viewpoint becomes visible. To actors themselves, their experiences are real and solid, their world is fixed and permanent. Stepping back from that world enables the sociologist to see its arbitrary, constructed, incomplete character. But equally, stepping back from the sociological analyst's world of scientific objectivity enables Bourdieu to see that this world, in its turn, is arbitrary and socially constructed.

This process of stepping back is strongly reminiscent of phenomenology. It comes as little surprise, then, to find that Bourdieu cites Husserl (see Chapter 7) and, especially, Maurice Merleau-Ponty (a French phenomenologist) as among his main influences. In the world of French social thought of the 1950s and 1960s, the objectivist stance was associated with the structuralism of Lévi-Strauss (see Chapter 9). Structuralism sought to represent social life as the outcome of the workings of sets of objective rules, which work behind the backs of actors. According to his own account of his intellectual development, after an initial flirtation with structuralism, Bourdieu's reading of Husserl and Merleau-Ponty led him to reject it as insufficiently reflexive and unable to theorise actors' intentionality, i.e. purposive consciousness (see Bourdieu 1990). However, though strongly influenced by phenomenology, Bourdieu never fully embraced it. He regarded it as falling into the opposite trap to objectivism, namely, excessive subjectivism, so that the only goal of analysis is to recapture the subjectivity of experience. Since every experience is made rather than given, any such attempt to recapture the true nature of soup from its taste, it might be said, is doomed to failure.

## Bourdieu's four key concepts

The four key concepts Bourdieu employs to resolve the dichotomy of objectivism and subjectivism are as follows: *habitus*, *practice*, *field* and *capital*. The relations between these concepts can be explained by considering them in turn, starting with 'habitus'. The world as it is seen from the point of view of the social actor appears objective and solid, as out there and independent of herself or himself. That it does so is due to the actor's habitus.

## Habitus

The habitus is a structure of dispositions to action, but also to thought, perception and understanding, which the actor acquires as a member of a social group or class. It is something like a mental and behavioural set (as psychologists would say), which the actor takes for granted and which structures the way he or she experiences the world and responds to it.

The notion of habitus is meant to fulfil an equivalent role to the notion of 'structure' in Lévi-Strauss's thought; it points to the set of deeply organising principles which frame and form the course of the individual's actions, without the individual being conscious of them. As with other French theorists, Bourdieu's position is affected by the legacy of Descartes and Freud with respect to thinking about 'the mind'. For Lévi-Strauss, structures operate through the unconscious part of the mind. For Bourdieu, this approach remains too closely linked to the Descartes/Freud legacy; it does not give enough importance to the body, so he finds himself rather closer to Foucault. For Foucault had opposed the idea that social control operates through the internalisation of thought, models of conduct, ideals and rules in favour of the idea of control through regulation of the body, on which are imposed patterns of strict routine and compliant reaction.

The habitus structures dispositions to action rather more than thought, and it works through their incorporation into the body: Bourdieu's emphasis is on the habitus as *embodied*. Different social situations, especially differences in social class, expose individuals to different environments, which instil certain patterns of reaction into individuals. The result is that the dispositions of individuals will vary, especially between social classes, in such a way that the individual's habitus plays an important part in the perpetuation of those differences. The kinds of dispositions the habitus endows individuals with are those which include, for example, very visceral reactions: responses of comfort or unease, which can be as intense as those of disgust and literal nausea. Bourdieu uses the metaphor of 'the feel for the game' for the way in which people are 'at home' and know 'just what to do' in certain base milieux. Those who move outside their usual class environment experience reactions of unease. The idea of eating, dressing or behaving like a middle-class person is repellent to many working-class people who are being exposed to the judgement of middle-class people. Similarly, Bourdieu suggests, the two classes may differ in their ideals of physique to which they aspire: the kind of bulked-up, muscular physique that Arnold Schwarzenegger personifies may seem disgusting to middle-class people, who value physiques which are trim and elegant rather than bulging muscles. The habitus therefore perpetuates the distance between and segregation of different social classes.

The invocation of 'the body' is widely considered the introduction of an important phenomenon, hitherto neglected by social theory, by opening up the opportunity to investigate all the ways in which social structural organisation is incorporated into individuals' ways of valuing, forming and adorning their bodies through dress, adornment, physical training, participation in sport, and health regimes involving eating and medications. Bodily replication of an established bodily pattern is similar to how an individual picks up a way of speaking, an accent, from other people as a completely thoughtless reaction, without ever being taught to speak that way.

It should be noted that Bourdieu is no more interested than Parsons in the physical or biological body. He is interested, however, in what Parsons would have termed the 'expressive' aspects of the body or what interactionists might term its 'social meanings', i.e. in contemporary sociology there is much interest in the way that the body expresses 'masculinity' or 'femininity'. The interest in the body, then, is in the way that people's attention to their own and others' physique is related to (shared) social values, to social identities and to culturally localised ways of doing things.

The habitus, then, involves general and durable dispositions to act in certain ways, which play the role, in Bourdieu's account, of connecting the 'objective' socio-economic conditions of class with stable patterns of action. These patterns are reactive and develop by exposure to these conditions and are acquired through socialisation. Socialisation itself is also shaped by these same conditions; it therefore transmits the accumulated effects of exposure to these conditions of life. The resulting (shared) dispositions are relatively stable and underpin the formation of stable ways of doing things. Habitus is also meant to integrate structure and agency, since the habitus-induced reactions do not dictate specific actions; in acting in response to a situation, there is need for the individual to engage in some improvisation of conduct. Nevertheless, there is not too much room for spontaneity, for these are 'regulated improvisations' (*Outline of a Theory of Practice*, 1977). In this way, individuals in the same class situation share common patterns of reaction, which means that acceptable ways of doing things can simply grow up and become standardised among them without anyone having consciously to work out or plan (and also without central direction) the arrangements which make up these ways of doing things. In Bourdieu's terminology, they are *practices*.

## Practices

These are not to be thought of in terms of means-ends rationality, i.e. as the most efficient or effective means for attaining some goal, since the practice as such is not in any way consciously thought out but is extensively what people find it obviously 'right' to do. A practice needs to be examined in the expectation that it will reveal its own endogenous (i.e. intrinsic or built-in) logic, and what will seem rational to one group will not necessarily seem so to another. It is wrong to think that practices are developed to any specific ends since, rather, they just grow up in response to surrounding conditions of life.

While each habitus is self-sustaining and provides for the common experience which members of a group share, it is grounded in the social position which defines the group and gives it its identity. This shared situation is what Bourdieu refers to as the *field*.

> **Fields**
>
> These are social environments inhabited by one or, more usually, by several groups. A group is constituted as such by virtue of its location within the field, which typically involves competitive relations with other groups in the same field.

The main structure of Bourdieu's thought is a combination of Marx and Weber, i.e. classes are seen as constituted out of the objective conditions of life, with their equivalent 'status groups' being the primary site of social struggle. The notion of 'field' connects to Bourdieu's central preoccupation, the relations of domination. The incorporation into hierarchical relations of inequality and differentiation of life patterns according to the habitus is what is important. Bourdieu's claim for the distinctiveness of his theoretical approach is that it fundamentally emphasises the relational constitution of all social phenomena. Hence *relations of domination* provide Bourdieu's central concern; he seeks to implement a combined Weberian *and* conflict theory conception of society seen as a struggle for pre-eminence among groups defined by (effectively) *life-styles*. Bourdieu seeks to preserve a sense of their strong affiliation to Marx's ideas by expressing them through the adaptation of Marx's notion of 'capital', which is now extended not merely to encompass the resources accumulated in the economic sphere, but also to include forms of accumulated *cultural* resources. Just as in Weber, domination is not a simple function of economic power, though the capacity to possess a given lifestyle presupposes the wherewithal to sustain it in the longer term. As Weber had pointed out, economic power does not automatically 'convert' into social standing and command; often, makers of 'new money' fail to achieve the social equivalence to and participation with holders of 'old money'.

This extension of 'capital' from the economic sphere is meant to reverse and subvert one of the underpinning attitudes of high cultural involvement, namely, that the world of art is wholly remote from that of commerce and finance. Deeply entrenched and powerful, this assumption shapes the hierarchical structure of society: those who are more distant from involvement in naked economic acquisition have more status than those who are less so (precisely the 'old money'/'new money' contrast and ranking). Extending the notion of capital recasts high cultural involvement as a kind of acquisitiveness. Bourdieu argues that the habitus ensures that all social life involves a maximising motivation, though maximisation is not to be defined in a narrowly economic sense, not to be identified with any general scheme of 'rationality'. Rather, each habitus engenders a pattern of reaction, a 'strategy', which, without being consciously chosen, leads people to act in ways that maximise on the opportunities available to their particular group, the rationality of that strategy being specifically appropriate to the group. On this understanding, high culture is no more remote from acquisitiveness than the pursuit of business and commerce; it is merely engaged in a different kind of acquisitive competitiveness.

Thus, in addition to economic capital, Bourdieu identifies social, cultural and symbolic capital, signifying his intention to treat them as resources in the general socio-cultural contestation. These different kinds of capital are connected to one another, in so far as they offer the potential for reciprocal conversion. For example, if we stay with the Weberian old money/new money dichotomy, old money has been able to convert its economic resources into prestigious personal attributes (or cultural capital), into appropriate educational background, social graces and refined artistic sensibilities, and has also been able to convert it into networks of personal connections with many other rich/powerful/prestigious people (such networks exemplifying 'cultural capital'). These people may, too, have converted that cultural capital into influential roles in the public sphere, into positions as social leaders, as occupants of powerful positions in administrative projects and political parties (symbolic capital). Such conversions do not work only one way, for something like sporting fame (symbolic capital) can be converted into economic capital (through advertising, being given positions on company boards, etc.).

Bourdieu's innovation here is to bring Weberian ideas about lifestyles to bear upon the place of 'culture' in the more traditional sense of 'high culture', e.g. going to the opera, visiting art galleries and buying expensive paintings. One strand of Bourdieu's argument involves applying to this topic a traditional critique of individualism from classical sociology. His view is that an emphasis on the great freedom of choice in respect of artistic options and preferences embodies an excessively individualistic conception, and overlooks the extent to which 'cultural taste' is deeply conditioned, with people's aesthetic preferences falling into conventional social grooves in accord with the dispositions of the habitus. The other strand of his argument is that the personal cultivation and public promotion of certain kinds of cultural taste are part of the contest for hierarchical pre-eminence. Within fields of cultural production much hinges upon 'distinction', upon the creation of discriminations that are subtle, refined, and not easily mastered by those outside the field. There is an attempt, through social struggle within and between fields, to promote the sensibility associated with those things into a higher-status and more powerfully exclusive position. In other words, the dynamics of high culture are to be understood in terms of a competition of prestige.

At the level of the society, the struggle is not between classes but between two 'fractions' of the economically dominant class, i.e. those predominantly possessing economic capital are the institutionally dominant fraction, and those who possess mainly cultural capital, such as academics and artists, are the less powerful 'fraction' of the dominant class. Other groups and 'fractions' within the society tend to be prestige-rated relative to these two dominant fractions and to one another to the extent they fail to possess the cultural characteristics of the dominant class.

## Class

> Class is the outcome and condition of struggles within and between fields, for those struggles generate and modify the alignment of people within the overall distribution of capital. At any moment in time there is a given structure to such distribution within which the possibilities and character of further struggles will be at least broadly delimited.

With respect to social structure, Bourdieu, like others, holds that social structure is produced and reproduced and, like many others before him, gives great weight to socialisation as the medium through which the existing structure is translated into actions. Accordingly, these actions have the effect or function of reproducing the outline of the structure, though not rigorously reproducing the exact configuration of the 'initial' structure.

The configuration of the prestige structure associated with the structuring of cultural taste is not absolutely stable. There is continual jockeying for position between 'fractions' of culturally active groupings, and readjustments in the relative standing of species of taste and of those possessing it. Nevertheless, on the scale of the society, the relative stability of the overall pattern reflects the success of dominant groupings. Part of the stabilisation of a society hierarchy consists in getting subordinated groups to accept the superiority of one's cultural taste, and in possessing a sensibility which puts one at ease with a specific repertoire of aesthetic and cultural distinction, which is converted into social distinction, namely, recognition of oneself – and one's type – as a special sort of person.

It was noted earlier that Bourdieu's approach to knowledge is consistent with social constructionism. His political ambitions are those of classic *Ideologiekritik*. His analyses perpetuate an even more widespread sociological inclination to suppose that something of consequence follows from exposing that things taken as 'natural' can be shown to be social products or, in another jargon, social constructions. In fact, Bourdieu's twin strategy is to show that (1) the socio-cultural hierarchy of (especially) French society is not a necessary manifestation of 'the way things are' but is a creation of the same social order that it supports; and (2) the position of 'high culture' within this hierarchy is based on false ideological premises. There is nothing new in trying to demonstrate such points, presumably on the standard assumption that something that is socially constructed is easier to change than something that is 'natural'. Bourdieu resembles social constructionists in another way: *in not giving serious consideration to whether this expectation really does follow from his demonstrations.*

We have pointed up predecessors of Bourdieu's ideas, as we have done with Giddens, in order to illustrate clearly that we call these theorists 'synthesists' because there is very little innovation in the *ideas* that make up their theories. Any theoretical originality in Bourdieu must depend on the way in which he reconfigures a set of existing elements into a unified scheme, rather than on novelty in the ideas he employs. Does Bourdieu succeed in overcoming the dualism of structure and agency, which he proposed to resolve through transcending the objective/subjective dichotomy? The most generous thing that could be said is that it is far from clear that he does so. Perhaps more than usually, there are complaints about the divergence between Bourdieu's claims about the nature of his approach, especially as a synthesis of structure-with-agency, and the detailed working out of the approach itself.

Many critics (e.g. Brubaker, 1984; Schatzki, 1987) think that Bourdieu signally fails to give agency any more room than it had in the classic theories of Marx and Durkheim, arguing that the great weight of his approach falls upon the 'objective' side of things, especially through the role of the habitus in fixing the possibilities within which action is possible. Marxists are apt to be disappointed with the use of 'capital' in Bourdieu's thought, since it severs the connection with Marx's original notion of the term as the accumulating product of exploitation. Instead, Bourdieu uses the term as a general category for 'resources', thereby identifying only those things that tend to be known in the vernacular as 'advantages in life'. Marxists see only a Weberian-style dissolution of Marx, a transformation of the notion of class into an equivalent of 'status'. Others see only a Marxist-style economic reductionism, which actually overwhelms the Weberian emphasis on the significant struggles over culture between economic classes. Equally, they complain that the supposed independence of fields in determining their own form of organisation is accompanied by an insistence that each field's character is dominated by the needs of the capitalist economy to reproduce itself. Such criticism sees Bourdieu's analysis of contemporary capitalism as essentially an exemplification of Althusser's strategy of 'relative autonomy' with 'determination in the last instance', but with the relative autonomy being so limited as to be negligible (cf. Alexander 1995).

More positively, Bourdieu may be seen as allowing room for 'subjective agency'. That is, he emphasises the fact that the habitus *structures* rather than *determines* the agent's pattern of action; the dispositions which make it up do not prescribe determinate courses of action on any given occasion, but set only the broad limits within which the individual will work out a specific course of action. Here, though, the question becomes whether, then, if this is the solution, there was ever a problem. Almost everyone is agreed that people are socialised, that they are 'prepared' to act within society. Consequently, they are able to anticipate and appropriately respond to a wide range of circumstances, though they are not prepared for *all* such circumstances, nor provided with precise prescriptions for conduct on each and every occasion. Even Parsons's notion of 'the social role' did not require that kind of specific predetermination of what an actor should do on a given occasion. Another precursor can be found in Schütz's description of 'the natural attitude', emphasising the extent to which, from the point of view of the actor, much of the social world is immutable, unchangeable by the actor's *individual* powers; only a relatively small amount of that world is (in more recent terminology) 'negotiable', i.e. it can be adjusted and modified to suit the individual's purposes, by the individual.

Bourdieu's substantive work centres on the analysis of superstructural phenomena such as education, art and literature. The use of the Marxist term is rather appropriate here, since Bourdieu's substantive analyses owe much to Marxist ideas of ideology and capital. But whereas in Marx, ideology is distinct

from capital, the one consisting in sets of ideas and the other in material phenomena, Bourdieu puts these two notions together and comes up with the idea
of *cultural capital*.

### Cultural capital

In each of the fields of education, art and literature, there are some
dominant sets of ideas that define what is culturally valued and
desirable. These definitions are often held right across society and
regarded as objective realities. On closer inspection, each set of
ideas is associated with specific social groups or classes and particular historical periods, but they transcend these origins and stand
as societally legitimate definitions of what is educationally or artis-
tically worthwhile.

The practices which constitute educational or artistic activity serve to reproduce
these definitions and therefore also the relations of dominance and subordination, by reproducing the cultural capital on which these relations depend. Subordinated groups may or may not challenge these relations. Frequently they do
not, sometimes because their alternative values possess little cultural capital,
and sometimes because their habitus involves assumptions which serve to legitimate the status quo, leading them to take for granted as natural, objective realities situations which place them systematically at a disadvantage in the struggle
for dominance. In Bourdieu's own words: 'the different classes and class fractions
are engaged in a symbolic struggle properly speaking, one aimed at imposing
the definition of the social world that is best suited to their interests' (1992: 167).

## Habermas as synthesiser

If Bourdieu is one of the two most influential of these recent, all-encompassing
theorists, then the other must be Jürgen Habermas. Habermas has sought to
construct not only pan-sociological theory, but also pan-disciplinary constructions that draw upon philosophy (especially moral philosophy and philosophy
of language), political theory, psychology and linguistics. Starting from the
synthesis of Marxist and Weberian concerns achieved by the Frankfurt School
(see Chapter 8), Habermas sought to construct an analysis of the structure and
dynamics of modern society which would combine the views of society as
objective and subjective phenomena. He treats analysis as something requiring
a dualistic methodology in order to comprehend society as both the subjective
understandings of its members and also a system of functionally co-ordinating
mechanisms that operate outside the individual's awareness. Society is therefore treated as a complex structure that operates at both a macro and a micro
level, being a combination of what Habermas calls, respectively, system and lifeworld (see below). It also involves both voluntarism and determinism in so far as

people are capable, under appropriate circumstances, of both acting freely and also being controlled, i.e. their actions are determined by the functional needs of the system. In terms of sociological positions, Marxist and Weberian elements (see Chapters 2 and 3) are complemented by Parsonian and interactionist contributions (see Chapters 5 and 6).

## Habermas and the Frankfurt School

Jürgen Habermas sought to renew the optimistic element – the aspiration to emancipation from authority – in the programme of critical theory, and, latterly, to mount a – qualified – defence of Enlightenment rationality against the depredations of the critique of reason. There were valuable elements in the Enlightenment project, especially the emphasis on reason as a means of emancipation, and therefore the Enlightenment project was not misguided but, so far, unsuccessful and unfinished. Habermas had undertaken his graduate studies at the Frankfurt Institute, after its return to Germany in the 1950s, and had, first, to oppose the despondency of the School's own post-war position, which, as we have seen, had become pessimistic and resigned. They saw that instrumental reason was so extensively and thoroughly installed in modern societies that it was a miracle that critical theory survived at all, its survival being more a matter of keeping a candle alight in dark times than of preparing for the imminent overthrow of instrumental reason. These discouraging conclusions could only be avoided if there was fairly extensive reconstruction of the framework of thought.

The key initial manoeuvre was to re-examine the conception of reason, and to find that both Marx and the Frankfurt School had taken too narrow a view of reason by recognising only two forms of it, the instrumental kind, associated with domination, and the emancipatory kind, associated with liberation. The Frankfurt School, seeing the emancipatory kind almost entirely subordinated to, and otherwise annexed by, the instrumental, had naturally drawn their pessimistic conclusion. Habermas proposed a third kind of human interest, in addition to those of producing well-being (instrumental) and freedom (emancipatory).

Habermas opposed the deeply entrenched idea that instrumental action is the most basic form of action, maintaining instead that it is actually *communicative action* that is basic. The idea that instrumental action is the basic form is, of course, appealing since it follows from, for just one example, Marx's idea that we must first survive in order to do anything else, and that we must therefore have ways of meeting our practical needs, must have an effective instrumental relationship to our environment. Habermas objects to this view because it suggests that all our actions are directed towards making our environment serve our needs and purposes, so that our actions are primarily oriented to dominating (i.e. controlling) things in our environment, including our fellow human beings.

A key element in Habermas's thought is the adoption of Immanuel Kant's conviction that morality involves treating human beings as belonging to the 'kingdom of ends'. That is, human beings are not *for* anything, they have no useful purpose, they are to be valued in and for themselves. They are not to be treated as means to an end, thereby providing the basis for extending the kind of notion of reason to include the third 'interest'. This interest embodies the fact that we are, or should be, interested in other people *for their own sake* and not in relation to any practical purpose that we might have. The relationship between parents and children is not founded in the *use* that each has for the other; parents take an interest in their children *because they are their children*. They want to know, understand and communicate with their children simply because they care about the children. Marx had not noticed this feature of human relationships in his theoretical scheme, an omission reflected in the fact that language played almost no part in his theories. Habermas, by referring to this third interest as 'communicative', indicates that he is taking 'the linguistic turn' at this point, thereby emphasising the significance of language for human life in a theoretical context in which it had been neglected. In Habermas's case the linguistic turn involves giving central place to the *communicative* character of action and reason, for language is the prime means of communication.

## Communicative action

Habermas initially rooted much of his critique of modern society in terms of the discrepancy between the ideals and the actualities of the society, e.g. the ideal of free and equal discussion was blocked by the actual inequities of the system. In the second and major part of his career, as he took the full linguistic turn in the 1980s, he made the emphasis he had placed on communication the basis for a much more comprehensive account, in which the potential for emancipation was rooted in the nature of communication itself. The systematic distortion of communication was described no longer in terms of the ideals of a particular kind of society, but rather as relative to the requirements for rationality built into the nature of communication itself.

Communication with our fellow human beings, in Habermas's view, is basically for its own sake. This does not mean that communication is purposeless, but rather that the purposes served are *intrinsic* to communicative relations themselves; since we want to relate to and understand our fellow creatures, there is therefore no built-in element of domination. If communicative action is taken as the most basic form of human action, then, it opens up the possibility of a society in which social relations are conducted on the basis of mutual recognition of one another as free and independent beings.

Habermas thinks that a considerable philosophical reorientation takes place as a result of this view of communicative action. Most importantly, it implies a fundamental shift in the understanding of knowledge, displacing the idea that knowledge is something that is acquired only individually with the view that it is developed *collectively*. It is this conviction that will eventually lead him to develop a generalised account of discourse, a 'universal pragmatics'.

## Lifeworld

The rationality exercised within the specialised institutions is instrumental, i.e. it gets things done, and done efficiently. In the spirit of Weberian rationalisation, it is increasingly oriented towards how people may be more effectively included within considerations of efficiency. Communicative action remains in place, however, in what Habermas, taking the term from Husserl, calls the life-world: that which is left over, left behind after differentiation has gone some extensive distance. Within the world of family life, of friendship, leisure activities and the like, people remain ends for one another, with the communicative inter-est predominant. They want to know how you feel, whether you are enjoying yourself, what you'd like us to do together.

## Lifeworld

The lifeworld is the repository of (at least the possibilities of) person-to-person relationships; in such relationships people are concerned to communicate, to achieve mutual understanding, to co-ordinate their reciprocal actions – in short, simply to associate with one another.

Communicative action involves these three dimensions of reciprocal relation-ship; the concern is with people's responses to one another and not with using people for some ends of action. In summary, the lifeworld is a site where people engage, through communicative action, in those activities that are vital to the reproduction of social life, i.e. those cultural and behavioural patterns for sharing and transmitting their understandings. People are endowed with the taken-for-granted understandings which form the basis for their day-to-day conduct. The lifeworld fulfils the functions of perpetuating cultural knowledge and equipping people to co-ordinate their actions, thereby furthering social integration and soli-darity, and also developing the personal identities of individuals.

Habermas does not want to say that an interest in using others as means to ends, in trying to influence them to do what you, rather than they, want to do, is entirely absent from the lifeworld. In his scheme, though communicative action is the essential and basic form of action, people in the lifeworld are also con-cerned to get other people to do things that involve what Habermas terms *strate-gic action*.

## Strategic action

This involves people in trying to influence one another, and the men-tion of influence does indeed involve a direct allusion to Parsons's notion of generalised media. Influence is one such medium; power and money will shortly make their appearance.

The lifeworld is the main venue of socialisation – in this theory once again a key contributor to the reproduction of social organisation – where the enculturation of individuals and, thereby, the renewal of culture takes place. However, in a complex, differentiated society, the organisation and integration of the society's affairs can no longer be conducted through interpersonal relationships embedded in personal bonds such as those of kinship.

As we mentioned, Parsons was himself somewhat of a synthesiser, and he drew from Durkheim, Tönnies and others the idea of social development as a matter of social differentiation. Within small societies, all of the main activities are carried out through the ties of kinship; there are no specialised social organisations devoted to work, religion, politics and so on. Larger and more complex societies progressively develop more and more specialised social organisations for the conduct of activities, and people specialise in some of these activities. Work takes place in plants and offices removed from the family residence, and formerly was done primarily by the male adult in the family; nowadays often it is both adults. Within the simple society, the production and reproduction of social order is, therefore, all done through relationships of kinship, and much of that involves the enculturation of the small child through family ties. The practical affairs of the society were threaded through with communicative reason, but increasing differentiation means that it is progressively separated from instrumental reason.

In short, the predominant features of 'the system' are organised through impersonal and instrumental relations, which are conducted in terms of the generalised media (Parsons) of, respectively, money and power.

### The relationship of system and lifeworld

Habermas views this relationship from the point of view of the perpetuation ('reproduction' is the term nowadays more commonly used) of society and assumes that, for a modern, complex society, only part of the perpetuation can be effected through the lifeworld.

Here, Habermas attempts to conjoin the often counterposed elements of structure and agency. Alternative and often closely parallel designations are 'society as seen through the eyes of its members' and 'society as seen by an objective, external observer'.

Both these dimensions are necessary to a comprehensive understanding. Society is, after all, a meaningful phenomenon and works through symbolic communication between its members. Therefore, essential to understanding how it works is what Weber would have termed 'explanation at the level of meaning'. Such explanation alone, however, is not enough, since the activities that reproduce the cultural patterns of the society do not thereby provide for the reproduction of the society as a whole. People's actions in the lifeworld are directed towards, and carried out in terms of, their effect upon one another, not towards the organisation and perpetuation of the society itself. Thus the ways of perpetuating the whole society cannot simply be understood as a product of people's conscious purposes and intentions; rather, they must be effected through the consequences of what people do, the ways the actions themselves fit together in patterns that none of the participating individuals intended. While the members of the society can comprehend the connections that their intended actions make, they do not have the capacity to understand the way in which the *unintended* consequences of their actions interplay across the range of a large association of people, and the overall organisation of a complex society is largely generated through the unintended consequences of individual action. Accordingly, Habermas differentiates between *social* and *functional* integration.

## Social and functional integration

The former is the kind achieved within the lifeworld, on the basis of the conscious awareness of the participants, while the latter is outside of and beyond their awareness; it is an upshot of, rather than any purpose of, their activities. The issue of functional integration is to be comprehended by the theorist in terms of the idea of the boundary-maintaining system.

## System: decoupling and colonisation

The notion of system is the point at which Habermas appropriates the Parsonian conception of the social system, which he treats, however, as giving a *partial* description of society, i.e. it captures the aspect of its functionalist integration. It is true that modern society is an increasingly complex system, much of which is differentiated into specialised spheres, and articulated by the generalised media of money and power, which are the media of impersonalised and instrumental relationships.

The system is the domain within which instrumental reason achieves pre-eminence. For Habermas, the Frankfurt School's pessimism resulted from their failure to recognise that any alternative to instrumental reason could persist within modern society, and to see that the lifeworld, home of communicative reason, necessarily persists into modern society, i.e. lifeworld is not displaced by system. Rationalisation, in the more usual Weberian sense (see Chapter 3), continues apace in both system and lifeworld but the two forms of rationalisation are somewhat different, and do not necessarily develop in parallel. The development of the system as a largely unintended product of individual actions means that the form of its development is driven by functional needs, rather than by the requirements of the lifeworld, and so the system is organisationally *independent* of the lifeworld. Habermas therefore argues that the system elements tend increasingly to develop autonomously, to become progressively detached from the lifeworld. He terms this process a *decoupling* of the two.

## Decoupling

The two are not simply disconnected; rather, the system elements seek to reshape the lifeworld in their terms. They seek to pursue the thorough rationalisation (in terms of instrumental reason) of all social organisation.

Hence the dominance of instrumental reason does mean that the system begins to make the lifeworld over into its own image. In Habermas's word, it seeks to 'colonise' the lifeworld, to extend the circulation of its generalised media – money and power – into the relationships of the lifeworld. It is a continuation of the thorough extension of the process of rationalisation (exploiting the growth of technical and scientific knowledge) throughout the society that Weber had initially identified and that the Frankfurt School had made their major theme.

## Colonisation and its effects

The intervention of the system in the lifeworld, and the attempt to subject it to rationalisation, will bring pathological consequences.

The disruption of the processes of communicative action will mean that at least some of the requirements of social integration will not be fulfilled, and the kinds of consequences that Parsons – and Merton (see Chapter 5) – attributed to inadequate socialisation and anomie will result on a significant scale: people's sense of the rightness of the social order will be eroded; aspects of social life will become meaningless to them, or will cease to appear as legitimate; people will lose what sense of common purpose they have and become disaffected, losing commitment to their obligations. Conflict and deviance in social relations and psychic strain – even mental illness – in individuals will occur. Further, the impact of the systems of money and power upon the lifeworld will be such as to create crises, the consequences of which will be borne by people in their capacities as workers and as citizens. These crises *could* result in growing class conflict, but have not done so because the workers/citizens have been bought off through social welfare and services, which have also substituted for real citizenship participation in the state. In other words, rather than relating to the system as citizens, people are, instead, put in the position of clients (of the administrative/state structure), or of consumers (through the 'bribes' of the economic sector).

Further still, system integration leads to increasing consolidation of learning and culture in the hands of experts. Their increasing remoteness from the wider public means that specialised spheres do not contribute to or feed back into the general culture. The development of modern society has reduced the possibility of the formation of political ideologies around which dissent could grow. People are highly specialised and individualised in their outlooks, making for a fragmentation of consciousness, rather than the development of a common one. Such colonisation can only be disruptive of the functioning of the lifeworld, creating problems in the renewal of culture and consequently engendering social crises of the sort that we are even now seeing with respect to, for example, loss of faith in governments and anti-globalisation riots. These developments comprise what Habermas terms a *legitimation crisis*.

**Legitimation crisis**

Ever-expanding state intervention extends control into more areas of social life, but it also raises expectations that it cannot satisfy. In addition, and at the same time, state intervention also disrupts and dissolves the bases on which the state's legitimacy has traditionally rested.

The increasing development of the colonisation of the lifeworld has led to the legitimation crisis mentioned above, and to the development of mechanisms that attempt to counter the progressive colonisation of the lifeworld. Here Habermas refers to the rise of *new social movements*.

**New social movements**

These are the various forms of protest, paradigmatically exemplified by opposition to nuclear weapons, which now form around many libertarian and environmental issues. The organisations that form around these issues develop outside established political structures and present a challenge to them.

These movements arise outside the established state structures of power and are much more concerned to be democratic in the sense of being participatory movements, in which discussion rather than power or money is the basis for policy formation. They do not have economic/material objectives, but consider the quality of life, often conceived as protecting and restoring ways of life under threat. For Habermas, the need is to restrict the influence of the system and to reassert the needs of the lifeworld. In a complex modern society, it obviously cannot be a matter of abolishing the system, for our lives are too massively dependent upon it. Instead, the system has to be put back in its proper place, and counter-institutions set up to represent the lifeworld, and to contain and inhibit the system's colonisation efforts. There is a limit to the extent to which the system can colonise, in so far as the lifeworld simply cannot be reproduced except, to a significant degree, through communicative action. Indeed, this conflict between the system's mode of rationalisation and the nature of communicative action produces the pathological distortions of the lifeworld.

## The public sphere

There is thus a tension between system and lifeworld, with the system having differentiated out beyond the control of the lifeworld. If there is to be a connection between system and lifeworld, such that the lifeworld exerts restraint on the instrumental tendencies of the system, then the role of the public sphere is crucially involved. The public sphere is that part of the society within which free and open discussion among the members of society speaking in their personal capacities (and not as functionaries of corporate or state organisations) can take place. This is the domain for the enactment of the Enlightenment ideal in bourgeois societies, a place where *reason*, in the form of argument, is the medium of discourse, where the participants stand as equals, and where the discussion defines its own limits, instead of having them set by authority or tradition. Through such unrestricted discussion, it is possible for people to arrive at ideas that can influence policy decision-making. The lifeworld can have an input into the steering operations of the system. However, Habermas argued that decision-making was increasingly being handed over to large organisations, i.e. the state itself and business organisations, and to their technically trained staffs, who were also becoming much more sophisticated in manipulating the formation of 'public opinion'.

For Habermas, the politics of modern society is very much about the place of the public sphere. At the very best in bourgeois society, it has really allowed only the bourgeoisie unreconstructed participation, but also, and worse, has often had its space restricted or even suppressed. Moreover, a strong Frankfurt School theme, it has been increasingly manipulated through the media of power and money. Hence, optimism about emancipation must reside in the reassertion of the public sphere, i.e. in an increasing *and authentic* democratisation of the society.

## The universality of reason

Habermas claims that there is an 'unfinished project of modernity' which is worth taking forward. It depends upon being able to justify the claim that *the potential* for emancipation persists within modern society, and involves him in defending the very (Enlightenment) idea of reason that has been under assault in French social thought. The capacity for emancipation resides in the universality of communicative reason, and in its character as a form of reasoning that is directed toward reaching *consensus*. The potential for emancipation is built into language, or, rather, into linguistic discourse itself, which is why Habermas claims to deliver a 'universal pragmatics', where 'pragmatics' relates to the organisation of language in discourse. Since this potential is built into discourse as such (and not just into particular discourses such as French, English or German) then it is (potentially) available to all and therefore universal.

However, it extensively remains a potential because in actual societies there are obstructions to exercising it. In modern society there is *systematically distorted communication* as a consequence of the way in which the system has come to dominate the lifeworld. The distortion is introduced into communication through the insertion of interests and ideology which restrain and dictate the course of thought. The limitations on the public sphere in bourgeois society are not usually through explicit restrictions on what people can say but, rather, unconscious influences on what they can actually think, where domination is manipulative rather than directly coercive.

To make his case, Habermas must here traffic in counter-factual considerations, for in modern society it certainly appears that instrumental reason is predominant. Marx argued that history was an expression of human nature, but only a distorted one. Hence one could not extrapolate what human beings are essentially like from their present conditions, but only by understanding what human beings would be like if they were able to live under conditions of freedom. Similarly, Habermas cannot argue that the conditions of emancipation are being met in activities as they are currently organised, for, of course, were these conditions being met, then there would be emancipation. Hence he must argue in the counter-factual terms that the conditions of emancipation are built into the nature of human communication; these conditions would apply if people were able to relate to one another under certain conditions, which he sometimes calls an 'ideal speech situation'. This approach gives Habermas the leverage which a critical theory needs: existing circumstances fall short of what they could be, and the recognition of the ideal speech situation gives us something towards which we can aspire as an alternative to the existing state of things. In other words, it gives us a basis for saying what is wrong with the existing state of affairs, and indicates policies by suggesting what needs to be worked for to bring that ideal speech situation closer to reality.

## Ideal speech situation

This would be a situation in which genuinely and totally free dialogue would be possible, in which all the participants were able to engage on a wholly egalitarian basis, exempted from *all* external constraining and distorting influences such that their discussion could be truly co-operative, where nothing else would be at stake other than the search for the truth through scrupulously conducted debate. Such a situation is 'ideal'; it will never be fully actualised in reality.

For Habermas as for Hegel, then, the idea of the discussion or debate as a way of arriving at truth is a generally influential model. In forming the idea of dialectical logic Hegel generalised the model to the whole of history, while Habermas makes it basic to his conception of how emancipation is possible in modern society. Habermas is insistent (we are tempted to say, dogmatically) upon the capacity of reason to arrive at universally valid conclusions in respect both of empirical knowledge and of morality, but, of course, it is not to be expected that these conclusions have yet been reached. The ideal is built into discourse, since people tacitly accept it whenever they seriously and sincerely enter into an argument. Habermas's idea is that there would be little point in serious, sincere argument if we did not believe that the point of the discussion is to identify the better argument, that the considerations invoked on behalf of the sides in the argument should be all those that are relevant to making its case (we shouldn't be prevented from saying things that matter for the argument because we are afraid to do so), that we should give up a point if the opponent faults it and not insist on it even though we know it is faulty just because we want to win the argument. In other words, the point is to use argument to get a *right* result, and not just to win the argument, and, in that sense, the parties to a disagreement are to be thought of as more like collaborators in an inquiry dedicated to reaching the truth than as rivals struggling for victory in a head-to-head contest. There can be no room in such a discussion for *imposition*, only for agreement and acceptance; a point is established only in so far as the parties agree that it is right, not because one of them can force others to go along with it. Thus the outcome of such a discussion would be a truth that would be accepted by all the parties to it.

For Habermas, then, the ideal of a completely free discussion is presupposed by the organisation of argument itself, and the conditions for the fulfilment of that ideal are also built into the conduct of argument. It is easy to see why he envisages an ideal speech situation, for real-life discussions vary in degree away from this ideal. At the same time, we can recognise that the ideal is presupposed in the idea of constructive discussion. Moreover, in important ways it is presupposed in the operation of science conceived as a search for truth, which is truth as agreement. Borrowing the idea from C. S. Peirce (1839–1914), an American philosopher, Habermas assumes that truth in science equates with arrival at general agreement. We do not have it in science now, but the guiding ideal there is that if all scientists freely participate in the exercise of their reason, in the gigantic discussion which is the community of science, they will eventually converge upon certain common doctrines, arrived at progressively, through scientific debate which eliminates their disagreements. The outcome will be the same as reaching the truth, i.e. the truth (in science) is that which is finally and generally agreed among scientists.

## Universal reason

Habermas's idea is, then, that in entering into discussions in social life we take for granted such ideals; our free, reasoned participation will arrive at conclusions which we can all accept and are universal in this sense. The claims of the ideal speech situation only make sense if they hold for everyone – there is no point in hoping to arrive at truth through discussion if others are going to try to get agreement by lying, bullying, etc.

If actual arguments are not like this, then one reason is that the conditions of society do not allow it, since, there, argument is often a vehicle for imposing one person's view on another, propelled by the needs of instrumental reason, not communicative action. The presupposition of a proper discussion is that the parties are entirely equal in respect of everything except perhaps the force of their reasoning. Of course, in modern society people are not equal, and they do not necessarily have the right or power to participate in public discussion. They may not be allowed to take part in discussions, may not have the capacity, or may be afraid to do so. If they do speak, their contributions may be disregarded because they are not socially valued persons and not to be taken seriously. Moreover, if they engage in discussion, it may be on the basis of power and resources that cannot match those of others in the discussion. With such systematic limitations on the presuppositions of the ideal speech situation, it is not to be expected that discussion can indeed arrive at authentically universal results.

It can be counter-argued that the ideals Habermas proposes are not so much derived from the presuppositions of actual communication as projected on to discursive structures by Habermas's own theoretical presuppositions. His purpose, after all, is to further the democratisation of politics in modern societies by establishing the constitutive nature of reason in human affairs in terms which, as noted earlier, are consistent with a Kantian ethical stance. Habermas simply assumes, however, that politics as conducted is a frustrated effort to achieve the kind of 'dialogical' organisation devoted towards the dispassionate search for truth that is purportedly exhibited in philosophical inquiry. The consequence is a vision of political argument in which, in the words of one critic (Newey 1997), 'the politics has to be done before the politics'. Newey's point is that Habermas's conception assumes that the very things that make politics the phenomenon it is – vested interests, ideological commitments, limited information, practical constraints, demands for immediate action and so forth – are contingent features which have already been overcome before the disinterested dialogic search for consensus begins. Little wonder, then, that for some critics Habermas's achievement amounts not so much to explaining politics as assuming it away.

## Kinds of integration

Notwithstanding these problems, Habermas's attempt to integrate and thereby overcome the persistent dichotomies of social thought is by far the most impressive example of synthesis theorising. His poststructuralist critics have pointed out that his conceptualisation of reason as a communicative phenomenon, from individual and mental to intersubjective and linguistically based, does not fundamentally alter the role that reason is held to play in human affairs as the final arbiter of truth and deliverer of liberation. In this sense, Habermas's thought remains firmly rooted within the Western Enlightenment tradition; for all his intellectual distance from Descartes (see Chapter 6), they are fellow travellers on the same pilgrimage. Habermas and Bourdieu can be seen as occupying opposed positions with respect to – of all things – human nature. Bourdieu's portrait is painted in rather Hobbesian terms, a picture of fundamentally selfish individuals who pursue their own ends in a relentlessly rational manner unless they are subdued by others or are deceived into mistaking some other's interest for their own. To this extent, Bourdieu's relationship to Marx is peculiar, as it often seems as if he regards capitalism as just another form in which human acquisitiveness is expressed rather than, as Marx regarded it, as avarice, which emblematically expresses the capitalist system itself. Habermas seems to owe much more to Jean-Jacques Rousseau's conception of humanity as essentially noble and thus to be closer to Marx's own assessment, both conceiving individuals to be essentially benign and indiscriminately sociable and co-operative. Unfortunately, basic values are distorted by the distorting effect of social structures on the expression of this essence of being a human being. In short, the respective attempts of Habermas and Bourdieu to bring structure and agency together reflect their different starting points, which ensure that they remain poles apart.

## The network as metaphor

The 1990s and 2000s were the age of the network. The development of the internet, in particular, was remarkable in its speed and influence: from simple transmission of data between remote computers, through the development of the World Wide Web, to the ubiquity of smartphones and tablet computers, connecting through increasingly rapid mobile telephone networks and wireless bases, this has been a remarkable transformation. Although many sociologists (and others) advanced all kinds of utopian and dystopian claims about what this would mean for the world (see Cavanagh 2007 for a sceptical overview of these claims), the network as a metaphor was taken by some to represent a new way of thinking about social organisation and the social world (Castells 2000; Terranova 2004).

Actor-network theory (ANT; Latour 2005) has proved to be the most influential 'network' approach. Derived from sociological studies of science and technology, ANT portrays the world as a series of performed relations between elements, each of which can be understood as a network itself, and each series being itself an element in a further network. Emphasising process over structure, Latour's descriptive approach owes a debt to the symbolic interactionist and ethnomethodological traditions. It is, however, also based in a (rather slippery) notion of systems theory, wherein networks of performed relations make up 'bigger' networks and are, themselves, composed of 'smaller' ones. Actor-networks are, in this latter sense, somewhat akin to Durkheim's 'organic' view of social solidarity: heterogeneous networks connect up to comprise society as a whole, and 'actors' who are not so connected are, therefore, not social.

ANT has been controversial for its lack of political commitment, its apparent inability to address concerns of power and stratification, and its relativist approach to the social world – most of all because of its unwillingness to distinguish analytically between human and non-human 'actors' (or, indeed, between animate and inanimate objects). In practice it is often both sceptical and relativist, as in Latour's *Science in Action* (1987), where 'what scientists say' and 'what scientists do' are portrayed as opposites. 'What scientists say' tends to be definitive, objective, and grounded in commitments to proper method. 'What scientists do', on the other hand, is shown to be messy, ambiguous, situated in everyday mundane laboratory practices, and driven by careerist and other 'extraneous' motivations. This 'Janus-faced' picture of science, Latour argues, illustrates the 'translation' of one set of meanings to another, translation being the central means through which elements in a network fasten together.

This highlights a key problem for ANT analyses. Because human, non-human and inanimate objects can be 'actors', and because connections are characterised by 'translation', it is difficult to determine what does and what does not constitute a network or the elements within it. Human actors' perspectives are sometimes treated as central and sometimes as peripheral. The person doing the description, the theorist, ultimately gets to determine which is which. This is fairly conventional: much of the ethnomethodological critique of mainstream sociology is based on the idea that the 'actor's point of view' is neglected in social theory – hence the use of Schütz's phenomenological reading of Weber. What ANT lacks, however, is a clear commitment to any theoretical determination of the social world: while for Parsons it is about social order, and for Marx about social conflict, ANT can have no such grand overview. Describing relationships becomes an end in itself: 'the great danger of critical sociology is that it never fails to explain' (Latour 2005: 251). But without either the 'actor's' point of view or a pre-existing theoretical commitment, ANT can start to resemble the poststructuralist playing with meaning, despite its avowed rejection of these games:

> ANT has been confused with a postmodern emphasis on the critique of the 'Great narratives' and 'Eurocentric' or 'hegemonic' standpoint. This is, however, a very misleading view. Dispersion, destruction, and deconstruction are not the goals to be achieved but what needs to be overcome. It's much more important to check what are the new institutions, procedures, and concepts able to collect and to reconnect the social.
>
> (Latour 2005: 11)

Actor-network theory emerged from the sociology of science 'fully formed'. In parallel, however, and with a clearer tradition in mainstream sociology, in recent years *social network analysis* has become increasingly popular and influential. In this approach, the factual connections between different actors in a network are quantified and represented diagrammatically to produce a 'picture' of what a network looks like. Crossley (2008), for instance, generates a diagram of the relationships between key figures in the development of British punk rock in the 1970s. The density of connections around particular actors and the relatively peripheral nature of others allow for quantitative determinations of how they relate to one another to be made. Furthermore, different kinds of connections can be found and examined: actors may be tied to others with whom they have a lot in common (class, gender, educational background, etc.) or to apparently very dissimilar actors. The extent to which a network is homophilic (actors connect with those similar to themselves) reveals a great deal about its nature, resilience and possible future.

This approach has been criticised for its *referential/representational* confusion (Knox *et al.* 2006). It is unclear what the diagrams of connections mean: are they meant to represent the social world or reveal its underlying patterns? Are they 'referent' or 'representation', the 'real nature of the social world' or a particular picture of it? Just what, in short, *are* these diagrams?

The use of the network as metaphor – or as representation – has certain key strengths. First, it allows for the representation of real connections between actors without those connections relying exclusively on either their own accounts or on a predetermined theoretical scheme. Second, it sits outside the micro/macro, structure/agency, free will/determinism dualisms that Giddens, Bourdieu and Habermas sought to dissolve. Finally, it offers the potential for empirical data to control what can and can not be said about particular social worlds, thereby avoiding the criticisms of 'grand theory' that have been levelled against the post-Parsonian thinkers considered earlier in this chapter. Whether it will resolve into something beyond this is, however, unclear at present. Latour has, in recent years, played down the 'network' element of ANT, and social network analysis is increasingly associated with its practical applications: the tracking of users of social networks like Facebook and the mass surveillance of mobile phone and internet use conducted by the National Security Agency in the 2000s. The criticisms levelled at ANT and social network analysis have not prevented their practitioners using these approaches, but equally have not been answered. In this sense their impact has mirrored that of the theorists considered earlier in this chapter.

## Conclusion

The theorists outlined in this chapter have attempted to respond to the views of poststructuralist and postmodernist thinkers who question the possibility of a general theoretical account of the totality of society and attempt to dispel disciplinary demarcations, whereas the 'synthesists' reassert the claims of sociological theory as more traditionally understood. None the less, all of them have also assumed that if sociological theory is not to be dissolved, then it must be reconstructed in order to remove the tensions, if not outright inconsistencies, which have been persistent sources of dissent and fundamental dispute within sociology. Their attempts at reconstruction have been made not through radical innovations in foundational assumptions but, instead, largely by the recombination of existing elements into purportedly more inclusive schemes. Whether their strategy has been successful is, like everything else in sociology, a matter for argument, and these various reconstructive proposals have both their enthusiasts and their critics. The latter, as we have indicated, are apt to see these reconstructions as preserving within themselves the very oppositions which they aim to transcend, covering over rather than fundamentally confronting the problematic issues, and leaving unanswered the questions that the Continental social theorists have raised.

## Questions

1  Parsons did not address Marx's arguments as he thought of them as too 'utilitarian', while Marxists have tended to neglect Parsons's work for its 'functionalism'. How might Marx be understood as a utilitarian and Parsons as a functionalist? To what extent can one understand aspects of Marxian theory as themselves functionalist? Does looking at Marx this way make sense? If it were not for the threats of postmodernism and other 'post' theories would it make any sense to see Marx's work in this light?

2  Define neo-functionalism. How do Mouzelis's and Alexander's theories relate to 'classical' functionalism? How does each transcend it? Are they right? Given the criticisms of functionalist thought would it not make more sense simply to defend functionalism *as it is*? What differences, if any, would there be between a functionalist and neo-functionalist analysis of a contemporary social phenomenon of your choice?

3   How many 'dualisms' can you think of in social theory? Are they 'problems'? Why? Were earlier social theorists like Marx, Weber, Durkheim or Parsons unaware of these 'problems'? In what ways do symbolic interactionist and ethnomethodological approaches offer alternative ways of overcoming these 'problems'?

4   What is 'communicative action'? Why does Habermas make it so central to his theory? To what extent does his analysis of 'communication' and meaning differ from its treatment by structuralists and Marxists?

5   In what ways do *each* of Bourdieu's concepts – habitus, practice, field and capital – serve to overcome the opposition of subjective and objective? Why is this opposition important in Bourdieu's thought? Is he right to make it so central to his argument? What alternative positions might there be? How does his theory allow one to undertake 'better' studies of the social world?

6   What is 'cultural capital' in Bourdieu's thought? How does this relate to Habermas's arguments about ideal speech and the roles of culture and the media?

7   How, if at all, do any of the theorists examined in this chapter meet the challenges to general theory made by Foucault, Derrida, Lyotard or Baudrillard?

## Next steps

Giddens's (1984) *The Constitution of Society* is the major statement of structuration theory, and Bourdieu's (1977) *Outline of a Theory of Practice* of the latter's approach. Outhwaite (1996) collects the most important of Habermas's texts.

Colomy (1990) offers an excellent comprehensive selection of neo-functionalist writings. Good introductions to Giddens, Bourdieu and Habermas are offered by Craib (1992), Jenkins (1992) and Edgar (2006), respectively. A more critical collection of papers is Martin and Dennis (2010).

## CHAPTER FOURTEEN

# From class to culture: do we need new theory for new societies?

**Chapter overview**

Social and institutional changes in Britain and the USA led to particular emphases being changed in sociological thought in the 1970s and 1980s. As well as the rejection of much of Parsons's thought, a re-invigorated Marxism spread throughout the discipline, emphasising culture and ideas over the economic 'base' of social organisation. Changes in class structure – the decline of the traditional working class and the rise of the service sector – required analysis, and the development of *globalisation* brought new challenges to how individual societies could be understood. These trends have meant that the *topic* of sociological theory has shifted, just as the modes of inquiry sociologists use have altered over time.

## Introduction

Thus far in the book, we have discussed, examined and re-examined the basic theories and their ramifications which inform the project of 'doing sociology'. We have seen how very dependent they are on the 'founding fathers', namely, Marx, Weber and Durkheim, despite all attempts – intended or unintended – to mask their basic concepts with elaborated concepts and terminology. In this chapter and the next we offer a change of register in two ways.

First, in this chapter we wish to provide a historical and political sketch in order to provide a backcloth against which the development of sociology, particularly in Britain, can be gauged and assessed. Just as we need to insert a human figure in a photograph we are taking of a large monument, e.g. the Pyramids, so we need this backcloth in order to see sociology in due proportion, although the background is the Pyramid and sociology the (small) figure.

Then, in the next chapter, we examine how sociological theory has been applied to areas that many people regard as urgent problems for the application of social theory, the issues (or minefields) of gender, sex and ethnicity. Conceptually, these areas might seem less abstract than many of those considered in earlier chapters. None the less, as we shall see, discussion of them draws on many of the familiar basic tools of analysis that we have been describing throughout the book.

## Marxism and the rise of British sociology

Owing to the extensive influence of Marx-derived ideas in all the topics that follow, it is probably helpful to emphasise the fact that the influence of Marx in British (and American) sociology has had only a short and relatively recent history. Our attempt to show the continuity of the Marxist tradition through 'Western Marxism' should not leave the false impression that there is such continuity in British sociology. American sociology did have a significant continuous history from the end of the nineteenth century, but Marx had no significant influence upon it until the 1960s, at which point British sociology, as we now know it, first came into existence. The development of sociology in Britain really has quite a short history, which can be dated from the early 1960s and the expansion of the universities that followed the publication of the Robbins Report on education at this level. There had been British sociologists before this, of course, but there was little representation of them in the universities, the only professors being at the London School of Economics. In social history and even in anthropology, however, there were strong Marxist tendencies, which antedated these events. Furthermore, many of the new appointees in sociology were influenced by the ideology of the 'New Left', a political tendency originating in a breakaway from the British Communist Party as a reaction to the Soviet suppression of the 1956 Hungarian uprising.

The Robbins expansion led to rapid and massive growth in the number of sociology appointments as departments of sociology were created in all of the then existing universities. The sudden institutional expansion of sociology coincided with two political events: first, American society experienced – and exported – the rise of the 'counterculture' as a reaction to the Vietnam War; subsequently, in France, there were the events of May 1968 and the defeat of the student movement. These developments powerfully influenced the intellectual direction of British sociology, as did those of the later 1970s and after, when Alexander Solzhenitsyn's revelation (1974) – to French intellectuals at least – of the persecutory and inhuman nature of the Soviet Gulag (system of political prison camps) led to the final disintegration of all faith in the emancipatory capacity of Marxism, which had been declining in any case.

In intellectual terms, these developments in British sociology involved the rediscovery of (in many respects, the discovery of) and subsequent disillusionment with Marxism. None the less, this discovery converted British sociology to a dominant conviction that it was an essentially 'critical' discipline, a conviction that has remained prevalent since the late 1960s, though the conception of the nature and basis for the criticism has continually been revised.

The way that these developments have shaped sociology's theoretical course has prompted us to organise our story of the deployment of sociological theory since the 1960s very much in terms of its relationship to Marxism. Changes in society led, first, to the rediscovery of Marxism, which was very much the discovery of existing European traditions in the interpretation of Marx, and to the eventual retreat from it, i.e. at least from explicitly Marxist ideas, though, as we will repeatedly suggest, the critical tradition is always at least significantly continuous with them. The rapid growth of British sociology in the 1960s entailed the appointment of very young and inexperienced individuals. Moreover, there was little in the way of indigenous sociology for them to draw upon, so that the materials for the formation of their views were those which were already available within American sociology or those – given the expanding market for sociology books – newly translated from the French (mainly), German and Italian, resulting in a wide range of Marxist theorists suddenly becoming available. The Marxist Perry Anderson (1980) has castigated English culture for being anti-intellectual, untheoretical and parochial, meaning that it has produced hardly any 'big' ideas; most influential 'English' ideas have come from immigrant intellectuals such as Karl Popper and Ludwig Wittgenstein. Indeed, the course and growth of British sociology might be seen as a consequence of, and in accord with, the situation Anderson describes. We need to point out that Anderson did not go unchallenged: the New Left historian of the English working class, Edward Thompson (1978), certainly contested his views, especially the value Anderson placed on 'theory'.

The expansion involved a rapid leftward shift in the standards used to appraise sociological arguments; for a time, the criterion for conservatism was that almost anyone was conservative who was – to exaggerate slightly – to the right of the International Marxist Group, which was then one of the more extreme Marxist splinter groups. Émile Durkheim, who was a bit of a socialist, if anything, was condemned as a conservative – the 'radical' Durkheim only gaining belated recognition (see Pierce 1989) – as was Talcott Parsons, who, politically, was a left-leaning liberal.

The Vietnam War had a radicalising effect on American universities partially because university faculty were seen to have been compliant with 'the American war machine'. Much university research funding derived from the Department of Defense, and in the 1950s and early 1960s anthropologists would routinely and unremarkably act as informants on the regions in which they worked to the CIA. There were very few Marxists on American university campuses before the Vietnam campaign, when resistance to being drafted into the armed services radicalised the student body. One important exception, resident in exile at the University of San Diego in California, was Herbert Marcuse, a German philosopher associated with the 'Frankfurt School'. Marcuse, along with others from the School, had found ways of perpetuating the relevance of Marxist ideas even in the extreme affluence of California, with (1) an emphasis on the way in which the structures of affluence were producing a homogenising, reductionist culture; which (2) dissipated dissent but (3) where that occurred, converted it into a commodity, e.g. bestselling books, thereby defusing it. The new culture was one of 'repressive tolerance': it presented itself as endlessly tolerant, anything but repressive, seeming to allow all points of view to flourish, but this was appearance only – the very tolerance itself was a way of drawing the teeth from dissent. In the light of their affluence and their absorption into this 'one-dimensional' culture, the working classes were no longer to be looked to for providing revolutionary impetus, which would now have to come from students – universities were to become 'red bases'.

From the newly radicalised student point of view, university faculties were frequently compliant in accommodating to the growing dominance of the 'military-industrial complex' that C. Wright Mills, very much a 'New Left' thinker in spirit, had warned about. Indeed, he followed an earlier warning given by Dwight Eisenhower, himself a former military general as well as being the retiring Republican president. Mills was deeply critical of the intellectual as well as the political condition of American sociology in the 1950s and early 1960s (see 1959a, 1959b).

At this point we must stress that although we talk about 'sociology', the tendencies we are discussing were often pan-disciplinary, meaning that institutional sociology absorbed individuals with different disciplinary affiliations, and that other disciplines incorporated many 'sociological' ideas. Attempting to keep the term 'sociology' consistent with disciplinary divisions would complicate our story beyond practical possibility, given that it is, itself, no more than an introductory sketch of main tendencies.

The radicalisation of the US campuses, following on student-run campaigns for racial integration in the American South and expedited by the Vietnam War, meant that the universities came to be regarded as tools of an oppressive state. Significantly, they were also seen as a point of vulnerability, a soft underbelly of the state, which was why it was strategic to make them into 'red bases'. The polarisation of the political situation took on the tone of 'those who are not with us are against us'; on this new scale of evaluation, academics who did not radicalise therefore became reactionaries. They were not seen as passive victims themselves of the rise of a military-industrial complex, but understood, rather, as active agents of the state's control. Their ideas were labelled 'conservative' because anything less than resolute and sustained opposition would allow the status quo to stand, and not necessarily because they firmly and positively endorsed the existing order.

This stance entailed a thorough revaluation of existing sociological ideas: ideas that did not expose and could not be used to expose the oppressive nature of the state could not be correct, but could only be misleading; their falsity could be seen not as incidental, but as functional. The role of these ideas was to mislead people, to distract them from and to obscure for them the fractures in American society that the tensions over Vietnam had brought into such plain view. Alternative ideas that would enable the criticism of those existing ideas and a different portrayal of social realities were to be embraced. This alienation from university 'establishments' was rapidly communicated, in a world of expanding international media, to the campuses of Europe.

## Searching for victims: the case of Talcott Parsons

The first and major intellectual *sociological* victim of these changes was Talcott Parsons. Although he sometimes played the part of public intellectual, he was mainly dedicated to professionalising American sociology, to giving it an accepted and respected place among the mature disciplines – science, medicine, law – on campus. Yet this determination was critically understood only as an ambition to enable sociology to accommodate to the powers that be.

One of Parsons's other 'failings' was that he wrote abstractly and, for many, quite obscurely. Wright Mills placed Parsons as the central target of his critique of contemporary American sociology. So did another radicalised academic, Alvin Gouldner, in *The Coming Crisis of Western Sociology* (1970). Much of Mills's critique consisted in denunciation of Parsons's laborious writing style. Its difficulty, however, did not create such obscurity and unintelligibility that Mills was prevented from making extended criticisms of the substance of the work.

Mills himself saw sociology as divided into two unrelated and equally futile parts, which he termed 'grand theory' and 'abstracted empiricism'. The notion of 'grand theory' was meant to indict especially Parsons, whose work was used as its leading example; large tracts of Parsons's writings were cited to illustrate how wordy, obscure and, when decoded into simple English, trite it was. Grand theory is highly abstract and purportedly general, but it says nothing of empirical significance. Abstracted empiricism is at the other extreme: lots of empirical reports, but no guiding ideas or standards to connect the empirical findings together or to construe their significance. These two approaches co-existed but did not, and by their nature could not, meet. Further, for Mills, they lacked the engagement with public issues that he saw as essential: sociology should not be a self-contained academic pursuit, preoccupied with its own technical problems; instead, it should provide people generally with a way to understand how their own 'private troubles' were connected with the larger structures of social organisation (and public issues) that were generating these seemingly personal but, in fact, common difficulties.

## New directions for Marxism

The fevered climate created by the political and cultural turbulence of the 1960s demanded that sociologists take a politically activist direction, with a common requirement that they provide guidance as to how insurrection against the existing social order might be brought about. An alternative to the 'orthodoxy' of the Parsonian establishment was therefore sought, on two levels:

1   Sociology in the universities had presented an essentially false picture of itself, as a technical pursuit that stood outside the tensions and divisions of the social order, aspiring to achieve a scientifically objective and politically neutral analysis of that order. The idea of 'science' was much akin to that which underpinned the natural sciences. To dissenting students, however, it was plainly false in so far as the natural sciences themselves were anything but neutral and were involved in extensive collaboration with the state, especially the military. It was held that the image of science had been outdated, that no longer did lone scholars pursue the truth as they saw it. With 'Big Science', state and business sponsored research that used scientific

investigation as a way of solving the problems that its sponsors faced. The earlier idea of science – the so-called 'positivist' idea – had to be rejected in favour of a new understanding of what knowledge is.

2   The idea that sociology was primarily a form of theoretical analysis was also rejected as a way of absorbing and paralysing intellectual commitment that would be better devoted to overthrowing a social order that was increasingly regarded as oppressive. There was a need to overcome the separation of theory from practice, of intellectual inquiry from political engagement.

There was, however, something of a ready-made alternative. Marxism, on some readings, is understood to be that very attempt to achieve the unity of theory with (political, even revolutionary) practice. In creating a theory that has overtly direct implications for political action, sociologists can follow the Marx who had famously proclaimed that the philosophers had attempted to understand the world, when the aim should be to change it. By this standard, the test of social theory should be not the soundness of its empirical predictions, but its capacity to serve the wholesale transformation of the social order.

This was music to many ears. After all, as we have mentioned, the rediscovery of Marx was, for many, really a discovery.

## The 'end' of nineteenth-century capitalism

Marx's name had certainly circulated previously within British sociology, but the consensus had been that his theories had been superseded by the development of capitalism itself. If his theories had any truth to them, then it was with respect to the structure of nineteenth-century capitalism, as Ralf Dahrendorf (in the late 1950s) and James Burnham (in the USA as early as the 1940s) prominently argued in their different ways. Far from discovering general truths about society, at best Marx had captured the truth that power in early capitalism was related to specific position, especially of ownership, within the system of production. The individual capitalist was the owner of industrial property, and the capitalist class had considerable political power in their contemporary society. But, argued Burnham, by the 1930s ownership and control had become separated, and power within capitalist production was increasingly concentrated in the hands of professional managers who did not own the companies that employed them. There had been a revolutionary, albeit non-violent, transfer of power within capitalism, but passing power to the newly dominant class, the managers. Making a similar point, but more conceptually, Dahrendorf criticised Marx for mistaking the economic inequalities as the basis for class structures. In Marx's own time, it was a reasonable mistake in so far as the structures of economic inequality and power had coincided, but it concealed the need for an analytical separation between the two since class antagonisms are the product of power differentials, rather than economic inequalities as such.

Others, going further in the direction that Burnham pioneered, began to argue that the very term 'capitalism' had itself become outmoded, that the class structures and conflicts which had fed Marx's model of social change had changed beyond all recognition, that class conflict had been mitigated and that the form of the new stockholder-owned, professionally managed corporations had replaced 'capitalist' businesses: better to think of modern society as 'industrial society'. Radicalisation soon reversed this tendency: capitalism was back in use and remains so everywhere today. One of the cracks in the façade of agreement on treating Marx as outmoded was the manifest collapse of the 'end of ideology' thesis (see Bell 1960).

### The end of ideology

This is the notion that Marxism generates ideology; as it weakens, so the power of reason and 'clear', i.e. non-ideological, thinking can flourish.

'Ideology' had come to mean the kind of zealously held political beliefs (see Chapter 2) that drove Stalinist communism in the Soviet Union and Fascism in Germany. The 1930s saw the intensification of ideological struggle between the left and the right, which often came to fighting in the streets in Western societies and led to violent suppression in Germany and the Soviet Union, and civil war in Spain. World War II was propelled by such ideological struggle; its aftermath had put an end to this kind of intensely polarised ideological opposition within Western societies, but world politics was still polarised between East and West on a strongly ideological basis, i.e. 'liberal democracy' versus 'communism'. Politics in the Western societies had acquired a 'civil' tone, contrasting with the 'uncivil' one that ideologically polarised opposition creates, and the opposition between private property and socialist appropriation had been dissipated by a new governmental consensus on the 'mixed economy', i.e. some nationalised industries but much of the economy in private hands, with state support for the privately owned, all combined within an interventionist welfare state. The ideological struggle of *extreme* left and *extreme* right was supposedly over, but hardly had its termination been announced than, as described, it immediately erupted again because of the impact of Vietnam.

The idea that Marx had been disproved by the development of industrial society then itself came to be regarded as an ideological (mis)conception, one designed to downplay the divisions and tensions which still existed in modern societies, and to obscure the fact that there remained real potential for revolutionary transformation. The idea that economic inequality and injustice had been eliminated by post-war prosperity was a superficial and false picture. Yet the emerging forms of standard theoretical analysis in sociology were unable to represent the capacity for radical change in the overall structure of society. Suggestions that industrial society/capitalism had fundamentally changed its character were vigorously resisted. An example was the 'embourgeoisement thesis', the claim that 'we are all middle class now', i.e. the working class is being increasingly absorbed into middle-class lifestyles – and even middle-class positions: see Ferdinand Zweig, whose *The Worker in an Affluent Society* (1961) was denounced by John Goldthorpe and David Lockwood in *The Affluent Worker in the Class Structure* (1968). The working class remained a distinctive entity, and a potential basis for forceful political action, if not necessarily revolutionary initiative.

Further, the understanding of Marx that had been widely circulated since around 1914 came to be condemned as false or, at best, as very crude. There were available – in little-known European scholarship – many other, and much more sophisticated, interpretations of Marx than the 'vulgar' versions that had been propagated by interpreters who often came from the orthodox, Stalinist-dominated international left. Marx had been rethought by numerous theorists, almost invariably in ways which denied that the value of his thought depended on predicting a working-class revolution in capitalism, or denied that his analytical ideas consisted in 'vulgar' reduction of all human activity to economic motives, or denied both of these views. Clearly, if Marx had not predicted a working-class revolution, then his theory was not falsified by the absence of one. At the same time, the fact that it had not yet materialised did not mean that one was no longer possible. Rather than seeing the increasing irrelevance of Marx as a result of the progressive disappearance of class struggle, we were witnessing changes in the way in which class struggle was carried on, and Marx's general ideas were misunderstood if it was imagined that they were designed only for the analysis of class in nineteenth-century Britain, rather than for the analysis of social struggle in all its forms. The idea that class struggle was no essential feature of social organisation was itself the false, and ideological, one. In this way, the revisiting of Marx's thought was accompanied by an enthusiasm for showing that modern society was, despite outward appearances, the host of class struggle and of the alienation that accompanied it.

## The rise of 'cultural Marxism'

This revisitation of Marx initiated a period of exploring the possibilities of 'Western Marxism'. It provided an alternative to Stalinist simplifications by introducing 'humanist' renderings of Marx, which had been influentially rejected altogether. We are here looking at the engagement of intellectuals with Marxist theory and the beginnings of a shift in its application towards their own cultural concerns, namely, the attempt to develop Marxist theories of art, painting, the novel and so on. It required a protracted shift of emphasis from the analysis of overt political struggles and social disturbance towards the evocation of the implicit ideological structure of high, subsequently high and low, cultural artefacts. Lucien Goldman (a French Marxist) published *The Hidden God* in 1964, which according to its subtitle was a 'study of the tragic vision in the *Pensées* [Thoughts] of Pascal and the tragedies of Racine', a form of inquiry inspired by the work of Georg Lukács, a Hungarian Marxist who published his first major contribution to rethinking Marx in 1923, and who pioneered the use of Marxism as a form of literary criticism, perhaps partly as a way of being not entirely a Stalinist Marxist in Stalinist Hungary. Alvin Gouldner, mentioned above, published *Enter Plato*, a study of 'the origins of social theory' in classical Greece, in 1965. As public and university revolutionary activism rapidly exhausted itself, this approach was another sign of the way in which Marxism was to be developed in the academy. It was to become a tool of academic controversy in the form of an increasingly elaborated cultural critique as the prospects of serious working-class militancy failed to material-ise; the working class simply failed to respond to – even if workers were aware of – the academic theorists' newly found enthusiasm for revolution. In the period after World War II, senior members of the Frankfurt School themselves – apart from Marcuse – had been in deep despair about the possibility of revolutionary transformation. Remember that Marcuse himself regarded students, rather than workers, as the bearers of revolutionary possibility.

It must be noted that even as the enthusiasm for European Marxism was get-ting to full steam in the UK, its hold on French social thought was beginning its slow disintegration. It would be the 1970s and after before the hold was almost entirely lost, but communism had been a much bigger social force in France than it ever would be in the UK. Paris was a global centre of attention for a few days in May 1968 when there were violent student demonstrations there. For some, it seemed, for a moment, as though students might bring the French government down, but this was probably as much wishful thinking as informed political ana-lysis. The 'days of May' marked the beginning of disillusionment with Marxian thought. Attempts to draw the workers into student activism were – with limited exceptions – pathetic failures. The French Communist Party and its leading theo-rists, especially Louis Althusser, whose work was shortly to grip British sociologi-cal thought, played a minimal role in supporting student activism.

### Value consensus versus false consciousness revisited

In the Anglo-American context of sociology, however, dissatisfaction with Parsons's thought was the focal consideration, and his work was open to assault and even ridicule.

Parsons's own foundational work, *The Structure of Social Action*, attempted a synthesis of major social thinkers from the late nineteenth and early twentieth centuries, including Durkheim and Weber, but excluding Marx. Marx was exclud-ed on the basis of his continuing affiliation with the 'utilitarian' tradition of social thought, which in Parsons's view was a stumbling block to the development of sociological theory. Durkheim and Weber tried to throw off this restraint, but Marx had not. Nevertheless, Parsons did not thereby reject Marx's views about the institutional structure of capitalism and the inequalities built into the capital-ist employment relationship (see Parsons 1937: 119).

Parsons rejected the utilitarian tradition – as, he argued, Weber and Durkheim had done – because as it assumed that individual ends were (analytically) ran-dom, it could not account for the existence of social order (see Chapter 5).

The 'problem of social order' had been a preoccupation of social thought since at least Thomas Hobbes. The problem was to understand how society is possible, certainly not to understand why it was politically quiescent, if indeed it was. That is, the 'Hobbesian' problem is to understand why individuals are not at one another's throats, rather than to understand – in the first instance – why class groupings might be engaged in a death struggle.

Much of the contestation with Parsons emphasised the difference between values and interests (often as a form of the difference between 'the ideal' and 'the material'. There were at least two possible lines of thought here: (1) Parsons exaggerated the extent to which a society is united around a single set of values, overemphasising the extent to which the order of society was consensual, and underestimating the degree to which it was coercive; and (2) Parsons placed exclusive emphasis on the integration of society at the level of values and excluded the possibility that society might be much less integrated at the level of interests (this last line of thought is spelled out by David Lockwood 1964). The fact that the society, despite some periods of intense trade union activity, showed little sign of developing toward a revolutionary polarisation countered the insistence upon the reality of different material interests arising from economic inequalities. Consequently, from a Marxist or near-Marxist point of view, the resort to the idea of false class consciousness was an appealing way of dealing with this uncomfortable support of value consensus.

The tradition of Western Marxism – especially with Gramsci's notion of hegemony, to which Althusser acknowledged a debt (see Chapter 9) – could provide a source that demonstrated that the level of ideology had 'relative autonomy' from economic conditions. Furthermore, the struggle for *cultural* domination was as important to perpetuation of capitalist dominance as overtly economic conflicts. *Even if* there should be a value consensus in society, it would not signify a spontaneous social agreement, but would constitute an imposition from above upon the dominated groups, i.e. the inculcation of a false consciousness. Such false consciousness might inhibit class struggle, but it would not achieve complete control of all subordinated groups. Attention was therefore shifted towards the identification of 'resistance' to dominant cultural forms. This line of analysis owes much to the Birmingham Centre for Contemporary Cultural Studies – note the name – and is well represented by both Paul Willis (1977), who paints a picture of alienated working-class youth whose delinquency in respect of school discipline is portrayed as a form of resistance to the empty, narrowing and meaningless possibilities that the capitalist labour market offered them, and by Stuart Hall and colleagues, in *Policing the Crisis* (1978), an analysis of a 'moral panic' in the media about 'mugging', a form of street robbery. Here media reaction was examined as symptomatic of underlying political tensions resulting from economic inequalities and fraught ethnic relations.

None the less, it was a fact that the working class became proportionately less significant as middle-class occupations, comprising the growth of what is now often called 'the service class', continued to expand. The middle classes had often, though rather casually, been conceived as a stabilising influence in society, inclined to identify with their social superiors rather than to make common cause with the working classes. Did their expansion therefore signify an end to class struggle in any significant degree? In terms of Marx's economic categories, Marxists sought to examine where the middle classes fitted into processes of exploitation and surplus value, in order to license arguments that the middle classes were objectively a proletarian grouping, and that radicalisation of white-collar workers was a serious prospect (see Carchedi 1977).

## The rise of the service sector and its consequences

The rise of the 'service sector', however, is associated with other important developments: consumerism, de-industrialisation, digitisation and globalisation.

After the fall of the Labour government in 1951, British politics saw a period of conflict within the Labour Party between its 'left' (mainly based in the local constituency branches of the party) and its 'right', located in the parliamentary party and in many less militant trade unions. However, the left suffered a double defeat, for the attempt to shift power from the right to the constituencies was defused, and Labour itself lost power in 1979 to the Thatcher government. This government was, in part at least, inspired by the idea that the universities, and especially the social sciences, were guilty of cultivating a British anti-business culture that was to blame for Britain's relative economic decline. As Simon Jenkins (1995) has documented, Thatcher's programme was actually strongly centralising, but it was conducted in terms of doctrines about diminishing the role of the state and thoroughly individualising the society so as to eradicate all forms of collectivism. Thatcher's explicit politics were very much those of empowering 'the sovereign individual', which meant that power should reside in the hands of individual members of the society rather than the state. If Thatcher centralised the state, she sought to empower the sovereign individual in the form of the consumer: individuals, as consumers, should have the capacity to influence organisations through the power of choice, by being able to shift their preferences to those suppliers of goods and services who would offer them the better bargain – therefore, consumer choice should be interjected into all forms of provision, private or public. It could be achieved either by privatising public-sector organisations or by introducing analogues of market relations into those services that the state continued to provide.

The Conservative regime, led by Thatcher for the first eleven years, was not an especially popular one at any point, but the Conservatives did defeat Labour at three consecutive elections. In this period the powers of trade unions were legally limited, the showdown with the coal miners' union marking an end of major trade union militancy, and there were considerable economic contractions which resulted in high levels of unemployment and the shrinking of the industrial base, including the export of machinery abroad. The regime might have been pro-business, but it was not, in practice, necessarily pro-manufacturing, and it promoted the increasing dependence of Britain on its (economically liberalised) service industries, e.g. great efforts were made to protect the country's status as a global financial centre.

Some Marxists and sociologists viewed the Thatcher period as involving an irreversible shift of political ground; it put an end to serious working-class resistance, thereby terminally obstructing traditional leftist politics. Politics had gone 'beyond left and right' (Giddens 1994), by which title Giddens meant that the emerging politics must take a 'third way' with respect to the traditional oppositions that had demarcated left from right. Amitai Etzioni (1995), late in his long sociological career, provided some inspiration for the 'third way' with 'communitarian' views, which called for a corrective to the recent, radically individualising politics in order to recreate bonds of social solidarity. He wanted to resurrect some collectivist forms in order to provide real bases of community existence.

All proposals are very reminiscent of Durkheim's anxieties, a century before, about the lack of intermediary relations between the individual and the society (see Chapter 4).

Developments in what soon was to become 'the former Soviet Union' were also important in reconfiguring the political scene. The abrupt arrival into the 'post-communist era' was quite a surprise for most sociologists, apart from Randall Collins. According to Outhwaite and Ray (2005), not only did sociologists not foresee the disintegration of Soviet power but also, fifteen years later, they are still without any explanation for it. Francis Fukuyama in 1989 instantly declared that this disintegration was 'the end of history' (see Fukuyama 1992)! In fact, this thesis was probably even more instantly disproved than 'the end of ideology' thesis by events which quickly followed the demolition of the Berlin Wall in 1989.

## The 'end of history'

As we have seen, Hegel (Chapter 2), with the apotheosis of the state, and Lukács (Chapter 8), with the overcoming of subject and object, talked about 'the end of history'. Now Fukuyama saw that the end of history meant that the long-running struggle, the stuff of history, so to speak, concerning preferable forms of government was now over: liberal democratic regimes had inevitably triumphed over communism, and future developments would be the largely peaceful universal extension and consolidation of liberal regimes.

However, political conflict was not long in breaking out, especially over the political ambitions of fundamental Islamic elements, which Huntington (1996) quickly labelled as a clash of civilisations. Whether so or not, it was at least clear that opposition to liberal democracy was not over, and that its opponents were not prepared to go quietly.

One response to 'de-industrialisation' was to note that class certainly ceased to function as the manifest marker of public identity. Not only were there relatively fewer workers in industrial production, but also there were others not active in the labour market for such reasons as early retirement and rising levels of sickness benefits. The government changed the way of counting unemployment, perhaps to keep the figures down, but certainly to deal with the fact that a growing proportion of the population was in either long-term or even permanent withdrawal or exclusion from formally paid employment. People's identities were less and less definitively shaped by their position in 'the sphere of production', and the possibility of identifying people's class position by their physical appearance was diminishing. The basis for identity, it can be argued, used to be rooted in the sphere of production, and one's identity was dominated by one's occupation (which is why 'class' was such a powerful predictor in survey studies, since an individual's life pattern and style would follow from occupation). The basis for identity has shifted to consumption; in an affluent society people have purchasing power (obviously within limits) to possess whatever markers of identity they might prefer to buy. This shift is not from class to status, in Weberian terms, for the whole point about status groups is that the markers of their identity are not available in the market; they cannot be bought. The changing proportion between work and leisure time and the extension of affluence to more people mean that consuming takes up a greater part of their lives. In short, people's lives as consumers are much more significant to them and powerfully formative in their self-conceptions. Indeed, individuals are ever more importantly 'consumers', and their visible identity is more within their own control: they can attempt to purchase whatever is necessary to claim it.

It is generally accepted – albeit with some differences, in degree, in how far this is subscribed to – that economic class inequalities matter far less publicly in the political structure of British society than they did half a century ago, just as the working class is far less significant as a political force than it was then. Of course, there is also ample room for variation in judgement as to whether 'the UK working class' was ever as significant a force as Marxists might like to think it. After all, some scholars in the 1950s were interested in the extensive political conservatism of much of the working class (see McKenzie and Silver 1968).

Nevertheless, an ideology of consumerism as a solution to the problems of inequality, injustice and autonomy was never going to be acceptable in British sociology. Any idea that freedom to shop, even to shop for one's very identity, was the fulfilment of human potential immediately runs into the Frankfurt School-style distaste for commerce. Consequently, it meets with the response that freedom to shop does not represent relief from subordination, but merely the latest form of it. Hence notions of domination and, therefore, of inequality *in power* rapidly move to the forefront. Large-scale structures of power are still in place: the nation state – although *perhaps* now fatally beleaguered by forces of globalisation – remains the prevailing form of political organisation, and structures of political power within nation states remain in place. The capacity of people to 'have a say' in the determination of their individual and collective lives is seen as limited, but limited in the same way in which, under consumerist ideology, for example, individuals fail to recognise that their 'free' purchasing choices are in fact restricted within a pre-given framework that defines their options for them.

The critical emphasis was progressively shifting from a focus upon material impoverishment and economic exploitation to the theme of individual subjection to external shaping, certainly in part as a combative response to the idea that a sovereign individual could be realised through consumerism. The cumulative effect of the picture sketched above can seem to make the individual truly sovereign, to give those with the resources (and in an 'age of abundance', that is very many of them, at least in the Western world) huge command over their lives: all possibilities are open to them, at the click of a switch or the insertion of a credit card number. The world is a contended one in which people enjoy unparalleled freedom. However, within sociology this conclusion is apt to be seen as an ideological wish, rather than the portrayal of a reality. Rather than being a medium of autonomy, self-determination and spontaneity, consumerism is seen, rather, as a form of passivity. The ideology of consumerism emphasises the freedom of individuals to create themselves, rather than the ways in which they have already been formed as subjects by the whole infrastructure within which they live. Here Michel Foucault was crucially important in opposing the idea that control of the society stems from 'the centre', that society is held together by the coercive or hegemonic powers of the state. The 'modern individual' is the product of a whole apparatus of shaping, disciplining, supervising and controlling influences which have been largely the creation of the professional and administrative middle classes through their participation in central institutions such as educational, legal, military and medical ones. They have created an elaborate apparatus of social regulation that works with refinement in the finely detailed habituation of individual conduct. Individuals may think of themselves as free to choose, but their identity is deeply penetrated by external formative influences, meaning that they actually move only within the narrowest of socially defined spaces and, above all, that they do so with utter docility: it does not occur to them to act otherwise, to break out of the space within which their dispositions have been confined.

## Globalisation and digitisation

In the 1950s a Canadian academic had argued that the rise of electronic media – he had television in mind – would exercise decisive influence upon the overall structure of social reality, producing what he called 'an electronic global village' in which the divisions of physical distance had been shrunken to negligible significance by the near-instant nature of electronic communication. Marshall McLuhan (1962) saw the rise of television as signifying the end of 'the Gutenberg era', a period in which society had been decisively shaped by the appearance of print (Gutenberg was the inventor of effective typesetting), the shift marking a transition from a 'linear' or 'logical' way of thinking associated with the linear structure of the written text to one in which many dimensions of experience are available simultaneously. The electronic computer and the internet can be thought of as fulfilling, more decisively, McLuhan's speculations, and have encouraged further reflections on the end of an era, the end of 'the modern' period of history.

One of the consequences of digitisation, and the shrinking of distance, has been the relatively recent intensification in processes of *globalisation*.

### Globalisation

This means that the world has 'shrunk' in two respects: (1) in physical communication via huge improvements in transport, making the world closer to being a single market, especially with the drive for 'free', i.e. unrestricted, trade; (2) in electronic communications; technological developments, especially email and the web, facilitate – and even generate – trade in services as well as in goods, and again transcending national barriers. This is perhaps the intensification to final completion of the process of unification of the whole world in a single integrated system of socio-economic relations begun in the seventeenth century.

Thus the links between all societies have been extended and elaborated, not least because the diminished significance of distance has enabled manufacturing to shift from the traditionally leading capitalist economies to parts of the world where labour is cheaper, and, moreover, even many 'service' activities are being outsourced there, e.g. British railway inquiries handled in India. Similarly, the conversion of many economic relations into electronic form diminishes the significance of location. Globalisation is not, of course, to be thought of as a general and spontaneous form of development, but as one that originates in and is propelled by the traditionally capitalist and formerly colonialist societies. Business organisations have increasingly been adopting a multi-national character, losing their sense of affiliation to the interests of one nation state or another.

The nation state has been the dominant political form of the modern period since the seventeenth century and, from a Marxist point of view, it was conceived as necessary to the development of capitalism. Yet if capitalism is (once again) revolutionising its form, the nation state may be dispensable. Even from a non-Marxist point of view, the rise of multi-nationals may seem to mark a significant shift in power, with companies moving outside the control of national governments altogether, thereby divesting governments of their capacity to manage their internal economies, which has been one of the central contemporary functions of government. The nation state is also being bypassed (from below, so to speak) by the vast growth in international electronic communications, which allow individuals and organisations to communicate with one another across all boundaries, with little possibility of any effective regulation by governments, as perhaps illustrated by the collapse of the Soviet empire. The fundamental political form of the modern period is under threat, so these developments can be viewed as epoch-defining.

A key element in the movement from class to culture can be found in the Italian Marxist tradition of the 1960s and 1970s, *autonomia*, which became more influential in English-speaking countries in the 2000s with the publication of Hardt and Negri's (2001) *Empire*. In this approach, class is redefined as a broader set of relations than in conventional Marxism, the term 'multitude' being preferred (Virno 2004). The heterogeneous nature of those who materially *and culturally* are disadvantaged by capitalism – including students, housewives, the unemployed, migrants, and so on – is emphasised, and their autonomous (for themselves) struggles reconstituted as struggles against capitalist social relations. Rather than seeing class as a strictly economic position – one's relationship to ownership of the means of production – the multitude is understood as a fluid and dynamic category, which may erupt into rebellion in unexpected ways and at unexpected times, dissolving back into apparent quiescence in between. Construing contemporary capitalism as 'Empire', a Leviathan-like monster that is only held at bay by the actions of the 'multitude', Hardt and Negri attempt to reframe Marx's argument that the world is increasingly divided into two contending classes in a looser and more dynamic framework. This, however, opens up questions about whether Marx was wrong, whether things have changed since Marx wrote, and what modernity might mean. Hardt and Negri offer a convincing way of looking at the world, but what the historical limits of this way of looking are is left vague.

## Defining the epoch

Quite how the epoch is to be defined, then, is another question. Is the modern period over? Or is the epochal change drastic but remaining within the boundaries of modernity? This notion has been termed 'high modernity' by Giddens, and 'liquid modernity' by Bauman (see below). In addition to its progressive expansion and increasing penetration of all areas of social life, one of the effects of the digitisation of communications is that all kinds of social boundaries are disintegrating; everything is made available to anyone with access to the right media, more or less instantly, at the click of a switch. Some see these developments, as we mention below, as requiring no more than an updating of Marx: digitisation is only the bearer of the final expansion of commodification, of converting everything into things that can be bought or sold. Digitisation has now made possible the thoroughgoing conversion of information into the commodity form. An early book on the idea of the postmodern was called, in a direct quotation from Marx, *All That Is Solid Melts into Air* (Berman 1983), a reference to the way in which commodity relations dissolve fixed and lasting social demarcations, releasing and making available their hallmarks to anyone with the purchasing power. 'High modernity' emphasises the increasing erosion of all vestiges of tradition, i.e. de-traditionalisation, and 'liquid modernity' points to increasing fluidity of social forms, their mutable and transient character.

It is *the depth* of ideological penetration that is the progressively implicated conclusion of such arguments: so intricate, detailed and thorough is the ideological constitution of the whole life of individuals that it becomes meaningless to think that there can be head-on confrontation with ideology, that one can mount a non-ideological view of the world to oppose an ideological one. None the less, it is possible to become aware – raise consciousness, in another phraseology – of the extent to which social existence is ideologically saturated, to recognise the manner in which things are ideological, to attenuate their manipulative reach by exposing their presence, but resistance to their domination acquires more of a negative character, one of refusing, evading or subverting ideology's pretended neutrality, objectivity or necessity (wherever one can). No longer does ideology seem an obstacle to objective understanding of reality, for the very idea of objective understanding is itself increasingly seen as an ideology that sustains, rather than dissolves, the critical task. Hence, *the* political task has become that of bringing to light the infusion of ideology throughout the culture, down to its very finest details. It involves throwing out the old, hallowed distinction between high and low culture and focusing on the critique of ideological schemes embedded both in the culture's most respected artefacts and in its most populist ones. Critical attention is directed to the ways in which 'the consumer' passively self-regulates through the ingestion of the ideological presuppositions which are incorporated in the branding of their sportswear, or the episodes of favoured soaps; in short, into the very fabric of language itself (e.g. Fairclough 1992).

As part of this movement, the conception of ideology itself has been shifting, so that its primal form is no longer seen as being that of the (misleading) doctrines and theories that people have about reality. Instead, it moves towards a conception of ideology that is being built into the seemingly non-doctrinal and non-theoretical ways in which people talk about reality in their everyday discourses. Ideology is built into the classificatory terms that people unreflectively employ as though they provided the only natural terms in which to identify features of the world. For sociologists, critique of ideology becomes increasingly critique of classification, a matter of undermining the idea of a unique, immutable and essential demarcation of things into an eternal – and, essentially, hierarchical – order. Frameworks of classification are to be understood as socially provided and entirely conventional in character; they offer only one (of many) possible ways of classifying things; they put them together on a basis that suits the needs of the enframing social organisation rather than reflecting divisions inherently natural to things themselves. Furthermore, such classifications do not necessarily capture real divisions at all; they are understood to be often in conflict with reality itself. They seem to provide a grid showing an orderly division among things, but on closer examination are revealed to give a false impression of fit, which only seems to apply because features are *forcibly* brought under its schemes, because natural diversity, heterogeneity and irregularity are suppressed. In these ways the hierarchical valuation of some over others is reinforced.

This shift in the conception of ideology was interwoven with the development of a politics increasingly focused upon relations between social categories and the oppressive role of social separation. The idea of a society tending towards a polarisation between two internally uniform and solidary classes in reciprocal opposition was giving way to an emphasis on cultural diversity, on what is now often called the multi-cultural character of the working classes. The traditional Marxist idea of ethnic differences as providing a distraction from the unity of interest within people in equivalent proletarian positions was replaced by the idea of social categories such as gender or ethnicity as authentic sources of identity. Hitherto, differences and relations had been – falsely – represented as unique, eternal and natural and, as we have seen, in a hierarchical fashion. The counter-campaign was to establish equivalence of value among different social categories, to deny that there were essential differences that distinguished men from women, or the members of one ethnic group from another, or that identified heterosexual practices as being especially in accord with nature (see Chapter 15).

An overall conclusion – though not universally accepted – was that the social preconditions of 'modern thought' were disintegrating, and that the *artificial* structure of modern thought was becoming increasingly so apparent as to ensure that its most fundamental presuppositions would lose their hold. The centrepiece to modern thought was the assumption that it had captured the single and essential nature of reality itself, an assumption that sustained the presence and achievements of science itself. The nature of scientific thought provides by far the most explicit and thorough exhibition of what form a grasp upon reality takes – must take. Science works towards one single, relentlessly thorough, thoroughly unified, all-embracing point of view. Indeed, its most advanced contemporary strivings are towards the appropriately named 'theory of everything'.

Critical attention did remain on the way in which scientific findings might be connected with the interests of, say, employers rather than employees, but its focus intensified on the very idea of scientific rationality itself. The extension of scientific rationality to all aspects of society's affairs had long been thought to be the hallmark and primary ambition of 'modern' societies. Science provides the only and final word on reality, and the constituents of its thoughts must therefore be divisions that are permanent, intrinsic, unvarying, essential and rigorously separated. Science thereby unites everyone within a single, global rationality. Disillusionment with science grew after the 1960s, not least because of the association of physics with the creation of the atomic bomb, and, as the idea of critical sociology unfolded, critics were quick to notice that the unifying rationality is only the other face of exclusion, i.e. rationality is denied to whole categories of other people, e.g. women and the members of non-Western societies had long been regarded as irrational. The idea of scientific rationality as reflecting the very nature of things began to seem less persuasive than the thought that it reflected, rather, the priorities of its social setting. It is the production of a nation state unified around a single, central, authoritative and controlling point of view that governs attempts to establish the wide-reaching and deeply penetrating standardisation of social practices and the uniformity of individuals.

The nation state is seen as associated with the attempt to impose itself – through imperialism – upon the whole world. Characteristically, through subordination, violence and suppression both at home and abroad, it seeks to eliminate all those who do not fit with the demands of the (political and intellectual) centre – a single, centralised framework upon the whole world. The treatment of scientific rationality as an artefact of a potentially dissolving modern form of social organisation suggests that thought itself might also be entering a postmodern period and that, therefore, the kinds of theoretical developments we will be looking at are themselves products of these changing social conditions.

## Conclusion

The events of the 2000s, while transformative in many spheres, have had little impact on the tendencies outlined in this chapter. The al-Qaeda-sponsored attacks on the World Trade Center in New York in 2001, and subsequent wars in Afghanistan and Iraq, have dominated approaches to international relations, questions about the legitimacy of governments, and debates about the relationships between globalisation (in particular the supply of oil) and the nation state. Such issues, however, have tended to be folded into existing claims about the 'clash of civilisations', and pro- and anti-globalisation theoretical tropes.

Anti-globalisation protests in the 1990s and 2000s, across much of the Western world – often organised to coincide with international summits – also generally failed to move beyond these debates. At the thirty-first G8 summit in Gleneagles, Scotland, in July 2005, for instance, these issues were played out in dramatic fashion. Commitments to reduce African nations' levels of debt were made, and rapidly shown to be tied to privatisation of state provision – or even simply new presentations of already existing pledges. Agreements on key issues, such as global warming, could not be reached because individual leaders, acting in apparently national interests, blocked them. Meanwhile, while the summit was going on, a series of co-ordinated suicide bombings occurred in London (the day after that city won the bid to stage the 2012 Olympic Games). In Scotland itself, opposition to the G8 was strong but diffuse. Some non-governmental organisations were allowed to take part in the summit deliberations. Others organised a somewhat ridiculous pop concert to raise awareness of the issues being debated. Others attempted to blockade the conference venue and disrupt the proceedings altogether. Each set of protesters debated the pro- and anti-globalisation issues, peaceful versus violent strategies, and so on, reproducing the debates playing out in the summit itself and those outlined in this chapter.

The global financial crises of 2007 onwards equally failed to move the terms of reference onwards. Duncombe's (2007) badly timed but well-meant book *Dream* outlined the issues: politicians and policy-makers increasingly came to hold the opinion that 'reality' was something they shaped and determined. The wars in Afghanistan and Iraq did not require justification by facts, because what counted as 'fact' was itself determined by those doing the justification. Duncombe was horrified but drawn by this development: why, he asked, had progressive political forces not engaged with this new, plastic, approach to defining the nature of the world? Why should imagination be restricted to those pursuing conservative, reactionary, policies? The publication of the text at the same time the world financial system collapsed, leading to years of stagnation and a confused (to say the least) policy response, was unfortunate. Nevertheless, Duncombe's point stands: nearly ten years later there is little in conventional sociological thought that has moved radically beyond the debates of the 1990s, and those who administer the world have similarly failed to rethink the assumptions they were working on at the turn of the millennium. The rise of 'emancipatory' forms of sociology, discussed in the next chapter, appears to be a sign of this stagnation coming to an end.

## Questions

1  Taking the criticisms levelled at Parsons in Chapter 5, and the work of Mills and his followers, to what extent have his original ideas survived? Which criticisms are 'fair' and which misrepresent his ideas? Is Parsons a scapegoat or a villain?

2  What is 'globalisation'? Why might some forms of social theory be better than others in understanding it? Which theoretical perspectives are least useful? Does that mean they are wrong? How does the concept of globalisation trade on, and differ from, Marx's ideas about the spread of capitalism or Weber's about rationalisation and bureaucracy?

3  Is there a native British sociology? Which ideas in the British tradition come from America? Which come from other parts of Europe? Is this a problem?

4  What is 'the end of history'? How does this differ from the 'postmodern condition'? How would Hegel and Fukuyama construe this era? Which, if either, is right and why?

What empirical examples can you think of that would support either of their positions?

5  Has Marxism died? What are the implications of this for British and American sociology? Have the financial crisis and other contemporary social and economic developments reasserted the economic basis of social life?

6  What is 'cultural Marxism'? How is it different to other developments in Marxian thought? How does it relate to ideology? To what extent does it parallel critical theory arguments about the culture industry? What are its implications for the study of other social phenomena?

7  Is the individual now finally finished as a concept? To what extent are the developments outlined in this chapter attempts to reassert 'traditional' sociological views against the threat of postmodernism? How do they relate to the theories outlined in the preceding chapter? Have sociological theory and sociological practice now become detached from one another? Is this a new development or has it always been the case?

## Next steps

The tendencies described in this chapter are rather diffuse. A flavour of the debates can best be found in Berman (1983) and Etzioni's (1995) collection of papers. Pierce (1989) is a good statement of the radical possibilities opened up by Durkheim's thought.

Huntington (1996) is a controversial account of the 'clash of civilisations' hypothesis, while Outhwaite and Ray (2005) provide a clear overview of the theoretical responses to the social changes of the 1980s and 1990s respectively.

## CHAPTER FIFTEEN

# Emancipatory sociology: stratification beyond class?

## Chapter overview

Sociology has always had a complex relationship to radical social movements, and to social change. Debates about the validity of Durkheim's or Parsons's works often centre on their alleged 'conservatism', for example. The changes in social thought and social organisation outlined in the last chapter have led to changes in the ways social change and radicalism are understood, however. The movement away from class analysis has favoured 'identity politics', wherein non-class categories (gender, sexuality, ethnicity, and so on) are frequently seen as more salient to political and social change than they were in the past. Theories based on these kinds of identities typically go through three phases: 'inclusionist' (emphasising the equivalence of dominant and subordinate identities), 'separationist' (emphasising the differences between these identities) and 'transgressive' (emphasising the porous nature of identity boundaries and disrupting them). These phases are used to organise a discussion of three important forms of emancipatory sociology: feminist sociology, queer theory and postcolonialism.

## Introduction: social theory as emancipation

In this chapter we consider so-called 'emancipatory social theories': feminism, queer theory and postcolonial theory. We refer to these as social theories, rather than 'sociological theories', to mark the fact, noted in earlier chapters, that conventional disciplinary boundaries are increasingly viewed as artificial, limiting and redundant. Indeed, leading thinkers in all three branches of emancipatory theory are as likely to be formally associated with disciplines such as philosophy, English or history as with sociology. Furthermore, as we will show, the transgression of boundaries, intellectual as well as social, is a central theme and strategy of contemporary emancipatory theorising. Indeed, theorists wish to emancipate us not only from disciplines, but also from the traditional distinction between 'pure' and 'applied' theory. Since these approaches focus around specific categories of social actors and the social features that define those categories, they might be described as 'applied theory'. The categories in question include women, gays and lesbians, racial and ethnic minorities in Western nations, and the inhabitants of the 'developing world', this last designation being condemned as an expression of patronising and hierarchical prejudice. Furthermore, these theories are committed to the cause of the category that the theory concerns; they are designed to emancipate the occupants of these categories, if not from the categories themselves, then from all unnecessary impositions upon them as women, gays or other 'minorities' that result from the social regulation of the categorisation of people in society. Nevertheless, the theorists whose ideas we will be discussing would emphatically reject the label of applied theory. It is their view that moving these categories to the centre of the sociological stage involves reorienting social inquiry around a new set of master themes: gender, sexuality, and 'race' and ethnicity. Furthermore, this move is meant to be nothing less than a paradigm shift, involving new ways of thinking about the very nature of sociology, even though, as we shall see, their line of thought follows from, owes much to and elaborates upon selected strategies of critical theory. The emergence of this kind of emancipatory theorising reflects the sidelining of social class as a single, central axis of injustice.

The emergence of new master themes of gender, sexuality, race and ethnicity in contemporary theory is therefore seen as representing much more than simply the creation of new substantive topics for social science to investigate. What is being argued for by emancipatory social theories is not just the addition of new topics but a different conception of sociology as a form of inquiry, one in which empirical inquiry is to be subsumed within a larger moral and political project of *emancipation*. It is in these developments that the politicisation of sociology we have made reference to in earlier chapters is most thoroughly carried through. Theory and politics are symbiotic here: the point of theory is not detached understanding but informed action; the test of a theory is its capacity to shape effective action.

## Praxis

In Chapter 2, we saw that Marx argued that philosophers had to do more than understand the world: they had to change it. Theory was practical, i.e. the notion of 'praxis'.

It may seem hard to reconcile this conception of theory with the notion of sociology as an academic discipline, but for many contemporary sociologists there is no contradiction here, and a direct affiliation with Marx's views on the unity of theory and practice is easily discerned. The argument is again, as it was in the 1960s, that sociology has always been and cannot avoid being political, that any appearance of 'objective neutrality' is only a top dressing which conceals ideological, hegemonic and oppressive functions. The crucial, indeed the only, question is: what kind of politics should sociological inquiry serve?

To refer to such a change as 'applied theory' therefore misses its significance for those who promote emancipatory sociologies, since this label suggests that

(1) action is subservient to and follows from prior knowledge; and (2) sociology has an agreed body of systematic knowledge about society, from which can be derived explanations pertaining to specific social groups and the relations between them. They precisely deny this label, and regard the very work of theorising as itself a combative, disruptive assault upon the categories that the wider society is apt to treat as given and fixed.

As we have seen, sociology since the 1960s has been marked by increasing theoretical disagreement and fragmentation, from which the moral could be drawn that sociology, conceived as a systematic and rigorous form of inquiry generating comprehensive knowledge of society, has failed. It has been exposed (by the Frankfurt School among others) as little more than an ideological fig leaf for an oppressive capitalist status quo. Sociology's pretensions to provide a disinterested, objective analysis of social life have been exposed as a sham and its theories are revealed as serving political and moral purposes. Sociology is an intellectual prop for a society in which social inequality and oppression are not incidental and remediable, but, rather, are deeply and ubiquitously entwined throughout the social order. As a result of this critique the rationale for doing sociology has to change. No longer is it about building a 'scientific' understanding of society; now the point of doing sociology is to challenge the forms of oppression. By constructing a theoretical analysis of their sources, resistance to prevailing understandings, categories and practices can be both produced and further promoted. Consequently, both those who are the victims of ideologically engendered oppression *and* those who are ideologically motivated into oppressing others can be emancipated from the misconceptions which lead them to think of certain kinds of people, e.g. gays, women, blacks, as essentially different and inferior.

## From class politics to identity politics

These arguments are not new, of course. As our reference to the Frankfurt School suggests, the critique of social science taken up by the 'new' emancipatory social theories was inherited in large measure from the 'old' one: Marxism. We have suggested in earlier chapters that recent developments in sociological theory are best understood in terms of their relationship to ideas preceding them and from which they take inspiration. This is especially true of the emancipatory sociologies. It is no coincidence that the decline of Marxism as a direct intellectual and political force, which we discussed at length in the previous chapter, roughly coincided with the rise of these sociologies. As the direct influence of Marxian theory receded and the class structure of Western societies was seen as increasingly fragmented, the desire for a politically engaged, radical sociology has attempted to retain much of Marxism's radical thrust but, as we noted earlier, has turned towards Weberian categories. For example, the idea of 'status groups' (if not necessarily the term) has replaced 'class' as the vehicle of critical social thought. With this turn, the oppressive character of Western societies was now to be reconceptualised in terms of what are often called 'minority groups' such as those of gender, sexuality, race and ethnicity, rather than class, the distinction of and discrimination against these groups being a matter of social exclusion rather than economic subordination.

## Identity politics

This shift from class to minority groups is sometimes described by referring to a change from *class* politics to *identity* politics.

Nevertheless, Marxism provided much of the logical infrastructure of the reasoning involved, and while most practitioners of these sociologies would not identify themselves as Marxists, as we shall see, the figure of Marx continues to loom large in the background.

Less obviously, perhaps, these developments are also preoccupied with a very Durkheimian theme, that of demarcation in terms of social boundaries. Although we have just mentioned Weber, the shift from class to identity politics is more usefully understood as a change from a predominantly Marxian radicalism to a fundamentally Durkheimian one. This suggestion might seem odd, since Durkheim was, was he not, the leading advocate of that conception of sociology as the empirical science of society whose rejection is fundamental to the emancipatory critique? Yet there is another dimension to Durkheim's ideas that has direct relevance to the notion of sociology as emancipatory inquiry, and to the 'identity politics' version of that view specifically, namely, his view of society as a moral order. As we saw in Chapter 4, for Durkheim, society is defined by shared moral sentiments among its members. What makes an individual a member of society is that he or she is accepted as such by others, perceived as part of the moral community. Social membership thus is a matter of moral boundaries; those individuals seen as possessing 'normal', positively valued identities are accepted within the social boundary while those who are not (Durkheim's leading example is criminals, you will remember) are treated as outside the boundary, conceived as diminished, abnormal creatures, denied full membership of society, and made the subject of moral sanctions. For Durkheim, of course, the maintenance of such moral boundaries was essential to the stable operation of society; by 'policing' them, society sustains its moral coherence, but it does so by, in a later jargon, 'demonising' those it excludes.

But what if, instead of viewing things from the point of view of society, as Durkheim does, one takes the viewpoint of those who are defined as unacceptable and less than fully social and therefore are socially excluded? Here one can see something of the rationale for the shift to 'identity politics': social boundaries relate to the way in which people think of themselves and others, and those who belong to 'society' in Durkheim's account think of themselves as right and proper people, unlike those reviled and degraded people who live beyond the conventional boundaries. Those who are socially excluded are assumed, in Durkheim's scheme, to accept society's definition of them as lesser, undesirable beings. We can also see here the origins of the idea of 'the Other', as those on whom proper members of society can project their fears and hostilities and, by dissociating from 'the Other', can reassure themselves of their own rectitude.

However, if one begins to look at social exclusion from the point of view of those who are excluded, it might seem that they are no longer understood as excluded because of their intrinsic, distinctive and *inferior* natures (labelling theory ideas are echoed), but only for socially functional reasons. There is no reason why society's 'outsiders' should accept society's definition of their nature, of who they are. From that viewpoint the moral boundaries imposed by the majority are likely to be experienced as wholly arbitrary; exclusion from the institutions of the society is unwarranted and oppressive, since only those points on which the excluded differ are emphasised and all those respects in which the excluded are just like the rest of us are denied. The identities upon which such exclusion is based will be regarded as things to be resisted, and alternative identities will be championed in their place, ones that reverse the moral definitions involved. What is defined by the majority as discreditable or repugnant will be redefined as worthy and desirable, while what the majority regard as normal will be scorned. The moral boundaries of society are to be challenged at every opportunity. Transgressing those boundaries becomes a positive political act.

There arises, too, a need to rewrite entirely the understanding of society's relations and histories in order to subvert the idea that 'society' was ever really more than the partial view of 'mainstream' (or in feminist condemnations, 'malestream') or 'conventional' people, one which sidelined, ignored, suppressed and denied those it selected, overriding their will and making them serve as its 'Other'. Re-examination of social life without these 'mainstream' conceptions will show that the literatures of orthodox sociology, history and the humanities have all thoroughly misrepresented the actual situation, have intolerably exaggerated the evidence for the superiority of men, of Western reason, of heterosexuals and so on.

Given this spin on Durkheimian preoccupations, it is not surprising that the concept of identity figures large in the programmes of emancipatory sociologies, hence the kind of politics they presuppose is, as already noted, often characterised as 'identity politics'. Gender, sexuality, race and ethnicity have all served in their various ways to constitute the principal 'Others' against whom both the dominant elements in Western society and their academic accomplices have defined themselves. The adequate theorisation of these identities will expose fundamental truths about such societies and will show that what have previously been taken as such are merely lies, thereby releasing some people from misconceptions and others from oppression based on those misconceptions. That, at least, is the hope and intention of emancipatory sociologists, whether they be feminists, queer theorists or postcolonial theorists. The key question, of course, is what is to count as 'adequate theorisation'?

## Three phases of emancipatory theorising

Although feminism, queer theory and postcolonial theory are distinct, most notably in the identities they respectively accent, they are united by a common theoretical thread and display a similar pattern of intellectual development. Therefore, the following account of the emancipatory social theories will present that development as consisting in three phases, marked by different takes on the Durkheimian theme of the relations between dominant, morally affirmed identities and subordinate, morally denied ones, and different portrayals of the processes of boundary creation, enforcement and transgression that define the relations between these identities. In the *first phase*, which we will call the 'inclusionist' phase, theory emphasises the moral equivalence and social congruence of dominant and subordinate identities. The central task of emancipatory theory is to critique societal ideologies and institutions that police a rigid moral boundary between these identities and thus devalue and dehumanise the subordinated ones. Emancipatory theory in this phase is driven by a concern to break down the barriers between identities, in order to promote social and moral equalisation. It does so by making a strong appeal to *empirical facts*. The exclusion of subordinate identities from the society's major institutions is shown to be arbitrary and unjustified, based on assumptions that have no factual foundation. Typically, the authority of science is invoked to substantiate the conclusion that the characteristics attributed to these identities by dominant groups are false and ideological. A more scientific understanding of society's structures will reveal their skewed nature and provide the platform for their reform.

A shift towards a more radical politics, rejecting the reformism of the inclusionist approach, marks the emergence of the *second phase* of theorising, which we will call 'separationist'. Emphasis is now on the *differences* between identities, and opposition to majority values. Inclusionism is critiqued for its acceptance of mainstream conceptions of the subordinated category, which is now condemned as 'Uncle Tom-ism'. There can be no genuine incorporation of the values and interests of the subordinated category, only a false accommodation that will inevitably result in their re-absorption into the moral and social 'slavery' of marginalised category membership.

Resistance demands that they are recognised as a morally and socially autonomous group, with its own independent, distinct and authentic values and interests. This group is conceived in terms of an *ethnic* model; in other words, the members of the category are viewed as forming a community in its own right, separate from the communities formed around other categories, e.g. heterosexual ones. The foundation of this autonomy is said to be the uniquely shared experience of the subordinated category's members, which sets them apart from all who do not possess the identity and, therefore, cannot possibly share that experience. Adequate understanding of such experience is only possible 'from within'; that is, by those who share the category identity and the experiential realm conjoining it. All attempts to theorise 'from outside' the properties of this realm and the relations of those who share it are doomed to failure; such attempts can never be more than an oppressive imposition of alien ideologies upon the category's members. Separationists (in line with an increasingly sceptical culture) question the impartiality of science, arguing that what passes for neutral, objective scientific knowledge is the product of partial assumptions and skewed methods. Therefore, autonomy demands the creation of a separate 'successor' science.

The separationist approach supports a politics of withdrawal from and confrontation with mainstream society and its institutions. However, such a politics is easier to theorise than to put into practice. The difficulties reflect those postulated by much critical theory, namely, that one cannot alter society by frag-mentary reform – or piecemeal social engineering, as Karl Popper (1957) termed it – but only through the transformation of the whole. Refusal to work within mainstream institutions tends to have the effect of leaving power in the hands of the oppressors, since autonomy is never more than partially achievable. There-fore, as a programme of practical politics, separationism fails to attract large-scale support among the subordinated category's members. The relative failure of the separationist approach motivates a critique of its theoretical assumptions and the quest for a more nuanced theory, one that can inform a broader-based politics.

The outcome is a further shift, this time towards a 'transgressive' phase of emancipatory theory. In this *third phase* the reality of boundaries as fixed and stable entities is thrown into question; theory emphasises their fragility and impermanence. Boundaries may appear firm, but this appearance is illusory since it simply reflects the paucity of trangressive responses. Once pressure is put upon those boundaries then their less-than-definite, provisional and ephem-eral character is shown up. The locations (i.e. identities) marked out by such boundaries have no solidity rooted in reality itself; they endure only so long as they are *worked at*. The emancipatory project becomes one of demonstrating the porous nature of all boundaries by transgressing them at every opportunity and in all conceivable ways (much of this being done through the use of disrup-tive artistic forms).

In terms of critique, the emancipatory theorist, by giving up any notion of a fixed point from which to survey society, forgoes any foundation that can under-pin a critical distancing. There is no magic bullet; rather than a single direct refutation of the general logic of oppressive representation and practice, innu-merable, multifarious, 'localised' tactical and pragmatic acts of subversion must be pursued. Earlier separationist ideas are now condemned as 'essentialist'. The idea of autonomy assumes a uniformity of identity among the members of the subordinated category, and clear-cut boundaries between their and oth-ers' identities, thereby buying too much into dominant thinking. Both assump-tions are now rejected. It is emphasised that identities are not 'objects' with an inherent nature independent of and prior to linguistic representation (as presup-posed by separationist theory); rather, they are purely linguistic constructions. Poststructuralism has preached that language involves no intrinsic meaning or stable references, only those that can be fixed in the specific circumstances of occasions of linguistic use. Hence the very notion of identity as something fixed and determinable is undermined; identity exists only in its use, exists only where it can situationally be 'made to stick'. There is nothing enduring 'behind' that use to give it solidity and permanence. If reality *is* language, there can be no other reality underpinning language and no 'subject' who is the 'master' of the language, and who imparts definitive meaning to speech.

It also follows that separationism's critique of science did not go far enough, since the notion of a successor science retains the assumption of stable objects to make up the subject matter about which such a science can generalise. Yet if nothing is ever really fixed, if the boundaries that define identities are by their very nature fluid and subject to continual change, then there is nothing for there to be a science of. In political terms the denial of fixed boundaries opens the way to the formation of alliances among members of different subordinated categories. The denial of the subject means that anyone is free to collaborate with anyone else, based on a purely pragmatic and highly specific calculus of common interests. As a result, resistance to oppression increasingly takes the form of 'rainbow alliances' created in response to immediate issues and local priorities.

In the remainder of this chapter we fill out this schematic account of the common pattern of emancipatory social theories, with brief histories of feminist theory, queer theory and postcolonial thought. Since feminist sociology is the most long-standing and influential of the emancipatory sociologies, we will discuss it first and at greatest length, dealing with queer theory and postcolonial theory more concisely.

## The rise of feminist sociology

The emergence in the 1960s of the women's liberation movement as a significant political force had major consequences for sociology. Women's liberation sought to expose the patriarchal nature of society and make women aware – raise their consciousness – of their oppression. The key task was to encourage women to see themselves as an oppressed group, with a shared fate and common interest in resisting their oppression. Feminism's critique of society as patriarchal, involving domination of the institutions of society by men, and the systematic exclusion of women from socially significant roles, was accompanied by the rallying cry: 'the personal is the political'. This slogan captures what was distinctive about women's liberation as a social and political movement. The path to liberation begins with the realisation that every aspect of a woman's life is dictated by a male-dominated social order. To accept traditional views of 'a woman's place' is to acquiesce in the general oppression of women as a group. Women should no longer accept the idea that 'biology is destiny' and that their social position 'naturally' results from biological differences from men. The roles and activities assigned to them are not an inescapable result of those biological differences, and women should recognise how their ordinary lives, in many different ways, manifest and sustain their subordination to men. Therefore, resistance begins with decisions to change one's own life, since if women can change their lives, patriarchy will disintegrate.

Consequently, women's liberation as a movement was characterised less by mass demonstrations and political lobbying, though these occurred, and more by the involvement of women in consciousness-raising groups. From the beginning, however, it was realised that practical action alone, whether in the form of consciousness-raising or more conventional political protest activities, was not enough. If the feminist cause was to tackle the social and intellectual edifices of patriarchal society then practical action required theoretical underpinning. Feminism, it was believed, needed a theory of gender and society that could show how a radically different arrangement between the sexes was possible. In the 1970s and 1980s feminist sociologists took up this task.

## Feminist theory: the first phase

The development of feminist social theory exemplifies the three phases of emancipatory theory outlined above. In the first phase, the issues taken up initially involved challenging conventional sociological accounts of women and demonstrating the arbitrariness of women's exclusion. This meant, among other things, documenting the 'absence' of women from sociology's conception of society. Orthodox sociological analysis emphasised as central to society institutions monopolised by men, such as the economy and polity, while the importance of institutions in which women played a central role, such as the family, was downplayed. It was pointed out that the analysis of modern society, to be found in the classical writings of Marx, Weber and Durkheim, laid stress on features such as authority, rationality, calculation and self-interest, features that were characteristic of 'public' institutions rather than the 'private' realm in which women made their principal contributions to social life. It was not simply that the contribution of women was rarely mentioned in the writings of the 'founding fathers'; 'society' was thought of as consisting only in things that men did, and, in rare discussions of women, they were usually defined as less fully 'social' creatures – more 'natural' – than men. For example, Durkheim, in line with a view widely held in the nineteenth century, spoke of women's contribution to society as primarily determined by their biological nature. Women, he claimed, are '*to a far greater extent the product of nature*'. Men, on the other hand, could overcome the constraints of biology and play a fully social role; they are '*almost entirely the product of society*'.

Feminists derided this view of women, seeing it as an ideological construction that served the function of legitimating sexual inequality. Feminist social theory took what we now refer to as a 'social constructionist' perspective, based on a posited distinction between 'sex' and 'gender'. The former is a pre-social, biological fact; individuals are usually, but not always, born with either male or female sexual organs. This natural fact, however, has no *necessary* connection with the way men and women are defined and perceived as members of society. This latter phenomenon, *gender*, is socially created. Simone de Beauvoir in *The Second Sex*, an early feminist classic, posed the question 'What is a woman?' Her answer, affirmed by subsequent feminist thinkers, is that womanhood is not a 'natural' outcome of female biology, but the product of social and historical forces that have shaped society along patriarchal lines. De Beauvoir was arguably the first social constructionist feminist thinker, though she did not, of course, use that terminology. She argued that the characteristics of 'womanhood' and 'femininity', taken by many to be natural in origin, were acquired through social learning, beginning at birth and continuing through childhood and adulthood. This view became accepted wisdom within the feminist movement. 'Women', as they are socially defined and perceived, are the result of processes of socialisation embedded in the institutions of patriarchal society, especially the family. That members of society routinely treat sex and gender as one and the same, thereby regarding women as 'naturally' different from men, is a feature of that kind of society – patriarchal society – in which women are systematically subordinated to men.

In such a society, attitudes towards women meet the criteria Durkheim laid down for a 'social fact' – they are universal, context-independent and constraining – and so are no less social facts than others studied by him. Consequently, much feminist work was concerned to document the socio-historical processes that had produced women's 'gendered' role in society. Other writers (e.g. Mitchell 1974) turned to psychoanalysis, in order to construct an explanation of the psychological construction of gendered identities. In a move that mirrors Parsons's use of Freud to theorise the process of 'identification' by which individuals become socialised, normatively competent actors, feminists sought to explain the formation of gender identity. However, the feminist view of psychoanalysis was ambivalent. On the one hand, Freudian theories themselves, with their emphasis upon the Oedipal character of infantile social development, were critiqued as reflecting patriarchal assumptions. On the other, an appropriately revised psychoanalysis held out the prospect of explaining the psychological mechanisms by which deeply rooted gender identities were created and experienced as compelling and necessary. Knowledge of such mechanisms could point to how such identities could be transformed.

## The debate over the family and domestic work

The political significance of the argument that gender is distinct from sex and is a social and historical product is clear: if gender is a construction of social and historical processes then it can be changed by such processes. Women's exclusion from society's major institutions has no objective basis and can be reversed. Furthermore, a reassessment of the institutions in which women are prominent might show these institutions, and the roles women play in them, to possess a quite different significance from that previously recognised. Thus feminist sociology critique argued for an alternative analysis of social institutions, redefining the activities of women and thereby recognising their importance to society. The key issue here was the nature of the modern family and the status of women's domestic activities. Parsons (1942) and other functionalist sociologists had argued that the 'nuclear family' had evolved around a biologically based division of labour between men and women. The structural basis for this division lay in the dual function of the family. On the one hand, the family provided physical and social support for society's workforce. The economy requires a motivated and emotionally adjusted body of social actors able to meet the demands that economic roles place upon them, involving 'universalistic' and impersonal norms of conduct and the maintenance of emotional neutrality. The family guarantees this motivation and adjustment by providing workers with an intimate, highly personal setting in which social relations are based on emotion, and the norms associated with the workplace are lifted and replaced by particularistic standards. The family's second function, according to the orthodox analysis, is to provide for the continuity of society through the raising of children. It constitutes a social environment in which children are cared for and socialised so that they internalise social values and develop a sense of social identity.

The identity that children develop through primary socialisation in the family is gendered, reflecting the sex role division between husbands and wives.

The two functions of the family are reflected in this sex role division, since men fulfil the externally oriented, 'instrumental' role that links the family with the world of work and the wider society, while women fulfil the internally oriented, 'expressive' role of managing the social relations within the family.

Feminists rejected this functionalist analysis of the family as nothing more than an ideological justification for women's domestic servitude (though Parsons himself had – in the 1940s – pointed to what he called 'strains' in the structural position of the American family which made the position of domestic servitude very unsatisfying to women and consequently unstable). The alleged symmetry of family roles between men and women was a sham, since men as workers determined the social and economic resources available to the family and therefore the social status and life chances of its members. So long as the activities of women as wives and mothers were defined as purely expressive and internal they would always be devalued by comparison with men's world of work and 'public affairs'. Social status is primarily defined by position in the occupational structure, and since most women had no 'occupation' but were 'only housewives', their status was diminished (again all echoing points that Parsons identified in his analysis).

It was for this reason, of course, that radical feminists advocated complete rejection of marriage and the family and preached a doctrine of 'women-only' social relations. But some feminist sociologists took a different line, seeking not to abandon women's family role but redefine it, hugely emphasising the point that women's household contribution involved *work*, no less than did the male's participation in an occupation. The 'domestic labour debate' (Barker and Allen 1976; Tilly and Scott 1978), as it became known, dominated much feminist theorising in the 1970s and was concerned to de-trivialise the work that women do in the home. The goal was to conceive women's domestic work as productive, *theoretically equivalent* to paid work done mainly by men, and therefore demanding recognition as labour and part of the economy of society. After all, cooking, cleaning, tidying, washing, ironing and so forth are physical work and can be quite arduous at that. There were several possible objections to this feminist conception. The first and most obvious is that housewives are not formally employed; they are not recognised in any official sense as part of the economic workforce and are not paid. Feminists replied that it was the patriarchal assumptions underpinning these facts that were in dispute. They turned the functional analysis against itself and argued that, regardless of the lack of societal recognition accorded domestic labour, the economy could not operate without the work women do. Marxist-leaning feminists argued that the Marxian concept of labour should be extended, since 'the housewife works for the maintenance of capitalism rather than simply being a worker for her family' (Glazer-Malbin 1976: 919). In other words, industrial capitalism can only operate as it does if there is someone doing the unpaid work that enables the paid worker to turn up fed, clothed and otherwise cared for.

Another argument concerned the meaning of women's domestic work. It could be argued, for example, that women viewed housework in a quite different way to the instrumental attitude of workers doing paid work in the economy. In line with the functionalist analysis of the family, it might be thought that women, as wives and mothers, derive expressive satisfaction from housework.

They might not regard it as 'work' at all, but simply as a means to express their emotional commitment to their husband and children, literally a 'labour of love'. In countering this argument a key text was Oakley's *The Sociology of Housework* (1974), one of the first sociological studies to investigate empirically women's domestic activities. Oakley interviewed forty 'housewives' and reported that very few of them invested housework with positive emotional meaning. Jobs like ironing, washing up and cleaning were regarded negatively, as 'chores' that had to be done and from which no intrinsic satisfaction was derived. Anything that could be done to reduce the physical labour involved and alleviate the tedium of such tasks was grasped at, hence the demand for domestic devices like vacuum cleaners, washing machines and dishwashers. Oakley argues that for most women housework is viewed in a broadly similar emotionally neutral way to that associated with paid work.

## The second phase: feminist standpoint theory

The main direction of feminist sociology up to the mid-1970s was inclusionist and 'corrective', in the sense that studies mainly were concerned with exposing and correcting the gendered omissions and misrepresentations of sociology. The aim was to 'bring women back in', to adapt a phrase of George Homans, i.e. to represent more adequately the contribution they made to social life and insist on their full membership in society. But a more radical, separationist feminism overtook this approach. We refer here not simply to the radical politics that advocated women's *practical* disengagement from patriarchal society, such as the setting up of women-only communes and the rejection of heterosexual relations. Congruent with these political moves was an intellectual shift towards a separationist social theory. The inclusionist approach assumes that 'adding' women to the sociological picture can rectify the gendered misrepresentations of sociology. For many feminists, this approach did not address the fundamental issue: sociology itself is the product of, and reflects, patriarchal society. Simply modifying sociology's account of women does nothing, these feminists argue, to challenge the essentially gendered nature of that account. Studies such as Oakley's were characterised as 'feminist empiricism', which accepted a conception of sociological inquiry that must be rejected if women's experience is to be adequately represented. It is not simply the *content* but also the *form* of sociological knowledge that devalues women's experience; it draws upon an essentially male idea of what it is to know something worth knowing. Sociology is gendered from its deepest starting points, in its conception of knowledge and of what counts as empirical inquiry (which is why, of course, women have not been recognised).

The form of sociological knowledge depends on a commitment to an ideal of knowledge that valorises objectivity, conceptualisation and generalisation. The social world is rendered comprehensible by means of scientific processes of inquiry; these processes justify sociology's claims to have established empirical knowledge since they ensure the neutrality and objectivity of knowledge. Positivist social science was committed to a clear distinction between facts and values, therefore distinguishing between scientific inquiry, on the one hand, and moral and ideological pronouncements on the other. From this positivist point of view, feminist arguments, while they might have some valid things to say about sociology's neglect of women as a topic for investigation, amounted to *non-science*, being viewed essentially as a set of political and moral claims. As such, while feminism might have relevance for the *use* to which sociological knowledge is put, it has no relevance to its *form*, i.e. sociology's methods and hence the kind of knowledge that those methods make available.

To challenge this view it was necessary for feminists to make a case that feminism was more than just a moral and political stance, and to place into question the distinction between facts and values that grounded the positivist view of scientific knowledge. Thus feminist theory turned in the direction of the sociology of knowledge. If the conception of sociology as objective knowledge was to be undermined, then feminism had to be shown to have *epistemological* implications. By the mid-1970s, of course, the idea of scientific objectivity was already under attack from various quarters. The positivist view of sociological knowledge had come under fire from a range of critics. Some, like the Frankfurt School, argued that the idea of objectivity was little more than an ideological rationalisation of capitalist materialism. Others, like symbolic interactionists and ethnomethodologists, argued that the phenomena of the social world could not be grasped by the supposedly 'objective' methods of sociology and thus were not amenable to understanding in these terms. Feminists gave a further twist to these critiques by arguing that sociology's scientistic view of knowledge was a 'masculinist' social product. Far from being a universal and necessary conception, it reflected male interests and orientations. Thus even to *study* women in orthodox sociological terms was to impose an alien framework upon them, one that could not do other than misrepresent their experience. Consequently, feminists, as sociologists, found themselves working within a framework of disciplinary inquiry that was inimical to their interests and experiences as women. Dorothy Smith expressed this dilemma:

> As women members of an intelligentsia, we had learned…to work inside a discourse that we did not have a part in making, that was not 'ours' as women. The discourse expresses, describes and provides the working concepts and vocabulary for a landscape in which women are strangers. That strangeness is an integral part of the socially organized practices constituting it.
>
> (1987: 52)

The 'bifurcated consciousness' (Smith 1990) that characterises the lives of feminist intellectuals reflects in extreme form a more general division in the lives of all women. Smith argues that throughout society a divide exists between women's 'opinions' and their 'experience'. In her view, there is a fault-line between the ideas and values women typically espouse, which have their source in the dominant patriarchal ideologies women imbibe, and the 'lived experience' that makes up their daily lives. The latter, which is pristine and primitive, has no representational form or shape which would enable it to be articulated. The former is nothing but form and shape; it is form without substance. The substance it appears to have is a chimera since it is one that women's experience *could not possibly possess*.

The patriarchal, 'malestream' nature of intellectual disciplines like sociology presents a fundamental challenge to feminists. To escape from this framework requires them to engineer a more radical change to their sociological thinking than the 'corrective' studies had proposed. It demands nothing less than a paradigm shift in which orthodox approaches to inquiry are abandoned and replaced by a sociology constructed in such a way as to be consistent with the 'standpoint' of women. The task is not to modify orthodox sociology but to create an alternative 'sociology for women', as Smith called it. She endorses the ethnomethodological view that orthodox sociology is characterised by a pervasive gap between its concepts and theories on the one hand and the ordinary experience of members of society on the other, adding that it is in relation to women that this gap is most pronounced. But whereas ethnomethodology sees no way or, really, need to close this gap and therefore adopts a radically different conception of sociological analysis, Smith argues that a sociology for women must be theoretical; it will build theories to account for the contexts of women's lives, but unlike orthodox sociology it will do so in ways that accentuate rather than negate women's ordinary experience. The result, she asserts, is a new and different kind of sociology.

Underpinning this paradigm shift is an alternative epistemology. The positivist view of scientific knowledge is rejected in favour of the view that all knowledge is socially determined, shaped by the social location of the knower. There can be no neutral, detached understandings, since what the world is like depends on the location from which it is viewed and there is no such thing as an absolute or detached location. The conceptual imagery is important here since the very idea of 'location' presupposes that every knower 'stands somewhere' and experiences the world as a consequence of that standpoint. All understandings are relative to their location and in this sense all knowledge is 'local knowledge', to borrow Clifford Geertz's phrase.

The feminist writers who advocated 'standpoint theory', as it became known, drew intellectual support from Marx. Two of his ideas in particular are central to their arguments. First, Marx is cited as anticipating the critique of positivism in his concept of 'praxis' and his rejection of the notion that knowledge can be neutral and detached. Knowledge is a social phenomenon: it consists of ideas created, sustained and promulgated by members of society. Therefore, the nature of such ideas and the use to which they are put inevitably plays a part in sustaining or challenging society's order. 'Theory' cannot be separated from 'praxis', in Marx's view. Second, he is credited with originating the standpoint view of knowledge.

## Standpoint theory

This simply states that we cannot really understand what it is to be a member of a social category unless we have lived it as a member.

Marx argues that the experience of the proletariat creates the potential for an understanding of the essential nature of capitalism, an understanding not available to members of other classes. Given the position of the proletariat in the economic system, the iniquities of capitalism would be so 'in their face' that an understanding of its essential nature would eventually be forced upon them. This argument, elaborated by Lukács in *History and Class Consciousness* (1971), was borrowed wholesale except that 'women' were substituted for proletariat and 'patriarchy' for capitalism. By virtue of their oppressed position, it was argued, women have the potential to develop an understanding of the patriarchal character of society and the forms of dominance that such a society imposes. Such an understanding is not available to men, since their 'standpoint' renders the workings of patriarchy largely invisible. Men do not *experience* patriarchal oppression, and therefore, unlike women, they have nothing on which to build a theoretical understanding of how it works. Furthermore, no criteria derived from 'malestream' social science can be legitimately applied to feminist standpoint accounts of women's lives.

## Problems with standpoint theory

Standpoint theory raises the question, of course, of what criteria are applicable to assess such accounts. Critics of standpoint theory, both within the feminist movement and outside, point out that any theory has to be judged against standards of theoretical adequacy. Rejecting malestream theory criteria, such as consistency with the known empirical facts, does not relieve one of the obligation to specify the alternative means by which one's theory is to be judged acceptable or otherwise. It is one thing to argue, as standpoint theorists did, that malestream social science is incapable of representing women's lives, its abstract, formal character rendering it unable to capture the concreteness and immediacy of their experience. It is another matter to state precisely how feminist theory is grounded in this experience while at the same time theoretically representing it. In other words, critics suggested that standpoint theory faces the same difficulty as malestream theory, in so far as it aims for a theoretical analysis rather than simply a simulation of women's experience. Theory necessarily involves concepts, so how are the concepts of standpoint theory *epistemologically different* from those of conventional social science? If standpoint studies are to constitute a 'successor science' (Harding 1991) to orthodox sociology, an explanation is required of how the concepts and methods of such studies actually are fundamentally different from those that sociology currently employs.

In the absence of this explanation, or examples of studies that display radical conceptual and methodological features, standpoint theory is open to the criticism that it is 'old wine in new bottles' (Button 1991). Furthermore, it is vulnerable to feminist critics such as Stanley and Wise (1993), who argue that standpoint theory is rooted in the same assumptions as the so-called 'feminist empiricism' it purportedly rejects:

> Feminist empiricism at basis aligns itself with other forms of empiricism – the feminist (social) scientist joins her male scientific peers; while feminist standpoint approaches both share and depart from traditional foundationalism by insisting that, while the feminist (social) scientist has a privileged

access to real social reality, this is because the oppressed have epistemological privilege and can see people and events as they really are.

(Stanley and Wise 1993: 200)

In other words, the standpoint approach remains empiricist, since the appeal to a pristine 'women's reality' only guarantees the statements of the theory if it is assumed that this reality 'speaks for itself' independently of theoretical interpretation.

Standpoint theory has also been accused of essentialism because its notion of a 'women's standpoint', common to all women, pays insufficient attention to the differences in social position among women. Differences in social environment undermine the notion that some essential standpoint is shared by all categories of women: the social location of a middle-class, university-educated white American woman bears little similarity to that of a poor black woman, to cite just one example. 'Women's experience' is a spectrum rather than a unity, and gender identity is cross-cut by other social identities, such as race, ethnicity, class and age, in complicated ways. How can there be a universal basis on which to build a general feminist programme for social change, since it runs against the sheer diversity of women's lives and outlooks? To argue that a common oppression experienced by women provides such a basis is, in the view of some critics, to equate the incommensurable. Standpoint theorists, who were white, university-based intellectuals to a woman, stood accused of arrogance by other feminists in assuming that they were able to speak for all women, many of whose experience bore little if any relationship to their own. In its own political terms, then, standpoint theory must be judged a failure; it did not succeed in establishing a rationale around which all elements of the women's movement would unite.

Underlying these political difficulties is a basic theoretical problem concerning the distinction between 'sex' and 'gender'. We have remarked in an earlier chapter (Chapter 13) that social constructionism is prone to exhibit the syndrome 'have one's cake and eat it too', i.e. it wants to argue for the socially created nature of phenomena while at the same time it presupposes that at least some phenomena have a natural foundation. The sex–gender distinction had served a useful purpose, enabling feminists to argue that, whatever the *natural* differences between men and women, these had no bearing on the social roles accorded to them by society. This separation between the natural and the social was itself argued to be the product of a philosophical tradition associated with 'modernism' (Butler 1990; Haraway 1991). This tradition assumes a dualism between mind and body, and thus between nature and society, that has no ultimate validity. It derives from the idea of the body as a natural, pre-social entity and is a symptom of *foundationalist* theorising, namely, the wish to ground knowledge in some absolute and undeniable source.

Standpoint theory is seen to exhibit this foundationalist tendency, wanting to ground its rejection of gendered social definitions of women in a posited unity of consciousness specific to women by virtue of their *being women*. But what is it that makes women *women*, if not socially constructed definitions? And what counts as 'women's experience' if those definitions differ from one social context to another? Given the variability of gender definitions, the only theoretically available alternative is to ground the feminist project in biological sex. The fact of women's common biology lies at the root of their distinctive experience as women and provides for the unity of the feminist cause. Hence the critics make the charge of essentialism, i.e. looking for the underlying reality.

## The third phase: postmodern feminism

Such considerations led to the third phase of feminist theorising, often referred to as 'postmodern feminism' but which we are calling the *transgressive* phase. Whereas standpoint theory proposed a distinctive and coherent 'woman's perspective' based on the common experience of oppression shared by all women within a patriarchal society, postmodern feminists argue that the very concept, 'woman', has no fixed and stable meaning. The key move here is the linguistic turn that we have discussed in Chapter 9 when considering structuralism. We noted there that the traditional view of meaning – that the meaning of any word is determined by its referent, the thing to which the word intendedly refers – is rejected. Meaning is neither a necessary relationship between word and object nor the product of an intentional act by a 'subject'; instead, it is properly conceived as *internal* to language itself. But not language as a system, since the poststructuralist claims that language is a multiplicity of discourses that link in shifting and unpredictable ways, rather than a unified and fixed system. To search for definite, clear-cut demarcations is nothing other than an attempt at political imposition, an exercise in forcing an indeterminate reality to fit within a rigid, fiercely policed and ideologically asserted set of categorical demarcations.

In line with this view, postmodern feminists argue that there is no single definition of 'woman', but many, as many as there are different discourses of gender relations. Furthermore, all definitions of women – like all definitions generally – are variable and fluid, having only brief and temporary application and lacking permanence. According to Judith Butler, the leading postmodern feminist, 'women' designates an undesignatable field of differences, one that cannot be totalised or summarised by a descriptive identity category (1994: 166). The definitions of 'women' are not determined by any 'underlying reality' such as biology, since biological definitions are also mutable and negotiable. For example, think about how sex change operations have become almost familiar occurrences nowadays. Butler rejects the sex–gender distinction as a theoretical resource since it implies a pre-social 'body' upon which gender is immutably inscribed by external cultural forces. Yet the body itself is only another culturally constructed phenomenon; it too is a product of signification and is manifested within discourse. The sexed body and gender identity are both aspects of the same discursive orders. On this basis Butler proposes a 'performative' conception of gender identity. Drawing heavily on Foucault, and in a typical poststructuralist move, she argues that since the processes that realise gender identity are linguistic, gender is best understood as something that is 'performed' in and through speech and other related practices of discourse. Furthermore, various discourses may conjoin, overlap or be discrepant. Therefore, just as women are 'spoken of' in many different ways, so also there are various ways of 'speaking as' a woman.

Butler's arguments have political significance in terms of the emancipatory project of feminism. The deconstruction of the subject, 'woman', poses a profound challenge to the idea that effective feminist politics needs to be founded in a unified conception with which all women can identify and around which all will rally. Butler argues that

the presumed universality and unity of the subject of feminism is effectively undermined by the constraints of the representationalist discourse in which it functions. Indeed, the premature insistence on a stable subject of feminism, understood as a seamless category of women, inevitably generates multiple refusals to accept the category.

(1990: 7)

Feminist politics, then, has no universal foundation. Collective action cannot be justified in terms of some common experience that can be attributed to all those who are identified as 'women'. Political action has to take account of the variety of identities persons possess and how these can shift, overlap and reform.

The postmodern approach answered the need for a rethinking of the status of feminism as a political programme. By the 1990s the women's movement had lost much of the impetus it had had in previous decades; the separationist position in particular had lost much of its force. In this context the transgressive arguments of the postmodernists pointed in a more practical and pragmatic direction, suggesting accommodation to and alliance with other forms of identity politics. If boundaries are not fixed but contingent, determined not by anything permanent but only by local social action, then deep principles are eschewed and tactical judgements rule. Butler's emphasis on the performative, boundary-transgressing approach to gender points to a strong connection between feminism and queer theory, which we discuss below. To many contemporary feminists, the feminism of the 1960s to the 1980s, while productive of important social changes, was intellectually prescriptive and politically restrictive. It failed to make common purpose with other oppressed groups in society and placed obstacles in the way of cross-category action. In particular, it was excessively gender-polarised and failed to recognise sufficiently the links between the causes of sexual freedom and gender freedom. For these feminists, the ideals of the gay and lesbian movement are integral to their conception of feminism, especially since gay and lesbian theory had, by the 1990s, arrived at the same postmodernist perspective. Consequently, postmodern feminism and queer theory are both politically aligned and theoretically contiguous.

## Sexuality and emancipation

Like women's liberation, gay liberation has been around as a political movement since the 1960s. For much of that time, however, the two movements had little connection. The view taken by many in the women's movement was that sexuality was subsumed by and was an aspect of their feminism. Radical feminists tended to regard lesbianism as homologous with feminism; commitment to feminist ideals and rejection of patriarchy demanded expression through withdrawal from heterosexual relations (a stance exemplified in the expression 'a woman needs a man like a fish needs a bicycle'). By the 1980s, however, gay men and lesbian women increasingly made common cause, and the 'gay and lesbian movement' emerged as a distinct political entity, separate from, though allied with, feminism. This political development heralded a new focus for emancipatory theorising: sexuality. Sexuality joined gender as a major theme of theorising about social oppression. The trajectory of this theorising was in many ways a rerun of the feminist theorising discussed above. Steven Seidman, a leading queer theorist, notes that

> [f]rom the beginning of the homophile movement in the 1950's through gay liberationism and the ethnic nationalism of the 1980's, lesbian and gay theory in the United States has been wedded to a particular metanarrative. This has been the formation of a homosexual subject and its mobilization to challenge a heteronormative society.
>
> (1997: 153)

In the nineteenth and much of the twentieth century, homosexuality was a largely hidden presence in society. Gays and lesbians strove to lead outwardly 'normal' lives that gave no hint of their sexual orientation, reserving their sexual activities and the social relations surrounding them for a secret world whose activities were kept beyond the notice of heterosexual society. This submerged social world and the gay subculture that shaped it were largely unknown to the rest of society. It was not that gay concerns never entered the public culture, but that when they did so it would be in disguised and allusive ways. Public figures such as politicians, writers and intellectuals carefully managed their homosexual lives to maintain a barrier between them and the straight world in which their reputation was built.

Like so many other things, this situation began to change significantly in the 1960s. The politicisation of homosexuality that originated in this period involved the explicit and public rejection of conventional morality, transforming gay identity from something concealed into something to be proclaimed with 'pride'. This political development was accompanied by the rise of gay and lesbian theory, which, like feminist arguments concerning women from which gay and lesbian writers took much of their inspiration, sought to oppose dominant conceptions which perceived homosexuality as a 'lesser' form of social being. The mainstream view, associating homosexuality with sexual perversion and psychological abnormality, was supported by science in the form of medical and psychiatric 'accepted wisdom'. This orthodoxy was countered initially by asserting its opposite, i.e. same-sex desire is natural and normal. In support of this alternative view it was argued that homosexuality is and always has been far more prevalent and more socially significant than conventional morality recognises. The homosexual is not, as he is standardly depicted, an inconsiderable, inconsequential figure consigned to the margins of society. Just as feminist writers had sought to expose the patriarchal biases of orthodox historical accounts and to re-evaluate the place of women in history, so also gay and lesbian writers produced revisionist histories of politics, literature and philosophy that sought to show how homosexuality is always resident at the very centre of society, an ever-present but officially unacknowledged force.

At this stage, theory was still wedded to an individualist view of sexuality: the notion that sexual orientation is a property of individuals, a product of their 'inner' physical and psychological make-up. Allied with this notion is the assumption that homosexuality and heterosexuality are mutually exclusive, oppositional states. The Aids crisis of the 1980s and the reaction of straight society to the so-called 'gay plague' convinced many gays that an unbridgeable gulf existed between the gay and straight worlds and that gays could only resist the forces of oppression focused upon them by separating themselves from mainstream society. In a move that paralleled the separationist feminism of the time, many gays argued for an 'ethnic' view of gay life in which gay communities would be self-sufficient and independent of the straight world. The Castro district of San Francisco came to be regarded as the model for such an independent gay community.

Some gay thinkers challenged the assumption of a clear and rigid dichotomy between gay and straight sexuality, in which individuals are 'naturally' the one or the other, thereby rationalising and underpinning these separatist developments. While some writers accepted such an 'all or nothing' view of sexuality, others argued against the view that individuals are naturally hetero- or homosexual, one or the other. After all, the pioneer of modern sexual research, Alfred Kinsey, proposed that an individual's sexual orientation is never wholly the one or the other, but rather a balance between conflicting underlying impulses. According to Kinsey *et al.* (1948), sexuality is always to a degree ambiguous, and heterosexual men are simply those who have managed to suppress, to a greater or lesser extent, the homosexual side of their nature. The significance of Kinsey's views is that he was one of the first to invoke the authority of scientific research to question the notion of a clear boundary between hetero- and homosexuality. On the other hand, he and those who argued against him shared the assumption that sexual orientation was to be understood primarily in individualistic terms. By the 1960s and 1970s, however, a more social conception began to develop. Sociological studies of homosexuality from within the labelling theory tradition (e.g. Gagnon and Simon 1967; Kitsuse 1964; Humphreys 1970) emphasised the role of learned behaviour, thus implicitly challenging the assumption of sexual orientation as an innate propensity. They also contributed to an understanding of gay lifestyles as rational responses to a hostile social environment.

By the 1980s the individualist view had given way to a full-blown social constructionist conception of sexuality. The argument that homosexuality is a 'natural' orientation, at least for some, was supplanted by the view that *all* forms of sexuality are socially created; nothing is natural. Social constructionism offered a more nuanced and sophisticated alternative to the strategy of direct refutation of the conventional moral definition: 'homosexuality bad – heterosexuality good'. Constructionist ideas challenged the antithesis of sex and society and insisted on sexual identity as a wholly social and historical phenomenon.

The emergence of gay culture and gay politics is understood as a purely socio-logical phenomenon, the impetus for which is to be found in the moral reaction of mainstream society to the perceived moral threat posed by homosexuality. As with feminism, constructionist theorising about sexuality followed the course of constructionist thought more generally within sociology. The 'moderate' con-structionism represented by symbolic interactionism and labelling theory gave way to a more radical poststructuralist variety. This development is not unre-lated to the fact that many of the leading gay and lesbian theorists are not soci-ologists but professors of English, the academic field in which poststructuralist ideas have had greatest impact and influence. The outcome, firmly established by the 1990s, was the approach known as 'queer theory'.

## Queer theory

In essence, queer theory consists in the application of poststructuralist argu-ments to the question of the nature of gay and lesbian identity. The key fig-ure in the emergence of queer theory is Foucault, himself gay. His late work *The History of Sexuality* is the single most important theoretical inspiration for queer theory. Since we have discussed this work in some detail in Chapter 11, we briefly recap his main points relating specifically to the question of homo-sexual identity. Foucault entirely rejects the idea that sexual identities reflect any underlying human essence; for him, such a view is itself a historically speci-fic phenomenon. It underpins the modern categories of sexuality, especially hetero- and homosexual, and, like them, originated in nineteenth-century ideo-logy and practice. Prior to this period sodomy was regarded as a sexual act, albeit typically a deviant one, without any implications that its practitioners were to be identified in moral and social terms as a distinctive 'type' of human being. Foucault argues that

> [t]he nineteenth century homosexual became a personage, a past, a case his-tory, a life form…Nothing that went into total composition was unaffected by his sexuality. It was everywhere present in him: at the root of all his actions…because it was a secret that always gave itself away.
>
> (1980: 43)

Foucault's argument concerning homosexuality mirrors his earlier analyses of mental illness and crime. Like the mental patient and the criminal, the homosex-ual is a social creation, the product of an essentialist discourse that presupposes a necessary link between forms of conduct and an inner 'self' from which that conduct emanates. The label 'homosexual' is invented to concretise this link, thereby constituting the homosexual as a *subject* of medical and scientific inves-tigation. Foucault charts the rise of psycho-medical discourses on sexuality and shows how these resulted, among other things, in 'sexology', the programme of research into the psychology and sociology of sex in the nineteenth and twenti-eth centuries, involving thinkers as diverse as Freud, Krafft-Ebing, Havelock Ellis, Reich and Kinsey. Central to the programme of the sexologists was the mapping of the various 'sexual pathologies', prominent among which was homosexuality. In conceiving homosexuality in these terms, sexology gave scientific authority to the hegemony of heterosexual discourse and contributed to the assumption of sexual identity as an objective reality underpinning sexual behaviour.

Central to queer theory's goal of problematising sexual reality is consideration of the homosexual–heterosexual dichotomy as a cultural theme. It seeks to chart the sexual thematic of modern culture and show how the mutual dependence between these two oppositional identities plays a major part in the cultural order of nineteenth- and twentieth-century society, in literature and the arts as well as in much popular culture. In an argument strongly reminiscent of Durkheim, queer theorists argue that public rituals of scandal and moral outrage have the effect of defining the cultural order by realising the opposition of heterosexuality and homosexuality as a social reality. This opposition is revealed as an artefact of cultural practices such as 'outing' and shaming, which serve the function of giving definition to the sexual order of society. Through this analysis queer theory deconstructs the very idea of sexual identity; neither homosexuality nor heterosexuality have any reality *except that which is imparted to them by contingent social practices*.

For queer theorists, Foucault's concepts provide a key theoretical resource in problematising the sexual order and challenging hegemonic heterosexual discourse. They also inform an alternative view of gay politics. Like postmodernist feminists, queer theorists reject the view that emancipatory politics requires a 'unified subject' around which political action is mobilised. Such a view presupposes the stability and distinctness of sexual identities, an assumption that queer theory seeks to problematise. From its postmodern stance there is nothing that fixes such identities, therefore nothing that differentiates so-called 'gay men' and 'lesbians' from so-called heterosexuals other than the social definitions enforced by society. Such definitions are seen as *internal* to a particular discourse, heterosexual discourse, which just happens to predominate in contemporary society but which can have no claim to 'truth'. The opposition between gay and straight is fundamental to that discourse, therefore it is insufficiently radical simply to assert a gay identity over against a straight one. Gay Liberation, Gay Pride and other similar movements thus are seen as 'playing the hegemonic game' in so far as they are premised upon the same dichotomy as the heterosexual orthodoxy they oppose.

In this respect, then, queer theory goes beyond postmodern feminism's view of 'woman', since it seeks to do more than open up the question of what it means to be 'gay' or 'straight' to alternative interpretations. It insists that the very terms 'gay', 'lesbian' and 'straight' are to be seen as boundary-drawing, and as reinforcing the limitations enshrined in *both* dominant *and* subordinate sexual ideologies. The task is to open up all possibilities and resist all boundaries. In Seidman's words:

Postmodernists give up the 'modernist' idol of complete human emancipation in favour of deconstructing false closure, prying open present and future social possibilities, detecting fluidity and porousness in forms of life where hegemonic discourses posit closure and a frozen, natural social order.

(1997: 44)

## Postcolonialism

The third emancipatory social theory, postcolonialism, focuses upon the phenomenon of imperialism and the relationship between colonial rulers and those they rule over. Just as feminism challenges definitions of gender, and queer theory challenges conventional sexual categories, so postcolonialism seeks to problematise the idea of ethnic difference and the relation between dominant and subordinate cultures across the globe. As with feminism and queer theory, postcolonialism denies the objectivity of sociology, finding it dependent on ideological assumptions that lend support to an oppressive social order. Like the other emancipatory approaches, postcolonial theory presents a critique of classical social theory as one-sided and neglectful of major social divisions, in this case the divisions created by imperialism. Classical theory, it is argued, is 'Eurocentric'; it casts everyone else in its terms, disregarding and overriding the ways non-European social actors think of themselves. Consequently, classical theory took as its problem the nature and dynamics of industrial societies, i.e. the societies of the West. In so far as it took any interest in societies elsewhere in the world, in the main it was simply to view them as a contrastive background to highlight the social and economic processes shaping the West or to puzzle over why these societies had *failed* to develop in the Western pattern.

The underlying assumption shared by classical theorists was of a universal process of social evolution; all societies develop according to the same broad principles of social and economic change. Although it originated in the West, the direction of this change was seen as universal, such that the application of sociology's analysis to non-Western societies was theoretically unproblematic. This universalistic, Eurocentric vision is taken to be exemplified by Durkheim in his conception of social change in terms of the transformation from mechanical to organic solidarity. Even Marx, who paid more attention to capitalism's imperialist aspect and was more critical of its effects on the 'underdeveloped' world than any other classical theorist, was in no doubt that these societies would be incorporated into the same global process of capitalist development and come to form part of a single world system (see Chapter 14 and 'globalisation'). At the same time, however, Marx's analysis of the role of imperialism in Western capitalist development is the inspiration for much anti-imperialist theory. The universalistic assumptions of classical social theory are said to provide an ideological foundation for the political and economic policies of imperialism. Those policies are aimed towards, and justified in terms of, 'progress'. If social development is a universal process that is led by Western industrial societies, then the 'mission' of imperial nations is to facilitate the emergence of progressive (i.e. Western) structures and institutions in the societies they rule. Indigenous cultural and political forms, such as tribal organisation, are by definition obstacles to progress and, as such, must be eliminated. Consequently, the path of colonial 'progress' inevitably involves violence, not just violence towards individuals who refuse to give up traditional ways, but 'cultural violence' (i.e. disregard and denigration) towards the traditional ways themselves. While classical social theory legitimates this approach by conceiving the individual in abstract, universal terms as a 'member of society', in practice imperialism presupposes an absolute difference between rulers and ruled. Anti-colonialist writers such as

Franz Fanon (1968) emphasise that the dehumanisation of indigenous peoples and their cultures is at the heart of imperialism. The 'native' is represented in colonial ideology as less than human, as a 'savage', thus justifying policies to transform him into a social being. That such policies involve the obliteration of everything that makes the native society what it is appears from the colonial point of view as a *positive* move, as the removal of something that has no value in itself.

While Marx is a major influence in anti-colonial thought, Fanon and other writers find Marxist theory inadequate to explain the phenomenon of imperialism. Marx's view of class struggle as the motor of history fails to account for the way in which imperialism transforms the difference between Europeans and non-Europeans into a racial divide as well as a social and economic one. In particular, Marx's theory of ideology, linked as it is to the concept of class, is judged incapable of explaining the dynamics of imperialist thought. Anti-colonial theorists thus sought an alternative form of analysis that could explain imperialism more adequately. The outcome of this theoretical quest is postcolonialism. Postcolonial theory seeks to do more than simply document the oppressive character of imperialism; it seeks to apply the insights of poststructuralism to an understanding of the ideological structure of colonialism. A key figure in this intellectual quest is Edward Said.

## Edward Said and 'Orientalism'

Arguably the most important thinker of postcolonial theory, Edward Said was, until his death in 2004, professor of English Literature at Columbia University. A Palestinian by birth, Said spent most of his career in American universities. *Orientalism*, his key book, was published in 1978. It examines Western literary and historical representations of the East from the seventeenth to the twentieth centuries and argues that these representations project an image of 'the Orient' that is a construction of Western interests and ideology; the Orient really exists only in the Western mind. In this image the societies and cultures of Asia and the Middle East are all lumped indiscriminately together, and depicted in wholly negative terms by contrast with the positive characteristics attributed to the West, the Occident. While the Orient is seen as overwhelmingly barbaric and cruel, backward and authoritarian, static and unchanging, the Occident is enlightened and civilised, progressive and democratic, dynamic and forward-looking. Orientalist cultures are supposedly dominated by mythology and magic, in contrast to the predominance of reason (in the form of science) in the Occident.

Said's argument is that this positive–negative contrast is central to how Western societies define themselves. In other words, the Orient is an imagined 'Other', a necessary intellectual invention that enables Western societies to conceive their culture as distinctive, and in self-congratulating terms. It has also been a powerfully influential invention since it has guided and shaped the colonial policies of Western powers towards their Eastern empires for three hundred years. The contrast between Orient and Occident is entirely weighted in favour of the West, since Eastern cultures are described in terms of 'absences', as the lack of this or that feature which is regarded as definitive of Western cultures.

In social science, from Marx through Weber and on to twentieth-century writers such as Wittfogel (1957), the societies of the Orient are said to lack, among other things, scientific rationality, a democratic political tradition, a history of revolutionary change, an entrepreneurial middle class and 'this-worldly' religious belief systems.

Although Said's own examples are taken mainly from French literature, the paradigm of the literary representation of Orientalism probably is Joseph Conrad's novel *Heart of Darkness*, famous as the inspiration for Francis Ford Coppola's 1979 film *Apocalypse Now*. Conrad's book, set in the Congo Free State at the end of the nineteenth century, conceives Africa as a model for the 'darkness' of the human soul, and exemplifies Said's point that writers have created the Orient (in this case Africa) as an inversion of Western culture and values. The argument strongly echoes Foucault, as Said asserts that the two sides of a discursive opposition are mutually defining. In other words, colonialism shapes the cultural world of the colonisers and the colonised, defining the nature of both parties. The idea of Europe and of 'European man' is created within the same discourse that creates the 'native'. Said also agrees with Foucault that every form of power creates its own form of resistance. Thus colonialism necessarily but unwittingly gives rise to the anti-colonial movements that oppose it.

### Spivak and the subaltern

Although Said's influence within postcolonial theory has been enormous, his ideas have been criticised. A common complaint is that his very own analysis puts too much emphasis on the Western side of the colonial dichotomy and pays insufficient attention to the colonised themselves. Such an emphasis neglects, it is said, the ways in which colonised peoples responded to colonialist discourse, sometimes modifying or even challenging it. Following the work of a group of radical Indian historians who sought to revise historical thinking about colonialism and to analyse anti-colonial activities and viewpoints previously neglected, this shift of focus has come to be referred to as 'subaltern studies' (a subaltern is a junior officer in the military; in the Indian army, the senior officers were exclusively European). The aim of subaltern studies is to write colonial history 'from below', i.e. to examine and articulate the points of view of oppressed peoples that have been unavailable to mainstream accounts (Amin and Chakrabarty 1996; Chaturvedi 2000).

The Indian-American theorist Gayatri Spivak (1988) has critiqued such studies from a poststructuralist perspective. In her view, subaltern studies are unduly restricted if they address only the 'voices' of those who explicitly opposed the colonial powers. Equally, or even more, significant is the 'silent voice' of those who are unable to express their point of view, since the power of colonialism consists in its ability to prevent an oppositional discourse arising. Contra Foucault and Said, it is a fact that there is no oppositional voice to be heard that needs to be explained. Somewhat ironically, as with Said, Spivak's analyses focus mainly upon Western literature (for example, on Jean Rhys's novel *Wide Sargasso Sea*). However, Spivak's most famous example of such a silent voice is that of Indian women who participate in the ritual of suttee, the self-immolation of a widow upon her husband's funeral pyre. Such women are, by definition, silent; they cannot be interviewed to discover their attitude towards the ritual. To the colonial authorities, suttee was clear evidence of the barbarity of indigenous beliefs and rituals, and colonial debates on its abolition took for granted the coercive basis of women's participation. In this way the subjectivity of women was subordinated to the liberal colonial ideology. As a committed poststructuralist, Spivak is careful to deflect the charge of 'realism': she makes no claim that the analysis she gives captures the widow's point of view or corresponds to what such a woman 'really thinks'. Indeed, her key point is that there is no point of view there to be captured, since the conditions within which such a view could be formulated are systematically withheld from such women. Thus Spivak is no standpoint theorist; she rejects the notion that the theorist can recover the standpoint of the subaltern and accuses of 'romanticism' those who seek such a standpoint. Instead, she argues that the task of the theorist is to 'represent' the subaltern's silence, while recognising that such a representation is an artefact of the analysis.

## Conclusion

We noted earlier in this book (in Chapter 14) that the direction of sociological thought in the 1960s, when it was becoming established as a university subject in Britain, was shaped by the political and economic circumstances of the time. We went on to suggest that the path taken by sociology over the last half-century is best understood by seeing it in its political and economic context, as a series of responses to events and movements in the wider society. This path is most visibly the case in relation to the theories considered in this chapter. Feminist theory, queer theory and postcolonial theory are attempts to shape sociological thinking in order to provide it with a critical perspective on what are perceived to be fundamental political and moral developments in contemporary society. The task of social theory is twofold: (1) to 'theorise' these developments so that a proper understanding of their nature and significance is available; (2) to promote at the same time the furtherance of moral and political agendas that challenge the liberal-democratic status quo. These aims are, of course, much the same as those that inspired sociologists half a century ago to take up the task of building a neo-Marxist theory of modern society. It is clear, then, that while the politics may have changed, the sociological vision has not. The notion of sociology as a 'critical' discipline, popularised in the 1960s, still holds sway.

This does not mean, however, that this vision is understood and implemented in the same manner as it was previously. As we have seen, the idea that a critical sociology presupposes possession of a general theory of society and history, taken for granted by Marxist-oriented sociologists, is eschewed by contemporary emancipatory thought. It is not simply that class politics is overtaken by identity politics, but that the totalising framework and global span of Marxism are replaced by a fragmented, localised perspective. Where there was strategy there are now only tactics; politics as historical action has been replaced by politics as *ad hoc* spontaneity. Where theory once sought and claimed to find grounds for certainty, it now emphasises the partiality of knowledge, the limitations of the possible and the imperfections of resistance. Emancipation no longer has history on its side.

## Questions

1 What is 'standpoint theory'? How does it relate to notions of objectivity and realism in methodology? Is it an individualistic or a collective position to take? Does this matter?

2 Do gender, sexuality and ethnicity have enough features in common to be treated together? Is this chapter biased in its treatment? Are the differences between feminist theory, queer theory and postcolonial theory more important than their similarities?

3 What is the 'Other'? How does it relate to previous uses of the same term by older theorists? How might it apply in the fields of gender, sexuality and ethnicity? How might it overlap across these fields in particular cases?

4 Is it appropriate for sociology to set itself up as a tool for emancipation? How might Weber's arguments about value-neutrality relate to this issue? What about Marx's point about changing the world rather than simply understanding it? What would happen if an analysis of a social phenomenon revealed something to the disadvantage of a discriminated-against group? How would this relate to 'underdog bias' and/or ethical considerations?

5 What is new and innovative practically in emancipatory sociology? What aspects reiterate existing theoretical tropes? Is this a paradigm shift or a new topic for theoretical consideration? Give examples that concern gender, sexuality *and* ethnicity.

6 Is emancipatory sociology just an updated Weberian analysis of status groups? How is it similar and how is it different? Has class therefore been abolished or is it still relevant – and if so, how?

7 What are 'identity politics'? Are they important? Why? Does someone's incumbency in a particular social category give them a different view of the nature of society as a whole? Is this view right or wrong? Why?

## Next steps

Standpoint theory and its critics are well covered by Smith (1987), Harding (1991), and Stanley and Wise (1993). Butler (1990) remains the classic statement of gender and identity. Foucault's ideas dominate queer theory, in particular in his *History of Sexuality* volume 1 (1980). Chaturvedi (2000) provides a good selection of postcolonial and subaltern studies.

There are few clear commentaries on the 'emancipatory turn' as a whole, but Seidman (1997) covers much of the ground in terms of gender and sexuality. Sullivan (2003) on queer theory and Young (2003) on postcolonialism are good critical introductions.

## CHAPTER SIXTEEN

# Conclusion

The last edition of this text concluded with a question: what kind of sociology might we reasonably expect to see? The fragmentation of the clear 'perspectives' that animated earlier editions was already evident. The influence of what we have called 'post-sociological' approaches was still increasing. Finally, attempts to develop 'new' approaches to social theory, whether based on overcoming dualisms (Giddens, Bourdieu, Habermas) or on giving voice to those routinely silenced (feminist sociology, queer theory, postcolonialism), did not live up to their claims when scrutinised closely, though they each retain enthusiastic supporters and thereby add to the heterogeneity of current sociological ideas.

If our introduction to this edition is a little more optimistic, it is because sociology *itself* seems to be under pressure, from demands for answers to questions coming from outside that seem to us to be legitimately sociological, and from internal questions about the nature of the discipline that seem to chime with those demands. We hope that these pressures will lead to some interesting developments in the discipline over the next few years or, at least, to some interesting sociological work being undertaken, whether under the banner of 'sociology' or not.

Sociology would not be sociology without some scepticism, however, and so if our introduction is a little more optimistic it is incumbent upon us to make the conclusion less so. Sociology might appear, as we argued in the conclusion to our last edition, to be something with an integrating narrative. The work of Foucault strongly resembles that of Weber, the concerns of Habermas resemble those of Parsons, and the commitments of the actor-network theorists resemble those of the ethnomethodologists. That is not to say that things have not moved on – they have – but to emphasise the extent to which sociologists often forget their own history. 'New' developments often turn out to be remarkably similar to older ones, with the same problems and weaknesses (and strengths), and subject to the same fate. The criticisms levelled at the 'conservative' Durkheim or Parsons are similar to those levelled at Giddens; Marx's 'neglect' of culture (in contrast to Weber) is reflected in the attacks on economic determinism that followed Althusser's appearance in the 1960s.

In rewriting and re-editing this text, however, it has become clearer to us that the problems identified and opened up by the poststructuralists and postmodernists have not gone away. Emancipatory sociology is animated by a tension between relativism and fixity of meaning, between a desire for theoretical closure and a suspicion that such closure may always be illusory. Just as symbolic interactionist ideas have become incorporated into mainstream sociology – transforming the mainstream and dissolving symbolic interactionism as a distinctive approach – it seems to us that the poststructuralist and postmodernist 'turns' continue to have an effect on even those sociologists who overtly disavow their doctrines. The post-postmodern world is not the same as the pre-postmodern: Pandora's box may have been closed but the sprites are out and cannot be put back.

The perspectives we touch upon in the final part of this book seem now, to us, to either seek to ignore the challenge of the post-sociological positions or to try to maintain those positions without drawing the corrosive, relativist conclusions they imply. Like the pointy-haired boss in the cartoon *Dilbert*, when asked whether sociology should be empirical in scope and based on a general theory, or suspicious of the existence of the real world and treating theory as just another story, contemporary sociologists often have the same answer. Do both.

# Glossary

**AGIL** The phases through which a social system operates over a period of time: adaptation, goal attainment, integration and latency.

**Alibi** The use of an object's 'use value' to justify wanting or having it, when its real role is a sign in circulation rather than something with intrinsic utility.

**Alienation** An estrangement from oneself and from what makes one human. For Marx, losing control over one's capacity to transform the world (by working under the instruction of others for wages) and therefore of one's 'species being'.

**Anomie** Insufficient social regulation of the individual, caused by sudden social changes.

**Autopoiesis** The self-organising nature of systems, understood as independent of values and goals: systems reproduce their own features as an end in itself.

**Base and superstructure** The idea that the economic structure of a society is the foundation on which the rest of it (e.g. its laws, its culture, media, etc.) is built.

**Biopower** The power the state has is derived from its total population, which it manages, viewed as an asset in its own right, and not merely from its military strength.

**Bourgeoisie** The class that own the means of production, such as factories, corporations, mines, transport systems, etc.; the ruling class.

**Bricoleur** Someone who puts something together with whatever happens to be at hand, and can do so expertly, rather than working from a fixed plan that requires specialised materials or knowledge.

**Bureaucracy** An administrative system wherein specialists in particular fields are appointed to administrative posts, characterised by impartial and expert administration and management.

**Carceral society** A social organisation based on the prison, where people are subjected to, and subject themselves to, constant surveillance.

**Career** A development through time punctuated by *turning points* rather than a smooth progression of events.

**Charismatic authority** Domination based on the power of a leader's personality.

**Class (Bourdieu)**   Both the outcome and the conditions for struggles within and between fields, generating and modifying the alignment of people within the overall distribution of capital.

**Class (Marx)**   A social group that has a particular relationship to the means of production: the proletariat (who have to sell their labour power) and the bourgeoisie (who own the means of production and buy that labour power).

**Class (Weber)**   A category of people with a common characteristic, which the members of the category may or may not orientate to themselves, determined by the social theorist.

**Colonialisation**   The intervention of the system into the lifeworld, subjecting the latter to rationalisation and therefore damaging it.

**Colonialism**   'Progress' led by Western industrial societies that depends on the destruction and denigration of indigenous cultural and political forms.

**Common-sense attitude**   An attitude towards the world that takes for granted a multitude of things that are obvious, self-evident, trivial, and so on, and which require neither investigation nor comment.

**Cultural capital**   Socially legitimate definitions of what is culturally worthwhile, which are tied to particular groups or classes in historical contexts.

**Culture industry**   The institutions of the mass media, which provide people with their ideas.

**Deconstruction**   The analysis of a text by cultivating incongruities and paradoxes, revealing where aspects of the text resist, confound and unravel the 'single' meaning that seeks to impose itself on the whole.

**Dialectical logic**   The idea that truth is achieved (or approximated) through argument: two opposing positions on a matter will generate a superior answer that incorporates elements from both – this will then form the next position to be argued about, and so on.

***Différance***   A term that points towards the contrasting (differing) and postponing of meaning (deferring) aspects of language.

**Discourse**   Ways of speaking and thinking that are patterned and socially accepted, and historically contingent.

**Disenchantment**   A diminution in our ability to find meaning in the world and to understand our place in it, paradoxically tied to increased material satisfaction.

**Division of labour**   The specialisation of work, where more gets produced more efficiently by dividing tasks into categories which are undertaken by different groups of people.

**Egoism**   The social isolation of the individual.

**Emergence**   The outcome of a course of action emerging through its being carried out, rather than according to a predetermined plan or particular goal.

**Episteme**   A matrix of presuppositions that restricts what it is possible to say or think in a particular historical period.

**Fatal strategies**   Developments that will become extreme and ultimately devastate themselves, e.g. the increasing dependence on carbon-emitting power sources is leading to climate change and will ultimately require major social restructuring.

**Field**   A social environment inhabited by one or more groups, who are typically in competitive relationships with one another.

**Functionalism**   An approach to the social world that stresses its coherent nature, and the ways in which its institutions operate to preserve its integrity.

**Genealogy**   The analysis of the buried history of thought, with the specific objective of revealing the link(s) between knowledge and power.

**Generalised other**   The standard outlook of a community, rather than the opinions and beliefs of specific people, internalised to form part of each community member's personality.

**Globalisation**   The 'shrinking' of the world through improved communications (physical and electronic) and the decline of the nation state.

**Grand narrative**   An attempt to provide an overarching, comprehensive account of the development of science.

**Grounded theory**   An approach to theory generation that emphasises case studies as a means of generating theoretical insights, which are then refined through other case studies.

**Habitus**   A structured way of seeing the world in a taken-for-granted way, given through being a member of a particular social group or class.

**Hegemony**   The collection of ideas that prevail over other ideas, where intellectual activities are understood as an arena of social struggle, of domination and resistance.

**Historicism**   The idea that ideas are socially and historically situated.

**Humanism**   The notion that social life is made up of the creative powers of a society's members, or can be best understood in terms of the actions of individuals.

**Hyperreality**   The realm of the world of signs (in particular images on television and computer screens) that has supplanted the 'really' real – the world of everyday life.

**Ideal speech situation**   A situation in which free dialogue is possible on an egalitarian basis, without any external constraining or distorting influences – 'ideal' because it can never exist in this pure form in reality.

**Idealism**   The idea that history, society and human development can best be understood in terms of the development of thought or ideas (in contrast to, for instance, economic forces or technological developments).

**Ideology**   A system of ideas that systematically misrepresent reality, serving the interests of a particular social group (the ruling class).

**Individualism**   Prizing the distinctness and independence of human beings, their freedom and autonomy, in contrast to their social responsibilities and subordination to collective authority.

**Internalisation**   Making the requirements of a position part of one's personality, building them into one's beliefs about what one should do.

**Intersubjectivity**   The notion that the world we share constitutes reality: we do not have personal 'versions' of the world but (sometimes slightly) different perspectives on the same one.

**Labelling**   The public identification of deviants, which socially fixes them as deviant, e.g. being found guilty of a crime.

**Legitimation crisis**   As the state extends into more and more areas of social life, it raises expectations that it cannot satisfy and dissolves the bases on which its legitimacy has traditionally rested.

**Lifeworld**   The repository of person-to-person relationships in which people seek to associate with one another.

**Materialism**   The idea that the world can best be understood in terms of the ways people transform it, through their labour and the ways in which that labour is organised.

**Moral entrepreneur**   Someone who lobbies for new regulations out of a sense of right, in contrast to someone who has to enforce prohibitions as a bureaucratic role.

**Motivated compliance**   Doing things not because failing to do so would lead to punishment, but because one actually *wants* to do them and believes them to be right.

**Natural attitude**   The attitude towards the world that takes for granted its existence as an external world. This is divided into the common-sense attitude and the scientific attitude, which are subtly different.

**Other**   The contrastive element in determining identity: for instance, for there to be sane people there have to be 'Others', the mad.

**Paradigmatic**   The meaning of words not being inherent to them, but down to their relationship to other words which are not themselves spoken.

**Party**   An organisation self-consciously put together for the pursuit of power.

**Performativity**   The standard of practical efficiency, in particular in the economic realm.

**Positivism**   An approach seeking to find law-like relationships between phenomena (often causal in form), modelled on the workings of the physical sciences.

**Postmodernity**   A historical period or epoch beyond modernity, in which the notions of modernity will no longer be thinkable.

**Power/knowledge**   A term used by Foucault to emphasise the ways that knowledge develops in close conjunction with power, meaning neither can be treated independently.

**Practice**   A rational course of action, specific to a particular group, with its own built-in logic, in contrast to actions undertaken with strict means-ends rationality.

**Praxis**   Theory as practical action, as a tool to change society.

**Proletariat**   The working class; that class of people who have to sell their labour power (work for wages) to support themselves.

**Rational (or rational-legal) authority**   Domination by incumbents of formal offices, often elected or appointed through formal processes.

**Rationalisation**   The organisation of social activities in accordance with a particular plan, worked out in advance and controlled consciously.

**Rationality**   A commitment to particular ends or goals which informs how one conducts oneself. These ends can be instrumental (means-ends) or value-based.

**Reality**   Something is real if it is external and constraining: it exists outside our consciousness and sets limits to our actions.

**Reductionism**   Reducing every kind of phenomenon to just one, e.g. making all social phenomena out to be manifestations of economic relationships.

**Reflexivity**   The feature of social reasoning that it both takes place in settings, and is an integral part of what constitutes those settings.

**Reification**  The misrepresentation of the world as something that operates independently and according to its own laws, even though it is really produced by people's own actions.

**Relative autonomy**  The idea that 'superstructural' elements of society develop in their own ways, but with the economic 'base' as the decisive shaping influence on the whole complex of society (the determinant in the last instance).

**Relativism**  The idea that what is true for one person or group of people may not be held to be true by others, and that there are no external criteria by which the 'real' truth can be established.

**Representationalism**  The notion that the function of words is to name or stand for things.

**Repressive tolerance**  Tolerance and freedom of expression understood as ways in which the capitalist system inhibits the possibility of change by neutering challenges to it.

**Scientific attitude**  A concern with knowledge over practical results, in particular with knowledge being sought for its own sake.

**Self**  Mead's term for the human mind, which develops in and through social interaction, enabling the human actor to acquire a sense of individuality.

**Simulacrum**  An image without an original, the real 'thing' it is an image 'of'.

**Situatedness**  The feature of courses of action that they take place in specific circumstances, and so are shaped by the contingencies of those circumstances.

**Socialisation**  Learning to be social, often achieved through the giving and withholding of affection and approval by parents to children.

**Standpoint theory**  The notion that unless one has lived as a member of a particular social category one cannot understand what it means to be a member of it.

**Status group**  A collection of people who recognise one another as equals, and who look up to or down upon other status groups.

**Status roles**  Knowing what a person with a particular status should do, what can be expected of them, and how one should behave towards them.

**Strategic action**  People's attempts to influence one another.

**Stratification**  Inequalities in society that are socially organised and patterned in nature.

**Structuration**  A generic term that emphasises that society is both produced and reproduced: society is produced by social actions, which become shaped by the conditions they produce, and thus tend towards perpetuating those patterns, *reproducing* that social organisation.

**Syntagmatic**  The meaning of words being dependent on what came before them and, crucially, what will follow.

**System**  A permanent social phenomenon that must maintain itself through transactions with its environment and by maintaining its internal relationships.

**Teleology**  The idea that things are done to achieve a particular end (often in contrast to the idea that things are caused by what preceded them).

**Totality (or social totality)**  The true identity of things can only be determined by their relationship to a whole, e.g. a worker is only a worker in terms of capitalist production.

**Totemism (Durkheim)**   The worship of things in the environment (e.g. animals or plants), and the making of representations of these things to use in religious rituals.

**Totemism (Lévi-Strauss)**   The use of natural phenomena to think with in 'primitive societies'.

**Traditional authority**   Domination based on precedent, a traditional entitlement to a powerful position with a traditional expectation of compliance from others.

**Universal reason**   The conclusions that emerge from an ideal speech situation which everyone would agree with and take for granted.

**Value (Marx)**   Commodities appear to have two kinds of values: what they are useful for (use-value) and how much they can be exchanged for (exchange-value). The latter is the form of appearance of *value itself*, the labour power embodied in the commodity.

**Values**   Cultural elements in society which indicate how things are, how they should be, and what people should do.

**Will to power**   The instinctive human drives to grow, develop in strength and potency, and gain power and dominance.

# Bibliography

Adorno, Theodor W. 1973. *Negative Dialectics*. London: Routledge.

Adorno, Theodor W., and Max Horkheimer. 1979. *The Dialectic of Enlightenment*. London: Verso.

Adorno, Theodor W., Else Frenkel-Brunswik, Daniel Levinson, and Nevitt Sanford. 1950. *The Authoritarian Personality*. New York: Harper and Row.

Alexander, Jeffrey. 1984. *Theoretical Logic in Sociology*, vol. 4: *The Modern Reconstruction of Classical Thought: Talcott Parsons*. London: Routledge.

—— ed. 1985. *Neo-Functionalism*. London: Sage.

—— 1995. *Fin de Siècle Social Theory: Relativism, Reduction, and the Problem of Reason*. London: Verso.

Althusser, Louis. 1971. *Lenin and Philosophy*. London: New Left Books.

Amin, Shahid, and Dipesh Chakrabarty. 1996. *Subaltern Studies*, vol. IX: *Writings on South Asian History and Society*. New Delhi: Oxford University Press.

Anderson, Perry. 1980. *Arguments with English Marxism*. London: Verso.

Baldamus, Wilhelm. 1976. *The Structure of Sociological Inference*. Oxford: Martin Robertson.

Barker, Diana, and Sheila Allen. 1976. *Dependence and Exploitation in Work and Marriage*. London: Longman.

Barthes, Roland. 1967. *Elements of Semiology*. London: Cape.

—— 1972. *Critical Essays*. Evanston, IL: Northwestern University Press.

—— 1973. *Mythologies*. London: Granada.

—— 1975a. *S/Z*. London: Cape.

—— 1975b. *The Pleasures of the Text*. New York: Hill and Wang.

—— 1977. *Roland Barthes by Roland Barthes*. London: Macmillan.

—— 1978. *A Lover's Discourse*. New York: Hill and Wang.

—— 1985. *The Fashion System*. London: Cape.

—— 1991. *The Grain of the Voice: Interviews 1962–81*. Berkeley, CA: University of California Press.

Baudrillard, Jean. 1995. *The Gulf War Did Not Take Place*. Bloomington, IN: Indiana University Press.

Becker, Howard S. 1964. *Outsiders: Studies in the Sociology of Deviance*. New York: Free Press.

—— 1967. 'Whose Side Are We On?' *Social Problems*, 14: 239–47.

—— 1970. *Sociological Work: Method and Substance*. New York: Aldine.

Bell, Daniel. 1960. *The End of Ideology*. London: Collier Macmillan.

Bendix, Reinhard. 1960. *Max Weber: An Intellectual Portrait*. London: Heinemann.

Bennington, Geoffrey, and Jacques Derrida. 1993. *Jacques Derrida*. Chicago: University of Chicago Press.

Berger, Peter, and Thomas Luckmann. 1967. *The Social Construction of Reality*. Harmondsworth: Allen Lane.

Berlinsky, David. 1968. *On Systems Theory*. Cambridge, MA: MIT Press.

Berman, Marshall. 1983. *All That Is Solid Melts into Air: The Experience of Modernity*. London: Verso.

Best, Steven, and Douglas Kellner. 1991. *Postmodern Theory: Critical Interrogations*. London: Macmillan.

Bittner, Egon. 1973. 'Objectivity and Realism in Sociology', in George Psathas (ed.), *Phenomenological Sociology*. New York: John Wiley and Sons, 109–25.

Blumberg, Abraham. 1969. 'The Practice of Law as a Confidence Game', in Vilhelm Aubert (ed.), *The Sociology of Law*. Harmondsworth: Penguin, 221–31.

Blumer, Herbert. 1969. *Symbolic Interactionism: Perspective and Method*. Englewood Cliffs, NJ: Prentice Hall.

Bottomore, Tom. 1984. *The Frankfurt School*. London: Tavistock.

Bottomore, Tom, and Maximilien Rubel, eds. 1970. *Karl Marx: Selected Writings in Sociology and Social Philosophy*. Harmondsworth: Penguin.

Bourdieu, Pierre. 1977. *Outline of a Theory of Practice*. Cambridge: Cambridge University Press.

—— 1990. *In Other Words: Essays Towards a Reflexive Sociology*. Cambridge: Polity.

—— 1992. *Language and Symbolic Power*. Cambridge: Polity.

Bronner, Stephen Eric, and Douglas MacKay Kellner, eds. 1989. *Critical Theory and Society: A Reader*. London: Routledge.

Brubaker, Rogers. 1984. *The Limits of Rationality: An Essay on the Social and Moral Thought of Max Weber*. London: Allen and Unwin.

Bruun, Hans Henrik, and Sam Whimster, eds. 2012. *Max Weber: Collected Methodological Writings*. London: Routledge.

Burawoy, Michael. 2005. 'Presidential Address: For Public Sociology', *American Sociological Review*, 70: 4–28.

Butler, Judith. 1990. *Gender Trouble: Feminism and the Subversion of Identity*. London: Routledge.

—— 1994. 'Feminism and the Question of Postmodernism', in Steven Seidman (ed.), *The Postmodern Turn*. Cambridge: Cambridge University Press, 153–70.

Button, Graham, ed. 1991. *Ethnomethodology and the Human Sciences*. Cambridge: Cambridge University Press.

Carchedi, Guglielmo. 1977. *Of the Economic Identification of Economic Classes*. London: Routledge and Kegan Paul.

Carver, Terrell. 1982. *Marx's Social Theory*. Oxford: Oxford University Press.

Castells, Manuel. 2000. *The Rise of the Network Society*. Oxford: Blackwell.

Cavanagh, Allison. 2007. *Sociology in the Age of the Internet*. Maidenhead: Open University Press.

Chaturvedi, Vinayak, ed. 2000. *Mapping Subaltern Studies and the Postcolonial*. London: Verso.

Cohen, G. A. 1978. *Karl Marx's Theory of History: A Defence*. Oxford: Oxford University Press.

Collins, Randall. 1975. *Conflict Sociology: Towards an Explanatory Science*. New York: Academic Press.

—— 1981. 'On the Microfoundations of Macrosociology'. *American Journal of Sociology*, 186: 984–1014.

—— 1986. *Max Weber: A Skeleton Key*. London: Sage.

Colomy, Paul, ed. 1990. *Neofunctionalist Sociology*. Cheltenham: Edward Elgar.

Connerton, Paul, ed. 1976. *Critical Sociology*, 2nd edn. Harmondsworth: Penguin.

Craib, Ian. 1992. *Anthony Giddens*. London: Routledge.

Crews, Frederick. 1986. *Skeptical Engagements*. Oxford: Oxford University Press.

Crossley, Nick. 2008. 'Pretty Connected: The Social Network of the Early UK Punk Movement'. *Theory, Culture and Society*, 25: 89–116.

Dahrendorf, Ralf. 1958. 'Out of Utopia: Toward a Reorientation of Sociological Analysis'. *American Journal of Sociology*, 64: 115–27.

Dawe, Alan. 1970. 'The Two Sociologies'. *British Journal of Sociology*, 21: 207–18.

Dawkins, Richard. 1976. *The Selfish Gene*. Oxford: Oxford University Press.

Deleuze, Gilles, and Felix Guattari. 1987. *A Thousand Plateaus*. Minneapolis, MN: University of Minnesota Press.

Derrida, Jacques. 1986. *Glas*. Lincoln, NE: University of Nebraska Press.

Drury, Shadia. 1994. *Alexandre Kojeve: The Roots of Postmodern Politics*. London: Macmillan.

Duncombe, Stephen. 2007. *Dream: Re-Imagining Progressive Politics in an Age of Fantasy*. New York: New Press.

Duneier, Mitchell. 2000. *Sidewalk*. New York: Farrar, Straus and Giroux.

Durkheim, Émile. 1951. *Suicide*. London: Routledge.

—— 1961. *Moral Education*. London: Collier Macmillan.

—— 1966. *The Rules of Sociological Method*. New York: Free Press.

—— 1976. *The Elementary Forms of the Religious Life*. London: Allen and Unwin.

—— 1984. *The Division of Labour in Society*. Basingstoke: Macmillan.

Durkheim, Émile, and Marcel Mauss. 1973. *Primitive Classification*. Chicago: University of Chicago Press.

Edgar, Andrew. 2006. *Habermas: The Key Concepts*. London: Routledge.

Elster, Jon. 1985. *Making Sense of Marx*. Cambridge: Cambridge University Press.

Etzioni, Amitai, ed. 1995. *New Communitarian Thinking: Persons, Virtues, Institutions, and Communities*. Charlottesville, VA: University of Virginia Press.

Fairclough, Norman, ed. 1992. *Critical Language Awareness*. London: Longman.

Fanon, Frantz. 1968. *The Wretched of the Earth*. Harmondsworth: Penguin.

Fine, Gary Alan, ed. 1995. *A Second Chicago School? The Development of a Postwar American Sociology*, 2nd edn. Chicago: University of Chicago Press.

Foucault, Michel. 1967. *Madness and Civilisation: A History of Insanity in the Age of Reason*. London: Tavistock.

—— 1970. *The Order of Things: An Archaeology of the Human Sciences*. London: Tavistock.

—— 1972. *The Archaeology of Knowledge*. London: Tavistock.

—— 1973. *The Birth of the Clinic*. London: Tavistock.

—— 1977. *Discipline and Punish: The Birth of the Prison*. London: Tavistock.

—— 1980. *The History of Sexuality*, vol. 1. New York: Random House.

Fukuyama, Francis. 1992. *The End of History and the Last Man*. New York: Free Press.

Gagnon, John, and William Simon. 1967. *The Sexual Scene*. New York: Aldine.

Garfinkel, Harold. 1967. *Studies in Ethnomethodology*. Englewood Cliffs, NJ: Prentice Hall.

Geertz, Clifford. 1983. *Local Knowledge*. New York: Basic Books.

Gellner, Ernest. 1985. *Relativism and the Social Sciences*. Cambridge: Cambridge University Press.

Gerth, H. H., and C. Wright Mills, eds. 1948. *From Max Weber: Essays in Sociology*. London: Routledge and Kegan Paul.

Giddens, Anthony. 1978. *Durkheim*. London: Fontana.

—— 1979. *Central Problems in Social Theory*. London: Macmillan.

—— 1984. *The Constitution of Society: Outline of the Theory of Structuration*. Cambridge: Polity.

—— 1994. *Beyond Left and Right: The Future of Radical Politics*. Cambridge: Polity.

Glaser, Barney G., and Anselm L. Strauss. 1967. *The Discovery of Grounded Theory*. New York: Aldine de Gruyter.

—— 1968. *Time for Dying*. New York: Aldine.

Glazer-Malbin, Nona. 1976. 'Housework'. *Signs: Journal of Women in Culture and Society*, 1: 905–22.

Glucksmann, Miriam. 1974. *Structuralist Analysis in Contemporary Social Thought: A Comparison of the Theories of Claude Lévi-Strauss and Louis Althusser*. London: Routledge.

Goffman, Alice. 2014. *On the Run: Fugitive Life in an American City*. Chicago: University of Chicago Press.

Goffman, Erving. 1961. *Asylums: Essays on the Social Situation of Mental Patients and Other Inmates*. New York: Anchor.

Goldman, Lucien. 1964. *The Hidden God: A Study of Tragic Vision in the Pensées of Pascal and the Tragedies of Racine*. London: Routledge.

Goldthorpe, John, and David Lockwood. 1968. *The Affluent Worker in the Class Structure*, vol. 1. Cambridge: Cambridge University Press.

Gouldner, Alvin. 1965. *Enter Plato: Classical Greece and the Origins of Social Theory*. London: Routledge and Kegan Paul.

—— 1968. 'The Sociologist as Partisan: Sociology and the Welfare State'. *American Sociologist*, 3: 103–16.

—— 1970. *The Coming Crisis of Western Sociology*. New York: Basic Books.

Grathoff, Richard, ed. 1978. *The Theory of Social Action: The Correspondence of Alfred Schutz and Talcott Parsons*. Bloomington, IN: Indiana University Press.

Hall, Stuart, Chas Critcher, Tony Jefferson, John Clarke, and Brian Roberts. 1978. *Policing the Crisis: Mugging, the State, and Law and Order*. London: Macmillan.

Hamilton, Peter. 1983. *Talcott Parsons*. London: Tavistock.

Haraway, Donna. 1991. *Simians, Cyborgs and Women: The Reinvention of Nature*. London: Free Association Books.

Harding, Sandra. 1991. *Whose Science? Whose Knowledge? Thinking from Women's Lives*. Ithaca, NY: Cornell University Press.

Hardt, Michael, and Antonio Negri. 2001. *Empire*. Cambridge, MA: Harvard University Press.

Harland, Richard. 1987. *Superstructuralism*. London: Routledge.

Heath, Joseph, and Andrew Potter. 2005. *The Rebel Sell*. Mankato, MN: Capstone.

Held, David. 1990. *Introduction to Critical Theory: From Horkheimer to Habermas*. Cambridge: Polity.

Heritage, John. 1984. *Garfinkel and Ethnomethodology*. Cambridge: Polity.

Holton, Robert, and Bryan Turner. 1986. *Talcott Parsons on Economy and Society*. London: Routledge.

Humphreys, Laud. 1970. *Tea Room Trade*. New York: Aldine.

Huntington, Samuel. 1996. *The Clash of Civilizations and the Remaking of World Order*. New York: Simon and Schuster.

Jameson, Fredric. 1972. *The Prison of Language*. Princeton, NJ: Princeton University Press.

—— 1984. 'Postmodernism, or the Cultural Logic of Late Capitalism'. *New Left Review*, 146: 53–92.

—— 1991. *Postmodernism, or the Cultural Logic of Late Capitalism*. London: Verso.

Jenkins, Richard. 1992. *Pierre Bourdieu*. London: Routledge.

Jenkins, Simon. 1995. *Accountable to None: The Tory Nationalization of Britain*. London: Hamish Hamilton.

Johnson, B. S. 1969. *The Unfortunates*. London: Panther.

Kamuf, Peggy, ed. 1991. *A Derrida Reader: Between the Blinds*. New York: Columbia University Press.

Kinsey, Alfred, Wardell Baxter Pomeroy, and Clyde E. Martin. 1948. *Sexual Behavior in the Human Male*. Philadelphia, PA: W. B. Saunders.

Kitsuse, John. 1964. 'Societal Reaction to Deviant Behavior: Problems of Theory and Method', in Howard S. Becker (ed.), *The Other Side: Perspectives on Deviance*. New York: Free Press, 87–102.

Knox, Hannah, Mike Savage, and Penny Harvey. 2006. 'Social Networks and the Study of Relations: Networks as Method, Metaphor and Form'. *Economy and Society*, 35: 113–40.

Kołakowski, Leszek. 2008. *Main Currents of Marxism*, 1-vol. edn. New York: W. W. Norton.

Lanchester, John. 2010. *Whoops! Why Everyone Owes Everyone and No One Can Pay*. Harmondsworth: Penguin.

Latour, Bruno. 1987. *Science in Action: How to Follow Scientists and Engineers Through Society*. Cambridge, MA: Harvard University Press.

—— 2005. *Reassembling the Social: An Introduction to Actor-Network Theory*. Oxford: Oxford University Press.

Lemert, Edwin M. 1967. *Human Deviance, Social Problems and Social Control*. Englewood Cliffs, NJ: Prentice Hall.

Lenin, V. I. 1963. *What Is to Be Done?* Oxford: Oxford University Press.

Letkeman, Peter. 1973. *Crime as Work*. Englewood Cliffs, NJ: Prentice Hall.

Lévi-Strauss, Claude. 1962. *Totemism*. Harmondsworth: Penguin.

—— 1963. *Structural Anthropology*. New York: Basic Books.

—— 1970. *The Raw and the Cooked*. London: Cape.

—— 1972. *The Savage Mind*. London: Weidenfeld and Nicolson.

—— 1973. *From Honey to Ashes*. London: Cape.

—— 1978. *The Origin of Table Manners*. London: Cape.

—— 1981. *The Naked Man*. London: Cape.

—— 1988. *The Jealous Potter*. Chicago: University of Chicago Press.

Lockwood, David. 1964. 'System Integration and Social Integration', in George K. Zollschan and Walter Hirsch (eds), *Explorations in Social Change*. London: Routledge and Kegan Paul, 244–56.

Lukács, Georg. 1971. *History and Class Consciousness*. London: Merlin Press.

Lukes, Steven. 1975. *Émile Durkheim: His Life and Work*. Harmondsworth: Penguin.

—— 1982. 'Relativism in Its Place', in Martin Hollis and Stephen Lukes (eds), *Rationality and Relativism*. Oxford: Blackwell, 261–305.

Lyotard, Jean-François. 1984. *The Postmodern Condition: A Report on Knowledge*. Manchester: Manchester University Press.

McCarthy, Timothy. 1978. *Marx and the Proletariat*. Westport, CT: Greenwood Press.

McKenzie, Robert, and Allan Silver. 1968. *Angels in Marble: Working Class Conservatives in Urban England*. London: Heinemann.

McLellan, David, ed. 2000. *Karl Marx: Selected Writings*. Oxford: Oxford University Press.

McLuhan, Marshall. 1962. *The Gutenberg Galaxy: The Making of Typographic Man*. London: Routledge and Kegan Paul.

McNay, Lois. 1994. *Foucault: A Critical Introduction*. Cambridge: Polity.

Major-Poetzl, Pamela. 1983. *Michel Foucault's Archaeology of Western Reason*. Chapel Hill, NC: University of North Carolina Press.

Manis, Jerome G., and Bernard N. Meltzer, eds. 1972. *Symbolic Interaction: A Reader in Social Psychology*, 2nd edn. Boston, MA: Allyn and Bacon.

Marcuse, Herbert. 1955. *Reason and Revolution*, 2nd edn. London: Routledge.

—— 1964. *One Dimensional Man*. London: Routledge.

Martin, Peter J., and Alex Dennis. 2010. *Human Agents and Social Structures*. Manchester: Manchester University Press.

Marx, Karl. 1976. *Capital: A Critique of Political Economy*, vol. 1. Harmondsworth: Penguin.

Mayhew, Leon H., ed. 1985. *Talcott Parsons on Institutions and Social Evolution: Selected Writings*. Chicago: University of Chicago Press.

Merquior, J. G. 1991. *Foucault*, 2nd edn. London: Fontana.

Merton, Robert. 1957. 'Social Structure and Anomie', in *Social Theory and Social Structure*. New York: Free Press, 131–60.

Mills, C. Wright. 1959a. *The Power Elite*. New York: Oxford University Press.

—— 1959b. *The Sociological Imagination*. New York: Oxford University Press.

Mitchell, Juliet. 1974. *Psycho-Analysis and Feminism*. Harmondsworth: Allen Lane.

Mouzelis, Nicos P. 1990. *Back to Sociological Theory*. London: Macmillan.

—— 1995. *Sociological Theory: What Went Wrong*. London: Routledge.

Newey, Glen. 1997. 'Gassing and Bungling'. *London Review of Books*, 19: 14–15.

Norris, Christopher. 1990. *What's Wrong with Postmodernism? Critical Theory and the Ends of Philosophy*, new edn. Baltimore, MD: Johns Hopkins University Press.

Oakley, Ann. 1974. *The Sociology of Housework*. London: Martin Robertson.

Outhwaite, William, ed. 1996. *The Habermas Reader*. Cambridge: Polity.

Outhwaite, William, and Larry Ray. 2005. *Social Theory and Postcommunism*. London: Blackwell.

Paglia, Camille. 1993. *Sex, Art and American Culture*. London: Viking.

Parsons, Talcott. 1937. *The Structure of Social Action*. New York: Free Press.

—— 1940. 'An Analytical Approach to the Theory of Social Stratification'. *American Journal of Sociology*, 45: 841–62.

—— 1942. 'Age and Sex in the Social Structure of the United States'. *American Sociological Review*, 7: 604–16.

—— 1951. *The Social System*. New York: Free Press.

—— 1953. 'A Revised Analytical Approach to the Theory of Social Stratification', in Reinhard Bendix and Seymour Martin Lipset (eds), *Class, Status and Power*. New York: Free Press, 92–129.

—— 1966. *Societies: Evolutionary and Comparative Perspectives*. Englewood Cliffs, NJ: Prentice Hall.

—— 1969. *Political and Social Structure*. London: Collier Macmillan.

—— 1971. *The System of Modern Societies*. Englewood Cliffs, NJ: Prentice Hall.

—— 1978. *Action Theory and the Human Condition*. New York: Free Press.

Parsons, Talcott, and Edward Shils, eds. 1951. *Toward a General Theory of Action*. Cambridge, MA: Harvard University Press.

Pierce, Frank. 1989. *The Radical Durkheim*. London: Unwin Hyman.

Piketty, Thomas. 2014. *Capital in the Twenty-First Century*. Cambridge, MA: Harvard University Press.

Poetzl, Pamela Major. 1983. *Michel Foucault's Archaeology of Western Reason*. Hemel Hempstead: Harvester.

Popper, Karl. 1957. *The Poverty of Historicism*. London: Routledge and Kegan Paul.

Poster, Mark. 2001. *Jean Baudrillard: Selected Writings*, 2nd edn. Cambridge: Polity.

Rabinow, Paul, ed. 1986. *The Foucault Reader: An Introduction to Foucault's Thought*. Harmondsworth: Penguin.

Rock, Paul. 1979. *The Making of Symbolic Interactionism*. London: Macmillan.

Rose, Arnold M., ed. 1962. *Human Behavior and Social Processes: An Interactionist Approach*. London: Routledge and Kegan Paul.

Rosenberg, Justin. 2000. *The Follies of Globalisation Theory: Polemical Essays*. London: Verso.

Runciman, W. G., ed. 1978. *Max Weber: Selections in Translation*. Cambridge: Cambridge University Press.

Said, Edward. 1978. *Orientalism*. London: Routledge and Kegan Paul.

Savage, Stephen P. 1982. *The Theories of Talcott Parsons: The Social Relations of Action*. London: Macmillan.

Schatzki, Theodore R. 1987. 'An Overdue Analysis of Bourdieu's Theory of Practice'. *Inquiry*, 30: 113–35.

Schütz, Alfred. 1962. *Collected Papers*, vol. 1: *The Problem of Social Reality*. The Hague: Martinus Nijhoff.

—— 1964. *Collected Papers*, vol. 2: *Studies in Social Theory*. The Hague: Martinus Nijhoff.

—— 1966. *Collected Papers*, vol. 3: *Studies in Phenomenological Philosophy*. The Hague: Martinus Nijhoff.

Seidman, Steven. 1997. *Difference Troubles: Queering Social Theory and Sexual Politics*. Cambridge: Cambridge University Press.

Sharrock, Wes, and Bob Anderson. 1986. *The Ethnomethodologists*. London: Tavistock.

Shils, Edward. 1978. 'Centre and Periphery', reprinted in Peter Worsley (ed.), *Modern Sociology*. Harmondsworth: Penguin, 566–78.

Sica, Alan. 1991. 'The California-Massachusetts Strain in Structuration Theory', in Christopher G. A. Bryant and David Jary (eds), *Giddens' Theory of Structuration: A Critical Appreciation*. London: Routledge, 32–51.

Simmel, Georg. 2009. *Sociology: Inquiries into the Construction of Social Forms*, vol. 1. Leiden: Brill.

Skinner, Quentin, ed. 1985. *The Return of Grand Theory in the Human Sciences*. Cambridge: Cambridge University Press.

Skolnick, Jerome H. 1966. *Justice Without Trial*. New York: John Wiley.

Smelser, Neil J. 1959. *Social Change in the Industrial Revolution*. London: Routledge.

—— 1962. *Theory of Collective Behaviour*. London: Routledge.

Smith, Dorothy. 1987. *The Everyday World as Problematic*. Lebanon, NH: Northeastern University Press.

—— 1990. *The Conceptual Practices of Power: A Feminist Sociology of Knowledge*. Lebanon, NH: Northeastern University Press.

Solzhenitsyn, Alexander. 1974. *The Gulag Archipelago*. London: Collins.

Spivak, Gayatri. 1988. 'Can the Subaltern Speak?', in Cary Nelson and Lawrence Grossberg (eds), *Marxism and the Interpretation of Culture*. London: Macmillan, 271–312.

Stanley, Liz, and Sue Wise. 1993. *Breaking Out Again: Feminist Ontology and Epistemology*. London: Routledge.

Stone, Gregory P., and Harvey A. Farberman, eds. 1970. *Social Psychology Through Symbolic Interaction*. Waltham, MA: Xerox College Publishing.

Strauss, Anselm L., Leonard Schatzman, Rue Bucher, Danuta Ehrlich, and Melvin Sabshin. 1964. *Psychiatric Institutions and Ideologies*. New York: Free Press.

Sullivan, Nikki. 2003. *A Critical Introduction to Queer Theory*. New York: New York University Press.

Sutherland, Edwin. 1961. *The Professional Thief*. New York: Holt, Rinehart and Winston.

Terranova, Tiziana. 2004. *Network Culture: Politics for the Information Age*. London: Pluto.

Thomas, Keith. 1973. *Religion and the Decline of Magic*. Harmondsworth: Penguin.

Thompson, E. P. 1968. *The Making of the English Working Class*. Harmondsworth: Penguin.

—— 1978. *The Poverty of Theory and Other Essays*. London: Merlin Press.

Thrift, Nigel. 1985. 'Bear and Mouse or Bear and Tree: Anthony Giddens' Reconstruction of Social Theory'. *Sociology*, 19: 609–23.

Tilly, Louise A., and Joan W. Scott. 1978. *Women, Work and Family*. New York: Holt, Rinehart and Winston.

Turner, Jonathan H., and Alexandra Maryanski. 1979. *Functionalism*. San Francisco: Benjamin Cummings.

Turner, Roy, ed. 1974. *Ethnomethodology: Selected Writings*. Harmondsworth: Penguin.

Virno, Paolo. 2004. *A Grammar of the Multitude*. Cambridge, MA: Semiotext(e).

Wagner, Helmut R., ed. 1970. *Alfred Schütz on Phenomenology and Social Relations: Selected Writings*. Chicago: University of Chicago Press.

Weber, Max. 1978. *Economy and Society*. Berkeley, CA: University of California Press.

—— 1987. *The Protestant Ethic and the Spirit of Capitalism*. London: Routledge.

Willis, Paul. 1977. *Learning to Labour*. Farnborough: Saxon House.

Winch, Peter. 1964. 'Understanding a Primitive Society'. *American Philosophical Quarterly*, 1: 307–24.

—— 1990. *The Idea of a Social Science and Its Relation to Philosophy*, 2nd edn. London: Routledge.

Wittfogel, Karl. 1957. *Oriental Despotism: A Comparative Study of Total Power*. New Haven, CT: Yale University Press.

Wolpert, Lewis. 1992. *The Unnatural Nature of Science*. London: Faber and Faber.

Young, Robert J. C. 2003. *Postcolonialism: A Very Short Introduction*. Oxford: Oxford University Press.

Zweig, Ferdinand. 1961. *The Worker in an Affluent Society*. London: Heinemann.

# Index